MW01193549

TORAH STUDY

A Survey of Classic Sources
on Timely Issues

Yehudah Levi

TORAH STUDY
A Survey of Classic Sources
on Timely Issues

Rendered into English by
Raphael N. Levi

Philipp Feldheim, Inc.
Jerusalem – New York
5750 – 1990

First published 1990

Hardcover edition: ISBN 0-87306-555-7

Philipp Feldheim Inc.
200 Airport Executive Park
Spring Valley, NY 10977

Feldheim Publishers Ltd.
POB 6525 / Jerusalem, Israel

Printed in Israel

The author gratefully acknowledges
the support by
the Rav Dr. Joseph Breuer Foundation
towards the publication
of this volume

Table of Contents

Part 4   155
The Purpose of Torah Study

Part 5   177
Formulating a Torah Study Program

Endorsements, by Outstanding Torah Authorities, of the Hebrew Edition

יעקב קמנצקי

RABBI J. KAMENECKI
38 SADDLE RIVER ROAD
MONSEY, NEW YORK 10952

בע"ה

כבוד ידידי הרה"ג הנעלה יקר הרוח מוה"ר יהודה הלוי שלו' וברכת כ"ט.

עברתי על ספרו "שערי תלמוד תורה". והנה דבר גדול עשה כ' במה שליקט הרבה מדברי חז"ל, ראשונים ואחרונים בכמה סוגיות חשובות בעניני ת"ת. ומה טוב עשה שלא הסיק מסקנות בדבר, שהרי כמה מן הסוגיות משתנות לפי העניינים שהזמן גרמם, כגון דרך הלימוד. ואפי' בזמן הש"ס מצינו דרבה ורב יוסף שהיו חברים ואעפ"כ הי' הא' עוקר הרים והב' סיני, הרי שחלוי ג"כ בכשרונות האדם. עם כל זה, לדעתי יש חשיבות גדולה בעצם ליקוט וסידור החומר, ובטוחני שעולם לומדי התורה יחזיקו טובה גדולה למר על מה שעמל לערוך הדברים לפניהם בצורה כה מאירת עינים. ויתן ד' שיוכל לזכות את הרבים מתוך מנוחת הנפש והרחבת הדעת כעתירת ידידו מוקירו.

הכו"ח ב' ניסן תש"מ. פה מאנסי

יעקב קמנצקי

The following endorsements are listed alphabetically

RABBI PINCHAS MENACHEM ALTER
Rosh Yeshivath Sefath Emeth (Gur)
Jerusalem

פנחס מנחם אלתר
ראש ישיבת "שפת אמת"
ירושלים

ב"ה, ירושלים ו' עש"ק פ' בראשית תש"ם לפ"ק

לכבוד הרבני החשוב והנכבד, חו"ב כו' כו', מהר"ר י'הודה לוי שי' לאוי"ט, שלו' רב !

עברתי על ספרו הנחמד "שערי תלמוד תורה", — והנה נהניתי מאד, איך שכב' מסביר, מסדר ומבאר — בחמשת השערים הראשונים — את הנחוץ והטעון בירור ופרסום בין המוני בנ"י, לזרזם, להדריכם ולהבינם הל' ת"ת, שעלי' אחז"ל : "גדול תלמוד שהתלמוד מביא לידי מעשה". (—והגם שבעניני סדר הלימוד כבר אחז"ל : "לעולם ילמוד אדם במקום שלבו חפץ — וכ"א יכול לבחור לו איזה דרך שנפשו חשקה בו, למען תתרבה התמדתו — אבל מי שהוא נבוך, באיזה דרך יבחר — הנה ברורים לו השיטות של הקדמונים כמו שכתב וביאר היטב) — ומלאכה גדולה וחשובה עשה כב'. ברך ה' חילו ופועל ידיו תרצה ; יישר כחו.

בענין שני השערים האחרונים — תורה עם ד"א, ותורה עם חכמות חיצוניות, כמובן, הענין צריך זהירות גדולה ; (—אני מקוה שכב' יבין אותי. אני חונכתי במסגרת אחרת, — כב' גדל והתחנך על שיטת הרה"ג רש"ר הירש ז"ל "תורה עם ד"א"—) בראותי את הכותרות — בתחילה נרתעתי אינסטינקטיבית — (בעיקר בשער האחרון) — וכבן אשר רואה בפעם הראשונה את אמו החורגת אשת אביו, אשר כמעט אי אפשר שלא ירגיש מועקה בלבו — עד כמה שתהי' צנועה וטובה בעיני אביו ובעיני כל העולם, ועד כמה שהוא חייב לכבדה כדינא מדינא כאשת אביו, והגם שזהו כבוד אביו וצורך אביו, אי אפשר שלא יעלה על לבו אהבת אמו וזכרה. כמו כן תורה"ק, חיינו ואורך ימינו, שזה עתה חבקנוה ונשקנוה בהקפות שמחת תורה. וכמשל שלמה המלך ע"ה, על החכמות של הטבע כאשה זרה, והתורה — תורת אמך.

והנה כפי שכ' כותב בהקדמה, הספר הוא ליקוטים מדברי חז"ל. וזוהי להלכה, אבל למעשה לדעתי — צריך כ"א להתייעץ עם רבו — או עם מורה הוראה ירא שמים, כדי להתאים לו את הדרך המועילה, ולכוונו במישור התורה והיראה, כי בפרט בדור שלנו הדבר צריך זהירות יתירה.

בסיכום, ספרו חשוב ביותר וייש"ר כחו.

והנני ידידו ומברכו בכט"ס ובשנה מבורכת

פנחס מנחם אלתר

RABBI AVRAHAM FARBSTEIN
Rosh Yeshivath Hebron, Jerusalem

ט״ז אייר תשמ״א ירושלים תובב״א
לסדר אם בחוקותי תלכו שתהיו עמלים בתורה.

ראה ראיתי את קונטרסי הספר שערי תלמוד תורה של הרה״ג יהודה הלוי
שליט״א החכם המופלג בתורה וי״ש.

והנה כלו מחמדים, אוסף כעמיר גורנה שיטות ראשונים ואחרונים
בדברים העומדים ברומו של עולם מעטירים בפנינים משלו, שזכו לו לחלקו
מהשמים.

ומקום הניחו לו להתגדר בו ולגלות עיניהם של לומדי התורה ות״ח
לעורר מחשבתם ועיונם בדרכי קנין התורה בדורנו הלכות שהם הליכות
עולם ואף על פי שעל הכלל כולו נאמר הנה להם לישראל שאם אינם נביאים
בני נביאים המה, הרשות ניתנה ליחידים לבור להם דרכם דרך התורה לשם
שמים וע״ז נאמר אחד המרבה ואחד הממעיט ובלבד שיכוון לבו לשמים.

הכותב והחותם לכבוד התורה ולומדיה.

א. י. פרבשטיין
ראש ישיבת חברון

RABBI AARON SOLOVEITCHIK
Rosh Yeshivath Brisk, Chicago

אהרן הלוי סולוביציק
ראש ישיבת בריסק בשיקגו

תלמידי המצוין איש האשכולות בעל תורה וחכמה ויראתו קודמת לחכמתו
ה"ה ר' יהודה ד"ר לוי שליט"א חבר חמר של חיבור בשם "שערי תלמוד
תורה". החיבור הזה הוא חיבור מעניין ומצוין עד מאד ויש בו ליקוט של דעות
הראשונים וגם של אחרונים בקשר עם תלמוד תורה. ידעתי את האיש מכמה
שנים שהוא גברא רבא שכל חכמתו ומחשבתו צמודים עם יראת ה' טהורה.

החיבור הזה יש בו ערך רב לצעירי עמנו ואפריון נמטיה ליה לר' יהודה
לוי שליט"א שעמל ויגע כדי להרבות כבוד שמים.

אהרן הלוי סולוביציק

(הערה מאת רו"מ ראה לקמן עמ' נו)

Chief Rabbi of Israel
RABBI OVADIAH YOSEF
עובדיה יוסף
ראשון לציון הרב הראשי לישראל

ב"ה ירושלים ט"ז שבט תשמ"ז
שנת צרור המור לפ"ק

ה ס כ מ ה

הובא לפני הספר "שערי תלמוד תורה" מעשה ידי אומן, נטע נאמן, צנצנת המן. חכו ממתקים וכולו מחמדים. תהלתו בקהל חסידים. הרה"ג היקר הנעלה מיחידי סגולה. יראת ה' היא אוצרו. ועליו יציץ נזרו. כש"ת רבי יהודה לוי שליט"א. עברתי בין בתריו, ונהנתי מאמרותיו, כי כביר מציאה ידו לאסוף כעמיר גורנה העניינים השייכים להלכות תלמוד תורה, בטוב טעם ודעת. וכל דבריו נכוחים למבין וישרים למוצאי דעת. צוף דבש אמרי נועם לנפש ומרפא לעצם.

לא נצרכה אלא לברכה למהדורא החדשה בתוספת נופך. יהי רצון שיזכה לברך על המוגמר בקרב ימים ועוד יפוצו מעינותיו חוצה להגדיל תורה ולהאדירה ברבות הטובה גם עד זקנה ושיבה. וכל אשר יעשה יצליח.

כברכת התורה

עובדיה יוסף

FOREWORD

Torah study is the lifeblood of Judaism. Just as the heartbeat must be carefully regulated and coordinated with the needs of the individual and his environment, so must Torah study be attuned—in the choice of subjects and methods, its intellectual level and its targets—to the specific legitimate needs of the "Talmid."

Throughout our history, in each period and each region, our Torah leadership instituted such forms of Torah study that were suited to the specific time and place. But behind these varied forms there were always basic concepts regulating *talmud Torah*, firm, yet flexible enough to function under all circumstances.

It is our goal to clarify these basic concepts and, in this way, to avoid a fairly widespread mistake, which is, to give to a particular form of study, as practiced at a particular time, the attribute of permanence, of a lasting, unchangeable nature. This erroneous claim would deprive *talmud Torah* of its unique character, its ability to be alive, profoundly productive, under every and all circumstances.

Of course, some obvious conflicts will come to the fore. Many decisions have to be made, and many questions answered.

How should we divide our time between the competing demands of Torah study and the requirements for assuring a livelihood to our families? Is it more important to dedicate a maximum of time and effort to the deepening of our knowledge of Torah, or rather to teach Torah and Mitzvoth to the many who are still removed from genuine Jewish life? How should we proceed when we are confronted by Chumroth

xviii

(stringencies) that are sometimes difficult to comprehend? In our Torah study should we emphasize breadth or depth? Deduction (Pilpul) over induction (Sevara)? What is the attitude of our Torah authorities to secular studies, college, and university and their effect on Torah study?

The background material needed to clarify the essential aspects of these questions is scattered throughout our literature. We have tried to collect this material and to place it before the reader "like a set table."

It is our hope that this collection, in which we have attempted to present all viewpoints, will help the reader — guided by his Rabbi or Rosh Yeshiva — to clarify his duties to Talmud Torah.

The Hebrew edition of this work was published in 1981, when the author's unforgettable mentor, HaRav Joseph Breuer, had explicitly expressed the wish that the author's notes and essays be presented in a comprehensive and coordinated Sefer. Entitled "Sha'are Talmud Torah," its three editions have received the warm endorsement of eminent Torah leaders in Israel and abroad.

ACKNOWLEDGMENTS

It is a pleasant duty to thank my dear brother Raphael for translating the Hebrew version into English. He performed this massive and difficult task with both great devotion and skill. I am sure I speak for the reader as well as myself, in expressing my great appreciation.

I take this opportunity to express my deep appreciation and gratitude to my dear nephew David Kahn, who selflessly devoted untold hours of painstaking critical analysis to help make this book into what it is.

I wish also to thank the editors, Mrs. Karen Paritzky, David Hornik, and Tzvi Ofer for their valuable contribution.

My heartfelt thanks also go to the Jerusalem College of Technology, with which I am affiliated, and to its founder, Professor Wm. Low (Zeev Lev) and its present head, Mr. Tzvi Weinberger, for their generous encouragement.

Finally, I wish to thank my dear wife, whose valuable advice—both managerial and literary—has contributed so much to this work—all this, in addition to the "logistic support" she supplied most beautifully.

Leo Levi
Jerusalem, Adar 5750

PART ONE

TORAH AND THE WORLD —
IDEA AND REALIZATION

Torah study is not just another mitzvah—it is, in a sense, the very foundation of Judaism. This work constitutes an in-depth analysis of several of the more crucial facets of this mitzvah, to help us integrate it effectively into our daily life.

We commence by clarifying the Torah's role in the scheme of creation. Our Sages tell us that the Torah predated the creation of the world and served as its blueprint. This suggests that the world was created to be a setting for the Torah, providing it with a domain for expression, for translation into reality. Torah and the world are thus interdependent component parts of one system. This explains Moses' reply to the angels when they sought to keep the Torah in Heaven. He challenged them: "What good is the Torah to you?...Do you then engage in business?...Do you perform work?..." In effect, Moses was telling the angels that for them, in Heaven, the Torah is a theoretical abstraction alone. Only on Earth can the Torah's divine ideas be imposed on more or less compliant matter, molding and shaping it, thereby becoming reality. Hence it seems that a person can truly live a full Torah life only if he is involved in the world, shaping it to the Torah's demands and using it in the service of God.

Here we investigate the Torah's view of worldly matters, especially the issue of earning a livelihood. Specifically we present the opinions of the Sages and Torah authorities throughout the generations regarding the obligation to learn a trade, the importance of work, allocation of time for work and Torah study, and the prohibitions of engaging in Torah study for material gain.

1
Derekh Eretz

1. The Importance of *Derekh Eretz*

Derekh eretz means everything required for life in this world—especially
social interaction. It encompasses culture;[1] sociability, including courtesy;[2] sympathy, love and tolerance of one's fellow man;[3] and earning a
livelihood.[4] R. Samson Raphael Hirsch[5] generalizes:

> *Derekh eretz* includes everything that results from the fact that
> man's existence, mission and social life is conducted on Earth,
> using earthly means and conditions. Therefore, this term espe-
> cially describes ways of earning a livelihood and maintaining
> social order. It also includes the customs and considerations of
> etiquette—which the social order generates—as well as every-
> thing concerning humanistic and civic education.

The Talmud contains several revealing statements concerning the
interrelationship between Torah and *derekh eretz*. Our Sages inform us[6]
that *derekh eretz* preceded the giving of the Torah by twenty-six generations. This seems to imply that Torah, which certainly embodies the
ultimate goal of our existence as Jews, must be preceded by *derekh eretz*
to ensure its success, as the Mishnah says:[7] "If there is no *derekh eretz*,
there is no Torah." Moreover, we are advised:[8] "Be involved in two
disciplines—Torah and *derekh eretz*." *Orchoth Tzadikim* expresses this
view even more explicitly:[9] "You must mediate between the two functions, setting aside time for Torah and for work of this world...this is for
your good and the good of your future—and let neither undermine the
other." R. Ya'akov Emden[10] interpreted the Talmudic words of Bar
Kappara, "On which brief Scriptural passage does the entire Torah
depend?—'In all your ways shall you know Him,'" as referring to
derekh eretz. And Maharal, in the concluding statement of his *Nethivoth*

'*Olam* goes so far as to state that *derekh eretz* is the very foundation of the Torah. In R. Hirsch's view, *derekh eretz* is the raw material to be shaped by the Torah.[11]

R. Simchah Zisel Ziv, one of the foremost leaders of the Mussar movement, describes *derekh eretz*, involvement with the needs of society, as the bottom rungs of the Torah ladder, leading from earth to heaven. He emphasizes that one cannot hope to ascend this ladder without first climbing the lower rungs by being involved with the needs of society.[12]

From the beginning, the Creator decreed that man must not only serve Him spiritually but also impress the seal of His will on the physical aspects of this world. In this vein, Netziv writes:[13] "And [Adam] performed agricultural work, thus **fulfilling the purpose of Creation**." Similarly R. Ya'akov Emden stated:[14] "For God always wanted man to arise early for his labors, to support his household." Even before Adam sinned, he was placed in the Garden of Eden "to work it and to guard it." In the words of the *Baraitha*:[15] "Adam did not taste of anything until he had labored [for it], as the verse says, 'and He put him in the Garden of Eden to work it and to guard it.'" To quote *Chovoth HaLevavoth*:[16] "To follow the commandment of his Creator, who ordered man to concern himself with the way of the world—agricultural work, plowing and sowing."[17]

That work is at the core of man's being can also be deduced from the fact that a person is identified with his place of work rather than his place of domicile; this is evident from Naval, who lived in Ma'on but was called "the Carmelite," because his work was on Mt. Carmel.[18]

Also, there are two types of mitzvoth. There are mitzvoth (such as fasting on Yom Kippur) that go against nature, that is, frustrate one's natural desires. Then, again, there are mitzvoth (such as enjoying a Sabbath meal) that are in accord with human nature and *derekh eretz* and bring the physical into the domain of sanctity. According to *Beth HaLevi*,[19] these latter mitzvoth are superior. Further along this line *Meshekh Chokhmah*[20] notes: "The halakhah is ... that we should use [the words of the Torah] in line with *derekh eretz*, for this is God's basic intent."

The above *Baraitha* concerning Adam continues: "Furthermore, God did not permit His Presence to dwell within Israel until they had performed work [the construction of the Tabernacle]." This confirms that physical labor is of exalted importance and not merely a curse imposed on Adam. Scripture does seem to imply that the necessity for labor was caused by Adam's sin; but the key phrase in the punishment is "by the sweat of your brow"—i.e., after the sin, he was able to provide for himself only with painful toil. This inference is supported by the statement of the Tana:[21] "Have you ever seen either bird or beast practicing a trade? They can provide for themselves without painful toil.... Therefore, would not I too have been able to do so, had I not perverted my deeds and ruined my livelihood?" In other words, the objection is to the suffering involved in earning a living, whereas work itself is beloved by God.[22]

God diminishes the effects of Adam's punishment and reduces the burden of *derekh eretz* for each person according to his merits. For example,[23] "Anyone who accepts the yoke of Torah is exempted from the yokes of governmental impositions and *derekh eretz*." Similarly, because of their special merit, the Early Pious Ones (*HaChasidim HaRishonim*) were blessed with success and able to sustain themselves with very little work each day.[24] And the Talmud further states that[25] "Whoever occupies himself with the Torah—his holdings will prosper."

According to Ramban:[26] "[Virtually the highest form of service of God is performed by] those who occupy themselves with the mitzvoth out of love [of God]...together with the concerns of this world, in line with the verse 'And your threshing will extend until your grape harvest.' They achieve a natural, good life in this world and their full reward is vouchsafed in the next world." R. Bachyay adds[27] that this stage is the way of the Patriarchs, who served God out of love as they engaged in sowing, cattle farming, and other physical concerns. Rambam explains[28] that the Patriarchs achieved perfection through their agricultural work: "Their ultimate intention [in shepherding and working the land] was to come ever closer to God, because they wanted to found a nation that knew God and served Him."

Of course, one must beware of viewing mundane matters as an end in itself, distinct from the service of God; rather, one should connect all his activities with Torah life. Then the mundane activities will strengthen Torah rather than conflict with it. One of R. Yitzchak Hutner's students who had completed his yeshiva studies, and was now dividing his time between working and Torah studies, wrote to the *Rosh Yeshivah* bemoaning the necessity of leading a "double life." R. Hutner responded with a particularly apt parable: "If someone rents one room as a residence, and another room in a hotel for temporary sojourns, he is certainly leading a

double life. However, if he rents a two-room apartment, he lives a full
life, not a double life."[29]

We proceed to examine various important aspects of *derekh eretz*.

(1) Perfection of the Nation

It has been said[30] that *derekh eretz*, involvement with the needs of
society, is an essential prerequisite to the development of a love of
chesed. At the same time, the very existence of society is dependent on
chesed. Based on the verse[32] "the world is built on kindness," the
Mishnah teaches[31] that *chesed* is one of the three pillars on which the
world rests. R. Yitzchak Abarbanel[33] comments that mutual acts of
kindness sustain the national community. The moralists (*Ba'aley Ha-
Musar*) consider industrial, professional, and commercial activity to be
"acts of kindness"—including the work of the farmer, the miller and the
baker, all of whom contribute to preparing our bread. Ben Zoma
marveled[34]: "How many labors did Adam have to perform to be able to
eat bread! Plowing, sowing, reaping, binding, threshing, winnowing,
removing pebbles, grinding, sifting, kneading, and baking—only after
all this could he eat. But I rise early and find all this done for me."
Although these activities were undertaken for monetary gain, they still
remain acts of kindness; only the degree of merit depends on the
intention.

The Sages obligate fathers to teach their sons whatever the national
welfare demands (*yishuv medinah*). They appear to have been motivated
by their concern for *derekh eretz* as an instrument for the welfare of
society.[36] According to R. Yosef Rozin,[37] this even includes the study of
science.

For the Jewish nation, these considerations have added importance.
R. Hirsch views the professions and crafts as an integral part of Israel's
role as a model to the nations, a kingdom of priests:[38] "Israel's mission is
to be a nation of agricultural workers, merchants, warriors and scientists, thereby demonstrating that humankind's mission, as revealed by
the Torah, is not restricted to certain occupations."

This view conforms with that of the Sages. They teach:[39] "Four
things need to be strengthened—Torah, good deeds, prayer and *derekh
eretz* [Rashi explains *derekh eretz* here to mean a craft, business or
military pursuits]... How do we know *derekh eretz* needs reinforce-
ment? Because the verse says,[40] 'Be strong and let us strengthen our-

selves for our people and for the cities of our God.'" This verse suggests
that *derekh eretz* is especially important in the Land of Israel. R.
Emden[41] expands on this theme:

> In the Holy Land [*derekh eretz*] is like a mitzvah for us. Our
> Sages comment on the verse "And you shall plant all kinds of
> fruit trees:" One should see to the planting of trees, for this was
> God's first concern at the beginning of Creation. Therefore, we
> too, on entering the Land of Israel, must be primarily con-
> cerned with planting... As others have planted for us, so should
> we plant for our children. Hence no one should exempt himself
> from developing the land, even if he is provided for and even if
> he himself will not benefit from his planting.

The "Chatham Sofer" writes:[42]

> "And you shall gather your grain" because of the mitzvah of
> settling the Land of Israel... [and this includes] not only farm-
> ing, but any trade useful in settling and advancing the Land of
> Israel, lest people say that there are no cobblers or construction
> workers in all the Land of Israel, and they will have to be
> brought from afar.

In these passages, R. Ya'akov Emden and the "Chatham Sofer"
remind us that, even though G-d desires the settling of the world in
general, this has even greater significance in Eretz Yisrael. In the diaspora our contributions to the economy help build up what is essentially
a non-Torah society. The same efforts in Eretz Yisrael make us partners
in the development of a society that is, potentially at least, the realization of the Torah's plan of a state which will serve as a model to the
nations.

The Sages esteemed wealth as an aid to the maintenance of society;
thus we pray[43] every month for "a life of wealth and honor." Likewise,
Rabbeinu HaKadosh and R. 'Akiva honored the wealthy[44] for their acts
of kindness and support of mitzvoth in the community. And though the
only virtue God felt He could bestow on Israel was poverty (to avoid the
moral dangers inherent in wealth),[45] the Sages declare that the Divine
Presence rests only on one who is wise, strong, and affluent.[46]

(2) Livelihood

The Sages explain[47] that the Scriptural imperative to "choose life" obliges us to acquire a trade. Another Talmudic passage[48] derives this obligation from the verse "See life with the wife you love," for just as a father must find his son a wife, so he must prepare him for a livelihood. Furthermore, Rashi comments that the verse "And you shall let them know [the way in which they shall go]" refers to the teaching of a trade for earning one's living.[49] Rashbatz[50] counts this instruction as a Biblical commandment, as does Mordekhay,[51] who states:

> Rabbeinu Tam explains that business activity apparently counts as a mitzvah. Hence one may embark on an overseas business trip even on Friday, in line with the Talmudic passage in the first chapter of *Kidushin*, where the verse "See life ..." is interpreted as referring to a trade; [the Sages] have also said[52] that the verse "And you shall let them know the way" refers to ... earning a livelihood from a trade.[53]

Rambam expresses this idea differently:[54] "The intelligent man first establishes himself in work that will support him; then he purchases a home; and only thereafter does he marry."

Furthermore, the Sages warn against becoming an economic liability, saying[55] that it is better to do unseemly work—and even to limit your Sabbath meals[56]—than to become a burden on others. To forestall such a predicament, they have forbidden the donation of more than one-fifth of one's property to charity.[57]

In this light, the following statement by Rambam[58] requires clarification:

> And not only the Levites, but anyone whose spirit has inspired him and whose insight has led him to separate himself, in order to stand before God and serve Him ... and who has freed himself from the yoke of the many [economic] calculations people seek—such a person has reached the pinnacle of sanctity. God is his portion ... and He will provide for him in this world, as He provided for the *kohanim* [and] the Levites.

At first sight, this could be understood to mean that a person who devotes himself entirely to God may demand public support. But this is not so. Radbaz comments on this passage as follows: "God will provide for his necessities but he should not impose himself on the public. Compare this with how [Rambam] explains the Mishnah[59] cautioning against using the Torah 'as a hoe.'" Rambam's interpretation of that Mishnah indeed confirms Radbaz's explanation. There, Rambam compares the scholars to the *kohanim* regarding privileges, but explicitly excludes financial support:

> Anyone who makes economic use of the honor of the Torah takes his life from this world...However, the Torah permits scholars to give their money to others to invest in profitable businesses [on the scholar's behalf]...and to receive priority in buying and selling merchandise in the marketplace. These are benefits that God granted them, just as He granted **the offerings to the *kohen* and the tithes to the Levite**...for merchants occasionally do such things for each other as a courtesy, even if there is no Torah scholarship to warrant it. A Torah scholar should certainly be treated at least as well as a respectable ignoramus.

R. Chaim Kanievsky[60] traces Rambam's words ["And not only the Levites..."] to the Talmudic dictum[61] that "the property of those who occupy themselves with Torah will prosper." This too implies that the support does not come from charity. Elsewhere, Rambam himself stresses:[62] "Anyone who intends to occupy himself with the Torah, not to do work, and to subsist on charity, has profaned [God's] name, disgraced the Torah, extinguished the light of the Law, brought evil upon himself, and taken his life from the world." And R. Mosheh Feinstein writes:[63] "A person is not only permitted but is even obligated to engage in business and work for a living. One is forbidden to say that, even if he does nothing, God will somehow provide for him."

In another context, R. Feinstein declares:[64] "A person should certainly provide for his upkeep, sustenance, and all his needs, together with those of his wife and dependents, so that he will have means available, not merely for a day, but for a long time. [In contrast, see R. Feinstein's remarks concerning Kolel students, cited below, Chapter 3, Section 2(3).]

Even if one has money, we find: "King Solomon cautioned a person to provide for his sustenance and not to rely on his riches, family connections or status."[65]

Rabbeinu Yonah[66] further addresses the importance of working for a livelihood:

> "See you a man busily engaged in his work"—King Solomon saw the great necessity to learn a trade in order to live, and he therefore urged, "Prepare your work outside." Our Sages say that work is great because it is ennobling. Many Sages were great artisans. They praise work profusely, pointing out that God ascribed [work] to Himself at the beginning of the Torah ...and that even one who occupies himself with the Torah —which exceeds all else in sublimity—will founder unless he also works or finds some other livelihood.

One must not only ensure that he himself has a trade but also teach one to his son.[67] This obligation is so compelling that a father may arrange an apprenticeship even on the Sabbath;[68] furthermore, he is not exiled if he inadvertently kills his son while teaching him a trade.[69] On the other hand, our Sages warn that one who neglects to teach his son a trade is essentially instructing him to steal.[70] The father's obligation to teach his son a trade is also cited by the later authorities.[71] The Sages even promulgated special rules to facilitate the study of a trade.[72]

The error of neglecting the obligation to teach one's son a trade is deplored by *Sefer HaBerith*:[73]

> The fathers [neglect this obligation] for the sake of Heaven, based on the words of R. Nehorai: "I forsake every trade in the world and teach my son only Torah."[74] They fail to understand that this is actually the prompting of the evil inclination, which is wont to cloak its nefarious suggestions in piety...and they do not know that this was not R. Nehorai's intent at all, as Maharsha has written.... Anyone who transgresses the words of our Sages in this matter and neglects to teach his son a trade will surely have to account for himself before the Divine Tribunal, and will certainly be punished.... The other nations say we sit idle and lazy and do no work; they accuse us of contaminating our surroundings by our swindling, deception, and usury and insist that all crafts are scorned by Israel. There is no greater profanation of the Divine Name—nor greater personal and general danger—than this.

Sedey Chemed[75] supported these remarks so ardently that he incorporated the entire chapter in which they appear into his own work.[76] Concerning the Biblical basis for this obligation, see *Mikhtav MeChizkiyahu.*[77]

Herewith the words of R. Shemuel Landau,[78] successor to his father, the "Noda' BiYehudah": "Everyone is obligated to teach his son the language and customs of his host country. And fathers should make sure their sons succeed in both Torah and *derekh eretz*; then the lad will retain both."

Work is so important that even the Torah scholar should steer his fellow Jews toward a proper livelihood. In the words of R. Ya'akov Emden:[79] "This matter is the responsibility of the Torah scholars especially—who should guide their flock with wisdom and insight to find a proper livelihood." He deduces this from God's command to Moses,[80] "'And you shall teach them'—That is their house of life, to teach them a trade for a livelihood," and from Jacob's establishing coinage (or marketplaces) for the people of Shechem.[81]

(3) Providing for One's Household

Although a person may waive his own personal requirements to some extent, he may not suspend those of others. Thus one must be careful not to deprive his wife, who depends on him for support, of her needs; for the Talmud states that she is to share in the benefits of a rise in his economic status but is not to suffer as a result of its decline. The economic standards to which she is accustomed determine his obligations toward her, even if he himself is satisfied with less. As R. Emden exhorts:[82] "[A husband] should not wait for a miracle...like [some saintly Sages did]." Similarly, the Sages interpret[83] the verse "He does kindness at all times..." to refer to one who provides for his minor children even after they have passed the age he is obligated to do so.

However, although one must provide for one's children, one may skimp on their support for the sake of Torah study, as the Talmud states:[84] "'Black as ravens'—Where do you find [the Torah]?...Rava says, in one who makes himself as cruel as a raven in providing for his children and his household."[85]

(4) Love of Work

But work is important not only for a livelihood; the requirement to work for its own sake transcends the obligation to provide for oneself and one's household. In the words of the Mishnah:[86] "Love work and hate officialdom [literally, "the rabbinate"]." This is explained as follows:[87] "If one has no work, what should he do? If he has a neglected courtyard or field, he should busy himself with it, for 'Six days shall you work and perform all your labor.'" Kaftor WaFerach[88] notes that "our Sages, along with the Torah, loved work." Rashbatz points out that this Mishnah[89] goes beyond the duty to support oneself; even if one has other income, he is obligated to work, "not only for the earnings involved, but out of love for it." One explanation offered for this obligation is the Talmudic dictum[90] that "idleness leads to neurosis." R. Ya'akov Emden rejects this explanation, suggesting instead[91] that one should love work because it is necessary for his physical well-being. Chida lists[92] two additional reasons: We should love work because God set us an example by doing work, and also because it helps to subdue our lusts.

The Sages adduce the importance of work from God Himself. They teach:[93] "A person is obligated to love work and engage in it. This can be adduced from the actions of God... Since even He performed 'the work that He did,' [when He created the world] how much more must this be man's obligation!" In fact, the Midrash actually equates work with imitating God:[94] "'You shall walk after God'—Can a man walk after God? [Scripture comes to teach us:] Just as God, at the beginning of Creation, occupied Himself with planting [the Garden of Eden] first of all, so you too, on entering the land, shall occupy yourselves with planting first of all." Clearly, work is beloved by God not merely as a means of man's survival, but because it sustains His creation.[95] Accordingly, we must love work because through it we serve the Creator, Who desires that we sustain His world and, as Rashi[96] explains, does not want His world to lack any trade needed to keep it running.

In instilling a love of work, the Sages also referred to the Prophets:[97] "Work is precious, for all the prophets engaged in it. Regarding Jacob, [Scripture] says: 'I shall return and pasture your sheep and guard them.' Of Moses it says, 'And Moses was a shepherd.' Of [King] David it says, 'and He took him from the sheep pens.' Amos is quoted, 'for I am a herdsman and I mix feed for them, but God took me away from the sheep.'"

Menorath HaMaor makes similar comments about the Tanaim:[98]

The Early Pious Ones worked for a living, and did not eschew humble occupations, even though some were princes, heads of yeshivoth and leaders. For example, R. Yosi was satisfied with carrying wood, declaring: "Work is great, because it warms the worker." Similarly, R. Yehoshua' was a charcoal burner, R. Yitzchak a blacksmith and R. Yochanan a cobbler. Abba Chilkiyah, a nephew of Hillel, dug up fields and vineyards as a day laborer; Abba Shaul dug graves and Hillel the Elder was a hewer of wood, even though he was the prince of Israel, the leader of his generation, and a descendant of the kings of Judea.[99]

Work is further praised for establishing a person financially. Asserts Rabbeinu Bachyay:[100] "[Work] is a good trait; it removes the shame of hunger and is the foundation of man's existence." Moreover, the Talmud states:[101] "Work is great, for the generation of the Flood was destroyed only because they neglected it and were drawn into robbery." Maharal[102] is even more explicit: "It generates love for God when the Torah scholar need not depend on others; [the converse, however] causes neglect of the honor of the Torah; for, if students did not sustain themselves [with public funds], the Torah would rise ever higher."

Indeed, according to Shulchan Arukh,[103] providing for oneself is considered a high spiritual achievement. This is deduced from a puzzling Talmudic passage:[104] "One who enjoys the fruit of his labors is greater than one who fears Heaven." This statement is somewhat obscure: If it refers to a God-fearing individual who toils, it is comparing two God-fearing individuals, one who toils and one who does not; then why mention fear of God at all? But if it refers to one who enjoys the fruit of his labor but is not God-fearing, how can such a one be greater than one who is? The commentators offer various explanations:[105]

Rashbatz[106] explains that a poor God-fearing man is superior to one who fears God under comfortable circumstances; the necessity to labor and the accompanying dependence upon God enhances one's fear of Him. Maharam Alashker, commenting on the above Mishnah, explains this statement as follows: "A person who studies half the day and works half the day should not think that his reward for the half day of work is less than for the half day he learns. Therefore [the Talmud] teaches us that [such a one] is superior to one who studies all day." R. Chaim of Volozhin[107] explains that one who earns his livelihood by working is greater than one who earns it by Torah study or serving as a rabbi.

But the most general explanation is that of Maharal,[108] who points out that it does not say "choose work", but rather "love work." This is because such love engenders thankfulness and love of Him Who provides the work. As serving God out of love is preferable to serving Him out of fear, one who loves work, and hence God, is greater than the one who merely fears God. This also explains why Maharal adds: "Work is the perfection of man," and "No one can love God perfectly unless he loves work, hates officiating, and shuns civil authorities." Maharal's observations may clarify an enigmatic Midrashic derivation:[109] "Work is more precious than patriarchal merit, for the latter preserved property, while work preserved lives." Or, as another Midrash[110] puts it: "The merit of labor withstands that which patriarchal merit cannot." True, labor saves one from hunger; but what great merit does one acquire through it? However, if labor contributes to man's perfection, as Maharal states, this accounts for its great merit.

Consequently, one should choose congenial and satisfying work, for this will lead him to happiness and love of God. Nowadays, most people devote a significant portion of their time to working for a living; the nature of this work, and their attitude toward it, will inevitably have a great influence on their personality and emotional state. *Chovoth HaLevavoth*[111] recommends that a person seek a livelihood to which he feels drawn, and R. 'Ovadiah Sforno[112] advises to select a profession for which one is particularly suited.

Acharonim too point out the spiritual advantages of labor which is a means to one's livelihood. The words of Shelah[113] are especially significant: "Therefore a person must seek some work or activity that will provide for him and his family, and should not...depend on others' generosity or loans; 'Blessed is the man who trusts in God.'" Shelah implies that relying on others for support diminishes one's trust in God; however, if one sustains himself by the fruits of his labors and is independent of others, his trust in God will grow.

In view of all the above advantages, it is not surprising that the Sages classified work *per se* as a mitzvah:[114] "'Six days you shall work': Rabi says, 'This is another commandment; just as Israel were commanded to rest, so were they commanded to work.'"

R. Yitzchak Abuhav[115] notes that the verse which commands us to work six days seems to be in direct contradiction to the verse commanding us to meditate in the Torah day and night. He resolves the problem by saying: "God established the reading of the Shema' morning and evening," through which we indeed "meditate upon Torah day and night."

The Tanaim are divided regarding the desirability of business versus physical work. Indeed, they go so far as to ask whether a father who teaches his son business rather than a trade has fulfilled his obligation of teaching him a livelihood.[116] Furthermore, note the contrast between the statement: "Minimize your business affairs and occupy yourself with Torah," and the statement advising rendering work (a trade) "secondary" to Torah but not necessarily minimizing it.[117] R. Yisrael of Salant[118] deplores the fact that most people denigrate the trades and prefer business, even though the former are more likely to strengthen one's trust in God and leave the mind free for loftier pursuits, whereas the latter frequently involves deceit and is distracting. On the other hand, Tosfoth Yom Tov[119] notes that according to the Mishnah, only one who engages in business dealings **excessively** will "not become wise, for without some dealings to keep his body alive, even his Torah will not survive."

(5) Appreciating The Importance of Property

We are commanded to love God with all our resources and to renounce our love of money for the sake of love of God. Nevertheless, the Torah warns us not to belittle our possessions. Indeed the Torah is mindful of the property of Israel, even that belonging to the wicked.[120] Thus, in the case of the plague of *tzara'ath* affecting houses, we are instructed to remove even inexpensive clay vessels from a house before it is pronounced *tamei* (ritually unclean), lest they, too, become irreversibly *tamei*. Similarly the urn that held the lots used in the Temple during Yom Kippur services was not sanctified, lest we be required to fashion it of silver or gold, thereby increasing public expenditure.[121] Only for the Yom Kippur service was the censer (*machtath haketoreth*) made of gold,[122] and only for Rosh HaShanah was the shofar fitted with a golden mouthpiece.[123] Similarly, the numerous show-breads (*lechem hapanim*), regularly required for the table in the Sanctuary, did not have to be made of fine flour.[124] Regarding the oil used in the Sanctuary, only that used for the candelabrum had to be of the highest degree of purity, but not that used for the *minchah* offerings.[125] According to one opinion, the *kohanim* would initially place but a small amount of oil in the candelabrum, adding more only if it did not last.[126] All these practices are rooted in the Torah's concern for our property.

Furthermore, the Sages maintain:[127] "The righteous value their property more than their lives...for they will not take what is not rightfully theirs." Because they are so meticulous about the means of acquisition, every asset acquired demands much effort; hence they treasure whatever they have earned.

Care of one's possessions is even considered piety. Thus the Amora Shemuel, who inspected his property only once a day, considered himself inferior to his father who used to inspect his property twice each day. Such care is laudatory: the time one deducts from Torah study for the inspection will prevent property losses, thereby saving far more time than actually invested.[128]

The protection of foreign holdings threatened by gentiles (along with Torah study and marriage) is a mitzvah for which one may leave Eretz Yisrael.[129] One may also leave for business reasons.[130] Some poskim rule that even when one has enough to eat, further acquisition — presumably for future needs — is considered a mitzvah.[131]

Utilitarian motives are not the only important considerations. In specifying that the Tabernacle's fine blue-wool tapestries be protected with goat hair cloths, the Torah teaches us that "one should be careful with beautiful objects."[132] Aesthetics, too, must be taken into account.

Although *chesed* (loving kindness) is a pillar of the world, "A person should donate no more than one-fifth [of his property] to charity...lest he himself become needy."[133]

Even though one generally values his life more than his possessions, one should respect one's property, as his life depends on it. And he who robs another's property is considered as if he has robbed his fellow man of his life:[134] "Such are the ways of all who gain by violence; they take the life of [the stolen goods'] owners." Indeed, "Anyone who robs his companion of [even] a penny is as though he has taken his life"—and even the life of his children.[135]

2. Reliance on God Versus Striving

The Torah is to be observed within the framework of the natural laws according to which the world runs. As Rava declared:[136] "One may not act in expectation of a miracle [to save him from harmful consequences]." Even in performing a mitzvah—which generally protects one from harm[137]—one must take reasonable precautions.[138] And even if someone is saved by a miracle, this is at the expense of his merits in heaven. Moreover, one who prays, when his wife is already pregnant, that she give birth to a boy, has prayed in vain.[139] This implies that a prayer for a miracle which contravenes the laws of nature is considered futile and a "false prayer."[140]

Even the Patriarchs did not expect miracles. Despite God's explicit promises of protection, both Abraham and Isaac, when entering an alien country, felt it necessary to present their wives as their sisters. Although they must have found it difficult to perpetrate a deception, they were not allowed to risk their lives by relying on God's help alone. Jacob, too, prepared to meet his hostile brother Esau "by equipping himself with gifts [diplomacy], strategic deployment, and prayer"—and did not depend on prayer alone.[141] Moses only slew the Egyptian after verifying that there were no witnesses. And the prophet Samuel hesitated to fulfill God's explicit commandment to anoint David, for "If Saul will hear, he will kill me," to which God responded by suggesting a subterfuge. *Chovoth HaLevavoth* comments:[142]

> This was not considered a lack of faith on his part; rather, [God's reaction] shows that caution is laudatory....For, had his faith been lacking, the reply would have been, "It is I who gives and takes life!"...as He said to Moses... "Who gives man speech?" And if Samuel, whose faith was perfect, was reluctant to put himself in even slight danger, despite a direct order from God...certainly, for an ordinary person to do so would be despicable....And what we have said regarding life and death also applies to health, clothing and shelter.

Furthermore, in the case of those mitzvoth for which a Jew is not expected to sacrifice his life, if he does so nonetheless, he is held responsible for his death,[143] even though he was motivated by saintliness and hoped for a miracle.

The Talmud teaches: "Everything is in the hands of God, except [the illnesses caused by] heat and cold"—because, as Rashi explains, these sometimes result from man's negligence.[144] In fact, independent of a person's decreed fate, any careless conduct can bring on injury or even death.[145] The Talmud recounts an incident[146] in which a woman (Miriam, the nurse) was mistakenly taken by the Angel of Death. The mistake was made possible by her placing herself carelessly in a somewhat dangerous situation. The Talmud proves by this incident that "there is death without justice." The same message seems to be conveyed by the Talmudic statement[147] "Once permission has been granted to destructive forces, they no longer discriminate between the righteous and the wicked."

There is no way to free ourselves from responsibility for our actions and their consequences. As Rambam[148] declares: "For not all of man's actions are decreed by God, [such as] 'who shall marry whom'...for if this were meant literally and marriages were predestined, why does the Torah say, '...lest he die in the war and another man marry [his betrothed]'?" Others,[149] however, believe that marriages are decreed.

We have been promised God's blessings:[150] "'And God will bless you'. Lest we think this is so even when we sit idle, the Torah continues—'in all that you do.'" God grants us His blessings if we work toward obtaining them by natural means. Similarly:[151] "The Patriarch Isaac, reasoning that labor is prerequisite to God's blessings, sowed, as the verse tells us." Again:[152] "One should not say: I will eat and drink and be well off without exerting myself, and God will provide. Therefore, we are told: 'You have blessed the work of his hands.'" Even in the face of an explicit Divine promise, such as the year of plenty that is to precede the Sabbatical year to compensate for anticipated agricultural losses, the "Chazon Ish" says: "The Torah did not mean for us to depend on this blessing and to refrain from those preparations called for by the laws of nature."

The Talmud[154] indicates that derekh eretz itself may, at times, be a sign of faith: "'Faith' refers to the Mishnaic order of Zera'im...for one who sows [shows he] has faith in God."

We are also commanded to act in compliance with the laws of nature and not to expect God to follow His plans regardless of our efforts. To quote Chovoth HaLevavoth:[155] "When one exerts himself, physically and mentally, on the basis of the laws of nature, he should bear in mind that he is fulfilling the Creator's commandment to occupy himself with the 'causes' acting in the world, such as agriculture, plowing, and sowing."

This requires some clarification. On the one hand, if man fails to conduct himself in line with natural law, he has to bear the consequences. He must earn a living, otherwise his livelihood will be deficient.

Even if he devotes himself to *talmud Torah*, he must combine it with labor, for "any Torah which is not associated with work will end in failure and cause transgression."[156] On the other hand, one must be aware, as *Chovoth HaLevavoth* puts it: "'Causes' [natural laws] alone accomplish nothing and [everything is only the result of] the Creator's decree." The message here seems to be that health and wealth etc., result not from autonomous laws of nature, but from Divine decree—for God in His wisdom decreed that the diligent would succeed. As it says: "He who is busy with his work will stand before kings," and "Laziness causes the roof to rot."[157] It is not that God established laws of nature, for these, in truth, are not laws at all, but expressions of the will of God, Who wishes His world to run according to set rules. He wills, in each case, that a released stone should drop—and we call this will "gravity," as if it were a law. Likewise, His will decrees that one who stands under a crumbling wall risks injury, and one who stands in the cold risks illness.

Ran describes this concept as follows:[158] "It is God's will that the world function as normally as possible. Nature is precious to Him, and He will only manipulate it when absolutely necessary." He continues: "[Events] result not from specific causes but from general ones, for God does not want nature altered for individuals." Hence anyone who ignores the laws of nature is as delinquent as one who eats a slaughtered animal without examining it for physical defects or one who lights the Chanukah lamp without filling it with enough oil.

This principle is implied in the Talmud:[159] "If one stole a measure of wheat and sowed it, by right it should not grow. But the world goes on as usual and those fools who act as spoilers will ultimately have to render account."

This however, does not contradict the fact that God directs the world according to His will. Rather, He directs it within the framework of the laws of nature. As *Meshekh Chokhmah* says:[160] "When a person walks straight in God's ways he succeeds naturally, and this is the meaning of God's benediction 'if you walk in My statutes...'—then the laws of nature also function in a straightforward manner. For all the ways of nature, as arranged by Divine wisdom, complement the ways of the Torah and its commandments."

These concepts may appear contradictory: If God maintains the laws of nature, how can He adjust them for the righteous? The solution to this puzzle is hidden in the uncertainties and ambiguities that God interwove with the very laws of nature, which control each and every particle in the world. This was discovered by contemporary scientists —to their astonishment, and in direct contradiction to fundamental and long-established beliefs. By incorporating uncertainty into the laws of nature, God has instituted a means for guiding the world in one direction or another without violating any natural law.[161]

All this means that God wants the world to operate in an orderly fashion. Even Ramban—who says that a righteous person should trust God to bend nature to his needs[162]—states that help only comes through natural means: "For the Torah commands [us to live] according to derekh eretz and God will covertly perform miracles for those who trust Him. He will only alter the natural order of the world when there is no alternative or in an occasional demonstration of His [Presence] to His enemies, as in the splitting of the sea and similar occurrences." Elsewhere, he writes:[163] "For the Torah does not depend on miracles," and therefore Moses was obliged to count the arms-bearing men in Israel, to prepare for war before they entered the Land. R. Yosef Albo, however, seems to differ. He states:[164] "That God makes nature subservient to those who believe in Him is a major Torah principle and a basis of our faith in God's intervention in individual destiny." However, even his views can be interpreted to conform with those of Ramban.

There is disagreement in the Talmud regarding a fundamental question: Is a physician permitted to heal the sick or is he, by doing so, considered as working against God, who caused the illness. Two opinions are presented in the following Talmudic passage:[165] "It is not the way of people to heal ['rather, they should pray for mercy'—Rashi]; it is merely a custom [to visit a physician]. Abayey says: One should not say this, for they taught in the house of R. Yishma'el, 'And he shall surely seek healing—hence a physician is permitted to heal.'"

Ramban concludes:[166]

One should not say: "God has stricken; how can I heal?" ...Rather healing is an obligation included in the commandment to save lives ["Ramban reasons that since healing is not prohibited, it must be an obligation because of the commandment to save lives"—Perishah[167]]. Saving lives is a great mitzvah...hence any skilled physician is obligated to heal. And if he does not, he is a murderer.

All this has become halakhah and is cited in Tur and Shulchan

Arukh.[168] Kaftor WaFerach[169] adds: "One who is diligent in this art is praiseworthy." Furthermore, the Torah obligates one who causes physical harm to pay the victim's medical expenses. From this we learn that we are expected to seek medical help, when needed — "The Torah did not make its precepts dependent on miracles."[170]

Rashba writes similarly:[171] "No sick person should depend on miracles by refraining from consulting physicians. He should actively seek remedies...Furthermore, it is forbidden to embark on a dangerous course, and depend on miracles [to save him]." Ran, too, declares:[172] "If one is in mortal danger and the experts insist that the Sabbath be desecrated for him [if he refuses to cooperate, this is not considered piety] and it is akin to suicide." Rambam railed against a misinterpretation of King Hezekiah's concealment of the Book of Healing[173] on the part of certain Torah scholars, who believe that when ill one should pray, rather than visit a physician.

> I have heard the following explanation: "[King] Solomon wrote the Book of Healing so that anyone stricken with any illness could seek it out, follow its instructions and be healed. And when [King] Hezekiah saw that people were not depending on God [for healing], he hid it." What harm this explanation has caused and how many errors are in it! How can they accuse Hezekiah of such foolishness?... According to their simplistic and erroneous opinion, when a hungry person, instead of relying on prayer, eats bread, he will undoubtedly be cured of a severe illness—hunger. In this way [according to them] he deserts his God and does not depend on Him. Let us rather say to them, "You fools! Just as I thank God when I eat, for enabling me to find that which satisfies my hunger, I should thank Him for letting me find the cure for my illness."

(Rambam's explanation is that Hezekiah concealed the Book of Healing because it was based on astrology and similar forbidden methods.)

The Acharonim, too, write in this vein. R. Yehudah 'Eyash[174] observes: "If a person sits idle and does not concern himself much with healing, his illness spreads until it envelops him completely and he dies, even though it is before his time. Similarly, one who enters a raging fire is surely consumed by it and dies prematurely. These words are obvious and only a perverse or fallacious thinker would dispute them." Chida[175] writes: "Apparently, nowadays we may not depend on miracles, and a sick person must follow the ways of the world and call a physician to heal him. He must not defy common practice and consider himself superior to generations of pious men cured by physicians. Such behavior is almost an [outright] transgression, either because he aggrandizes himself [by imagining himself pious], or because he relies on miracles in times of danger." *Shevet Yehudah* asserts:[176] "Seeking a physician is necessary and based on the Torah, and it is almost a strong obligation [sic] on the patient to do so. And if anyone defends himself and objects ...saying that God heals even the undeserving, this is only the opinion of the strange and foolish; it borders on recklessness, and he will be held accountable for it." The "Chazon Ish"[177] declares health care a mitzvah, like the obligations to perfect oneself, noting that some Amoraim patronized gentile and apostate physicians.

The obligation to seek medical aid can be deduced from many statements by the Sages. They mandated desecration of the Sabbath for medical treatment in life-threatening instances and praised alacrity in this regard.[178] Such praise would surely be inappropriate to one guilty of a shortcoming in his faith. Furthermore, the marriage contract requires husbands to provide for their wives' medical care. Additionally, according to the Talmud[179] certain afflictions are destined to be cured only by a specific doctor, and a specific medication, implying a decision from on High that physician and medication should provide the cure.

R. Yehudah HeChasid charges that anyone who could have studied medicine and saved lives but did not, is, effectively, a "murderer."[180] See *Lev Avraham*[181] concerning the seriousness of disobeying a physician's order in an effort to fulfill a mitzvah.

Relating to another aspect, Rambam[182] writes: "The medical profession is extremely important in perfecting man, and teaching him to know God and acquire true happiness. Its study and practice are among the greatest of [Divine] services."

However, excessive worry and preparation for the future are also reprehensible. In the words of the Sages,[183] "'Blessed the man who trusts in God'—That refers to Joseph, who [in general] did not appeal to the Egyptians. But because [of the one time] he asked the chief butler to remember him and mention him [to Pharaoh], two years were added [to his incarceration]." Joseph tried to get out of prison by normal means, which would appear to be wholly in order. Why, then, was he punished?

The "Chazon Ish" explained:[184] "As Egyptians were known not to remember [a favor] and not to do kindness, it was merely an act of desperation...for a true believer does not engage in such things." Only that which is dictated by reason is permitted—and obligatory; anything else betokens desperation and a lack of faith.

Also, when God provided the manna, He taught Israel to trust in Him and not to worry too much about tomorrow. The Sages tell us[185] that those who saved manna for the next day lacked faith, because it had been promised explicitly.[186]

It is clear from what has been written so far that work is an essential part of Torah life. What, then, is meant by the statement that God sustains His righteous by reason of their righteousness, as the Mishnah[187] states: "Whoever accepts the yoke of Torah is freed from the yokes of governmental imposition and derekh eretz?" The following passage offers clarification.[188] "If [the Early Pious Ones] spent nine hours each day in prayer, how was their Torah maintained and their work accomplished? Because they were pious, their Torah was kept intact and their work was blessed." In other words, though they were freed from the yoke of derekh eretz, they did indeed do work—but only a little, and it was blessed. This is also implied by the Talmudic statement:[189] "Whoever engages in Torah study, his property will prosper."

2

Derekh Eretz and Torah Study

1.   "And You Shall Meditate In It Day and Night"

How are we to resolve the conflict between the obligation to provide for ourselves and to "meditate in the Torah day and night?"[1] If we occupy ourselves day and night with Torah study, when can we earn a living?

The Jerusalem Talmud alludes to this dilemma:[2]

They asked R. Yehoshua': "What is the law concerning one who wishes to teach his son [the wisdom of][3] Greek?" He answered them, "Let him teach it when it is neither day nor night, in accordance with the verse 'you shall meditate therein day and night.'" [They countered] "But R. Yishma'el taught, 'You shall choose life—that refers to a trade,' [and if you take this verse literally:] it implies that one is prohibited to teach one's son a trade, because it says: 'you shall meditate...'" Rabi, the son of R. Chiya answered in the name of R. Yochanan, "[The Sages only forbade teaching the 'wisdom of Greek'] because [it may lead people to become] informers." [But they did not forbid teaching other things, such as a trade].

Hence, the obligation to meditate in Torah day and night does not conflict with teaching one's son a trade, and certainly not with providing for himself; only the teaching of seditious arts is frowned upon.

The Babylonian Talmud, in *Berakhoth*,[4] is more explicit:

Why does Scripture tell us, "And you shall gather your grain?" A [different] verse says, "This Book of Torah shall never leave your mouth." We might have taken this literally; therefore the Torah says, "and you shall gather your grain"—practice it according to *derekh eretz*. These are the words of R. Yishma'el. R. Shim'on ben Yochai said, "If a man plows at the time of plowing, sows in the sowing season...and winnows when the wind blows, what will become of the Torah? Rather, when Israel fulfill the will of God, their work is done by others, as Scripture says, 'and strangers will come and graze your sheep.' But when Israel do not fulfill the will of God, their work is done by themselves, as it is written, 'and you shall gather your grain'...." Abayey said: "Many followed the words of R. Yishma'el and succeeded—the words of R. Shim'on ben Yochai and did not succeed." Rava said to the scholars: "Please do not appear before me [i.e. come to the yeshiva] in Nissan [during harvest] and Tishrey [during the ingathering], lest you be preoccupied with your livelihood the entire year."

Since both Abayey and Rava followed the opinion of R. Yishma'el, the halakhah has been established accordingly. Thus Shulchan Arukh rules:[5] "After leaving the synagogue, one should go to the study hall ...Afterwards, he should pursue his occupation, for 'any Torah not combined with work will end in failure and lead to transgression.'"

The main discussion of the verse "This book of Torah shall not leave your mouth, and you shall meditate in it day and night" is found in *Menachoth*:[6]

R. Yochanan said in the name of R. Shim'on ben Yochai: "Even if one has only read the Shema' morning and evening, he has fulfilled this verse, but one may not tell this to unlearned people." Rava [supporting R. Shim'on] said, "It is a mitzvah to tell this to unlearned people." Ben Damah, the nephew of R. Yishma'el, asked his uncle: "What about a person like me, who has learned the entire Torah—may I study the wisdom of Greek?" R. Yishma'el answered him, "It is written: ... you shall meditate therein day and night. Go find an hour that is neither day nor night—that is the time to study the wisdom of Greek." [Thus R. Yishma'el's opinion here is that one must study literally day and night.] This opinion differs from that of R. Shemuel bar Nachmani, who said in the name of R. Yonathan,

"This verse ['You shall meditate...'] is neither an obligation nor a mitzvah—it is a blessing."

In Shulchan Arukh, this dispute is decided according to Rava,[7] that is, [in an emergency] one may satisfy the demands of this verse by reading the Shema'.

The last two Talmudic passages appear to contradict each other on two points:

a) In the first passage, R. Yishma'el favors *derekh eretz*, while in the second he takes literally the commandment to study Torah day and night.

b) In the first passage, R. Shim'on ben Yochai seems to oppose any activity other than Torah study, while in the second passage he is the most lenient.

Rishonim have already dealt with and resolved these contradictions.

R. Yehudah HeChasid explains:[8] "R. Shim'on ben Yochai, by saying 'If a man plows... what would become of the Torah?' did not mean that continuous study is an obligation [this is evident from his opinion in the other Talmudic passage]. Rather [he meant that study] is a generally meritorious action recommended to guard against neglect of the Torah." Rosh agrees.[9] According to these Rishonim, then, the difference of opinion in the second passage relates to the question of how to satisfy the absolute requirements of the verse under discussion: R. Shim'on believes that a **minimum** of learning by day and night is sufficient while R. Yishma'el contends that, in principle, the commandment is only fulfilled by learning **all** day and night, except for interruptions needed to fulfill other obligations, such as making a living, as he rules in the first passage. He forbade his nephew to study the wisdom of Greek, because this study was not for the sake of a livelihood nor did it serve any other mitzvah.[11] The controversy in the first passage, however, concerns Torah study as a means of achieving a higher level of perfection, for one who wishes to be "crowned with the diadem of the Torah."[10] Here R. Shim'on takes a maximalist position, whereas R. Yishma'el teaches that even if one studies in order to rise spiritually, he must still be concerned about his livelihood. On this question, Rava decides in accordance with R. Yishma'el, indicating that even if one wants to be crowned with the diadem of the Torah, he is forbidden to do so by totally neglecting the requirements of *derekh eretz*, even though admittedly he can achieve such elevation only by curtailing his *derekh eretz* as much as possible.

Acharonim suggest many other solutions, as summarized in the review at the end of this part.

We still must identify the "strangers" destined—according to R. Shim'on—to do Israel's work. Some might think that this refers to those who support Torah scholars, such as in the "Zebulun-Issachat arrangement" of the Midrash. But "Zebulun," the businessman who provides for the Torah student "Issachar," is no stranger. Zebulun even takes precedence over his brother in the blessings of Jacob (end of Genesis) and Moses (end of Deuteronomy). R. Chiya Pontrimoli[12] (and seemingly Rashi[13]) explains that the "strangers" are the gentile laborers hired by Jewish landowners.

Moreover, the verse cited by R. Shim'on ben Yochai speaks of a time when all Israel fulfill the will of God—that is, the end of days. (See review at the end of this part for an exposition of the arguments for and against this interpretation.)

Relating to Abayey's statement that "many acted like R. Shim'on ben Yochai but did not succeed," *Sefath Emeth*[14] asks: "This is indeed surprising; how can we say that one who acts like R. Shim'on ben Yochai does not succeed? Rather, they did not succeed in using worldly matters in the service of God, which is the primary task of humanity [and can be accomplished only in the way of R. Yishma'el]." This statement is not unique among the later authorities.[15] For a novel interpretation, see the review appended to this part [Section 4(1)].

Summarizing this discussion, R. A. Azulai[16] writes, "If the book of Torah never leaves his mouth day and night, but he does not wish to work, this, too, is an evil affliction."

2.   "Combining Torah Study with *Derekh Eretz* is Beautiful"

But not only does *derekh eretz* not conflict with our duty to study Torah day and night, on the contrary, *derekh eretz* is a necessary adjunct to Torah study, as proclaimed by the Mishnah:[17] "Combining Torah study with *derekh eretz*[18] is beautiful and all Torah which is not combined with work will end in failure and lead to transgression."[19]

Another Mishnah[20] declares: "Where there is no flour, there is no Torah;" that is, a livelihood is a prerequisite for Torah study[21].

The correlation between work and successful Torah study is also clear from the quotation from Shulchan Arukh cited in the last section.

This, too, is the meaning of the verse[22] "[Torah] wisdom is good with an inheritance [i.e. a source of income]." Likewise the Midrash:[23] "'To guard the way of the tree of life'—the way [derekh] refers to derekh eretz; [only] after [we have walked that path, can we reach] the tree of life, meaning Torah." R. Ya'akov Emden[24] makes the same point, in explaining why, when appearing before the Heavenly Tribunal, one is first asked: "Were your business dealings honest?" and only afterwards: "Did you set aside specific times for Torah study?" This, he teaches, is because one's Torah study must be preceded by some form of gainful activity. Moreover, he points out, "And if his business dealings were not honest, he is doubly in the wrong, for he trangressed and did not trust in his Creator, and this in turn destroyed the merit of his Torah study."

In this context, the following amazing passage[25] from *Tosafoth Yeshanim* bears clarification:

"Combining Torah study **with** *derekh eretz* is beautiful"—Rabbeinu Tam explains that *derekh eretz* is primary [if one matter is cited in connection "with" another, the latter is always primary and the former secondary]. But this leads to a difficulty: The verse says "See life **with** the wife you love"—and there we cannot say that "the wife" is primary to "life." The solution may be that [the word "life" in this verse refers to a trade]—and a wife is primary to a trade...But R. Elchanan said that Torah is primary [to *derech eretz*], based on: a) the statement that "the early [generations] made their Torah primary and their work secondary, and they succeeded;" and b) [the *Baraitha* in] *Pirkey Avoth* that lists among the forty-eight ways of acquiring the Torah "the reduction of *derekh eretz*." Furthermore, the latter part of the same Mishnah, "any Torah that does not have work associated with it will end in failure," indicates the opposite. [Work associated with it (Torah) implies that work is secondary to Torah.]

Rash, too, interprets the Mishnah like R. Elchanan[26] as does *Tosafoth Yeshanim*. *Machzor Vitry* explains that Torah and *derekh eretz* are equally important. Chida writes:[27] "*Derekh eretz* is primary, as the *Zohar* declares, because Zebulun is given precedence over Issachar."

R. Mosheh Alshikh[28] resolves the difficulty underlying the dispute between R. Tam and R. Elchanan as follows: "There are two kinds of people. Those whose primary concern is their work, to which Torah study is secondary, constitute the majority of Israel. Then there are a few, appointed by God, whose steady occupation, day and night, is the Torah. The Mishnah addresses both groups. To one group it says: 'Torah study should be combined with *derekh eretz*' and to the other: 'Any Torah not associated with work ...' "[29]

Alternatively, R. Alshikh[30] suggests: "While engaged in *derekh eretz*, one should meditate on and review his Torah studies—that is what is meant by Torah study associated with *derekh eretz*." R. Chaim of Volozhin writes similarly.[31] *Hafla-ah*[32] adds that rather than causing him errors in his business dealings, this preoccupation with Torah will ensure his success. R. Yehudah HeChasid,[33] however, discouraged this practice as potentially counterproductive; for, since he will not be giving a full measure of service, he may be guilty of "robbery" and, in spiritual terms, his loss will exceed his profit. Similarly, in discussing the Midrash which states that Enoch the cobbler "made with every stitch a special dedication to God," R. Yisrael of Salant[34] writes: "This cannot mean that he thought of Divine matters while he stitched, as it is forbidden by Torah law to distract oneself while working for others." *Beth HaLevi*[35] writes in the same vein: "Furthermore, one should constantly analyze his actions while working to ensure that they do not involve any trace of defrauding [his employer]." Thus, in accordance with these words of *Sefer Chasidim*, R. Yisrael of Salant and *Beth HaLevi*, one must be careful lest his efforts to be God-fearing (studying Torah while working) turn his good deeds into evil ones.

We conclude by recalling Rambam's sharp words of warning to anyone who might consider avoiding the above-discussed obligation quoted in the previous section under "Livelihood."[36] His words were cited subsequently by *Tur* and Rema in Shulchan Arukh.[37] In Section 2 of the following chapter, we cite opposing opinions by *Kesef Mishneh* and others.

3. How Much Should One Work?

We have seen that we must provide for ourselves by normal means, yet excessive industry is forbidden and perceived as a lack of faith. How much time, then, is one to devote to his livelihood, and to what standard of living may he aspire? Balancing Torah study and work, say our Sages,[38] is as perilous as traveling the narrow path between two roads —

one filled with fire and the other with snow. However, by following the words of Torah authorities, one can guarantee a safe journey on this precarious route.

One indication as to the ideal division of our time is found in the following midrashic passage:[39]

> Rabi said in the name of the holy congregation: "Secure for yourself a trade along with Torah. Why? [Because the verse says]: See life..." And why did he refer to them as the "holy congregation"? Because they included R. Yosi ben Meshullam and R. Shim'on ben Menasiah, who devoted one-third of their day to Torah, one-third to prayer and one-third to work. Others say that they toiled in the Torah in the winter and in their work in the summer.

Rambam,[40] in explaining the tripartite nature of learning (one-third Scriptures, etc.) cites as an example one who engages in a trade three hours a day and studies nine. Elsewhere, too, he writes:[41] "Whoever wishes to fulfill this mitzvah [of Torah study] properly and be crowned with the diadem of Torah, should not let his mind be diverted by other thoughts, nor feel that he can acquire Torah, wealth, and honor all together. 'This is the Torah way:...live a life of deprivation...'"

This much regarding the amount of time to be devoted to work. But there is also the issue of attitudes and priorities. The Mishnah assures us[42] that "Whoever accepts the yoke of Torah will be freed from the yokes of governmental imposition and *derekh eretz*. According to the Rishonim the "yoke of Torah" refers to Torah study.[43] We should not conclude from this that one is not to work at all; the question is one of emphasis only, as we are taught:[44] "The early generations made Torah [study] their fixed [occupation] and their work transitory—and succeeded in both. The later generations, who made their work fixed and their Torah study transitory, succeeded in neither."

What do the Sages mean by "fixed" and "transitory"? If the implication is that one should spend **more** time studying and **less** working, why is the holy congregation praised for allocating equal time to study and work? Moreover, had the Sages meant that one's work should be minimal, they would surely have used the term "minimize," not "transitory." Therefore, they apparently did not mean that work should be minimized, but rather that involvement with the Torah should be primary, basic and interrupted only to fulfill a mitzvah—including the earning of a livelihood. Furthermore, one should pursue this livelihood only until he accumulates sufficient means—hence the term "transitory." Rambam equates the term "transitory" with opportunity—"if he has the opportunity, let him avail himself of it."

The assignment of primacy to Torah study entails allocation of fixed periods to it. This is what Rashi[45] had in mind when commenting on the Mishnah, "Make your Torah fixed" — "Set aside definite times to learn four or five chapters every day." However, in another explanation of this Mishnah, Rashi says: "He should designate not just certain times for the Torah, but the entire day." Rashbatz[46] counters: "But this is impossible. Did not the Talmud say: 'Combine it with *derekh eretz*'?... Rather, the time you set aside for Torah should be primary and all other activities should merely support it." Elsewhere[47] Rashi himself explains: "'Did you set aside times?'—A person must engage in *derekh eretz*, for 'if there is no *derekh eretz*, there is no Torah.' Therefore, it is necessary to set aside specific times for Torah...lest the entire day be devoted to *derekh eretz*."

All the above refers to work. Regarding business however, which generally enhances a businessman's wealth rather than simply supporting him—our Sages taught:[48] "Minimize your business activity and busy yourself with the Torah" and that such minimization aids in the acquiring of Torah,[49] carefully chosing the expression "minimize," especially because business pursuits are liable to detract from Torah study.[50]

In the passage from *Berakhoth*, quoted at the beginning of this chapter, our Sages allude to the amount of work they consider proper. Rava instructs his disciples not to attend the yeshiva in the spring and autumn months, so that they can do the work necessary to support themselves the rest of the year. This is accepted as halakhah by *Sefer HaAgudah*, and R. Yehudah HeChasid[51] cites it as one instance in which "neglecting the Torah actually upholds it." He adds: "If one studies during the reaping and vintage, or at any time that he could earn money, and as a result has nothing to eat—it would be better for him to work first and study only afterwards, for 'Better is the end of a thing than its beginning.'[52] However, if he has much money with which to profit and sustain himself—then it is better that he engage in Torah study." Maharal[54] comes to a similar conclusion regarding the postponement of Torah study for earning a livelihood: "If a person limits his time away from Torah study—say, for a month or two [of work]—then he

should forgo his learning. Otherwise, certainly not." Actually, the Mishnah itself[43] hints at this: "If there is no flour, there is no Torah." Since it
speaks of neither grain—which implies long-term planning—nor bread,
which suggests a hand-to-mouth existence, but rather of flour, an intermediate foodstuff, it endorses an intermediate level of planning for
financial security.[55]

On the other hand, the Mishnah says:[56] "This is the Torah way [for
one who wishes to be crowned with the diadem of Torah—Rambam]:
'Eat bread with salt, drink measured water, sleep on the ground, live a
life of deprivation, and toil in the Torah." Similarly, the Talmud[57]
relates: "Ilfas and R. Yochanan were studying Torah, but were
oppressed by poverty. They said, 'Let us stop and go into business'...
[The angels said] 'Let us kill them, for they are abandoning life in the
next world for life in this world.'" R. Yochanan heard them and abandoned his plan; he eventually became the head of the Academy in Eretz
Yisrael. It appears that only someone willing to accept a life of sacrifice
is worthy of attaining greatness in Torah. (Ilfas' and R. Yochanan's
decision to go into business would seem to indicate that they had been
supporting themselves until that point by manual labor. If so, this
episode further reinforces the view of R. Yisrael of Salant[58] that a
manual trade is superior to business activity insofar as its impact on
talmud Torah is concerned.)

The above guidelines, along with the advice of one's Torah mentor,
should enable each person to determine his own appropriate measure of
work.

4.   "Torah Study Is His Steady Occupation"
(*Toratho Umanutho*)

The concept "Torah study is his steady occupation" requires clarification.
R. Chiya used to pray[59] "Let the Torah be our steady occupation." In
another Talmudic passage,[60] R. Yochanan explains that only people like
R. Shim'on ben Yochai and his companions are excused from interrupting their Torah study for prayers, since "their Torah was their steady
occupation; but people such as we, do have to interrupt [their studies for
prayer]." To understand this statement, we must first clarify what is
meant by "Torah was their steady occupation"—not just intensive, but
"steady." This cannot mean that R. Shim'on and his companions
earned their livelihood from the Torah, as this is expressly prohibited by

the Mishnah; moreover, even those who do allow it consider it only a second choice, and certainly not something to pray for.

Rishonim state explicitly that *Toratho Umanutho* refers to one whose Torah is primary and whose occupation is secondary. Rosh[61] comments: "Every scholar whose Torah study is his steady occupation...makes his Torah fixed and his work transitory, thinks about Torah constantly and does not forgo it for unimportant things, only for earning his livelihood, which is his duty—for 'combining Torah study with *derekh eretz* is beautiful and any Torah not associated with work will fail and lead to transgression'... [In the case under consideration] Torah was his steady occupation and he abandoned it only minimally, as needed for his livelihood." Nimukey Yosef[62] agrees. "These things were only said about one whose Torah is his steady occupation, that is, about a scholar whose Torah is fixed and whose work is transitory." Rashba[63] elaborates: "When Rosh said 'only as needed for his livelihood,' he evidently did not mean this literally, and anything one does to revive his soul is included...It is taken for granted that things can happen to a person, such as illnesses and the like, which require great expenses, and these have no fixed limit."

Korban Ha'Eidah[64] explains that one whose Torah study is his steady occupation is one who does conduct his business, but does not let it interfere with his study time, even when a special opportunity arises.

All the above shows that *Toratho Umanutho* means that one should treat the Torah with the dedication which people normally devote to their professions; it does not mean that he neglects his livelihood.[65]

The following statement is frequently cited as a basis for denying the obligation to acquire a trade:[66] "R. Meir said, 'One should ensure that his son learn a clean and easy occupation'...R. Nehorai said: 'I ignore every occupation in the world and teach my son only Torah.'" R. Nehorai does not seem to acknowledge a father's obligation to teach his son a trade. This is puzzling since in halakhah there is unanimous agreement on this issue. This is evident from the fact that a father is permitted to arrange for his son's apprenticeship on the Sabbath and that one who accidentally kills his son while teaching him a trade is not exiled. A careful reading of his words reveals however that R. Nehorai was not taking issue with R. Meir; rather, he apparently makes a strictly personal statement. The fact that Rif and Rosh quote both opinions in their commentaries also implies that they do not conflict.[67] Other commentators, too, insist that this obligation is accepted unanimously. In his Shulchan Arukh[68], R. Sheneor Zalman of L'ady states: "For he is obligated to teach his son a trade, after he has taught him Torah. This is evident because **there is no dispute in this matter.**" Maharsha[69] explains: "R. Nehorai...meant that he would ignore the constancy of all the trades in the world and teach his son Torah fixedly and a trade transitorily."

R. Ya'akov Emden[70] assesses the situation as follows: "Even according to R. Nehorai, everyone must work at a trade...and not depend on miracles... [He] merely assumes that by teaching his son Torah exclusively a father can fulfill his obligation to teach him a profession. But the son will certainly feel the need to enable himself to maintain his Torah, and will seek a livelihood on his own." R. Mosheh Feinstein[71] writes similarly and at length. But these latter interpretations entail a certain difficulty: If, as claimed, R. Nahorai believes that it suffices to teach one's son Torah, in what sense is the father obligated to teach his son a trade at all?

Peney Yehoshu'a explains that R. Nehorai speaks only for his son, an eager, exceptional student destined to become a perfect *talmid chakham* and a perfectly pious person, whose "work would be done by others." Presumably, the boy's enormous potential justified his father's decision. Also *Sefer HaMiknah*[72] explains that R. Nehorai apparently does not dispute the Sages' position on "any Torah not associated with work..." He seems to agree with *Peney Yehoshua'*.

Or Chadash interprets it thus: "He should [leave aside] all other trades and teach him only the Torah trade." He evidently endorses using the Torah as a trade with which to earn a livelihood. This would seem to contradict two Mishnayoth: "Any Torah not associated with work will end in failure," and "You should not make [the Torah] a hoe with which to dig." *Or Chadash* does not address this problem, which we discuss in detail in the next chapter.

Imrey Shefer suggests otherwise: "[R. Nehorai's statement applies] only to his minor-age son. But he concurs that when his son reaches puberty and approaches adulthood he must earn a livelihood... [and his father must] teach him a trade." Chida also considers[73] it untenable to maintain that R. Nehorai taught his son no trade whatsoever. He explains him to mean that "after teaching [one's son] a trade, one should make his [son's] Torah studies primary," which is similar to Maharsha's interpretation. We have already[74] cited *Sefer HaBerith*'s sharp warning that every father who disregards the Sages' words, neglecting to teach his son a trade, will eventually have to render account. He adds that such a father in attributing his actions to R. Nehorai, is only following his evil inclinations, for "this is not R. Nehorai's intent at all, as Maharsha has written."[75]

"Chatham Sofer"[76] writes:

> I might venture to say that R. Yishma'el held that the verse "and you shall gather your grain" applies only in the Land of Israel, when the majority of Jews live there. Then, farming is itself a mitzvah because it fulfills the requirement to settle the land and because [the farmer] helps it bring forth its holy fruits...But when we are scattered among the nations of the world because of our sins, and the more the rest of the world is built up, the more destruction is visited on our service of God, R. Yishma'el would concede to R. Shim'on ben Yochai [that one should endeavor to study Torah exclusively]. Therefore, we follow R. Nehorai...when he says that he will ignore every trade in the world and teach his son only Torah, for this was said outside of Eretz Yisrael.

This explanation raises the following difficulties: If R. Yishma'el's statement applies only to Eretz Yisrael, why does Rava, who lived in the Diaspora, caution his disciples not to come to him in the spring and autumn? Furthermore, it seems difficult to maintain that Mishnaic directives such as "love work" and "any Torah not associated with work will end in failure" apply only in Eretz Yisrael.[77]

Also in need of clarification is the "Chatham Sofer"'s explanation of the words of "Rabbi Ilai" [Nehorai],[78] indicating that a son should be taught a trade only if he does not succeed in his Torah studies, a view which the Rishonim[79] seem to contradict.

Many contemporary authorities have dealt with the question of a son who wishes to study Torah exclusively, while his father wishes him to study secular subjects as well, to prepare for a livelihood. They agree that in this case the son need not obey even if this causes his father pain.[80] How can this view be reconciled with the father's obligation to teach his son a trade? Perhaps this obligation was only mandated for the son's own benefit, and hence does not apply if rejected by the mature son.

3

The Prohibition of Deriving Material Gain from Torah Study

1. The Severity of the Prohibition

The Mishnah[1] says: "Do not fashion [the words of the Torah] into a crown of self-aggrandizement, nor into a hoe with which to dig. Thus, too, was Hillel wont to say: 'He who uses the crown will perish.' This teaches you that anyone who gains [materially] from the words of Torah takes his life from the world." R. 'Ovadiah of Bartinoro explains: "One who does so misappropriates the holy Torah, and is thus subject to Divine execution, as is anyone who misappropriates sanctified objects." This is based on the Talmud[2] which reasons as follows: If Belshazzar was killed by Divine decree (extinction) for using vessels looted from the Sanctuary, even though they had lost their sanctity, how much more must this punishment apply to one who makes personal use of the crown of Torah! The Mishnah[3] states: "One who accepts payment for rendering a verdict—his verdict is void." Similarly, R. Tarfon never forgave himself for once saving his life by exploiting the respect others had for his Torah learning, sorrowing:[4] "Woe unto me, for I have made personal use of the crown of Torah!" This prohibition is codified by Rambam, *Tur*, and Shulchan Arukh.[5]

Interestingly, all Rishonim who comment on this Mishnah (Rashi, Rambam, Rabbeinu Yonah and others), except *Machzor Vitry*, explain that the phrase "he removes his life from the world" refers to the next world. This would seem to contradict the Talmudic passage according to which Belshazzar—from whose fate this prohibition is derived—was killed that very night, that is, he lost his life in this world. To clarify this contradiction, we proceed to investigate several details of this prohibition.

Apparently, there are two proscriptions: a) **Benefiting** from the honor of Torah, that is, drawing on accumulated credit for Torah study in this world, thereby depleting the "balance" in the next, such as in the Zebulun-Issachar arrangement; and b) **using** the Torah for one's personal affairs, which constitutes degradation of a mitzvah (just like counting money by the light of the Chanukah lamp[6]), such as R. Tarfon did when he appealed to his status as a Torah-authority to obtain release from his captors. The derivation from Belshazzar concerns the latter aspect; this resolves the dilemma. The episode of Belshazzar is in the category of using the Torah for profane purposes, which is punishable by extinction. This is the subject of the first part of the Mishnah ("...nor into a hoe with which to dig"). The latter part of the Mishnah, on the other hand, speaks of benefiting materially from the Torah, which means receiving reward on earth and hence diminishing it in the next world.

This distinction enables us to understand some otherwise puzzling commentaries on our Mishnah.[7] Rashbatz writes: "[Benefiting materially from Torah] is totally permissible, but it is pious to refrain from doing so." This statement, which is in apparent contradiction to the Mishnah — and especially the Talmudic comment concerning Belshazzar's death — can be readily understood if we interpret "takes his life from the world" to mean only that the beneficiary is drawing on his account in the next world. He may do so; but he should know that his account there will be debited accordingly. Even more explicitly, *Midrash Shemuel* writes: "He takes in this world the [good] life that was credited to him in the next world."

In this context, Rashbatz, limits the prohibition to a) "One whose initial objective in occupying himself with [the Torah] is to earn a livelihood;" b) "One who avoids repaying a debt, by using the crown of Torah." R. Sheneor Zalman of L'ady quotes this stipulation in his Shulchan Arukh.[8] However, one may inquire why the prohibition is limited to these two points alone. Especially difficult is the implication of a) that Torah study must be free of ulterior motives from the outset. This opinion apparently contradicts the views of Rishonim who maintain that it is specifically at the beginning of one's learning that ulterior motives—*shelo lishmah*—are permissible.[9]

Rashbatz's reasoning apparently provides the basis of R. Sheneor Zalman: "If he studies *lishmah* and then finds that he has no livelihood other than teaching or serving as a rabbi, this is considered using the Torah for the Torah's sake, for if he has nothing to eat he will not be able to study properly." (To continue the Chanukah analogy: one may, with certain limitations, use one Chanukah light to kindle another without implying any degradation of the mitzvah). Rashbatz and R. Sheneor Zalman apparently disagree with Rambam regarding the permissibility of placing oneself in such a situation *a priori*. Although there seems to be no explicit prohibition in the Talmud, Rambam, cited by *Tur* and Rema, writes:[10] "Anyone who **intends** to occupy himself with Torah, not to do work, and to subsist on charity, has profaned [God's] name, disgraced the Torah, extinguished the light of the Law, brought evil upon himself, and taken his life from the world; for it is forbidden to benefit personally from the Torah in this world." He also notes in his "Commentary on the Mishnah:"[11] "And [the Talmudic sages] did not permit themselves to seek money from others, for they saw that it would be perceived as a profanation of God's name. The masses would deem Torah study just another occupation, and it would thus become contemptible in their eyes. Whoever took money would, therefore, be guilty of 'treating the word of God contemptuously.'"[12]

Maharal likewise criticizes[13] Torah scholars who accept money from the community:

> This practice destroys the dignity of the Torah, for if Torah scholars would not make their living this way, the Torah would rise ever higher and they would exert a positive influence on the public, for whose failings they are responsible; moreover, they would not show favoritism. Nowadays, however, because he needs [the support of the lay public], every rabbi acquires a master. That is why Shammai said, "Love work"... One should not consider work beneath his dignity—on the contrary, work dignifies men.

Elsewhere, Maharal laments:[14] "Laymen believe that the essence of the [Torah] student is to be supported by others."

Consider the words of R. Mosheh ibn Makhir:[15]

> Anyone who reveres God and pursues justice and kindness must support himself by his own handiwork and toil and may not become a burden on the public, lest he diminish the honor of God, the honor of Torah and of divine service, and his own honor in the eyes of the world. Moreover, Torah law, integrity, and reason all teach that it is improper to live off another... For

has not the Creator created me with hands and feet, just as He created my neighbor? Why, then, should I not seek peace of mind, doing the will of my Creator and living off my handiwork?

One might argue: "How can I work, thereby neglecting my [Torah] studies and service of God? How will I ever be able to fulfill my obligations to myself, for the sake of my soul—for the Torah 'is beyond earthly measure' and the day is short and the work to be done is considerable?" This objection appears legitimate; but if you examine it carefully, you will find it flawed and invalid. For God commanded us to study Torah and to work, so why should we neglect one for the other? Both are equally good and proper, and each is impossible without the other.

However, one should not make his work primary and his Torah secondary. Instead his work should be secondary, sufficient to sustain oneself from day to day. Rather than seeking luxuries, one should trust in God, Who provides wherewithal and sustenance for His creatures.

Keren Orah[16] assesses the situation as follows: "The Rishonim have exerted much effort in seeking ways for a Torah scholar to use the honor of the Torah for his own gain. But there is still no perfect solution, and that is why scholars are despised by the common folk."

R. Menachem Mendel Kargau[17] writes: "If a person chooses the easy way of providing for himself and his household [by not working], his Torah will have no permanence... Besides, this is not the proper approach for an upright person; it will not enhance his glory to eat the bread of indolence and be a burden to others. It would be better for all the Torah students of our day [to work]—even as peddlers—rather than adding to the desecration of the Torah by profiting from their studies."

R. 'Ovadiah of Bartinoro decried this practice in the strongest terms:[18]

Among the Ashkenazic rabbis, we witnessed a scandalous state of affairs. A rabbi, ordained as head of a yeshiva, is not ashamed to accept ten gold coins to spend a half-hour writing and presenting a bill of divorce; and the signatories and witnesses take another two gold coins, or at least one each. This rabbi is nothing but a thief and an extortionist, for he knows that he is the only one in his city empowered to grant a divorce, and the person who wants to give the divorce must pay whatever is demanded. I suspect that such a bill of divorce is invalid, for the Mishnah states: "One who accepts payment for rendering a verdict, his verdict is void; for testifying, his testimony is invalid."

His words are quoted in Shulchan Arukh;[19] however Rema disagrees.[20]

2. Permissible Circumstances

(1) The Honor of a Torah Scholar—The Individual

Although generally one may not benefit from Torah scholarship, the Torah scholar is entitled to certain privileges:

a) The Talmud says,[21] "A Torah scholar may demand that his court case be heard first, for Scripture refers to David's sons [who were Torah scholars] as *kohanim*—and just as *kohanim* have priority, so do Torah scholars."

b) In this context, the Talmud also permits a Torah scholar to seek special tax exemptions.

c) An indigent, sickly Torah scholar may accept whatever money he needs, even if it is given to him because of his scholarship.[22]

d) The Sages[23] praise those who invest a Torah scholar's money for his profit.

e) A Torah scholar was commonly permitted to sell his merchandise before others in the marketplace.[24]

According to Rambam,[25] these advantages "are benefits that God granted them, just as He granted the offerings to the *kohen* and the tithes to the Levite. For merchants perform these two acts [(d) and (e)] for each other as a courtesy, even if not warranted by Torah scholarship—and a Torah scholar should certainly be treated at least as well as a respectable ignoramus. Similarly, the Torah eases the tax burden for scholars...just as it exempts *kohanim* from paying the half-shekel." *Kohen* and scholar are likewise equated in the Talmudic story[26] of one Torah scholar's giving tithes to another even though he knew the latter was not a *kohen*.

f) A Torah scholar's fellow citizens must do his work for him, just as

Scripture first commanded Moses to build the Holy Ark and then enjoined the entire community to participate.[27] The simple interpretation seems to be that work refers to actual physical labor and not to economic support.

The Talmudic passage explains in detail that this privilege refers to a person whose "holy ministrations" for the public do not leave him time to take care of his own needs. Thus it seems to include such matters as food **preparation** rather than provision (see Rashi on this passage). The text refers to work which the Torah scholar does for his personal needs, not for a livelihood, such as erecting a railing on his roof or chopping firewood.

Other authorities, however, call for economic support for such scholars.[28] According to both Rashbatz and Meiri,[29] "scholars and disciples who waive their entitlements and provide for themselves by the work of their hands—or by making do with less—will see great reward for their efforts, which are considered as piety. It is better for them to take a little time from their constant study than to depend on the community for their livelihood." This implies that financial support, too, may be accepted at the discretion of the scholar.

g) Associating with Torah scholars is meritorious:[30] "'To cleave to Him'—Can a person indeed cleave to the Divine Presence? Rather, anyone who gives his daughter in marriage to a scholar, invests money on his behalf, or allows a scholar to benefit from his possessions is considered to be cleaving to the Divine Presence." Moreoever,[31] "Anyone who hosts a Torah scholar in his house ...is considered as if he has brought the daily offering in the Sanctuary." Similarly:[32] "He who wishes to pour the sacrificial wine onto the altar, let him quench the thirst of Torah scholars with his wine." "Anyone who presents a gift to a Torah scholar is like one who offers first fruits." "All the prophets prophesied only for him who gives his daughter in marriage to a Torah scholar, him who invests on his behalf, or him who lets a scholar use his possessions; but regarding the scholar himself [his reward for *talmud Torah* is beyond human conceptions]." Conversely,[33] "anyone who withholds his possessions from a scholar will never enjoy them."

Concerning Torah scholars, the Sages write:[34] "Whoever wishes to accept [the aforementioned benefit], let him accept it, as did Elisha. Whoever does not wish to accept, let him not accept, like Samuel." Nevertheless,[35] "Blessed is the Torah scholar who eats his own food, earns his own livelihood by the work of his hands, and accepts nothing from the public."

(2) The Honor of a Torah Scholar—The Spiritual Leader

The Talmud[36] relates that a sackful of coins was brought to the study hall and R. Ami took possession of it. His behavior was questioned as the verse concerning the gifts due the *kohen* states "and he shall give...," implying that the *kohen* should not take on his own. Presumably, the same applies to charity. The Talmud answers that R. Ami took the money not for himself but as charity for others. Another answer given is that an important personage is different [and may take] just as the *kohen gadol* is to be made rich by his brethren. The second explanation offered by the Talmud implies that the requirement of enriching a *kohen gadol* also applies to other great personages, such as the head of a yeshiva.[37]

As this principle is derived from the case of a *kohen gadol*, who was unique in his generation, presumably the only other "important personage" so entitled is the spiritual leader of the whole community. Thus, R. Sheneor Zalman writes in his Shulchan Arukh[38] that one who can provide for himself by working occasionally may not accept pay for his Torah "unless the public needs him because there is none like him in wisdom; then, he would be wrong to refuse, and he must permit himself to be chosen... whereupon the community must support him in a dignified manner, such that he need do no physical labor."

(3) Payment for Lost Time and Caretaking; Emergency Measures

In response to Rambam's strong condemnation of accepting payment for Torah study, *Kesef Mishneh* writes that the common practice is to accept such payment for services to the community. Thus, it is customary for a teacher of Torah to accept compensation for his loss of earnings during the time he teaches, just as the Amora Karna accepted such payment when rendering a verdict.[39] Referring to this case, the Talmud quotes a *Baraitha* stating that anyone who takes money to render a verdict is despicable even though his verdict stands. This, the Talmud continues, cannot mean taking money strictly for judging, as the Mishnah[40] states explicitly that under such circumstances the verdict is void. Therefore the *Baraitha* must be referring to compensation for lost earnings. If such conduct is indeed considered despicable, how could Karna have done so? The Talmud answers that if a clearly ascertainable loss is involved, as in the case of Karna, compensation may be accepted. Because of his unusual ability, Karna was paid a zuz for telling, from the aroma of a cask of wine, whether it was about to sour; this was his livelihood. Likewise, R. Huna, when asked to render a verdict, requested that someone draw water in his stead or that he be given money to pay for someone else to do it.

The Talmud relates that the legislators of Jerusalem were paid from the public treasury. According to Tosafoth,[41] this was justified because "he leaves all his occupations and business activities, which is presumably even more evident [a loss] than Karna's." *Shulchan Arukh HaRav*[42] deems such compensation valid even if the scholar has no other trade. In a second explanation, Tosafoth imply that the case of the legislators was an emergency situation. This appears to be Rambam's position as well.

The custom to support community leaders from the community budget apparently dates back to the Geonim, as Rabbeinu Yonah observes:[44]

> Because we now lack the intelligence to apprehend any wisdom in its entirety, and must [labor] day and night—so that one who toils in Torah cannot work [without] neglecting Torah altogether...the communities adopted the custom dating back to the Geonim...to support those who strengthen the Torah, lest they be compelled to work.[45]

Thus, the Acharonim permit a rabbi, *dayan* (Torah judge), etc. to charge for his services if this is his only income. As *Kesef Mishneh* states:[46] "Anyone who cannot sustain himself [by other means] may accept payment for teaching...and similarly, he may take money from the community to render judgement." Maharshal concurs:[47] "Since teachers and those engaged in holy ministration accepted payment from the public treasury, the same applies to us...for not everyone can study Torah well and simultaneously support himself." These decisions are cited by several authorities,[48] one of whom[49] adds: "One should try with all his might to sustain himself by his own efforts. If this is impossible, [he may accept the necessary funds from the public treasury; but] he should undertake to spend some time in public service to strengthen the three pillars of the world: Torah, service of God, and acts of kindness, by teaching children... [or] rendering judgements...without accepting additional payment."

Several major Acharonim state explicitly that permission to accept payment for Torah learning is an emergency measure. R. Yitzchak Abarbanel[50] compares it to the emergency measure of committing the Mishnah to writing. R. Yosef Karo[51] explains that "perhaps all the scholars agreed to this [as an emergency measure, because] if the pupils and teachers could not find sustenance, they would not be able to toil properly in the Torah, which might then be neglected."[52] Maharshal seems to agree.[53] The "Chatham Sofer" writes similarly.[54] R. Mosheh Feinstein[55] also implies that this practice is an emergency measure, adding however: "...those who take Rambam's strict view have been prompted by their evil inclinations to interrupt their learning and engage in work and trade until they eventually forget even the little they have learned and do not set aside even a limited time for Torah study."

Elsewhere he describes the emergency status thus:[56] "Every Torah disciple and student in the holy yeshivoth must constantly be aware of the terrible destruction of the Torah [in the Holocaust]. It is therefore a major obligation for every yeshiva student to try to **replace them** in Torah greatness, the ability to make Torah decisions, and reverence of God. This is imperative for the entire community of Israel."

Others, like *Shulchan 'Arukh HaRav*,[57] take a stringent view, even regarding compensation for a clearly ascertainable loss of earnings: "But if God has granted one the ability to sustain himself through his handiwork—if that is only secondary, while the Torah is primary—he may not earn a living from the Torah, even though he forgoes his occupation for it and any payment could be considered to be compensation for lost earnings. [This applies] even to a stipend [given to facilitate] the rendering of a verdict, which would guarantee him much free time in which to pursue his studies and become acquainted with all phases of the Torah...He may not use the crown of the Torah for this purpose." To explain why this is considered "using the crown," even though one is only recouping whatever earnings he lost, we recall the distinction between using the Torah and profiting from it, as elucidated in Section 1. Although compensation does not involve profiting from the Torah, it does mean using the Torah, which is punishable by extinction. However, if one has no means of support, and if, by refusing payment, he would have to stop studying altogether, then these funds are arguably not used for himself but for the benefit of the Torah.

One question remains: Does a paid student fulfill the mitzvah of talmud Torah? Chida replies:[58] "When a judge presides during study hours, it is as though he spent the time learning...but only if he is not paid for this function. Likewise, a paid teacher cannot count his teaching as studying...and a paid yeshiva student's learning is not considered time allocated for Torah study."

One who teaches children Scripture may charge for his caretaking services,[59] according to both Rif and Rosh.

(4) Accepting Payment for Torah Study — Halakhic Opinions

We have already cited Rambam's opinion prohibiting the deriving of benefit from the Torah, i.e. accepting gifts or charity for Torah study, except in the case of an old or infirm scholar unable to support himself otherwise. His remarks are quoted in Shulchan Arukh[60] in conjunction with the following more lenient views:

> Some maintain that even a healthy person is permitted [to accept payment for Torah study], and the custom has been established...that the rabbi of the city is maintained by the people of the city.
>
> Others are even more lenient and allow Torah scholars and students to accept stipends from those who offer them.

In other words, there are those who hold the lenient view that a rabbi is permitted to accept compensation exclusively from the community; this view conforms with R. Yitzchak Abarbanel's position. Others are more lenient and permit students to accept gifts, even from individuals, in line with the opinion of Rashbatz. We proceed to clarify where these three opinions differ.

As indicated earlier, Rambam concedes that the taking of evident loss-of-earnings compensation is permitted and that the legislators of Jerusalem were paid from the public treasury. In what way, then, does Kesef Mishneh disagree with him? Rambam seems to consider the latter arrangement an ad hoc emergency measure for outstanding national spiritual leaders (perhaps applicable only in Jerusalem, whence the word of God issues—hence he mentions the city twice). Kesef Mishneh, on the other hand, extends this ad hoc ruling to every rabbi and communal leader.

We should also examine carefully the Talmud's equating a *kohen gadol* who is enriched by the community, with an outstanding Torah sage. Rashbatz comments:[61]

The authors of the Talmud equated the law applying to an important personage [Torah scholar] with one which applies to the *kohen gadol*. This is a logical assumption, as the [Torah scholar] takes precedence in all matters—such as the saving of life or the return of lost property—over anyone, including a *kohen gadol*, as indicated by the Mishnah:[62] "The *kohen* supersedes the Levite...if they are equal [in scholarship]. But...a scholarly *mamzer* takes precedence over an ignorant *kohen gadol*"...and since a Torah scholar takes precedence over a *kohen gadol*, the enrichment due the latter is certainly due the Torah scholars in Israel as well.

This deduction, however, appears to be open to question. The *kohen gadol* is recompensed not for his Torah study, but for his public service, whereas extinction awaits one who makes use of the Torah. Moreover, demands on the *kohen gadol* are often greater than those on the Torah scholar—regarding marrying a divorcee, contact with a corpse or blessing the people, to note only a few, so that it should not surprise us if he also earns special privileges. Perhaps this is why Rambam does not adopt this argument.

Considering these reservations, we attempt to understand how Rambam would interpret the aforementioned Talmudic story of R. Ami and the sack of coins [above (2)]. He would reject Rashbatz's explanation that R. Ami was entitled to claim the money as head of the yeshiva, just like the *kohen gadol*. Rambam may have held that R. Ami applied the verse regarding the *kohen gadol*—"the *kohen* who is greater than his brothers"—to himself, literally, since we know from another Talmudic passage[63] that R. Ami was indeed an "important *kohen*," perhaps the most important. The fact that he was not ritually anointed is irrelevant, as throughout the period of the Second Temple such anointing was not practiced. Admittedly, this reasoning is a bit far-fetched and open to several challenges; nevertheless, it could render Rambam's position more comprehensible.

The most lenient opinion includes among those devoting themselves to "holy ministrations"—and therefore permitted to accept payment—even students who provide no service to the community, but spend all day studying Torah. Rashbatz presumably limits this dispensation, applying it not to just anyone who sets aside his affairs and concerns himself only with divine ones, but only to an accomplished Torah scholar, as stated in the Talmud.[64] Apparently, Rashbatz's opponents, such as Rashi,[65] maintain that the term "holy ministrations" refers only to one who serves the community (this is not necessarily the great personage entitled to enrichment; rather, as Rashi says, he is entitled to "whatever is necessary for his subsistence").

Rashbatz presents an additional argument to support his lenient view:[66] "A person important to the community may accept money from it... without violating the prohibition against benefiting from the Torah, for he is honoring the Torah, not using it." Similarly, in the words of R. 'Ovadiah Sforno:[67] "One who is supporting himself temporarily [through Torah], endeavoring to increase his knowledge and improve either his own or another's actions is comparable to one who uses sanctified utensils for the service in the Sanctuary." Perhaps this is also the opinion of the Acharonim[68] who wrote: "This permission is based on the fact that it enables those who study the Torah to maintain it."

R. Y. Abarbanel notes that since a leader also advises his community and conducts its affairs, he is entitled to payment.

We conclude with Rashbatz's words of apology and resignation:[69]

> All this is the basis for our practice of accepting a stipend from the community to serve as its rabbi... It is well known that our purpose in studying Torah was not to serve as rabbi or judge, for [in Christian Spain] we were propertied and had studied medicine, which can support one respectably there. But through the guilt of the generation, persecutions were decreed in all those lands... and if the profession of medicine had been able to support us in the country in which we have settled, we would not have come to this point, which is very low indeed.

(5) The Partnership of Issachar and Zebulun

The Midrash[70] states: "'Rejoice, Zebulun, in your going out' — This teaches us that Zebulun acted as an agent for his brother, buying from his brother and selling to the Canaanites, buying from the Canaanites and selling to his brother." This may indicate that there was a regular partnership between the two brothers, one of whom produced merchandise for the other to sell. However, it is well-known from another Midrashic source[71] that the tribe of Issachar was dedicated to Torah study. Therefore, the implication seems to be that Zebulun invested the tribe's money and shared the profits with its members.

There are, however, other Midrashic versions of their arrangement:

* "Why is Zebulun mentioned before Issachar [in the Torah], even though Issachar was older? Because Zebulun occupied himself with business and Issachar with Torah, and Zebulun supported him — therefore, he was accorded precedence."[72]
* "Issachar occupies himself with Torah while Zebulun goes to sea, returns and feeds him. Thus the Torah increases within Israel."[73]
* "Zebulun is mentioned before Issachar. Why? Zebulun occupied himself with business and Issachar with Torah; they agreed that Zebulun's profits would accrue to Issachar... And 'It is a tree of life to those who strengthen it;' therefore, Zebulun is mentioned before Issachar, for if not for Zebulun, Issachar could not occupy himself with Torah."[74]

These Midrashim imply that Zebulun also extended economic support and not merely services.

In contrast to these explicit Midrashim, the Talmud, in which the ultimate halakhic authority is vested, only hints at this type of partnership:[75] "Unlike Shim'on, the brother of 'Azariah, and unlike R. Yochanan of the princely household." Rashi comments: "Shim'on, the brother of 'Azariah is a Tana in the Mishnah of *Zevachim*; he learned Torah through [the help of] his brother, who engaged in business [and supported his scholar-brother] to share in the consequent reward of Shim'on. He is therefore identified as the brother of 'Azariah. Likewise, R. Yochanan studied through the Prince, who provided for him."

None of the principal early halakhic authorities (Rif, Rambam, Rosh) cites such an arrangement as permissible; neither was it included in R. Yosef Karo's Shulchan Arukh. Rabbeinu Yerucham[76] is the first to cite it, stipulating that a Torah student may credit part of his future learning to a businessman in return for some of the businessman's profits, but he may not "sell" his studies retroactively. Rabbeinu Yerucham bases this on the incident related in the Talmud[63] of Hillel's brother Shavna, who sought to make such a retroactive arrangement; but a heavenly voice declared: "If a man relinquishes all the riches of his house for love, he will be disdained."[77] Both arrangements are discussed in *Tur* and by Rema in Shulchan Arukh.[78] This type of agreement, when valid, perhaps even obviates the Mishnaic warning[79] that "any Torah not associated with labor will end in failure and cause iniquity."[80]

Zebulun's precedence over Issachar implies that Zebulun's merit is not only equal to that of Issachar but even exceeds it—and this is problematic. Clearly, Zebulun's merit is derived from Issachar's studying; how can the derivative be greater than the source of its greatness? We might suggest that Zebulun received his blessing first, not because his merit is greater, but because his contribution to Torah study, too, precedes that of Issachar. But this seems a bit forced and the Gaon of Vilna[81] states explicitly that the supporter is primary and the learner secondary.

Another difficulty: Issachar profited from his Torah studies, deriving his livelihood in exchange for his studies—yet the Mishnah said that such a person takes his life from the world.

The following proposal may answer both questions. Perhaps the Mishnah tells us simply that the physical benefits the recipient derives from his Torah scholarship are "debited" to his "account" of merit in the next world, as if he had withdrawn part of it. This may be R. Yosef Ya'abetz's intent when he writes[82] that the recipient "diminishes his sustenance in the next world." This would account for Zebulun's preeminence, for he accumulated merit through the arrangement, while Issachar's merits decreased. This is explicit in the words of Netziv:[83] "The dignity of the one who occupies himself with Torah is reduced somewhat and the dignity of his supporter is increased, until they sit together."

Indeed, Rabbeinu Yerucham implies that the merit of Torah learning Zebulun acquires is deducted from Issachar. This is explicit in the words of R. Yosef Karo:[84] "[The one who studies all day] may give half his reward for Torah study to another... and it is then as if he studied Torah for half a day." Shakh, too, makes the point explicit:[85] "They split evenly—the business profits and the reward for Torah study will be shared by both." Similarly, R. Yosef Ya'abetz comments on the Mishnah: "Undoubtedly, he divides his share in the next world with the one from whom he receives." R. Chaim of Volozhin seems to concur.[86] R. Mosheh Feinstein apparently takes this principle for granted:[87] "In all the details of the mitzvah of Torah study for which there is a reward... they share." (He also demands that this arrangement be explicit, with an even division of business profits.) The Midrash supports this concept:[88] "He who learns with travail earns a thousand; without travail, his reward is two hundred. Where do we see this?... The tribe of Naftali learned with travail and was rewarded with a thousand, as Scripture teaches: 'And from Naftali came a thousand princes.' But the tribe of Issachar, who learned without travail [because they were fed by Zebulun[89]] only gained two hundred."

R. Pinchas Horowitz (*Hafla-ah*), however, writes:[90] "Would a Torah scholar sell but a single hour in the next world, even for his entire life in this world?... Rather, each one receives his full reward, for just as a lit candle can be used to light other candles without diminishing its brightness, patrons receive their reward from God in heaven without diminishing the reward of the Torah scholars." He cites no source for this opinion. Note that R. Feinstein explicitly rejects this analogy[91].

The concept of trading in one's share in the next world needs clarification, especially considering the principle taught by Rambam,[92] that the reward of the righteous in the next world is their proximity to God, which accrues to them because of their knowledge of Him. Certainly one who studies Torah acquires this knowledge and consequent nearness to God, whereas one who engages in business does not, even though he supports the other. How, then, is it possible to "sell" one's share? As the Midrash states:[93] "Evil will naturally befall the evildoer and good will naturally reward one who does good."

Perhaps giving one's money to a student is such an act of self-effacement that it ennobles the soul of the donor, as the Sages write:[94] "'Good understanding to all those who do them' — Not 'those who learn them,' but 'those who do them.'" Regarding Issachar, the logic (as noted in the name of R. Y. Ya'abetz) is as follows: Because they derive their livelihood from Torah study, its elevating influence on them is only half as great as it would be if they provided for themselves.

R. Meir Auerbach[95] observes that the Rishonim seem to dispute the efficacy of the entire Issachar-Zebulun arrangement. R. Hai Gaon[96] deems it invalid to pay another to read the Torah in exchange for his merit. Does Rabbeinu Yerucham's endorsement of the Issachar-Zebulun arrangement actually contradict the Gaon? R. Auerbach thinks not. Rather, each mitzvah offers two rewards: subjective — enhancing and elevating one's soul, and objective — the reward a king gives his servants. R. Hai Gaon speaks of the former, which accrues only to him who performs the act itself. Rabbeinu Yerucham, however, refers to the latter, which belongs to him who toils to enable the student to study. Considering the above-mentioned suggestion, some of the subjective reward, too, accrues to a patron because of his dedication.

R. Feinstein[97] notes: "It is interesting that Rambam mentions neither the matter of Issachar and Zebulun nor the incident of Shim'on, the brother of 'Azariah... and neither did the author of Shulchan Arukh... Perhaps Rambam held that one who does not learn cannot be considered as having fulfilled the mitzvah of Torah study." How is it, that Rambam does not codify the above Midrashim? He may be of the opinion that these conflict with the Babylonian Talmud (see Section 1, above), which is decisive.

R. Yosef Karo writes: "Even if entered into from the beginning, such an arrangement is permitted only to one who does not earn enough to survive and who—if not for this agreement—would have to seek a livelihood and stop learning entirely." In other words, the arrangement entails the same conditions as any use of the Torah, as explained in connection with the legislators of Jerusalem [see above, nos. (3) and (4)]. According to the Midrash which indicates that this arrangement is hinted at in the Torah, it is difficult to describe it as an emergency measure which contravenes normal Torah rules. We are therefore left with the explanation of Rashbatz and R. 'Ovadiah Sforno:[98] it is not considered using the Torah since one does it in order to study.

On the other hand, *Shulchan 'Arukh HaRav* rules:[99] "One may not free himself from his own study obligation by supporting a wiser, more understanding man, if it is only his working on the man's behalf that is preventing his own learning." "But if it is his lack of mental capacity that prevents him from learning [Talmud]—[and his capacity] does not suffice even for learning the practical applications of the mitzvoth, even though he makes his Torah study primary—then he is a boor... Let him engage in business so that he can support those who study Torah day and night... and he will be treated as if he learns himself, and the others' learning will be credited to him."[100] That is, the business role in the Issachar-Zebulun arrangement is only permitted to a boor.

R. Yehudah HeChasid writes:[101] "If two friends have a business that can be handled by one of them while the other learns—and one of them will forget everything he learns while the other has a good memory—let the former engage in business while the other studies; and if the one with the good memory is indolent and the other diligent, let the latter learn." He evidently bases this counsel on a *Baraitha*:[102] "If one's son is diligent, sharp-witted, and retentive, his son takes precedence." The order in which the qualifications are listed seems to indicate that diligence is given priority over sharp-wittedness and memory.

(6) Supporting Torah Scholars

The last of the maledictions pronounced on Mount Ebal[103] was: "Cursed be he who will not uphold the words of this Torah in order to fulfill them." The Talmud[104] offers various interpretations of "upholding the Torah:" "The beadle who stands [on the podium to raise the Torah aloft];" "Because of this, King Josiah rent his garments and said: 'It is up to me to uphold it;'" "[Even] if one learned, taught, observed and fulfilled, but had the opportunity to strengthen [the observance of others][105] and did not strengthen it, he is included in the curse." Rabbeinu Yonah[106] explains: "One should observe the actions of his fellow workers [in the service of God]... encourage them, showing them how to act... and the Sages applied the verse: 'Cursed be the one who will not uphold...' [to one who fails to do so]." The Midrash elaborates:[107]

> Thus did God say to Moses: "Tell Israel: 'My children, busy yourself with the Torah and you need not fear any nation.'" Had the verse said, "It is a tree of life to those who **toil** in it," Israel's "enemies" [i.e., Israel itself] would not be able to stand their ground; but the verse says: "to those who **support** it."[108] Had the verse said: "Cursed be he who will not **study**," Israel's "enemies" would not be able to stand their ground; but the verse says: "... who will not **uphold** the words of this Torah." These are the words of Scripture: "It is a tree of life to those who **support** it."
>
> Rav Huna said: "If a person transgressed a commandment punishable by death by divine judgement, what should he do in order to live? If he used to learn one folio, let him learn two; if he used to study one chapter [of Mishnah], let him study two. But if he learned neither Scripture nor Mishnah... let him concern himself with public welfare and the distribution of charity, and he will live. For had the verse said: "Cursed be he who will not **study**," there would be no remedy—but it says, "Cursed be he who will not **uphold**..."[109] Had the verse said: "It is a tree of life to those who **toil** in it" there would be no remedy, but the verse says: "it is a tree of life to those who **support** it."
>
> R. Yirmiyah said in the name of R. Chiya: "If a person neither learned nor fulfilled, nor guarded nor taught, but when the opportunity arose, he supported and when the occasion arose, he prevented [another's transgression]—he is included

in the benediction."

R. Huna and R. Yirmiyah said in the name of R. Chiya bar Abba, "In the future [world]—in the Garden of Eden—God will prepare a shady place and a canopy for those who perform mitzvoth, next to those who are masters of the Torah..."

"Shim'on, the brother of 'Azariyah, said.."—Even though Shim'on was greater than 'Azariyah; because 'Azariyah engaged in business and supported him, the halakhah was said in his name. Accordingly,[110] "And to Zebulun he said, rejoice, Zebulun, in your going out, and Issachar, in your tents." [Why is Zebulun mentioned first] even though Issachar was older? Because Zebulun left his dwellings and engaged in business, and returned and provided for Issachar. Therefore, he was rewarded for his toil and the verse is in his name.

"Those who perform mitzvoth" apparently refers to those performing acts of kindness. Since this phrase is followed by the incident of Shim'on, the brother of 'Azariyah, acts of kindness presumably include support of Torah students. This may be the basis for the later authorities[111] who interpret "support" as providing for those who study. We may conclude that a Torah scholar is permitted to accept support because of his learning, since it would be unreasonable to maintain that providing this support is a mitzvah but accepting it is forbidden.

The codes cite a halakhah unique to one's son:[112] "If a man needs to learn and so does his son, but he cannot provide for both, then—if both are equal—he takes precedence over his son; but if his son is intelligent and understands what he learns better than his father, then his son precedes, but [the father] should not neglect studying altogether." In other words, a son may live off his father in order to study, and the father must curtail his own learning to enable his son to learn more. This seems to contradict Rambam's statement elsewhere[113] that one may not make use of Torah. Perhaps this difficulty may be resolved by recalling that the father himself has not completely fulfilled the commandment of Torah study until he teaches his son the entire Torah; hence there is room for the precedence of his son's learning.[114]

Rambam writes:[115] "If we probe the words of our Sages, we do not find them seeking money from others or collecting funds for the esteemed, precious yeshivoth, nor for leaders, judges, those who spread Torah, the great [Torah scholars] or anyone else." However, according to the Midrash,[116] R. Eli'ezer, R. Yehoshua' and R. 'Akiva all traveled to Antioch to raise funds for indigent scholars. And, in another Midrash, we are exhorted to give tithes to those who toil in the Torah,[117] and, in the Jerusalem Talmud, to support Torah students rather than building synagogues or study halls.[118]

Perhaps this difficulty can be resolved by noting that the instances cited apparently refer to charity cases (R. 'Akiva, for example, was in charge of dispensing alms[119]), and we may well argue that poor Torah scholars are certainly no less deserving of aid than other indigents. Indeed, Rambam himself writes that we cannot make assumptions based on Talmudic references to "handicapped or elderly people who cannot perform manual labor and have no recourse but to accept contributions from others—for otherwise what should they do, die? This the Torah does not demand."

R. Chayim Palaggi[120] deals with the difference of opinion between Rambam and Rashbatz regarding the permissibility of scholars' accepting monetary support for their studies: "According to the vast majority, there is no prohibition. Basically, it appears that [if one would otherwise have to neglect his Torah studies] it is better to accept support than to forgo even one hour of learning." But "the scholar [must] not ask for this support; a generous donor must **offer** it to the scholar for him to learn constantly." Unless this condition is fulfilled, "everyone agrees that this is expressly forbidden, and better he should live by his handiwork and study Torah only a little. About such circumstances, they said: 'Whether he does much or little, if only his purpose is for the sake of God.'"[121] He apparently bases himself on the Mishnaic ban on using Torah as a hoe; if remuneration is initiated strictly by the donor, it is no longer analogous to such misuse.

4

Summary

1. The world is constructed such that people must engage in *derekh eretz*. We should make it secondary, but not to the extent that it will hamper our ability to serve God.

   This state of affairs has certainly existed since Adam's sin; but the Rishonim imply that it was the Creator's intent from the start.

2. We are commanded to love work, not merely to perform it.

   Work is important for several reasons: it strengthens the body as well as the soul; it supplies one's necessities, so that he need not depend on others, and it enables one to meet his obligations toward others — specifically, toward his wife and family. Above all, by working, one "walks in the ways of God."

   The Rishonim advise that a person choose work he finds agreeable; according to Maharal, this will help strengthen one's love of God. Thus, one who enjoys the fruit of his labors is greater than one who fears God. Such was the ideal state attained by the Patriarchs (Rabbeinu Bachyay).

3. Even though God controls every aspect of the world, he does so according to a definite order — known to us as "the laws of nature" — which we are able and indeed obligated to discover in order to better perform God's will.

   We are enjoined not to expect miracles — and a prayer for a miracle is considered in vain.[1] Proper faith (*bitachon*) entails the recognition that whatever God metes out to man is good, but what man brings on himself — by either action or inaction — is not subject to *bitachon*.[2]

4. The Tanaim disagree regarding the verse "This book of Torah shall not depart from your mouth and you shall meditate in it day and night." The halakhah is as follows:

a) "Apply *derekh eretz* to them:" that is, a person must work to sustain himself, to a greater or lesser degree, as circumstances dictate. There is special merit in working to improve the Land of Israel.

b) Every Jew must study Torah, and even someone burdened with *derekh eretz* must set aside time to learn by day as well as by night. Only in emergency conditions can one fulfill this requirement by reciting the Shema' morning and evening.

c) One who excels in his studies is advised to make his Torah primary and his work secondary. This is what is meant by "his Torah is his steady occupation;" and anyone who accepts the yoke of Torah will be saved from the yokes of governmental imposition and *derekh eretz*. Anyone who wishes to be adorned with the crown of Torah should not aspire to acquire wealth and honor together with Torah.

d) One may diminish his Torah studies for a limited time to earn enough to study more later.

5. *Derekh eretz* and work not only help one serve God but also constitute a prerequisite for Torah study. Learning Torah without working, with the intention of accepting charity, is the cause of many transgressions, including the most serious of all: the profanation of God's name.[3]

6. It is forbidden to use the Torah as a hoe, and anyone who benefits from the Torah removes himself from the world. Despite the severity of this prohibition, later generations have been lenient in several cases:

a) Judges, rabbis, and teachers may accept evident loss-of-pay compensation if they neglect their trade to serve the public. Some Rishonim include one who neglects completely the pursuit of a livelihood to enter public service.

b) Those who do not serve the public but simply learn for themselves may also be permitted to benefit from the Torah, especially now that the level of Torah study has sunk so low that, God forbid, it may be forgotten. However, this is only an emergency measure.[4]

Special Review:
"And You Shall Meditate In It Day And Night"

Note:

> This review constitutes an extensive analysis of a contradiction
> between two Talmudic passages, which the reader may wish to
> skip on the first reading.

The meaning of the verse[1] "This book of Torah shall not depart from
your mouth and you shall meditate in it day and night..." is discussed
primarily in two Talmudic passages—in *Berakhoth* 35b and in *Menachoth* 99b. In both passages, R. Yishma'el and R. Shim'on ben Yochai
are the protagonists, except that they appear to have switched roles. In
Chapter 2, we discussed this difficulty, together with the opinion of two
Rishonim who explained that R. Shim'on's demanding stance refers
only to a "general mitzvah," while the actual obligation is fulfilled by
reading Shema' morning and evening. An amazing number of alternative ways of resolving the difficulty have been presented by Acharonim;
we present their views here, especially concerning the apparent contradiction in the words of R. Shim'on ben Yochai (acronym: Rashbi).

Their approaches may be divided conveniently into five categories:

1.   Textual Variations

One version of the passage in *Menachoth* reads: "R. Yochanan said in
the name of R. Shim'on ben Yehotzadok" instead of "R. Shim'on ben
Yochai [Rashbi]." According to this version, there is, of course, no
contradiction in the words of Rashbi—only a disagreement between

him and R. Shim'on ben Yehotzadok. *She-iltoth*[2] addresses this version,
as does Shakh[3]. (Chida,[4] however, cites the *Zohar* to prove the authenticity of the printed version,[5] as corroborated by Rashi[6] and the Munich
manuscript as well.)

Semag[7] attributes the statement: "Even if he has only read the
Shema' morning and evening" to R. Yochanan, without mentioning
Rashbi. *Seder Mishnah*[8] points out that according to this reading, there
is no contradiction in the words of Rashbi.

The text of the version in *Berakhoth* also has a variant. *Sefer HaA-
gudah* quotes "R. Shim'on ben El'azar" instead of "R. Yishma'el," and
"R. Yishma'el" instead of "Rashbi." According to this version, too,
there is no contradiction between the two passages.

2.   R. Shim'on Concedes to R. Yishma'el

Sedey Chemed[9] reconciles the discrepancy in the two versions by
saying that in the second one, Rashbi retracted what he said in the first:

> One statement was before the heavenly voice and one after...
> When R. Shim'on ben Yochai left the cave [where they had
> hidden from the Romans] with his son and they saw people
> plowing and seeding, he said: "They are sacrificing eternal life
> to engage in temporary existence!" Every place that they cast
> their eyes immediately went up in flames.[10] This certainly
> means that Rashbi considered it a requirement [to devote him-
> self to Torah study exclusively], for otherwise... should people
> be punished so severely and see all their property destroyed just
> because they did not fulfill a general mitzvah [as explained by
> the Rishonim]? Until a heavenly voice proclaimed: "Did you
> leave [the cave] to destroy My world?" Whereupon they
> returned to the cave... There, their minds settled, and they
> revised their opinion. Consequently, it is not far-fetched to say
> that the incident reported in *Berakhoth* took place before they
> heard the heavenly voice, whereas Rashbi's declaration that the
> basic commandment is fulfilled by reading the Shema' morning
> and evening was made after they had heard it.

Sedey Chemed notes that other difficulties in Rashbi's words are also
resolved by this explanation.

According to *Keren Orah*,[11] Rashbi concedes to R. Yishma'el that for one in need, *derekh eretz* is permitted; the latter concedes that one may not forgo Torah study any more than necessary for his livelihood. However, *Keren Orah* does not specify where Rashbi and R. Yishma'el would then disagree.

3. Two Mitzvoth of Torah Study

a) The Talmud in *Nedarim* (8a) states:

> R. Gidel said in the name of Rav: "If one says 'I will rise in the morning and learn this chapter, [or] this tractate [of the Mishnah], he has vowed a great vow to the God of Israel." But is he not already under oath [since Israel accepted the Torah under oath], such that once he is thus obligated, no additional vow has any meaning?... Therefore, we must conclude that since he can satisfy the [prior oath] by reciting the Shema' morning and evening, his present oath [which obligates him beyond this] is meaningful."

This appears to conform with Rashbi's view in *Menachoth*, and Rava's decision there, that the requirement of Torah study is satisfied by reading the Shema' twice daily. Rashi states this explicitly and Radbaz, too, explains it so at length.[12] But Ran understands the passage differently:

> This should not be taken literally, for a person is obligated to study day and night, according to his abilities. We learn this in the first chapter of *Kidushin*, where "and you shall inculcate them..." is interpreted to mean "that the words of the Torah should be incisive in your mouth, so that when someone asks you something, you do not stammer, but respond immediately." Evidently, the reciting of the Shema' will not suffice for this. Hence I see proof of my opinion, as stated elsewhere, that an oath can apply to [any commandment] derived by inference, even a divine commandment, if only it is not stated explicitly in the Torah. In our case, then, since by reciting the Shema' he can satisfy the explicit commandment to speak of

them "when you lie down and when you rise," his oath remains
meaningful [and can apply to the divine commandment of
constant study].

Based on Ran, R. Yehudah Ashkenazi reasons[13] that in *Menachoth*
Rashbi speaks only of the mitzvah of "[the words of this Torah] shall not
depart..."; but the demand "and you shall inculcate them" [*weshinantam*] prevents him from devoting time to agricultural work. Chida[14] and
other Acharonim[15] explain the matter similarly. However, this would
leave Rashbi's statement in *Menachoth* somewhat misleading.

b) Maharam Schick[16] explains that the verse from Joshua speaks only
of the obligation to study the written Torah, for which the recitation of
the Shema' twice daily suffices. But concerning the oral Torah, we need
"strangers [to] arise to graze our flocks to enable us to study
constantly."

c) R. M.D.A. Treves Ashkenazi[17] distinguishes between learning and
teaching. The former obligation is served by the twice-daily Shema';
regarding the obligation to teach, however — especially when the public
depends on someone for instruction — Rashbi said: "What will become
of the Torah?"[18]

d) R. Sheneor Zalman of L'ady[19] offers a fourth interpretation based on
the concept that the commandment of *talmud Torah* consists of two
mitzvoth: knowing the entire Torah and studying it. Knowing the entire
Torah becomes obligatory when one begins his studies, and applies to
"everyone with a good mind and a good memory, enabling him to
apprehend and remember the entire oral Torah." In his view, this
encompasses the Mishnah (decided halakhoth) "and, in brief [i.e., without in-depth investigation or pilpul], the reasons behind the halakhoth, their sources in the written Torah and their derivations by means
of the Thirteen Rules of Derivation, together with all the other derivations made either by the Sages or according to a tradition handed down
by Moses from Mount Sinai, or by logical reasoning or rabbinic decree,
to prevent abuses." According to his opinion, this mitzvah of knowing
the Torah is so great that it is not superseded even by a mitzvah that
cannot be performed by another.

Thus, *Berakhoth* deals with this mitzvah, and Rashbi expresses his
fear of what will become of the Torah if, from early youth, people must

devote their time to seeding, harvesting, and threshing. *Menachoth*, on the other hand, deals with the general mitzvah of Torah study, which pertains to either one who already knows the entire oral Torah or one who never will. According to Rashbi, in emergencies, it is sufficient for such people to recite the Shema' twice daily. According to R. Yishma'el, however, the mitzvah of pondering it day and night applies to them too, except that they are exempted as needed for *derekh eretz* and those mitzvoth which cannot be fulfilled by others.

4. Two Groups of People Subject to Differing Obligations

a) *Nezer HaKodesh*[20] maintains that the two passages speak about two groups of people. We are indeed obligated to study day and night. But since the verse ends: "and then you will act wisely," it evidently applies only to a person who has superior mental gifts and can soar ever higher through learning. Such a person may not ignore this obligation for even one hour—and his work will be done by others. Most people, however, lack the capacity for deeper insights and will not benefit from constant study. They need only set aside time to learn, so they can "guard and fulfill [the mitzvoth]." They should spend the rest of their time working, for otherwise the world would become a wasteland.

In the same spirit, R. Chaim of Volozhin[21] interprets literally the word "many" in the statement that "**many** emulated R. Yishma'el and succeeded, and **many** followed Rashbi and did not succeed." He writes: "The general public certainly cannot devote the entire day to Torah study without spending even a short time earning a livelihood. It is to such people that the Mishnah refers when it says: 'All Torah not associated with labor will come to naught.' But an individual who can devote all his time to Torah study surely may not interrupt his learning even briefly to earn a livelihood, as Rashbi has said."

Thus, in *Menachoth*, Rashbi speaks of the general public; in *Berakhoth*, however, he speaks of select individuals. These are classified as "not doing God's will" if they engage in *derekh eretz*. R. Chaim supports this interpretation by pointing out that the verse "and you shall gather your harvest" is in the singular.

b) Maharam Schick[22] also posits that the two statements of Rashbi refer to different groups of people. The twice-daily Shema' exempts one from further study—and satisfies the demands of the verse "the words of this Torah shall not depart..."—only if all one's other actions—including plowing and reaping—are done for the sake of heaven. Otherwise, as the other passage states, one must actually study day and night.

Note that this view is diametrically opposed to the opinions in Section (a) above and implies that those who are on a lower level must devote all their time to Torah study; for them, "strangers will arise to graze [their] sheep," and not for those who are on the highest moral level. At first sight, this conclusion appears somewhat strange.

c) R. Chiya Pontremali[23] explains:

> If one is poor and must work to live, then he has fulfilled his obligation even if he only recites the Shema' morning and evening—and this is what Rashbi means in *Menachoth*. But when he says, in *Berakhoth*, "is it possible that a person should plow...," he speaks of one who... can afford to employ laborers to do the work while he studies... and his work will be done by others. [To the poor, Rashbi] applies R. Yishma'el's question: "Are these words meant literally?" For he holds that a poor person is exempt [from this obligation] and need only recite the Shema' twice a day. If you ask: how can R. Yishma'el permit a person who is not poor to neglect his studies and engage in work that could be performed by others? The answer is that he heeds the words of R. Yochanan:[24] "Whoever wishes to squander his money should hire laborers and not stay with them"... [Therefore,] even if his work can be done by others, he must stay with them lest he become poor.

R. Shalom of Ragonto[25] resolves the contradiction similarly.

d) The preface to *Sefer Divrey Nechemiah* mentions a fourth way of distinguishing between two groups of people regarding their duty to study Torah (his explanation is similar to his grandfather's, R. Sheneor Zalman, cited in Section 3 above, except that instead of positing two mitzvoth of Torah study, he differentiates between two groups of people). In his view, *Menachoth* deals with one who has learned the entire Torah, as did ben Damah:

And such a person may engage in business extensively, fulfilling
his obligation by reciting Shema'. For all-day study is only a
rabbinic commandment; hence it can be minimized for the sake
of earning a livelihood, which is also a mitzvah... And R.
Yishma'el, who said "Go find a time...", was referring to the
study of other subjects [which is no mitzvah at all and for which
one may not interrupt Torah study]... *Berakhoth* deals with one
who has not yet learned and does not know the Torah. Rashbi
contends that he must study constantly, until he is well-versed
in all the laws; and he should expend no time on other matters,
for otherwise, "What will become of the Torah?" R. Yishma'el,
however, teaches that even [in such a case]... we follow *derekh
eretz*.

5. "Strangers Will Arise" as a Promise for the Future

Another possible explanation derives from the fact that Rashbi's
words appear to be not a regulation, but a boon promised to Israel if
they "do the will of God"—something dependent on the community,
not the individual. This nuance is reinforced by the use of the plural in
the phrases "Israel do God's will" and "strangers will come," which
refers to gentiles. This would be similar to Ramban's[26] commentary on
the reproof of King Asa for consulting physicians when he was ill:
"When Israel *en masse* are in a state of perfection, their fate does not
follow the course of nature at all, neither concerning their bodies nor
concerning their land, neither as a group nor as individuals." Accordingly, when Rashbi asks what will become of the Torah, he indicates that
it is impossible to grasp the full significance of the Torah until we reach
this perfection. However, the words of Abayey—"many emulated
Rashbi, but did not succeed"—seem to imply that Rashbi's words were
meant as a guidance to the individual. It may be, however, that Abayey
referred to people who **thought** that it meant to guide individuals and
that they, as individuals, had attained that level; they failed because they
were in error.

Perhaps *Sha-agath Aryeh* also has this in mind when he writes:[27] "We
must therefore say that Rashbi also permits one to engage in *derekh eretz*
and seek a livelihood... He differs with R. Yishma'el only in this: ... if

they would 'do God's will,' then their labor would be performed for them by others. But the Torah knows human nature and knows that they will not reach perfection, such that it will be necessary for them to do their own work." Hence having one's work performed by others is a potential boon, but not something on which one should base his course of action.

6. Resolving the Contradictions in R. Yishma'el's Words

To resolve the contradiction in the words of R. Yishma'el (who in *Berakhoth* supports the use of *derekh eretz* in conjunction with the Torah, but in *Menachoth* forbids ben Damah to study the "wisdom of Greek"), most commentators say the following: R. Yishma'el permits the interruption of one's study only in order to find a livelihood. He therefore forbade the study of the "wisdom of Greek" to ben Damah only because it was not for his livelihood, but for pure knowledge. Chida[28] explains that R. Yishma'el quotes the verse from Joshua not as a reason for the prohibition but to motivate his nephew. R. Shemuel Jaffe[29] suggests that R. Yishma'el forbade the study of the "wisdom of Greek" because of a special Hasmonean decree. *Sedey Chemed*[30] says that in *Berakhoth* he speaks of the general public, while in *Menachoth* he dealt with a studious individual.

Here, too, some seek to resolve the difficulty by means of textual emendations. In *Berakhoth*, they read "R. Yehoshua'" in place of "R. Yishma'el."[31]

PART TWO

THE TORAH:
THE SPIRIT AND THE LETTER OF
THE LAW

The Torah is often referred to as "the Law," and it does in fact contain mitzvoth—commandments and interdictions. However, these by no means comprise its total content. Only a small fraction of the written Torah, the twenty-four books of the Tanakh, is devoted to detailed rules of conduct, generally referred to as halakhah. By far the greater part consists of historical, moral, and ideological instruction. Our Sages declared: "The conversation of the Patriarchs' servants is dearer to God than the Torah of their sons," indicating that halakhic material is often much briefer than the passages dealing with historical and moral matters. Clearly the Giver of the Torah valued the spirit of the law no less than its letter and, in guiding us, the Torah endeavors to shape not only our routine actions but also our attitudes, feelings, and thoughts. It seeks to restructure our total personality. As awareness of this objective is an essential component of Torah study, we devote the second part of this work to the role of agadic material—and subjective judgment—in Torah.

1

Halakhah and Agadah in the Talmud as Meta-Halakhic Guidelines

Note:

According to *'Arukh* (s.v. *halokh*) the word "halakhah" denotes, in the most general sense, the way a mitzvah is to be fulfilled. Nowadays, however, the word "halakhah" is applied to matters whose conditions and limits are precisely definable and have therefore been stipulated by our Sages and the later authorities (e.g. the minimum length of a lulav), as contrasted with those which are not precisely definable and must be established by each person according to his own good judgment (e.g. how much kindness to perform). For example, one distinguishes between a "lecture in halakhah" and a "lecture in agadah." Similarly, in *Chidushey Agadoth*, Maharsha clarifies matters which are not delimited in the Talmud, even though they are explicit mitzvoth, such as the laws of *talmud Torah* (BT *Berakhoth* 38b) and performing acts of kindness (BT *Sotah*, end of Chapter 1); character traits and embellishing the mitzvoth (BT *Shabbath* 133b); appearing wise to other nations (ibid., 75a) and many more.

As the common usage of the word "halakhah" has changed, we too will employ the term in its popular sense, although it would be more accurate to say "delimited halakhah" or "defined halakhah" instead of "halakhah" alone.[1]

1. Halakhah and Agadah: Their Roles in Torah Study

The essence of the mitzvah of *talmud Torah* is to study Torah in order to fulfill it, i.e. to recognize our obligations in this world and have the words of the Torah guide us through its intricate pathways.[2]

This perception might lead us to conclude that the study of halakhah suffices. That, however, would obviously be wrong and would lead to several difficulties:

1. It would explain why study of the halakhic portions of the Talmud is obligatory, but not why we should study the agadic portions, which are the major part of Scripture and a substantial part of the Talmud as well.
2. In studying the halakhic parts themselves, why should we concern ourselves with opinions which are ultimately rejected? For instance, it is well established[3] that the opinion of Beth Shammai, when it contradicts that of Beth Hillel, is not accepted. Why, then, should we be obliged to delve so deeply into the former's words?

Moreover:

1. How many hours of our day are really taken up in fulfilling the patently halakhic mitzvoth — such as *tzitzith, tefillin, mezuzah, matzah, shofar,* and *lulav*? After all, we must devote the major part of our time to worldly pursuits (eating, sleeping, earning a living) and to those mitzvoth which have no set limit in halakhah (kindness, Torah study, etc.). Concerning these, there are relatively few halakhoth stipulating the precise amount of time to be devoted to them.
2. The halakhic part of the Talmud deals extensively with such questions as the legal responsibility of a person whose ox gores a cow alongside which a dead newborn calf is found, or the ownership of an object which two persons find at the same time. But the problems which tend to occupy most of our time in daily life are far more complex considerations. For example, may one disclose negative facts about others to prevent a loss to a third party, and if so, precisely what may be revealed and how? Another common issue concerns division of time between competing mitzvoth, e.g. the commandment to teach others versus the obligation to learn. Halakhah provides very little guidance in matters such as these.[4]

These two sets of questions actually answer one another, as there is much more to mitzvoth and other obligations in this world than halakhah alone. Agadah can indeed guide us in this meta-halakhic sphere, as elaborated below.

Contrary to popular belief, halakhah does not necessarily spell out all details of all mitzvoth. Some mitzvoth are explicitly detailed, whereas others are left to the individual's own judgment, based on his best understanding and guided by Torah scholars. Concerning these latter mitzvoth, the Torah provided us with general principles and examples alone; these are to be found in its agadic parts. Consequently, the study of agadah is necessary to guide us in fulfilling the incompletely specified mitzvoth, such as those which the Mishnah declares to have no fixed limit, the commandment to be holy, the development of balanced character traits, saintliness, etc. In fulfilling all of these, we use our intellect to set limits and determine all other details, relying on the agadah for direction.

Indeed, our Sages teach us explicitly that we may find guidance for our course of action in the agadah:[5] "'And you shall **do** that which is upright in [God's] eyes'—This refers to the excellent agadoth." And this applies explicitly to mitzvoth: "You should not say, 'I have learned the halakhoth; that is enough for me.' Therefore the Torah says 'for you should surely guard all these mitzvoth,' which refers to Midrash: halakhoth **and** agadoth."[6] Thus, not only study of the halakhah but study of the agadah, too, is necessary for the proper observance of the mitzvoth. Actually, as we shall see further on, some mitzvoth—which may be called "halakhic"—have most of their details spelled out in halakhah, while others—which we call "agadic"—have their details embodied primarily in the agadah.

Agadoth take many forms, but two are especially important: those which teach us fundamental principles—a world view—and those that provide us with historical and biographical information.

2. A Torah-Based World View

Elucidating the reasons for mitzvoth, R. Samson Raphael Hirsch explains that there are two tasks our intellect must fulfill in connection with the Torah:[7]

1. "To learn the entire content and extent of its laws so well that we know clearly what to do and from what to refrain in our life."
2. "To research God's words themselves and their derivation... so that

our spirit will become enlightened, through God's word, to an ever clearer understanding of this world and of our role in it... [so that we can recognize the] spirit of *Tanakh* and Talmud." That is to say: acquire a Torah-oriented world view.

R. Hirsch does not explain why such a world view is important. Evidently, its significance lies in the observation hinted at above: through this world view we can direct those of our actions which are not guided by the halakhic portions of the Talmud, especially in regard to establishing our priorities. The Sages themselves also based their actions on such a world view. Section 7(1) illustrates how the Sages handled a labor strike based on the view that "whatever God created, He created only for His honor." Furthermore, consider Rava's rebuke of R. Hamnuna for spending too much time in prayer: "Does one neglect eternal life to occupy oneself with temporary life?" apparently basing his criticism on the view[8] that "this world is like an antechamber to the next." Clearly, a proper world view is important to guide our actions.

Where are we to find this world view? R. Hirsch explains:[9] When, under the pressure of historical circumstances, the Sages were forced to commit the Oral Torah to writing, they proceeded very carefully. They clothed this "spirit of *Tanakh* and Talmud" in agadoth; the more sensitive ideas were cloaked in obscure terms and in "hidden ways and in the form of a code, so that only one who has the key can understand them."[10] (Apparently, they concealed their loftiest concepts in the Kabala, which is an invaluable mine of information on the spirit of *Tanakh* and Talmud. These concepts are so subtle that they fall into the category of subjects which are not passed on, even to an individual, "unless he is a scholar and understands on his own [the details, after having been taught the general principles]."[11] This Kabala is much misunderstood and many have erred in treating "internal phenomena and concepts as if they were imaginary external worlds."[12])

While turning to agadah as the major source for our world view, we should not forget that the halakhic portions of the "Talmudic ocean," too, can contribute in this area. Although their primary role is to guide us in halakhic questions, they can give us ideological guidance as well; from the details of a commandment, we can infer the intent of its Author. Furthermore, as all proponents in a Talmudic halakhic discussion base their arguments on the Oral Torah,[13] even the minority opinion may contribute to our understanding of the ideological substrate.

3. Narrative Portions of the Agadah

The Biblical and Talmudic narratives are significant in several respects, providing inspiration, instruction, and assistance in overcoming the influence of our baser nature.

It is easy to fall in love with the kind of personality our forefathers modeled for us. Their example shows what human nature is capable of and can inspire us to try to follow in their footsteps.

In addition, some of the messages that we are to glean from the agadah are so complex that it is difficult to express them explicitly, especially when they must be absorbed at various levels of intellectual and emotional maturity. In such cases, "a picture" can truly be worth a thousand words and the message will come across far more effectively in the form of a narrative. We elaborate on this in the next section.

A third need for agadah concerns the abstractness of general principles. The immature mind and the personality fettered by primitive desires will have great difficulty applying abstract principles correctly. We may misinterpret the intent or distort it to suit our own desires, without any means of detecting our errors. Here, the stories of our Biblical forefathers and Talmudic Sages make the abstract principles concrete and thus remove some of the uncertainty which may lead to error.

If we had the privilege of having these personages living among us, we would garner all these advantages to a much greater degree. However, under the given circumstances, we may only look towards inspiring personalities that Providence **has** granted us and rely on the narratives of the agadah concerning past giants of the spirit.

The Prophet Elisha is lauded for "having poured water over the hands of Elijah,"[14] from which the Sages deduce that "*shimush* [serving a Torah personality] is greater than studying [Torah]" — "because by observing one's teacher, one learns practical halakhah." The study of biographical anecdotes of the Sages, as presented in the agadah, is the closest we can come to serving them[15] and thus constitutes a reasonable substitute for *shimush*. According to this suggestion, the above Talmudic dictum implies that the study of agadah is, in a way, superior to the study of halakhah.

Several of the early and later authorities explicitly refer to agadic narrative as a guide to conduct:

Ramban:[16] "[The term] 'Torah' includes the narratives from the beginning of Genesis, for **this shows people the way** in matters of faith."

R. A.Y. Bloch:[17] "[Certain practical questions] are based on out-looks and opinions which are intimately connected with parts of the agadah [i.e. narratives]... and even though they contain several positive or negative commandments, they cannot be treated in the same way as the halakhic parts, i.e. rendering decisions which can be universally applied, for many times they depend on the nature of the person... as well as conditions of time and place."

R. A. Kotler:[18] "The entire Book of Genesis is nothing but negative and positive commandments, even though it contains only three mitzvoth according to the usual enumerations. For all narratives of the actions of the Patriarchs and all their traveling—even matters of manners or of secular concern—are Torah and great instruction. The narratives of the wicked [are important] also, so that we can distance ourselves from them."

4. Halakhic and Agadic Sources of Torah Obligations

Why is the Torah divided into halakhah and agadah? Why are some obligations codified in detail, whereas others take the form of examples and general principles?

In many areas, obligations may change widely according to circumstances and individual personalities and talents. Had these obligations been fixed in every detail by the halakhah, it would have been impossible for us to take the best course in all given situations. In the words of *Magid Mishneh*:[19]

The complete Torah provides rules by which men may perfect their character and conduct. For instance, obligating them to be holy—which is interpreted by the Sages as meaning: 'sanctify yourself by [refraining from] that which is permitted to you'—so that one does not become addicted to his passions; similarly, [the Torah says] 'and you shall do what is upright and good,' which means that a person should act well and with integrity towards others. **In all such matters, it is not feasible to spell out details,** for the mitzvoth of the Torah apply at all times and to all circumstances and we **must** [always] follow them. On the other hand, the required traits and the comportment of people **differ according to time period and personality.**

R. Mosheh Chaim Luzzatto writes in a similar vein,[20] indicating that although asceticism is obligatory, the details are left to individual discretion, as they are too numerous and varied to be codified and must therefore be decided on a case-by-case basis.

Not surprisingly, we can find the foundations for these ideas in the Midrash; we elaborate on this observation in the next chapter, in discussing obligations "which have no measure" assigned to them in halakhah.

Why, then, have so many laws been detailed? Couldn't they benefit from flexibility as well?

The answer is simple: these detailed "halakhic" laws are a vital part of Torah life, which would otherwise suffer irreparable damage. These laws are like the skeleton of the human body, without which the body would not have the rigid shape required to fulfill its functions. The other mitzvoth, however, are like the flesh, the skin and the spirit, which give man his individuality; these are elastic and change according to the pressures applied and the environment. Just as the skeleton could not fulfill its task if it were elastic, so too the flesh and skin could not fulfill their task if rigid. Thus, halakhah rigorously fixes the basic principles of our life as Jews. The other mitzvoth, however, which embody the real mission of our life, must remain subject to change as needed and cannot be defined exactly; yet it is just these mitzvoth, and the manner in which they are fulfilled, which characterize the wise and pious person.

The mitzvah of Sukah may serve as a good example. The setting up of three walls and placing *sekhakh* (covering) above them such that the shade exceeds the admitted light — all in accordance with the specified measurements — form the skeleton of the mitzvah. In contrast, decorating the Sukah and sitting comfortably and relaxedly within it constitute the flesh and skin. Finally, contemplating, while sitting in the Sukah, God's having protected our forefathers in the desert, embodies the spirit of the mitzvah, which is also an integral part of it.[21]

As halakhah is rigid, it takes priority over the other, more elastic obligations, whenever a conflict arises between them. This situation has given rise to the popular notion that the halakhah is more important. It is possible, however, that an agadic mitzvah is more important, whereas the halakhic mitzvah is more urgent — just as air for breathing is more urgent than food; yet it would be inaccurate to say that air is more important or more valuable than food.

2

Mitzvoth Not Defined by Halakhah

1. Setting Limits on "Matters With No Set Limit" such as Torah, Divine Service, and Acts of Kindness

Many of the mitzvoth in the Torah have been delimited by the halakhah; however there are others, as enumerated in the Mishnah, for which no measure has been set.[1] The Talmud on that Mishnah states explicitly that these mitzvoth have no limit whatsoever—neither upper nor lower. However, these bounds are absent only from a halakhic perspective. In fulfilling our obligations in the world each such precept obviously has a proper measure, and anyone who either exceeds it or fails to reach it is in error. This proper measure varies from person to person and from situation to situation, as indicated by the Sages.

The existence of a proper measure for every action, even when it is not specifically defined in halakhah, implies that, in principle, every act is either obligatory or forbidden. This is stated explicitly in *Chovoth HeLevavoth*.[2] R. A. Kotler explains:[3]

[Whether a halakhically neutral action is an obligation or a prohibition] depends on the end result of the action, whether it strengthens our service of God, or the contrary. For example, gratifying an unnecessary desire will reinforce one's passions and is likely to lead him to err. Hence one is forbidden to do so, even if the act itself is permissible. Anything which can give rise to evil consequences is in itself evil. However, [fulfillment of] desires which are necessary to strengthen the body and for peace of mind—and are thus means of serving God and of engrossing oneself in the Torah—is actually a mitzvah.

Assessment of the relative importance of these mitzvoth, and assigning priorities accordingly, may have a greater influence on our way of life than do the halakhic decisions, for the "matters which have no measure" include the three mitzvoth on which the world stands: Torah, divine service, and acts of kindness. We are dealing with the very foundation of the world, yet defined halakhah does not provide detailed guidance. We must rely on our reason (or that of our spiritual guides) and on the agadoth in the Torah, Talmud, and Midrashim for guidance. The parables of the Sages teach us that priorities in these matters must be established according to the needs of the place and time. Consider the following Midrash:[4]

> God said: "A person should not evaluate the mitzvoth of the Torah ... to see which mitzvah has the greatest reward and then fulfill that one..." A parable tells of the king who had an orchard, to which he brought workers. However, he did not tell them the relative values of the various plantings, for had he told them, they would have planted [only] the tree that has the greatest worth. As a result, part of the orchard would be bare, part planted. Similarly, if God had revealed the reward for each mitzvah, the result would be that some would be fulfilled and some would be abandoned.

What does the Midrash mean when it says that "some would be abandoned?" Does it imply that some halakhic mitzvoth—such as putting on *tefilin* or affixing *mezuzoth*—would be abandoned in favor of some others—such as *berith milah* or *tzitzith*? Or did it refer to mitzvoth which "have no fixed measure" in halakhah, such as abandoning Torah study in favor of, say, performing acts of kindness? Presumably, the Midrash was referring to the latter type, as fulfillment of "halakhic" mitzvoth generally does not require so much time that one would neglect them in favor of others. It seems that Rabbeinu Yonah, too, interpreted the Midrash so,[5] for he adds: "As you know, our Sages have said that 'one who occupies himself with Torah exclusively [and neglects other mitzvoth] is like one who has no God,' even though it is written that 'Torah study is equal to all of them.'" The first statement quoted by Rabbeinu Yonah was made by R. Chanina ben Teradyon[6] about himself, to explain why God would not deliver him from a terrible death, even though his whole life was consecrated to Torah study; he attributed this to the fact that he had failed to do acts of kindness to the extent appropriate to him. Since R. Chanina certainly did not neglect the observance of the halakhic mitzvoth, Rabbeinu Yonah clearly interprets the Midrash as referring to those mitzvoth which have no measure, making the failing of R. Chanina one of judgment only. Thus, the parable tells us that there are certain conditions which specifically mandate Torah study, whereas others specifically require acts of kindness — just as there are spots where a fig tree is appropriate and other places which can only be graced by a date palm. For example, it is especially appropriate to occupy oneself with those mitzvoth which are neglected by the multitude — in line with the statement of Hillel:[7] "In a place where there are no men, try to be a man." Thus wrote R. Yehudah HeChasid:[8] "Cherish the mitzvah which is like an abandoned corpse — a mitzvah which has no one to care for it [and its reward will be likewise great]."

Moreover, our Sages have suggested in the agadah that the establishment of priorities in mitzvoth depends on personal disposition. Just as people differ in their personality traits, so too do they differ in their obligations regarding mitzvoth. This is implicit in the Midrash:[9] "'Like raindrops on the sprouts' — Like the raindrops which descend on shoots and make them grow — some green, some red, some black and some white — so it is with the words of Torah — some [people] are rabbis [analytic], some are sages [knowledgeable], some are righteous and some are devout [men of great deeds]...."

In a dramatic illustration of how the choice of vocation depends on the individual and his abilities, our Sages have taught us[10] that any student who sees no signs of success in his learning after five years will never succeed. This moved Rav to tell his son Eivu: "I have toiled with you in learning and nothing has succeeded. Come, I will teach you the way of the world." The Talmud then describes how Rav instructed him in business methods.[11]

Netziv wrote:[12]

The form of service to God is not the same for all persons — one occupies himself with *talmud Torah*... and another... with divine service, and another with doing acts of kindness, but all for the sake of Heaven. And even in Torah study itself, not all methods of study are the same. Also in fulfilling the mitzvoth... and performing acts of kindness; not all those who perform

them have the same way of life, and if someone were to ask
which is the proper way... [the answer is:] "that which graces
[i.e. suits] the person"—the person who chooses will do so
according to his own nature, depending on whether he is tal-
ented in Torah, divine service, or performing acts of kindness.

R. Eliyahu, the Gaon of Vilna, wrote similarly:[13] "'He who walks in
his uprightness, fears God'—Each person has to walk in his own special
way, for people's characteristics are not all the same."

In the same spirit, Or Same-ach[14] wrote that all mitzvoth are applicable to all persons, from the least to Moses, our Teacher. [But] the
fulfillment of them may vary—one may simply pick up the *ethrog*; only
one who is particular will hold it all day; therefore, the Torah specified
character traits only in hints. ... Each person is to act according to his
own nature and his own spiritual capacity; for the obligation of Torah
study is not the same for the person who has a fine intellect and is eager
to study and the one who is intellectually more lethargic. As it is
evidently impossible to establish an absolute measure, the Sages formulated for us the basic obligation of the mitzvah of Torah study: if one
reads the Shema' morning and evening, he has fulfilled the commandment to study [Torah] day and night. That is why the admonition
regarding "the laws and judgments" [i.e. halakhic aspects]—which are
the same for everyone—is differentiated from the notion of "the paths
in which they should walk" [i.e. non-halakhic aspects]—which differ
from person to person.

The Talmud notes that certain personalities chose to pay special
attention to a particular mitzvah. For example, R. Shim'on ben Yochai
and his comrades were exclusively occupied with the Torah to such a
degree that they were exempt from the obligation of daily prayer.[15] On
the other hand, the Early Pious Ones spent nine hours of the day in
prayer—but because of their piety, their Torah knowledge remained
intact, even though they did not spend much time studying it.[16]

Perhaps the Amoraim too had this in mind when they advised one
who wants to achieve piety[17] to occupy himself with matters involving
the tractate of *Nezikim* (which deals with interpersonal relations, such as
kindness); others advised studying *Avoth* (which, in the main, provides
guidance regarding Torah study); and some said he should occupy
himself with *Berakhoth* (that is, prayers etc., a form of divine service).

In sum, only a small part of our time is guided by halakhah; we must apportion most of our time to Torah study, divine service, performing acts of kindness, earning a living, etc. according to our best understanding.

2. To Be Holy

There is another mitzvah which is basically non-halakhic: the mitzvah "You shall be holy."[18] To this Ramban comments:

> "You shall be holy" — Be restrained... for the Torah has warned us against immorality and forbidden foods, but has permitted conjugal relations with one's wife and the consumption of meat and wine. Thus a lustful person can indulge in perversion with his wife, or many wives, and revel in wine, eat meat to excess, and use foul language to his heart's content — for no prohibition against this is explicit in the Torah. Thus he would be "depraved with the Torah's permission." Therefore, after the Torah has enumerated what is entirely prohibited, it has commanded us, in general terms, that we should be restrained in that which is permitted. One should limit his conjugal activity, in line with the Talmudic dictum[19]... to the minimum required by his obligations. He should indulge in wine to a minimum, just as the Torah refers to a *nazir* as "holy," and he should remember what the Torah related to us in this context about Noah and Lot... He should also guard his mouth and his tongue from overindulgence in eating and in using vulgar language, which is referred to in the verse[20] "and every mouth speaks foulness." He should sanctify himself in this way until he reaches the stage of restraint, as they tell of R. Chiya,[21] who never spoke of unnecessary matters in his life. The general commandment ["You shall be holy"] instructs us in these and similar matters, after all the absolute transgressions have been enumerated.

This mitzvah thus essentially has no halakhoth at all; its details are founded on reason and the agadah (note the explicit reference to Noah and Lot).

3. Character Traits

We are commanded to walk in the path of God:[22] "And you shall walk in His ways." What are His ways? Our Sages have taught:[23] "Just as He clothes the naked... you, too, should clothe the naked. God visited the sick... you, too, should visit the sick. God comforted the mourners... you, too, should comfort mourners." All this is derived from the narrative part of the Torah. Elsewhere, they taught:[24] "'And I will praise Him'—Emulate Him—just as He is merciful and gracious, so should you too be merciful and gracious." Here, personality development is based solely on agadah, with no halakhah to guide us. Furthermore, R. A. Kotler interpreted the statement "The conversation of the Patriarchs' servants is dearer to God than the Torah of their sons"[25] as follows:[26] "Concerning character traits and proper manners—which are not readily definable in every detail, depend on the circumstances, and are basically subjective—the guidance and supervision of a wise scholar is essential... as [we are taught]: 'Serving [the sage of] the Torah is greater than studying it.'" This is possible through the agadah, in both the Written and Oral Torah.

Other agadoth concerning our Sages are similarly instructive regarding a variety of traits. We are told, for example, that Rabbeinu HaKadosh suffered years of terrible anguish as punishment for showing lack of compassion for an animal.[27]

The mitzvah of walking in the path of God—emulating His characteristics—is a major one. Rambam, in fact, lists it immediately after the basics of the Torah. Rabbeinu Yonah, too, enumerates among those who do not have a share in the next world[28] the four categories of persons who cannot receive the Divine Presence:[29] scoffers, liars, fawners, and talebearers. We find that only the last of these practices is explicitly forbidden by the Torah,[30] while the others "only" designate a lack of the character traits which we are commanded to acquire under the heading of "you shall walk in His paths." This, then, is one of the agadic mitzvoth; yet, failure to fulfill it is in the most severely punishable category of transgression. Similarly, the Sages say that a haughty person[31] is like one who denies [the existence of God]; God himself says, "I and he cannot dwell in the world [together]" and "he will descend to Gehinnom."[32]

A *ben Torah*, whose character traits are shaped by the Torah, will help others and thereby himself fulfill the mitzvah of love of God—perhaps the most basic of all mitzvoth. Our Sages interpret the verse "And you shall love the Lord your God" as follows:[33]

> The Name of Heaven shall become beloved through you; [this obligates a Jew to] study Scripture and Mishnah, serve scholars, conduct his business dealings honestly and converse with his fellow-beings in a calm manner. What do people say about such a person? "More power to his father who taught him Torah, more power to his teacher who taught him Torah, woe to those who did not learn Torah."

In his enumeration of the mitzvoth, Rambam actually cites such conduct as part of the mitzvah of loving God.

4. Desecration of God's Name

The Talmud continues: "and he who studies Scripture and Mishnah and serves scholars, but is not honest in his business dealings and whose conversations with his fellow-beings are not calm. What do people say about such a person? 'Woe to so-and-so for having learned Torah...'" This is included in the concept of desecration of God's name.[34]

In fact, this concept does have halakhoth connected with it, namely the requirement to forfeit our lives rather than allowing ourselves to be coerced into transgressing if the coercer's motive is to make us transgress — if we yielded to him, we would show greater reverence for him than for God. (Normally, this law applies only in public, i.e., before ten Jews, but in times of religious persecution, it is valid even in private.)[35] However, this instance does not encompass the entire interdiction. The passages cited above show that even in everyday conduct, we must consider the opinion of others, lest they suspect us of slighting any Torah commandment, including the requirement to walk in the ways of God. "What constitutes desecration of God's name? Said Rav: 'In my case, if I purchase meat and do not pay for it on the spot.'"[36] Thus this prohibition includes the obligation to guard against leaving ourselves open to the mere suspicion of a transgression. As the Mishnah states:[37] "A person must absolve himself before people, just as he must absolve himself before God." The Talmud on this Mishnah puts it thus: "In the Pentateuch, in the Prophets and in the *Kethuvim* [Hagiographia], we find that a person must absolve himself before people, just as he must absolve himself before God." In the Babylonian Talmud, this matter of being above suspicion is cited in connection with public servants: those responsible for the distribution of charity,[38] those who baked the show breads for the Holy Temple, and those who prepared the incense.[39]

The prohibition against leaving oneself open to suspicion applies even in our relations with gentiles.[40]

In a positive vein, this mitzvah entails an obligation to maintain the prestige of the Jewish people in the eyes of the gentile public. Thus, the mitzvah of calculating the seasons and the zodiac is also included in this category, as it is based on the verse " 'For this is your wisdom and your insight in the eyes of the nations' — This refers to the calculation of the seasons and the zodiac."[41]

Aside from applying this commandment to those responsible for the distribution of charity and Temple supplies, and perhaps to astronomical calculations, the Sages have not explained the details of the mitzvah. Using personal insight and the agadah, everyone can find his own way of fulfilling this important mitzvah, to which alone applies the pronouncement: "The guilt of desecrating God's name is not suspended by repentance, nor atoned for by Yom Kippur, nor cleansed by suffering. Rather, all of these [together] will suspend it and his death will atone for it." Furthermore, "both inadvertent and purposeful desecration of God's name [are punished publicly]."[42]

5. Mitzvoth Regulating Relationships with One's Fellow Man

In social matters, too, our obligations may depend very subtly on circumstances, so that it is impossible to establish all the applicable laws in the halakhah. Let us consider several general guiding principles in this area.

(1) Going Beyond the Letter of the Law

The mitzvah to go beyond the letter of the law (*lifnim mishurath hadin*) in interpersonal relationships is somewhat analogous to the mitzvah "to be holy" in our personal development.[43] Our Sages derived this mitzvah[44] from the verse: " 'And the actions that they shall take' — This means going beyond the letter of the law."

Lest this appear to be a minor obligation, note that R. Yochanan[45] cites its neglect as the reason for the destruction of Jerusalem: the Jews of that time, he says, were not prepared to go beyond the strict letter of the law. Semak even enumerates it among the 613 mitzvoth.[46]

The Sages do not define precisely what is included in this mitzvah. Only by turning to the Talmudic narratives and studying the actions of our Sages can we learn what they meant by "going beyond the letter of the law." For example, this category includes the returning of lost property and helping a stranded donkey-driver load his donkey—both under circumstances when this was not halakhically required;[47] compensation paid for a loss caused only indirectly, such that no legal claim applied;[48] and finally, returning a purchased parcel of land to the original owner who had reason to regret having sold it.[49] These are all instances in which a minor change in the circumstances would have made the act obligatory.[50]

In a similar vein, the Torah commands us:[51] "Do that which is upright (*yashar*) and good in the eyes of God." Based on this verse,[52] when selling a field, for example, one must accord priority to the buyer who owns an adjacent lot. As Rashi explains: "'And you shall do what is upright and good'—In a matter in which you will not suffer a major loss, for you can find real estate elsewhere, do not discomfit the one whose property borders on [the lot being sold] to cause his properties to be scattered." Elsewhere, the Sages require a claimant, who received a field in payment, to permit the original owner to buy it back when he obtains the necessary funds.[53]. (In both cases, we grant priority in acquiring property to the person to whom it is more valuable. However, I have not found that halakhic authorities define the mitzvah in these terms.) This mitzvah, too, is far from trivial. The Book of Deuteronomy is called *Sefer HaYashar* precisely because of this verse[54]—as if this mitzvah were the most important in the entire book. *Torah Temimah* explains[55] that this verse falls into the category of "What is hateful to you, do not do to your friend," which Hillel perceived[56] as encompassing the entire Torah. This means that we should treat our fellow as we would have him treat us, even if he does not have a legal claim.

Ramban explicitly classifies "doing that which is upright and good" with "going beyond the letter of the law:"[57]

[The Sages] called this a compromise beyond the letter of the law. They mean that, after having been commanded to guard

His decrees, we should keep in mind to do that which is upright
and good in His eyes, for He loves the upright and the good.
This is essential, for it is impossible to enumerate in the Torah
all the interpersonal relationships between a man and his
friends and neighbors, and all his business dealings and social
and political actions. But after [God] mentioned many of
them... He reiterated, in general terms, that we should do what
is good and upright in all things, including compromising and
going beyond the letter of the law. For example... in the
regulations of one who has an adjoining property, and even
when they tell us... to speak calmly with our fellow men.

Even though this mitzvah is occasionally called "halakhah,"[58] the
Sages formulated it according to their discretion, based on the general
mitzvah to be upright and good.[59] We too must establish similar limitations for ourselves, as explained at length by Magid Mishneh, cited at
the beginning of this chapter.[60]

The Talmud tells of Rabbah bar bar Chanah who hired poor laborers to transport his wine. After the laborers clumsily broke the barrel,
Rav instructed Rabbah not only to forgo his claim against them, but
even to pay them their wages. When Rabbah questioned the legality of
both of these decisions, Rav cited the verse: "You shall go in the way of
the good [people] and guard the paths of the righteous," implying, as
Rashi indicates, that he is to go beyond the letter of the law.[61] From the
context, it appears that Rabbah was forced to make these concessions.
On this basis, some authorities conclude that the court can enforce going
beyond the letter of the law in certain cases. Although some dispute this
conclusion, it does seem to be the accepted practice today.[62]

Obviously, one cannot accede to every demand. After all, under such
conditions, how are we to decide who is to yield to whom?[63] As the
Talmud stipulates no specific instructions in this matter, the later
authorities draw their conclusions from the agadah. Some say it applies
only to a wealthy defendant,[64] while others conclude that it is relevant
only to the case of a rabbi, who must serve as an outstanding example.[65]

A similar mitzvah[66] instructs us not to "withhold good from those to
whom it is due." Basic law forbids us from causing damage to another,
but does not prohibit us from denying him profit. However, the Sages
did prohibit such behavior, as implied by the verse in Proverbs.[67] Rabi's

dictum:[68] "A person may not spill the waters of his cistern if others require them," may indeed be based on this mitzvah as well.[69]

Preventing another from deriving benefit from one's possessions, when no expense or inconvenience is incurred by the owner, is called "Sodom-like behavior" by the Talmud. The authorities agree that the prohibition against such behavior is legally enforceable; it apparently falls into the same category as the other mitzvoth mentioned in this section. Based on the above verse in Proverbs, we have learned[70] that one may not prevent another from taking a shortcut through his field after his produce has been gathered; by allowing it, he benefits someone while suffering no loss himself.[71] This is the general Talmudic category of "one who has an advantage, while the other one has no loss." In any case, it appears that the source of this law is reason and the agadah. Its very name testifies to its origin in the historical records (agadoth) regarding the citizens of Sodom. If this trait indeed caused them to sink to such a low moral and spiritual level, then it is certainly proper for us to do all in our power to prevent it from gaining a foothold in Israel.

(2) Causing Pain to Others and Social Manners

The laws regarding one who causes physical or property damage to another are set down in the laws of torts and deceptions. At times, however, emotional damage too may be significant and even exceed monetary loss. Therefore, based on the verse: "You shall not hurt each other," the Torah treats "mental abuse" (ona-ath devarim) more severely than monetary abuse.[72] It is impossible to establish hard and fast rules in this context, as there are many ways of hurting one's fellow man — through devious actions, through words, or even mere hints or allusion. The Sages cite several examples:[73] One should not ask the price of an object if he has no intention of buying it; in speaking to a penitent individual, one should not remind him of his former sins; if a person is the son of a proselyte, one should not remind him of his lineage; if he is suffering, one should not — as did Job's friends — tell him that his sins are the cause of his suffering; when someone seeks a vendor, one should not send him to a person who never sold anything of the sort. Rambam[74] adds that if one is asked something regarding a scholarly subject with which he is familiar, he should not ask a third person whom he knows to be unfamiliar with it: "How would you answer this?" or "What do you think about this?"

It is important to note that the Torah prohibited us from causing any pain and embarrassment to our fellow man; the injunction is not limited to the examples specified by the Sages.[75] Rambam states explicitly "and [this prohibition applies] also to all similar cases." It is left to the best judgment of each individual to establish exactly what is covered by the prohibition. This is emphasized by *Sefer HaChinukh*:[76] "It is not possible to itemize everything that causes people pain, but one must be as careful as he can [and not plead that the offense was unintentional] for God knows [man's] ways and his intentions."

Understanding the prohibition against "mental abuse" in this broad sense can help resolve several difficulties. Three such instances are briefly discussed below.

The prohibition against causing property damage to another is not explicitly stipulated in the Talmud.[77] Perhaps it derives from the injunction regarding mental anguish. Similarly, all Talmudic passages which regulate social manners to prevent pain to one's fellow man—such as the ban on spitting in front of another or on returning a piece of food to the collective bowl once one has bitten from it—may well be covered by the prohibition against mental anguish.[78]

This prohibition may also include the rule forbidding unnecessary imposition on the public's patience. This rule is mentioned frequently in the Talmud, but without any scriptural source. To cite just one example: it was prohibited, even in the Temple, to scroll the Torah in public to reach the proper place, as this would not be in keeping with the dignity of the public ("who would have to wait and be quiet during this time"—Rashi).[79] This prohibition applies today as well, except in emergency situations.[80]

In a more modern vein, if one smokes and thereby causes pain and discomfort to his neighbor, it is certainly no less offensive than returning bitten food to a bowl (besides the physiological harm he may well be causing his neighbor and himself—see Section 8 (1), below). Hence contemporary authorities have forbidden smoking altogether, while others prohibit it at least in public places.[81] Jumping a queue, which causes others loss of time, frustration, and the discomfort of a longer wait, would appear to be in the same category. Although I have found no specific prohibition in the responsa, one may infer this conclusion from the words of our Sages.[82]

Similarly, one who borrows a book from a study hall library shelf, and does not return it, confronts the next person who seeks it with only two alternatives: either to forgo pursuing the subject he wants to study or to take time off from his learning and search for the book throughout the study hall. In either case, the offender causes significant *bitul Torah*. Accordingly, the strong words of our contemporary authorities do not sound exaggerated. For example, R. Aharon Kotler declared:[83] "Not returning a book [taken from a public place] to its proper spot, after having finished with it, leads to wasting [Torah study] time and involves monetary considerations, since the book is community property and one is preventing another from using it; furthermore, it involves robbing another of his time and inconveniences him." The "Steipler" expressed this in even more extreme terms:[84] "It is certainly **cruelty and wickedness**, to impose on others [to return, to its place, a book] which one has removed."

Few halakhic details are stipulated concerning such instances; most are based on reason, with additional guidance derived from the words of our Sages in the agadoth.

(3) Deliberation in Court

Even a judge in court is not always permitted to follow the simple interpretation of halakhah and must sometimes apply personal judgment — even if it actually contradicts the simple halakhah. Our Sages teach:[85] "How do we know that if a judge knows some testimony to be false, he should not say 'Since the witnesses have testified to it, let me decide [according to their testimony], and let the witnesses take the responsibility'? Because the Torah says, 'You shall distance yourself from falsehood.'"

The Talmud cites instances of judges who rendered their verdict against the rules of halakhah, based on their personal judgment.[86] Rambam concludes, "In monetary matters, a judge should decide according to what seems truthful to him, if he is firmly convinced that the matter is so, even if there is no clear proof for it. It goes without saying that if he has certain knowledge that the matter is so, he must decide according to his knowledge... And if he has faith in [the testimony of] a woman... [who is formally ineligible as a witness] and is firmly convinced [of the truth of her statement], he relies even on this and renders his verdict accordingly." Furthermore, the Talmud actually requires the judge to use his personal judgment in those cases where no clear halakhic guidance exists; this is called *"shuda de-dayana."*[87]

The court has the power to levy fines whenever needed to maintain the level of public morality.[88]

Encouraging litigants to compromise is another instance in which the court must use its "judgment." There is a difference of opinion among the authorities whether a judge should recommend compromise or whether strict justice is preferable. This dispute was resolved by the Sages' decision that it is a mitzvah to ask the parties beforehand, "Do you wish justice or compromise?" Furthermore, a court which constantly works out compromises is considered commendable.[89] But clearly, even in such cases, the judge must guard against abuse.

Halakhah spells out no rules for all these matters. Only the agadoth of our Sages can help prevent personal inclinations from influencing judgment.

6. Beautifying the Mitzvoth

The commandment to beautify the mitzvoth is also among those fulfilled according to personal judgment. The Talmud derives this mitzvah from Scripture and has even set financial guidelines for it.[90] Nevertheless, if a person has a certain amount of money and can spend it either on a poor person whom he knows to be in need or on a more beautiful *ethrog* — who will make the halakhic choice for him? Such questions can only be answered using one's judgment, based on study of agadoth.

7. Duties of the Heart

Most mitzvoth entail action, but some specifically require only thought or feeling; R. Bachyay Ibn Pakudah called these "duties of the hearts." Although such mitzvoth are basic to Judaism, they are treated only minimally by the halakhah. In his introduction to *Chovoth HaLevavoth (Duties of the Hearts)*, R. Bachyay suggests that these mitzvoth supplement the 613 commandments, which comprise only those performed by the body. Thus, his voluminous book on the duties of the heart is based entirely on the agadah. Regarding the Book of Genesis, which is almost exclusively historical (agadah), Ramban[91] indeed stated that "it is meant to guide us on the proper road in the matter of faith" (it is evident from his commentary that the other "duties of the heart" are included as well). We proceed to examine several of these "duties of the heart."

(1) Loving and Revering God

The Torah itself attests to the fact that reverence for God is the basis of all mitzvoth;[92] the love of God, too, is fundamental to Judaism. Our Sages teach us[93] that love and reverence of God are acquired through the study of Torah, including both halakhah and agadah; but they have also indicated that the best way "to gain an understanding of the Creator is through the study of agadoth."[94] The study of halakhah, too, can help us to become acquainted with God's wisdom and goodness, but our Sages concluded that the agadah is especially appropriate to this end — perhaps because it elucidates the characteristics of God and His ways in the world, the knowledge of which is clearly a prerequisite to loving and revering Him.

Furthermore, although the study of halakhah can bring us to love and revere God, it does not tell us how much time to devote to acquiring such love and reverence. Our only guidance derives from our own deliberations and from the agadoth. R. Chaim of Volozhin states this explicitly,[95] indicating that everyone must decide for himself exactly how much time he needs to expend for this purpose. After all, if one exceeds the required time, he is detracting from Torah study.

These mitzvoth are not merely abstract and theoretical, and our Sages derived from them guidance to solve complex problems of public affairs.

The Talmudic principle:[96] "Whatever God has created in the world, He has created only for His honor" (i.e. that He be revered) has, on first sight, no practical significance. However, the agadah reveals that our Sages derived important guidelines from this principle. The Talmud[97] relates the following incident: The Garmu family was skilled in baking the show-breads, used in the service of the Sanctuary, but refused to teach this skill to others. They were rebuked for this, and when they persisted, the Sages relieved them of their duties and brought in artisans from Alexandria, Egypt, to replace them. The work of these latter, however, was not as skilled as that of the Garmu family and — in contrast to the previous loaves — the bread became moldy during its week on the table in the Sanctuary. Basing themselves on Scripture, the Sages then said that "whatever God has created in the world, He has created only for His honor" and called the Garmu family in order to reinstate them. The family, however, refused to come. Thereupon the Sages doubled their salary and the Garmu family returned to work.

Two lessons may be learned from this incident:

a) The general rule is that one may not yield to unjustified disobedience from public workers, even when the public may suffer from the consequences.

b) But the rule differs when the matter concerns God's honor: The public must submit and not stand on its own dignity when it conflicts with the honor of God.

From the halakhic viewpoint, even the bread of the Alexandrian bakers was fit, but the halakhah did not suffice to establish proper conduct in public affairs; we must supplement it with reason and agadah.

(2) Faith and Trust in God

Both Rambam and Ramban teach[98] that the first of the Ten Commandments, "I am the Lord your God," requires us to believe that there is a supreme force and prime cause for all that exists; in addition, according to Ramban, we are commanded[99] "to be perfect with God." These mitzvoth include faith and trust in God, which are basic commandments of fundamental importance. Where can we learn the details of these mitzvoth, which are not stipulated in the halakhah, if not from our own reasoning and from the examples set down by our forefathers and Sages, i.e. from the agadah?

(3) Repentance and Rebuke

The mitzvah of repentance is extremely important; "an hour spent in repentance and good deeds in this world is better than the entire life of the next world."[100] This mitzvah is so great that, on occasion, it overrides a commandment of the Torah and can change a person's willful transgressions into meritorious deeds (for one who repents out of love).[101] How are we to attain this precious gift from God? We are motivated to proper repentance if we contemplate "whence we came and whither we are going" — and nothing is better able to arouse the heart to repentance than the agadoth of our Sages. When we hear of an occurrence that shows how one transgression brings about another, or how one mitzvah brings about another, how the sons of Korach repented and were saved from eternal disgrace, and so on, we may be inspired sufficiently to help us overcome even a lifetime of bad habits and to repent our transgressions.

The mitzvah of reprimanding others is also not an easy one. How can a person succeed at it if he does not know how to influence the emotions of someone else who has succumbed to error? Again, understanding, together with the agadoth, indicates how to fulfill this mitzvah.

(4) Mitzvoth Involving Remembrance

We are commanded to remember six events, each connected with a historical occurrence. Their general aspects are mentioned in the agadic parts of the Torah and the details derived from the agadoth of our Sages: a) the Sabbath; b) the Exodus from Egypt; c) the convocation before Mount Sinai; d) the treacherous attack of Amalek; e) the incident of the Golden Calf; f) God's punishment of Miriam for her derogatory speech.[102]

Fulfillment of all these mitzvoth is based on the agadah.

8. Worldly Concerns

Several important mitzvoth relate to worldly concerns, such as safeguarding one's person and earning a livelihood. In such matters, nonhalakhic guidelines far outnumber the few explicit halakhoth. Nevertheless, these mitzvoth are of marked practical importance, especially considering the great amount of time generally devoted to their observance.

(1) Safeguarding One's Person

We are obligated to guard our lives[103] and the well-being of our bodies. Part of this obligation is set down in the halakhah. Our Sages have taught[104] that saving a life obviates all the mitzvoth of the Torah (with the exception of three: idolatry, immorality, and murder). When a conflict arises between saving our life and that of our fellow man, halakhah forbids us from giving up our own life to save someone else.[105] Nevertheless, most of the details of this mitzvah are not set down in the halakhah.

Taking care of our own physical needs is even considered an act of kindness: Hillel, when going to bathe and to eat, applied to himself the verse "He who treats himself [fairly] is a man of kindness."[106] How are we to clarify the details of this mitzvah?

Essentially, one may acquire the guidelines for fulfilling this mitzvah by examining the physical world. The better acquainted with it we are, the better we can fulfill the mitzvah. In addition, we may deduce some of the details from the agadah and from the customs of our Sages. For example, the Sages, Rishonim, and Acharonim alike praised physical exercise.[107] Rav Shesheth engaged in moving beams and other heavy items, declaring that work is laudable because of the exercise it affords. Rashi is quoted[108] as saying that he did so for health reasons, expecially during the winter, in order to perspire. Rambam mentions[109] that exercise which is necessary for health—such as ball-playing or wrestling —may be looked upon by the foolish as a game, but not so by the wise. R. Ya'akov Emden wrote[110] that all the natural scientists agree that lack of exercise is the cause of most of man's ailments.

R. Yehudah HeChasid[111] chastises a person who has the opportunity to learn medicine but refuses to do so, likening him to a murderer. The Talmud rebukes[112] a person who treats the learning of hygiene contemptuously. The Talmud and the Rambam's writings[113] alike are replete with details concerning health matters.

On the other hand, the same health considerations enjoin us to be cautious about using the specific prescriptions cited in the Talmud. There is a prohibition against their use dating to the early authorities;[114] the Tosafists wrote explicitly that the prescriptions mentioned in the Talmud are not valid in our time because the nature of the body has undergone changes since then. This concept is found also in the writings of the Acharonim.[115]

We conclude with a modern example reflecting the influence of medical research on halakhic practice. Research into the effect of smoking on health has greatly intensified since 1950, with tobacco smoke increasingly implicated as a serious health hazard. (We cite here just one simple statistic: A study of the mortality rates of men aged 40 to 60 years showed the rate among smokers to be more than double that of nonsmokers.) Consequently, halakhic authorities have forbidden smoking at least to a limited extent. Their prohibitions range from banning smoking in public places if someone objects (R. Mosheh Feinstein) to prohibiting smoking altogether (R. E. Waldenberg).[116]

(2) Earning a Livelihood

Self-sufficiency is a major obligation. The Talmud states:[117] "Turn your Sabbath into a weekday [by forgoing the extra meal] rather than taking charity." Similarly, the Sages have obligated us to teach our sons a trade and have offered extensive advice on selecting the most suitable one.[118]

These guidelines were not stipulated as halakhah but rather presented as good advice on how best to fulfill this obligation. Everyone must clarify the details of this mitzvah[119] for himself. (This subject was treated at length in Part One.[120])

9. Protective Fences

The Torah obliges us to erect "protective fences" around its prohibitions, lest we transgress accidentally or carelessly. The best-known of these are the general safeguards which rabbis in every period of our history have decreed for the public as a whole.[121] However, these do not exempt us from erecting "fences" contingent on individual needs and on conditions that change with the times. Thus each individual should establish such safeguards for himself, in accordance with his understanding,[122] just as the spiritual leaders in each generation have established them for the general public. Here, too, we should be guided by the practices of our forefathers, as recorded in the agadah. At the same time, one must be careful not to "make the fence excessive," lest it cause more harm than good[123] (see the review appended to this part).

3

Obligations Which are Not Mitzvoth

1. The Tacit Will of God as a Source of Obligation

Amazing as it may seem, we are required to fulfill certain obligations, including some which concern day-to-day affairs, without having been commanded explicitly to do so.

Rishonim clearly stated that certain obligations are binding on us even without explicit commandments. Thus, R. Yehudah HeChasid writes:[1] "We find that anyone who is able to understand [that something should be done] even though it is not commanded, is punished for not heeding." By way of example, he lists Balaam's going to curse Israel, even though God had explicitly permitted his departure. When taken to task for it, he replied: "I sinned." Obviously, he realized that God had not wanted him to go and that this realization alone was enough to render him liable.

Similarly, Rambam says[2] that a person will be rewarded for following the dictates of reason, for doing what is right and honorable, and punished for any deed which he understands to be improper, even if not specifically forbidden. Similarly, Chizkuni states:[3] "There are several mitzvoth which people are obliged to fulfill by reason alone, even though they were not commanded to do so." Consider also the words of Rav Nissim Gaon, cited in Section 5 of this chapter.

The above observations indicate that we must rely on our own discretion not only to derive the details of the mitzvoth but also regarding matters which, strictly speaking, are not mitzvoth at all. Lacking clear direction, we can only base our actions on those of our forefathers and Sages, as handed down to us in the agadoth.

Bearing this in mind, we may answer an old question: There are several base actions (such as taking a loaf which a pauper was about to pick up; raising one's hand as if to strike another; making a vow, even though one fulfills it[4]) which stigmatize their perpetrators as "wicked."

May we indulge in these practices if we are prepared to accept that label? On the face of it, there is no reason to forbid these actions, as neither the Torah nor the Sages expressly forbade them. However, such behavior obviously incurs punishment, for God is "not a God who desires wickedness."[5] All the enumerated actions are against God's will, and their perpetrator is subject to chastisement. Presumably, one who inflicts unnecessary pain on himself—and is consequently called a sinner[6]—also falls into this category.

The following are several additional examples of conduct which, although not expressly mandated, is nontheless obligatory to some extent.

2. Piety

Chasiduth (piety) denotes doing more than one is required to do. Although the term "going beyond the letter of the law" (*lifnim mishurath hadin*) usually refers to civil litigation, Rishonim use it to describe piety as well, thus applying the term to all mitzvoth.[7] In other words, piety is the fulfillment of God's will beyond the performance of explicit commandments. Study of the halakhoth is not sufficient to determine God's will; one must also study the reasons behind the mitzvoth and the agadoth, i.e. the entire Talmud. This is the meaning of the Mishnah:[8] "An ignorant person cannot be pious." If he lacks the background, how can he know God's will? If such a person feigns piety, it is dangerous to live in his proximity.[9] Even if he has studied Scripture and the Mishnah, he is considered ignorant in this respect, unless he has studied the Talmud as well.[10]

We even find instances where punishment is meted out for lack of piety. Rambam[11] says that while it is permissible to leave Eretz Yisrael during a period of severe famine, it is not characteristic of the pious to do so, as we can see from the story of Mahlon and Chilion (in the Book of Ruth), who were the leaders of that generation and left the country under great pressure, yet were doomed to destruction by God. In a different instance, we find that Elijah the Prophet was displeased with R. Yehoshua' ben Levi; the latter had followed an explicit ruling, but was upbraided by Elijah: "Is this a Mishnah for the pious?".[12]

Rabbeinu Yehonathan[13] deduces from the Talmud that the minimum requirement for piety is care not to cause damage to another

—even unwittingly, being indulgent of others in monetary matters, and being devout in one's prayers.

However, this concept of piety also applies to other mitzvoth. For example, a pious person does not accept payment for something he did on Sabbath, even though it was permissible to do so, for it is a sign of piety to shun anything that has the slightest hint of transgression about it.[14]

From the words of Rambam,[15] however, it appears that general piety is not necessarily the highest level towards which one should strive. He says: "One who is punctilious about his actions and [therefore] strays somewhat from the median path in one direction or another—this is piety. However, if he walks strictly on the median path—this is wisdom. And we are commanded to walk on the median path, which is the good and straight way." This seems to indicate that the way of piety is not always the best way. The Talmud[16] apparently supports this view. It reports that a Tana once declared: "The pious are not happy with one who kills snakes and scorpions on Shabbath," and that he was answered: "The wise ones are not happy with these pious ones."

3. Stringency

Taking a position on the mitzvoth more stringent than the halakhah is *ipso facto* outside the field of halakhah. Laudable stringency is an aspect of piety, but it is not easy to determine precisely when stringency is indeed laudable.

On the one hand, our Sages have said[17] that "one who is exempt from doing something, yet does it nonetheless, is called a boor;" but on the other hand, in connection with the Chanukah lights, they describe, with implied approval,[18] those who enhance the mitzvah and even those who enhance these enhancements! Again, we have an Amora who claimed that he compares to his father as vinegar compares to wine, because he was not as stringent as his father in abstaining from dairy products on a day on which he ate meat. However, regarding the very same restriction, classical authorities state that he who innovates a stringency is close to heresy.[19]

We noted above that one who performs an act from which he is exempt is called a boor. This rule is cited as halakhah by many of the Rishonim[20] and in connection with a wide variety of stringent interpretations. The Rishonim labored hard to find the rules for determining which stringencies are laudable and which are censurable. Some could only solve the problem through reason and agadah. Thus, Meiri would apply the censure only to stringencies that are not morally or ethically motivated.[21] We must be very careful not to take the more stringent view just for "safety's sake" and should limit stringencies in accordance with the rules stipulated by our Sages. (For a detailed analysis, see the review at the end of this part.)

4. Additional Non-Formalized Obligations

Besides these general responsibilities, there are many specific obligations which were not formally commanded, yet we may assume confidently—through reason and the agadah—that they are indeed God's will. Below, we present a brief review of several such obligations.

(1) Peace

Peace is one of the three practices vital to the world's survival.[22] King David advised all those wishing life to "seek peace and pursue it."[23] Peace is so beloved of God that "even though Israel practice idolatry, as long as there is peace between them, God says, 'It is as if I had no power over them, for they are at peace with each other.'"[24] Conversely, anyone who maintains strife transgresses a prohibition.[25] Nevertheless, there is no explicit mitzvah to maintain peace. True, the Mishnah advises us[26] to be disciples of Aaron: to love peace and to pursue peace—and our Sages provide us with the details of how Aaron went about doing so. Still, none of this is couched in terms of a commandment.

Several additional observations imply that God desires peace:

a) God commanded that we be blessed with peace.[27]

b) He permitted His name to be obliterated for the sake of making peace between husband and wife.[28]

c) He even deviated from the truth somewhat for the sake of peace.[29]

d) "He makes peace in His heights."[30]

e) One of His names is "Peace."[31]

These observations show that the pursuit of peace is a great and sacred obligation.[32]

The Sages instituted many regulations "for the sake of peace." Thus for this reason many acts were classified as theft — even though legally they are not. "For the sake of peace" also plays a prominent role in the regulations governing our relationship with non-Jews.[33] Apparently, the Sages derived all these guidelines on the basis of reason alone.

The entire Torah is "for the sake of peace," as it is written: "Its ways are ways of pleasantness, and all its paths are peace."[34] Thus, striving for peace, although formally not a mitzvah, is nonetheless a most sacred obligation, and reward in both worlds is vouchsafed us if we nurture it.[35]

(2) "The Torah Comes to Counter the Evil Inclination"

Some acts are expressly permitted by the Torah, yet the Sages understood that, basically, it is better to avoid them. They referred to such acts when they stated: "[Here] the Torah comes to counter the evil inclination" — such as the law of the "beautiful captive"[36] or eating the meat of an animal which was ritually slaughtered while on the point of dying.[37] Our Sages have not told us how they came to their conclusions; it seems that they did so on the basis of their reasoning.

Again, not all that the Torah permits is proper conduct for us.

(3) Torah Study for Women

The Talmud exempts[38] women from the mitzvah of *talmud Torah*. Concerning a father's obligation to teach his daughter Torah, the Mishnah cites two opinions:[39] ben 'Azai says that a man is obligated to teach his daughter Torah, but R. Eli'ezer states that "he who teaches his daughter Torah is as if he had taught her levity." Rambam decides[40] in favor of R. Eli'ezer, but agrees that women earn reward if they learn; however, this reward is not as great as that of a man, in line with the general rule that more reward accrues to one who does a mitzvah obligatory upon him, than to one who fulfills a mitzvah voluntarily. He adds that the censure applies only to the Oral Torah, but not to the Written Torah; and while a father should not teach even the Written Torah to his daughter, it is not like teaching her levity if he does.

Other Rishonim make several distinctions.

R. Yehudah HeChasid[41] writes that a man is indeed obligated to teach his daughters the laws concerning the mitzvoth and that the prohibition applies only to delving deeply into the Talmud, studying the Kabala and the like. He demonstrates this from Scripture and the Sages. The author of Semak, in his introduction, cites among the reasons for writing his work: "to tell women the mitzvoth which apply to them, positive and negative ones; their reading and studying Semak will be as useful to them as the study of the Talmud is to men." Without explicit basis, either Scriptural or Talmudic, these authorities differentiate between studying in depth and learning the conclusions only—between those mitzvoth which apply to women and those which do not.

Further distinctions are made in the works of the early authorities. *Ma'ayan Ganim*[42] speculates that the censure may refer only to teaching women at a tender age, when their intellect is not firmly established. Later on, however, if they aspire to it, "let them ascend the mountain of God."

In a similar vein, *Perishah*[43] writes: "If they learn on their own, we can see that they are exceptional; this is what Rambam meant by saying that they do have reward if they learn properly... But a father is not permitted to teach his daughter... since he has no way of knowing [whether she is misinterpreting what is being taught]." Taz[44] raises the question of the mitzvah of *hak-hel*, according to which, every seven years, the king assembled the entire nation—men, women and children—and read to them from the Torah. He asks why women are obligated here and answers: "It seems to me that here the king only expounded the simple words, which is certainly permitted... as we see in common practice every day."

Accordingly, not only practical halakhah but "all work involving character traits and their improvement, all development and strengthening of the intellect, acquisition of reverence and of love [of God], and perfecting the way to repentance are all obligatory, based on simple reason, regardless of their status as general or specific commandments of the Torah."[45] And if these are binding on women, then certainly the Torah study required to acquire them is likewise obligatory.

It appears that in regard to teaching women, the later halakhic authorities made certain logical distinctions which were not stated explicitly by the Sages. Moreover, basically there is apparently no halakhah prohibiting a woman from studying, not even an explicit rabbinic injunction. Even the Rambam's formulation is not prohibitory. It appears that R. Eli'ezer is offering no more than advice; he held that one who wishes to teach his daughter Torah is likely to do more damage than good, a view with which Rambam agreed. Such advice is by its very nature time-dependent and its general application may change with circumstances.

Indeed, the most recent authorities have established practice in accordance with the perceived needs of the times, as the "Chafetz Chayim" writes:[46]

It appears that all this was written in bygone times, when everyone lived in the same place as his ancestors and the tradition of their fathers was very firm with them—to comport themselves in the ways of their fathers, in line with the verse: "Ask your father and he will tell you." In those circumstances, one can say that she should not learn Torah, but should rather depend on the customs of her righteous forebears. But nowadays, to our shame, when parental tradition is greatly weakened and it is also quite usual that people do not dwell in the same place as their fathers did—especially those [daughters] who have adopted the practice of studying the language of the nations—it is certainly **a great mitzvah** to teach them the Pentateuch and also the Prophets and *Kethuvim* and the ethics of the Sages, such as *Pirkey Avoth, Menorath HaMaor* and similar works, so that the truth of our holy faith be confirmed to them. For if we fail to do so, they may stray entirely from the path of God and transgress [even] all the fundamental laws, God forbid.

R. S.R. Hirsch points out that when expounding the verses regarding the obligation to teach Torah to one's children, the Sages made a distinction between sons and daughters only in regard to the verse which commands us to "teach" (*welimadetem*) but not in the verse which commands us to "inculcate" (*weshinantam*), "to teach us that the mitzvah of thoroughly inculcating the regulations applies to [daughters] as well."[47]

R. Y.Z. Ciechanowicz, like the earlier authorities, concludes[48] that it is not only permitted but even mandatory to teach women the laws which pertain to them; furthermore, concerning the laws which do not pertain to women, the censure pronounced by R. Eli'ezer only applies to one who urges them to study, but not if they come of their own accord to learn. In his view, moreover, only the father is forbidden to teach her; but others are permitted to teach women "without delving into the conjectures and argumentations, only the final, straightforward decision."

R. A.Y. Neumark[49] expresses views similar to those of the "Chafetz Chayim":

> Time [i.e. experience], which is the most reliable teacher, confirms [the Talmudic principle] that "both are the words of God" [meaning that among the Sages, there can be two conflicting opinions, both of divine origin]. The words of R. Eli'ezer... were valid as long as the general environment was permeated with the spirit of faith... but now that the destructive plague of atheism and materialism has begun to rule the environment and to ensnare souls, it is no longer permissible to abandon the daughters of Jacob and not raise them on the wellsprings of the Torah and reverence for God.

Citing the words of the Sages, R. Zalman Sorotzkin[50] explained beautifully how the course of instruction for daughters depends on the state of the world. We find, he says, that in a generation which does not have the proper faith in God, it is more important to teach girls than to teach boys. We learn this from our father Abraham: in the time of Nimrod, who caused the whole world to rebel against God, Abraham built the tent of Sarah — to convert the women — before he built his own tent — to convert men. That is why in that portion of the Torah the word "tent" is twice written in the feminine form, to impress on us that this is the proper way to nurture the faith in a faithless generation. Therefore, he continues, we are not permitted to keep our daughters away from the "cheder" (Torah school), for this would be tantamount to depriving them of eternal life.

Indeed, this is not an entirely new development, and Jewish historical records are replete with learned women. Chida mentions several:[51] The daughter of R. Chanina ben Teradyon disputes his son's opinion and the Sages accept hers;[52] moreover, the words of his daughter Beruriah are cited with praise.[53] Chida also quoted several responsa which attributed decisions to women.[54] And even the Tosafoth quote halakhoth in the name of women,[55] as do the later *poskim*.[56] R. Aharon Berakhyah of Modena[57] mentions that his grandmother taught him Torah wisdom, indicating that he therefore owed her the reverence one owes one's teacher. The author of the responsa *Rav Pe'alim*[58] relates that his grandmother was wont to learn eighteen chapters of Mishnayoth every morning before dawn.

On the other hand, R. Mosheh Feinstein[59] writes that one who teaches his daughter Mishnayoth "is as if he had taught her levity."

(4) Community Needs

We are not explicitly commanded to concern ourselves with community needs; our Sages derived this obligation from Moses, who, even when the day of his death was approaching, occupied himself with the needs of the People of Israel rather than with his own.[60] Anyone who concerns himself selflessly with communal affairs can be assured that his ancestral merits will be credited to him;[61] he is likened to one engaged in Torah study;[62] while occupied with communal affairs, he is exempt from the obligation to read the Shema' even if this means that he will miss it completely—which shows us that in this respect, concerning oneself with the needs of the community is even more weighty than Torah study.[63] Our Sages have also taught that those who engage in community service merit temporal greatness:[64] "Saul merited royalty only because his grandfather set up lights [on dark streets] for the use of the public." Similarly, the Sages derived from the Scriptures[65] that those who benefit the public will merit God's salvation. This provides an agadic foundation.

Furthermore, Maharal[66] says that whatever kindness is done on behalf of the community is accounted manifold, because of the multitude of people who benefit from it. This provides a logical foundation.

(5) "Those Who Have No Share in the Next World"

The most severe transgressions are those that cause the transgressor to lose his share in the next world. Rambam[67] enumerates fourteen sins in this category. It is surprising that the majority are not explicitly mentioned in the Torah, but are derived by reason or from the agadah. These are: the *epikorsim*;[68] those who deny the divine origin of the Torah; those who deny the future revival of the dead; those who deny the coming of the Messiah; those who segregate themselves from the ways of the community; informers (who enable gentiles to persecute a Jew); those who instill fear in the public for selfish reasons; and those who would undo their circumcision.

Rambam explains[69] that those who segregate themselves from the community, even though they do not transgress any law, are condemned because they separate themselves from Israel and do not fulfill the mitzvoth together with the community. The informers cause damage and endanger others in such a way that they cannot be held legally accountable; nevertheless, it is permitted to kill them without trial, if this is necessary to prevent them from endangering another through informing.

Furthermore, the Sages have taught that anyone who causes himself to entertain lustful thoughts will not be admitted to the presence of God.[70] The Sages continue there: "What is meant by the verse, 'Their hands are full of blood'? This refers to those who commit adultery with their hands." This transgression caused the death of 'Er and Onan;[71] and because of this God brought the Deluge to the world, destroying all life,[72] which shows that even non-Jews are destroyed because of it. And yet this prohibition is not mentioned explicitly in the Torah, but is derived by reason and from the agadic parts of the Torah only.[73]

(6) Making Derogatory Statements About the People of Israel

The prohibition on making derogatory statements against the People of Israel is not spelled out in the Torah; it is only from the agadah and by reasoning that we can deduce that God does not want his firstborn to be maligned. It was the duty of the prophets, and it is our duty as well, to "tell [God's] people their transgression"; but this means telling **them**, not about them. Our teacher Moses, Elijah the Prophet and Isaiah the Prophet were all punished for transgressing this prohibition,[74] despite the apparent ample justification for their criticisms: in the time of Moses, the people neglected circumcision and succumbed to immorality; in the days of Elijah, all but seven thousand were intentional idolators,[75] and in the days of Isaiah, God Himself called them a nation of sinners. We are told of the following incident:[76] When the city of Samaria was under siege and its inhabitants on the point of starvation, Elisha prophesied that "tomorrow a measure of fine flour will sell for a shekel and two measures of barley for a shekel at the gate of Samaria." The officer on whom King Ahab relied scoffed that "even if God will open trapdoors in the Heavens, can something like this occur?" Whereupon the prophet told him, "You will see it with your eyes, but you will not eat of it." And the next day, when the prophesy was fulfilled, the people trampled this officer and he died. The Sages tell us that he was punished so severely because he denied that the people would merit such a miracle, since they were sinners and idolators.

Despite the importance this matter is accorded and the severity of the punishment meted out to transgressors, the prohibition is not explicitly stated anywhere. Rambam[77] discusses this prohibition at length and cites numerous supporting arguments from the agadoth to emphasize its seriousness. He does this relating to the *anusim*, who outwardly accepted the Islamic faith to save their lives and were very severly castigated for doing so by a scholar of that generation.

The Sages hinted at this prohibition when they applied the verse "Do not malign a servant to his master" to the prophet Hosea[78] for maligning Israel; they reprimand him for this even though Israel had sinned. It is from this passage that several authorities[79] included the prohibition against maligning Israel in their enumeration of mitzvoth. Evidently, all these prophets were only punished because they should have understood on their own that it is not proper to calumniate the Nation of God—even when this nation deserved calumny. We may derive this prohibiton from all these agadoth.

Moreover, as *Mesilath Yesharim* says: "It is the will of God that the pious in Israel should exonerate and atone for those among them who are [spiritually] on a lower level... and to defend the entire generation."[80] He adduces further proof from the angel Gabriel and from Gideon, both of whom merited God's favor only after they defended Israel's conduct—"for God loves only those who love Israel." (See also Part 3, Chapter 5.)

5. Rationally Based Obligations Binding Even on Gentiles

As indicated at the beginning of this chapter, whenever God's will may be deduced rationally, such deduction is sufficient to obligate us. This rule is supported by the words of Rav Nissim Gaon in the introduction to his commentary on the Talmud: "All those mitzvoth which are rationally [or intuitively] derived, are applicable to all, from the day that God first created man on earth—they are obligatory on him and all his descendants, for all generations to come."

In this way, R. Avraham Grodzinsky[81] explains why gentiles were severely punished for transgressions from which they had not been expressly enjoined—for example, the generation of the Deluge [as well as 'Er and Onan] for non-coital emission; the people of Sodom for not supporting the poor and destitute; Ammon and Moab—who are forbidden to intermarry with Israel—because they did not welcome our forefathers with bread and water. Also, many nations were punished most severely for lacking proper character traits — Assyria and Babylon for haughtiness, Aram for cruelty in war.[82] In all these cases, R. Grodzinsky says that they were punished because they should have known better, as reason dictates these matters. R. Yehudah HeChasid[83] derived this same insight from the fact that, after having been given explicit permission to go, Balaam said, "I have sinned [by going]."

Also, compare Chizkuni's[84] explanation of why the generation of the Deluge was punished for something that was not forbidden to them.

4

The Role of Reason in Establishing the Halakhah

1. Deriving the Halakhah in Principle

Even though the Torah — in general and in specific detail[1] — was given at Sinai, many minor points are left for us to clarify. Furthermore, even that which was given explicitly must be analyzed in depth, using our best reasoning powers to extract the halakhoth. In the words of our Sages:[2] "R. Yanai said, had the Torah been given clear-cut, we would not have a leg to stand on. What is meant by 'God said to Moses...'? [Moses] said to Him, 'Teach me what the halakhah is' to which He answered, 'Decide according to the majority. If the majority exonerate him, he is exonerated; if the majority find him guilty, he is guilty,' in order that the Torah can be interpreted with forty-nine facets indicating 'unclean' and forty-nine facets indicating 'clean.'" This shows us that we must examine all aspects of a problem, from all sides, before we can arrive at a clear halakhah.

This is also the intent of the Talmudic passage[3] which, in connection with Rabah bar Nachmani, relates that the scholars in the Heavenly yeshiva disputed the opinion of God. Ran explains this difficult passage as follows:[4] Since they were empowered to make halakhic decisions, and since they decided — based on their reasoning powers — that a particular circumstance causes ritual impurity, it follows that this circumstance should indeed cause impurity because that decision is based on human reasoning. This is so even if the conclusion is objectively false, as God Himself wanted human reasoning to be decisive. Those who supported the other side of the argument, even though objectively correct, must follow the decision of the majority.

A similar point is made elsewhere in the Talmud,[5] relating that when Moses rose on High, he found God adding crowns to the letters in the

Torah. When Moses asked who required this of Him ("to add to what He had written"—Rashi), he was answered that there will be one man, called 'Akiva ben Yosef, who will derive mountains of halakhoth from every minute part of each letter. R. Mosheh Feinstein explained this passage,[6] saying that the "crowns" allude to sovereignty imparted to the letters, that is, the interpretation of the letters was made, to some extent, independent of their Author, and if, despite their best efforts, the Sages misinterpret the letters, their misinterpretation becomes halakhah.

The Talmud[7] also states that seventeen hundred [derived decisions] were forgotten during the period of mourning for Moses, but 'Othniel ben Kenaz reestablished them by his dialectics. This too shows that it is possible to clarify the words of the Torah by logical reasoning—even that which was not made explicit. Similarly, Rambam enumerates[8] among the types of mitzvoth a special group which is derived by reasoning. This thesis is repeated by Rambam in other places as well.[9]

The Sages also derived entire halakhoth solely on the basis of reasoning. Consider, for example, the very basis of civil litigation: "He who makes a demand on another's property bears the burden of proof." This rule is not derived from the Written Torah, but rather by reason: "It is the one who is in pain who goes to the physician"; similarly, he who feels financially deprived must be expected to take the initiative in court —as Rav Ashi argues.[10] Thus, too, the decision that one must suffer death rather than kill another is arrived at by reasoning:[11] "Who tells you that your blood is redder? Perhaps that of your friend is redder!" Many other such instances are enumerated by various authors.[12] Repeatedly[13] the Sages declare that in the presence of a logical conclusion, there is no need for a Scriptural source.

2. Clarifying the Halakhah in Our Day

All the above remarks apply in principle. In present practice, however, we are not qualified to expound verses and to extract new laws from the Written Torah. *Kesef Mishneh* comments on the above words of Rambam, noting that from the time the Mishnah was completed, it was decided that later generations would no longer be permitted to differ with it; a similar situation obtained when the Talmud was completed. Rambam himself writes that all decisions must be based on the Babylonian Talmud or, if no decision concerning the issue at hand is to be found, on the Jerusalem Talmud or the *Tosefta*.[14]

Nevertheless, there is still much room for applying logical thought in deriving halakhoth—by analogy—concerning new questions which arise daily.

Reason is also important even for clarifying old questions. Obviously, recognition of the paucity of our reason and the weakness of our intellect will constrain us to obey the words of the earlier generations. We might therefore believe that a rabbi should merely count the authorities who permit something and those who forbid it, and then decide according to the majority. In fact, however, this is not so. According to many opinions, the principle that the majority rules applies only when the authorities are in session together, face to face.[15] The "Chazon Ish," as well as R. Mosheh Feinstein, agreed that a majority of opinions which were expressed in different places and times is not binding in establishing the halakhah, and that we must not abandon reason in arriving at halakhic decisions.[16]

On one occasion, the "Chazon Ish" wrote:[17] "The halakhic decision always follows the most convincing evidence, and even though we [generally] follow the decisions of Shulchan Arukh, nevertheless we occasionally deviate from these decisions when later authorities did so, based on solid arguments... For every halakhah, we must investigate also the arguments of the later authorities, as **wisdom is the deciding factor in everything**, and only if the evidence for the two sides is balanced do we follow the decision of the greater authority; in such balanced cases, we follow the decisions of R. Yosef Karo and R. Mosheh Isserles [i.e., Shulchan Arukh]."[18] In another passage, the "Chazon Ish" puts even more stress on the subjective aspects:[19] "It is in the nature of intelligence to evolve and we should use our own intelligence as much as at all possible and seek that which is the most reasonable; no one has the authority to say 'Accept my opinion,' but we, ourselves, are bound by that [insight] which has been granted to us."

This emphasis on reason is entirely in accord with the Meiri's views:[20]

> The following is a principle binding on every thoughtful person, one in which I saw our present generation fail: An occasion arises in which a halakhah must be decided. Based on the law of the Talmud, [the act in question] is permitted... and they dispute the Talmudic conclusion on the basis of spurious reasoning, inventions, additions, gleanings and variant readings,

and then they whoop like cranes: "See, I found that such a one wrote thus," without knowing or caring whether the statement is valid and without finding support for their argument in the Talmud... [The proper approach is:] anything for which you do not know the reason, do not accept under any circumstance... Thus, in all halakhic issues, it is not proper to decide according to what has been written by a post-Talmudic authority... unless there is proof for it.

An important and revealing comment on this question is made by Maharal:[21]

It is more fitting and more proper that one should base his decisions on the Talmud, even though there is a risk that he will not reason correctly and therefore reach an incorrect decision. Nevertheless, a scholar can only deal with what his reason tells him, based on his understanding of the Talmud. If his understanding and wisdom mislead him, he is nonetheless beloved of God when he reaches decisions which are based on his reason, for "a judge can only decide on the basis of what he sees." This [method of arriving at the halakhah] is better than someone who reaches his decisions based on some halakhic compilation, without knowing any of the reasons, like a blind man walking along the road.

Although a realistic humility should compel us to accept as binding the decisions of earlier authorities, who were closer to the source of our tradition, the decision-making process may yet involve disputing the decisions of earlier authorities. In the words of Rema:[22] "There are those who say that if a judge and his contemporaries find—based on incontrovertible arguments—that the law is not as stated by earlier authorities, then they can disagree with [the earlier decision], provided it is not mentioned in the Talmud."[23] In the words of R. Avraham, the son of Rambam:[24] A judge is obligated "to make branches sprout from the trunk" through his reasoning power, which he developed through the study of the Talmud. He writes:

In brief, a judge who merely follows what has been set down and made explicit is weak and feeble. This would void the principle that "a judge can only decide on the basis of what he sees." It is not so; rather, the written words are the "trunk" and whoever wishes to reach a decision or render a judgment must consider them in the light of the circumstances of each individual case which comes before him, to draw analogies between similar laws and to make branches sprout from this trunk. The many stories in the Talmud, which illustrate some of the rabbinic regulations, were not set down in vain, nor were they meant to establish the rule in that particular case. Rather, by hearing many of them, the scholar should develop the power of sound judgment required for deciding actual cases.

We should not only deduce the law in a particular case from the stories related in the Talmud, but also use them to guide us in further decisions. Even halakhic anecdotes, then, give us much more general guidance beyond the particular case to which they refer.

3. "Its Ways Are Ways of Pleasantness" — A Source of Halakhah

The above verse has been frequently used by both the Sages and the later authorities as a basis for decision-making and as a source for clarifying the halakhah. Many have used it for rational derivation of new, reasonable halakhoth.

(1) Derivations by the Sages

The wisest of all men declared:[25] "Its ways are ways of pleasantness and all its paths are peace." From this verse, Abayey derived[26] that certain kinds of plants could not have been intended for the "four species" of plants which are used on Sukoth in conjunction with the *lulav* — because they abrade the hands. This verse is also used to exempt women from levirate marriage in certain cases — lest they become repulsive to their husbands.[27] *Or Same-ach* said that this principle is a cornerstone of tradition.[28]

A problem remains, however: The verse is from Proverbs and, according to tradition, Torah-halakhah can be derived only from the Five Books of Moses. Apparently, the derivation is not an actual deduction from that verse; rather, it merely enunciates what is accepted as a general basis for the entire Torah. In other words, we can call it "derivation of new laws from the reason underlying the law," on a Torah-wide scale. Based on this verse, the Talmud indeed states that "the entire Torah is for the sake of peace."[29] True, Tanaim disagree on the question of whether a halakhah can be based on a reason that we perceive as underlying a given mitzvah and the Talmud does decide that "we do not derive new laws from the reason underlying the law."[30] It appears, however, that this decision applies only to reasons for individual laws; in the case of a general reason, underlying the entire Torah, the practice seems to be undisputed.

(2) Derivations by Later Halakhic Authorities

The authorities following the completion of the Talmud also used this verse to derive details which had not been clarified before, primarily to bolster decisions which were derived on other grounds.

For example, several special laws concerning levirate marriage (besides those mentioned above) are derived from that verse, as are the details of the Torah's injunction against doing something on one's own property that will cause damage to another.[31] The authorities use this verse to establish the halakhah regarding numerous other laws as well.[32]

(3) Social Order

Many of the regulations of social order are based on the principles of (a) majority rule, (b) the power of the court to confiscate property, and (c) conjecture regarding the intent of the parties to the disputed agreement. In such cases as well, the halakhic authorities have established hard-and-fast rules based on the verse "Its ways are ways of pleasantness..."

(a) Even though the Talmud applies the principle of majority rule only to opinions expressed in a court of law, Rosh explicitly applies it to community decisions, which require the minority to accede to the decisions of the majority; otherwise, he says, community decisions would be impossible. While Rosh himself does not provide a source for this rule, the later authorities derive it from the verse in Proverbs.

(b) The validity of regulations of trade-unions, too, is based on this verse, in conjunction with the principle empowering the court to confiscate private property.[33]

(c) However, this principle is not limited to community affairs; regarding individual matters as well, we find that certain decisions are made and others rejected because something is, or is not, consonant with "ways of pleasantness." One example is the case of a man who signs over all his property to his wife and then dies unexpectedly; as it is clear that the man did not intend to disinherit his children, we act accordingly.[34]

(4) Clarifications of Rabbinic Ordinances and Customs

So far, we have only dealt with Torah laws, but the Sages, too, have instituted numerous ordinances which can also be clarified by applying this verse.

a) Radbaz wrote in very general terms[35] that "most of the rabbinic ordinances are in the nature of compassion and improvement of the quality of life, motivated by the verse: 'Its ways ...'."

b) According to Rambam,[36] our obligation to help the gentile poor along with the Jewish poor, to visit their sick and bury their dead, are all derived from that same verse, as implied by the Talmud itself.

c) R. Yosef Karo[37] wrote that the reason we permit a widow to sustain herself from her husband's estate (until she claims and receives her *kethubah*) is also based on this verse.

d) Regarding Rabbeinu Gershom's injunction forbidding a man to divorce his wife against her will, Maharashdam[38] wrote that "it is inconceivable that a man should be fettered hand and foot while his wife laughs at him. Heaven forbid, for there are several prohibitions against this and the 'ways of the Torah are the ways of pleasantness.' It never occurred to [Rabbeinu Gershom] to make ordinances in respect to this [situation of a totally rebellious wife]."

e) In the case of individuals taking over the estate of a proselyte who died without leaving heirs, *Tur*[39] — in the name of his father, Rosh — held that these individuals are no more obligated to bury him than is the general public. Bach objected to this, noting that the obligation of burial was already imposed on the estate during his lifetime, as the Sages have decreed explicitly that the four cubits around a person have the power to acquire property for him,[40] in order to avoid strife, "and such is precisely the case in this situation, for these people come to spend his property and others have the obligation to bury him. However, the Torah said: 'Its ways are ways of pleasantness and all its paths are peace.' It would therefore appear, in my humble opinion, that the proper judgment is that they should first bury him and then each can spend what he has."

f) R. Ya'akov ibn Tzur and R. Yedidyah Monsonego wrote[41] that although the Mishnah[42] forbade a husband to move his wife from town to town without her consent, this does not apply in a dangerous situation. When witnesses testify that by traveling to her home, the husband puts himself in danger, he is permitted to require her to come to his city, again because "Its ways are ways of pleasantness..."

g) In reference to the custom of leaving a son with his divorced mother until he reaches the age of six years[43] — R. Ya'akov Bardugo[44] writes that this does not apply if the mother is blind, because the child could suffer harm under such circumstances, which would be inconsistent with the words of the verse in Proverbs.

h) Concerning the testament of R. Yehudah HeChasid — who forbade a woman to marry a man who bears the same name as her father — R. Yechezkel Landau wrote[45] that the author could not have meant this to apply when the father's name was added at a later date, so that the couple would have to separate, "for this is neither the way of pleasantness nor the path of peace."

(5) The Reasons Underlying the Mitzvoth

We also find that some of the reasons adduced for various mitzvoth are based on this verse:

a) Radbaz[46] explains why the fine imposed on the "conspiring witnesses" ('eidim zomemim) is paid to the one against whom they testified: "For he was pained that they testified against him falsely, in order to hurt him financially... therefore, the Torah entitled him to recompense, for 'its ways are ways of pleasantness.'"

b) The obligation to "be fruitful and multiply" applies only to men. Basing himself on the above verse, Meshekh Chokhmah suggests that the Torah exempts women from this mitzvah because they risk their lives by subjecting themselves to childbirth and the Torah never obligates people to do anything beyond their capacity to endure.[47]

c) The 'Eiruv Chatzeroth is a halakhic device permitting the carrying of objects on the Sabbath in enclosed areas open to the public. It was instituted by the Sages "because of the ways of peace... in accordance with the verse 'Its ways are ways of pleasantness...'"[48] Maharsha[49] comments that according to the basic law, the Sages should not have permitted carrying on the Sabbath in a public courtyard and that they only did so—by means of the 'Eiruv—for reasons of peace, that is, to encourage social intercourse during the leisure hours of the Sabbath.

(6) Epilogue

The numerous Torah-based and rabbinic laws derived from this verse reflect its importance in Torah thought. It follows directly from the basic concepts of our faith. Since God is both the Creator of the world and the Giver of the Torah, the two—the Torah and the world—should complement each other to make one whole. In other words, we are obligated to observe the Torah to bring life in this world to perfection. Similarly, it follows that the Torah laws should not be physically or socially injurious to this life. Therefore, as long as there is no evidence to the contrary, this common-sense conclusion should guide our decisions. This is the significance of the principle: "Its ways are ways of pleasantness and all its paths are peace."

Considering this harmony between the Torah and the physical world, we may understand the Talmudic saying:[50] "Is that which the Torah forbade not sufficient for you? Do you wish to deny yourself other things as well?" Our thesis also easily explains the well-known, but surprising, statement[51] that "Each man will have to account for all that he saw with his eyes, but of which he did not partake." If one understands that the world was created for him[52] and for the fulfillment of the Torah, he will not scorn what it offers.

5

Summary

The above observations show that the Torah consists of much more than halakhah alone. We require reason, as well as the agadah, to clarify the path to be taken—even regarding halakhah itself. Furthermore, we note that many of the mitzvoth—notably those "upon which the world stands"—are largely outside the realm of halakhah. We have also discovered that Torah obligations occasionally go even beyond the scope of mitzvoth, and that some of our most important obligations may be in that category.

A Jew may not say: "I have fulfilled my obligation as it is specified in Shulchan Arukh—and this is enough for me," for Shulchan Arukh is only one part of Torah life. Neither should he say: "I have learned the halakhah, so my path is clear before me." Rather, he should fulfill the injunction to "study midrash: halakhah and agadah."

Special Review:
Praiseworthy, Boorish and Heretical
Chumroth (Stringencies)

One of the unique features of today's Orthodox scene is a tendency to accept *chumroth* which exceed previous practice in their stringency. The term *chumra* (plural: *chumroth*) is used here to mean an act which a person treats as forbidden even though it is permitted, or the performing of mitzvoth from which he is exempt. Those who accept *chumroth* are often not aware of the dangers inherent in this practice. To point out some of those dangers, without overlooking the potential benefits, we digress with a rather comprehensive review of the advantages and possible risks of adopting *chumroth*.

A *chumra* is a double-edged sword. It can raise one to the pinnacle of holiness or lower him to the level of foolishness or even heresy. The institution of a new *chumra*, which previous generations did not observe therefore requires wisdom and much learning, lest the loss exceed the gain. In the words of *Shevuth Ya'akov*:[1] "I am not happy with those recent compendia, such as *Lechem HaPanim, Gan Nata'*, and *Be-eir Heitev*... the authors of which merely copy from one book to the other, searching every nook and cranny, and when they discover some *chumra*, it is a great find for them to copy over. Do not rely on them at all; it is enough for us to follow those *chumroth* which were instituted by Rema and the other great authorities, who have the power to decide."

We proceed to investigate several *chumroth*, some laudable and others boorish or heretical.

1. *Chumroth* Observed by Our Biblical Forefathers and Sages

We find that the Patriarchs observed the entire Torah, even though they were not obligated to do so.[2]

After the Torah was given, many of the nation's leaders instituted safeguards in the form of *chumroth*.[3] Thus, we find that the Prophet Ezekiel[4] declared that he never ate the flesh of a fatally sick animal, nor that of an animal which had an anatomical defect and could be rendered permissible only after inspection by a rabbinic authority—even though both are wholly permissible and it may not even be an act of piety to avoid them.[5]

The Amora Mar 'Ukva said[6] that he considered himself as "vinegar, the son of wine" because his father, when he had eaten meat, would not eat cheese until the following day, whereas he himself merely refrained from eating meat and cheese at the same meal. The Amora Shemuel described himself similarly for patrolling his property only once daily, and not twice, as had been his father's practice. There are also Tanaim —such as the House of Rabban Gamliel[7]—who took the stringent view for themselves but the lenient view for others.

The Sages observed especially important *chumroth* regarding the rules governing interpersonal relationships.[8]

2. Praiseworthy *Chumroth*

Occasionally, the Sages praised those who observe *chumroth*, such as those "special individuals" who, at the time of a protracted drought, began to fast two weeks before the customary public fasts were declared.[9] They said that, whenever personal discomfort is involved, anyone who wants to make himself a "special individual" in that respect may do so and is to be considered praiseworthy. Similarly,[10] although it is permitted to step off the trodden path—after the rainy season—to avoid obstructions, even if one may thereby cause some damage to the fields, those who refrain from doing so are lauded. In this context, R. Ze'ira comments that one should practice this stringency only when he is alone, lest his companions—who may not wish to accept this voluntary *chumra*—feel shamed.

This attitude is also evident in connection with the Chanukah lights. The mitzvah requires only one light, each day, for the entire household. Nevertheless, the Sages have described the options of "those who enhance" and "those who enhance the enhancement."[11] Despite the wholly voluntary character of these extensions, the greatest of the Tanaim found them sufficiently significant to dispute their details, and the almost universal practice is according to "those who enhance upon the enhancement"—that is, to start with one Chanukah light on the first night and add another on each successive night.

The Talmud does not consider people who do not drink—even water—outside the Sukah [during the Sukoth holiday] to be arrogant, even though the halakhah only requires that meals be eaten in the Sukah. We find that Tanaim accepted this *chumra* and Rambam called it laudable.[12]

We are taught that the merit of one who is required to fulfill a mitzvah, and does so, is greater than the reward of one who fulfills it voluntarily. This implies that some reward is due even to the latter, although he was not explicitly commanded.[13] The Talmud, in fact, cites an opinion, later withdrawn, that the reward of the volunteer is even greater than that of the one who was commanded.

Beautifying the mitzvoth is mandated by the Torah; one should observe it by adding up to one-third to the required expenditure.[14] We also find the concept of "the choicest fulfillment" mentioned by the Talmud and later authorities in connection with numerous mitzvoth —for example, using an ox, rather than a lamb or a bird, for a sacrifice; using a ram's horn for the mitzvah of *shofar*; using olive oil for the Chanukah lights.[15]

Similarly, one must establish the safeguards he needs to protect himself from careless transgression. From the fact that a *nazir* is forbidden to partake not only of alcoholic wine, but also of anything that grows on the grapevine,[16] our Sages have deduced that a person must distance himself from "that which is ugly," from that which is similar to that which is "ugly," and even from that which bears a faint resemblance to that which is "ugly." The wording of the commentaries regarding the commandment[17] to build safeguards renders it clear that it is addressed to the individual and does not only instruct the Sages to establish safeguards for the community. This view is also supported by numerous other statements in Torah literature.[18] Occasionally, even asceticism is lauded; R. Eli'ezer held that anyone who fasts is considered holy, provided it causes him no harm. See also the discussion on saintliness in Chapter 3, above.[19]

On the other hand, there are several reasons for not adopting *chumroth*, as discussed below.

3. Appearing Arrogant and Other "*Chumroth* That Lead to *Kuloth* (Leniencies)"

Simple logic dictates that one may not accept a *chumra* to which he is not obligated if it leads to the transgression of a commandment, as this is a

chumra de-athy liyedey kula ("a stringency which leads to a leniency").
Specifically, this principle applies to any "ostentatious" *chumra* which
gives the appearance of arrogance—perhaps the character trait most
despised by God.[20] As a rule, we are not permitted to adopt, in public, a
chumra which is not generally accepted. Thus the reprehensible *chumra
de-athy liyedey kula* precludes most individual *chumroth*, unless they are
practiced secretly.

This is also evident from a lengthy discussion in the halakhah
concerning the issue of whether a groom may recite the Shema' on his
wedding night; considering that the Mishnah[21] exempts him, this may
give the appearance of arrogance. The consensus seems to be that he is
permitted to do so—but only because his *chumra* is not readily apparent, as he is simply acting like everyone else.

The Talmud relates an incident[22] which illuminates the matter at
hand. One regulation instituted by Joshua on entering the Land of Israel
was to allow people to avoid obstacles on the trodden path by encroach-
ing on the bordering fields, even if they contain unharvested produce, so
that the trespassing causes damage. Rabi and R. Chiya were once
walking along the edge of a field, availing themselves of this regulation.
When they saw someone in front of them walking on the path itself, Rabi
asked R. Chiya: "Who is that ahead of us who shows his [religious]
superiority?" The latter answered: "That must be my disciple R.
Yehudah ben Kenusa, and all his actions are for the sake of Heaven."
When they reached him and saw that it was indeed he, they told him that
had it been anyone else, they would have excommunicated him. Rashi
explains the word "superiority": "Because he shows us that he is so
God-fearing that he does not use the rule instituted by Joshua; such
conduct gives the appearance of arrogance."

Maharshal discusses at length the question of why Rabi wanted to
excommunicate R. Yehudah. He concludes:

> Here we have proof that a disciple who is arrogant in the
> law—and acts stringently in matters in which the public gener-
> ally act leniently—deserves excommunication (even if he did
> not slight his teacher by doing so in his presence), unless the
> teacher knows with certainty that the disciple acts only for the
> sake of Heaven... And even if the lenient practice is somewhat
> questionable, a person should not take the stringent view
> against his teacher unless he has strong reasons for doing so.

This opinion is cited by *Magen Avraham*.[23] R. Yisrael Bruna[24] was asked if there is a problem of arrogance with the young men who wear their *talith katan* over their garments in public, saying that they wish to observe the mitzvah publicly. He answered that this depends on the custom, the time, and the person. In those days, this practice was customary only among the rabbis and was in fact a distinguishing feature of the rabbinate. Hence, a young person's doing so would cause raised eyebrows and is therefore prohibited. This responsum is quoted[25] in connection with a more modern question: may one wear his *tzitzioth* outside the garment or might this lead to a desecration of God's name if the one doing so does not show similar concern in all his other actions?

From the above two cases, we may deduce that the appearance of arrogance does not apply to a person who is known for his piety. This is also evident from the incident which the Talmud relates[26] regarding Eli'ezer Ze'ira. He wore black shoes as a sign of mourning for Jerusalem and was imprisoned for it by the representatives of the *Reish Galutha*, who suspected him of arrogance; he was only freed after having proved himself an outstanding Torah scholar.

If one accepts an obligation which is not mandatory, and this entails an action of questionable propriety, such a stringency is certainly considered foolish and boorish. Moreover, the Sages declared that one who is exempt from an act, yet performs it nonetheless, is considered a boor (see the following chapter). Some halakhic authorities (*poskim*) included in this category a person whose actions arouse a suspicion of arrogance. He is considered foolish because he is trying to be saintlier than others and instead becomes guilty of a despicable character trait. One posek wrote[27] that those who wait until dark to recite their evening prayers (which, according to halakhah may be recited an hour and a quarter earlier) are suspected of arrogance and are called boors — unless they also assume a similarly stringent attitude towards their other obligations. Another posek wrote[28] that a person is allowed these extra *chumroth* in private but not in public, where they would make him appear arrogant and hence foolish. This view — relating the appearance of arrogance to the stigma of foolishness — is shared by a number of poskim. Others teach that the label of boorishness applies only to active *chumroth*.[29]

Our Sages have given us good advice on this subject by recalling the words of Elijah the Prophet:[30] "If you wish to be stringent, [be stringent in the obligation of humility and] act like your fellow men."

However, the stigma of foolishness is not limited to the arrogant; it applies to any *chumra* which entails the possibility of a forbidden action. One revealing application of this principle may be found in the rule that frees a Jew from his obligation to dwell in the Sukah when this would cause him discomfort. One who insists on dwelling in the Sukah despite his discomfort is called boorish. In *Chok Ya'acov*,[31] this is explained on the grounds that one who causes himself needless suffering is called a sinner. Thus, the person is stringent about dwelling in the Sukah at the cost of becoming a sinner, which is somewhat foolish. He effectively turns himself into a sinner in order to perform a ritual that is not required of him. Similarly, *Divrey Chayim*[32] considers it boorish to look into a mirror to make sure that the *tefilin* are properly centered on the head, because they are acceptable even if they are not exactly centered, while it is improper for a man to look into a mirror.[33] Many more examples of a similar kind can be found.

The "Chazon Ish" enumerates[34] several evils which can result from *chumroth*. He explains why the Sages permitted the sale of certain farming implements during a sabbatical year to those suspected of working during that year. The "Chazon Ish" asks: Are we not putting a possible stumbling block before the (morally) blind? As this is a divine prohibition, shouldn't the sale be forbidden even in the case of doubt? He answers that our refusal to sell might place an even more serious stumbling block before them and cause them to transgress even more severe prohibitions:

> The Sages permitted [such sales] despite the possible transgression, even though one is certainly forbidden to place even an ambiguous stumbling block before the blind so that, presumably, we should have been stringent in case of doubt. [It seems that they permitted these sales] because if we are stringent in these ambiguous cases [we are avoiding the stumbling block of their working the field in the sabbatical year, but at the same time], we are also creating a stumbling block by withholding kindness, livelihood and peace from ourselves and from them. They are only ignorant, and we are obligated to support them and to act kindly towards them, and certainly not to generate hatred and conflict between them and us. [Refraining from such sales results in] the transgressing of "Do not hate!" and several other prohibitions that are no less severe than the prohibition

[of working in the field during the sabbatical year] from which we are trying to save them.

This is entirely in agreement with the decision of Rabbeinu Yonah,[35] who permits the giving of food to a poor person even when the donor does not know whether the recipient will recite the required benediction — "because he intends to do a mitzvah and gives [the food] in the form of *tzedakah*... The good deed is certain, while the transgression is uncertain." Bach adds:[36] "And even if he knows that the recipient is an *'am ha'aretz gamur* [utterly ignorant and hence non-observant] and will certainly not recite the benediction—this is not sufficient reason to forgo the mitzvah of charity." We may find support for these opinions in the Mishnah,[37] which permits a strictly observant person (*chaver*) to eat—on the first Sabbath after the wedding—in the house of one who is suspected of not tithing properly. The Jerusalem Talmud indicates that the reason for this ruling is that it prevents social discord: "R. Avin said: here they permitted untithed foods, to preserve the peace." Similar decisions are to be found in other contexts.[38]

We proceed to examine several rabbinic regulations instituted to avoid shaming the less affluent, even though they relax, somewhat, certain ritual requirements. Here, insisting on stringency in observing the ritual law would entail leniency regarding the prohibition on shaming another person.

1. Someone whose Pesach sacrifice became unusable may not burn it with his own wood, but only with the wood set aside for the altar.[39]
2. It has become a universal custom not to bury anyone in expensive clothes. Even if a wealthy person attempts to do so, he is to be stopped.[40]
3. Similarly, certain communities have set limits on wedding expenses.[41]
4. If the merchants raise the price of fish on Fridays, it is proper to prohibit the purchase of fish for several weeks[42] (even though it is especially praiseworthy to eat fish on the Sabbath). This is based on the Mishnah which relates that R. Shim'on ben Gamliel was outraged at the excessive price demanded by the dealers for the bird-pairs required for the obligatory sacrifices in the sanctuary. Thereupon he and his court taught that a woman can fulfill her child-birth obligation[43] by bringing one sacrifice for several births,

thus reducing the demand for bird-pairs significantly and causing the price to drop from twenty-five dinars to a half dinar.[44] Here he decided to forgo a *chumra* in the laws of sacrifices to avoid a *kula* in the mitzvah of kindness—that is, failing to do his best to lighten the burden of mitzvah fulfillment for the public. For the same reason, a decision was made in the year 5679 (1919), during the severe post-war depression in Europe, declaring that all the rabbis of Poland should forbid the eating of fish on the Sabbath, "to free us from the burden of suspicion [of ill-gotten hidden wealth] and iniquity."[45]

According to R. Z. Bing,[46] we must apply the rule "all additions detract"[47] to all excessive *chumroth*. He continues: "All superfluous additions prevent a person from righteousness. This is what King Solomon had in mind when he said: 'God made man straightforward, but they sought many calculations.'[48] Furthermore, Scripture states: 'Do not deviate, either right or left,'[49] which means that one who keeps to the median path will stray neither right nor left."

He continues by enumerating the prohibitions involved when individuals take on novel *chumroth*, without consulting rabbinic authority, and concludes:[50] "There are many safeguards and cautions which must be observed in these matters. In brief, 'do not separate yourself...' A person should not make himself special by taking on additional *chumroth* of his own devising without consulting rabbinic authority or the advice of scholars, [lest] he establish prohibitions for things which are permitted and make the Torah appear as two Toroth."

In general, every *chumra* requires an expenditure of money, time or energy—all of which we are meant to devote to the service of God, in Torah study, acts of kindness, and the like. If we expend them on matters which are not required of us, we have less to expend on mitzvoth, and thus almost every *chumra* "leads to a leniency."[51]

If one goes a step further and declares the *chumra* to be "halakhah," the *chumra* may become an outright transgression. In the words of the Sages:[52] "Just as there is a prohibition against declaring the impure as pure, so, too, there is a prohibition against declaring the pure as impure." In explaining the verse: "Teachings of truth were in his mouth and injustice was never on his lips," *'Aley Tamar*[53] cites the Midrashic explanation: "Because he never declared the pure as impure, nor the impure to be pure; because he never declared the permitted to be forbidden nor the forbidden as permitted." He elaborates: "It appears that the explanation is as follows: 'Teachings of truth were in his mouth' — because he declared the impure as indeed impure and the forbidden as indeed forbidden; and 'injustice was never on his lips' — because he never declared the pure to be impure or the permitted to be forbidden — which would do injustice to the entire Creation, for 'God created goodly creatures and goodly trees, to give enjoyment to men.'" According to this explanation, the opposition to this kind of *chumra* arises from the fact that it will eventually lead to leniency by preventing proper utilization of part of God's creation. *'Aley Tamar* proceeds to make a case for a definite prohibition against this kind of *chumra*:

> It is apparent that one who errs on the side of leniency has only transgressed against God, while one who errs on the side of *chumra* is guilty of a dual transgression: a) a transgression against God by misinterpreting the words of the Torah; and b) a transgression against his fellow to whom he causes a loss — and the transgression of depriving another of his property applies, irrespective of the amount involved. Thus, he who declares as forbidden that which is actually permitted is guilty of the more serious offense.

In the same spirit, Maharal writes:[54] "Just as one should reject absolutely that which is improper acording to the Torah, so too is it improper to reject that which is not rejected by the Torah. The fool thinks that by adding such restrictions he strengthens the Torah, but, in fact, this is... only vitiation of the Torah."

We conclude this section with the words of Shakh:[55]

> Just as we may not permit the forbidden, so, too, must we not forbid that which is permitted, even if it is the property of a gentile and even if it does not involve a monetary loss. In most instances, we find that this will eventually lead to an unwarranted leniency. And even if this course of events is not apparent, it is forbidden nonetheless, because after a long chain of events, a leniency may result.

4. "He Is Called a Boor"

The Talmud relates:[56] R. Yeisa and R. Shemuel bar Yitzchak were eating together. When the time for the afternoon prayer came, R.

Shemuel rose to say it. R. Yeisa reminded him that R. Shemuel himself had taught that it is not necessary to interrupt the meal for this prayer, (since there will be ample time after the end of the meal) and that Chizkiyah had taught in a *Baraitha* that he who is exempt from an act but performs it [anyway] is called a boor. R. Shemuel countered that while there is a Mishnah which teaches that a bridegroom is exempt from reading the Shema' on the first night, there is another Mishnah stating that if he wishes to, he may do so nonetheless. Furthermore, "I can resolve this by quoting R. Gamliel, who said: 'I will not listen to you to absolve myself from divine rule for even a short time.'"

It thus appears that the disagreement between R. Yeisa and R. Shemuel concerned interpretation of the words of R. Gamliel, who had ruled that the acceptance of "divine rule" differs from other duties in that we are permitted to be stringent on its behalf without being stigmatized as boors. R. Yeisa holds that this applies only in the case of the Shema', while R. Shemuel holds that it applies to prayer as well. They both agreed, however, that in general, one who accepts an unnecessary obligation is called a boor.[57]

Many Rishonim cite this rule as halakhah, applying it to numerous laws. The following *chumroth* are stigmatized as boorish by Rishonim[58] (note that some of these reservations are disputed; a few of the *chumroth* have even been accepted as halakhah):

1. Standing while reading the Shema'.
2. Scoring the parchment for the writing of Torah scrolls or *tefilin*.
3. Sitting in the Sukah in spite of distress.
4. Recitation of *Havdalah* by a bereaved person, before the funeral.
5. A husband lighting Chanukah lights away from home, knowing that his wife lights them at home.
6. Avoiding the eating of meat after having eaten cheese.
7. Insisting on reciting the evening prayers after dark.
8. Young men wearing the *talith katan* over their clothes.
9. Women reciting the benediction for those mitzvoth from which they are exempt.
10. Women wearing *tzitzith*.

To these the Acharonim added:
11. Reading the Shema' while engaged in community work.
12. Reclining during the Pesach *seder* even if exempt from doing so.

13. Donning *tefilin* in spite of acute discomfort.
14. Singeing the wicks before kindling the Sabbath lights.
15. Reciting the *Tikun Chatzoth* in public. (*Tikun Chatzoth* is a midnight ritual, mourning the exile; it is practiced by especially devout individuals.)

Rambam's commentary on the Mishnah cites the above *Baraitha* of Chizkiyah which speaks of the "foolishly pious"[59] and explains the term as referring, among other things, to one who "does things which are not obligations, as if he were demented in his piety. And the Jerusalem Talmud says that one who does something in spite of being exempt from it is called a boor." Other commentators also[60] quote this *Baraitha* in connection with being meticulous about eating—even light refreshments—only in the Sukah, permitting this particular *chumra* only because it is specifically mentioned and allowed by the Talmud.

Nevertheless, we do find *chumroth* which were lauded by the Sages and the *poskim*—such as those cited above (Sections 1 and 2). We proceed to clarify which circumstances render *chumroth* laudable and which render them boorish.

When is a *chumra* considered boorish?

Regarding the issue of women pronouncing benedictions on mitzvoth from which they are exempt, Ramban writes[61] that the stigma of boorishness only applies in cases in which the obligation is innovative and not based on a Torah commandment, so that it appears to add new mitzvoth. However, those who fulfill mitzvoth properly, even if they themselves happen to be exempt—such as women—merit reward.

Ritba also holds that only acts which are mitzvoth for others are permitted.[62] However, he introduces the subjective element of "desirability": "But only mitzvoth that God commanded others, which He desires." He may imply that both conditions must apply: the act must be a mitzvah (for others) and desired by God in the case under consideration. This would make his opinion coincide with that of Meiri,[63] who writes that the voluntary performance of a mitzvah implies boorishness "only if everyone, under these circumstances, would be exempt from it and if it does not result in better sense, or morality, enhancement, humbling of the heart, etc."—all of which are aspects which render the act desirable.

A similar opinion is found in *Sefer HaTerumah*,[64] when disputing the censure of someone who scores the parchment for writing *tefilin* (see 2, above) "because [his writing] will be more beautiful and straighter if he scores [the parchment] and he is therefore not considered boorish."

Chida accepts this approach, stating[65] that *chumroth* are permitted when they are beneficial, acts of diligence or beautifications of mitzvoth. For this reason, some authorities[66] permit one to stand during the Torah reading, even though it is not required.

A number of Acharonim say that the Sages censured only those *chumroth* that apply to mitzvoth concerning the relationship between man and God. For mitzvoth concerning interpersonal relationships, however, the reverse is true; here, it is recommended to act stringently, in fulfillment of the commandment "to go beyond the letter of the law."[67]

5. "He Is Called a Sinner"

If a *chumra* involves afflicting himself, it earns him the name "sinner." The Sages interpreted the verses dealing with the Nazirite as follows:[68] "'And he shall atone for having sinned against the person'—Against which person did he sin? This refers to his depriving himself of wine. It thus follows logically: if one who deprives himself merely of wine is called a sinner, how much the more so one who deprives himself of many things? This shows us that one who fasts [unnecessarily] is called a sinner." Thus the Talmudic challenge:[69] "Do the prohibitions of the Torah not suffice for you, that you seek out others?"

The Talmud there continues that according to Shim'on the Just, there is no place for asceticism, except in special cases in which it may be necessary to overcome a tendency to conceit. But R. Eli'ezer is of the opinion that, as long as one can bear it, it is permitted.[70] Furthermore, we have already quoted the opinion that one who sits in the Sukah in the rain is called boorish—because this is a *chumra* which leads to self-affliction, which causes him to be regarded as a sinner.

Even though R. Yonathan Eybeschutz and R. Ya'akov Emden differed sharply on certain issues, in this case they are entirely of one mind. The former wrote:[71]

> When the Sages said: "Torah combined with worldly pursuits is good," they implied that any asceticism practiced by an individual should be such that it can be practiced by the entire nation without exception. However, asceticism which can be practiced

only by individuals, and not by the nation in general, ceases to further perfection and is considered inappropriate by the Sages.

R. Ya'akov Emden, in turn, declared:[72]

Even the angels who descended from on high conformed to the customs of the places they visited. Therefore, while you are still among men, do not attempt to be an angel, to survive without paying attention to your body; rather, eat and drink that which benefits you (for your good, for your benefit and for your true advantage) and face ever upwards, sow and build, buy and sell, do whatever you have the opportunity for, and follow the way of the world in everything.

Furthermore, asceticism also involves the denial of acts of kindness to oneself. In the words of King Solomon:[73] "A man of kindness benefits himself [as well] and one who hurts his body is cruel." The Midrash[74] relates that once, when his students asked Hillel where he was going, he answered that he was on his way to do a kindness for a house guest. When they expressed surprise that he had a guest in his house every day, he explained that this guest was himself, and he was obligated to feed him. Commenting on this Midrash, *Yefeh Toar* explains that benefiting one's own person is considered a kindness as much as benefiting another. Ralbag, in his commentary to the above verse, explains at length that one who mortifies his flesh and tortures his body is considered cruel, "and some people consider deprivation imposed on their body to be a service to God. But in fact it is contrary to God's wish."

We may assume that all this is so because "God looked into the Torah while He created the world,"[75] so that, in general, there will be no conflict between nature and the Torah. This is also evident from the halakhic applications of the verse[76] "Its ways are ways of pleasantness and all its paths are peace," to which we devoted an entire section in Chapter 4, above. On the one hand, we need to account for every place in which the Torah seems to contradict the demands of nature or of physical needs; on the other hand, we should assume that everything in this world must contribute something to Torah life. This is the message of the Sages when they stated:[77] "At the Final Judgment, every man will have to render account for everything he saw, but did not eat thereof." In this way, we can also understand why R. El'azar saved pennies so that he could taste every new fruit once a year.[78] One commentator[79] goes so far as to state that just as it is prohibited to eat that which is forbidden and impure, so too is it a mitzvah to eat that which is permitted and pure, that which was created by God for the enjoyment of man. But I have been unable to find any other authority who shares this view.

However, it appears that conscious intent to serve God is a condition for the act to be considered as a mitzvah. This is evident in the Talmudic passage[80] which declares that if, on the Sabbath, one hears that a child has fallen into the sea, spreads his net to catch fish and hauls in the child along with the fish, he is still adjudged guilty of fishing because his intention to catch fish was decisive. He is guilty even though the same act — spreading the net and raising the fish together with the child — would have been a mitzvah had his intention been to save the child. Similarly, a person's enjoyment of an earthly pleasure is meritorious only if the enjoyment is motivated by a genuine desire to improve his service of God.[81]

6. Casting Aspersions on Our Predecessors

By instituting new *chumroth*, one views earlier generations — which did not observe them — in an unfavorable light, suggesting, as it were, "that they desecrated the Sabbath, ate *tereifah*, trangressed rabbinic restrictions concerning *nidah*," etc.[82] Obviously, one must be careful to avoid such conduct.

Rav Ami and Rav Asi forbade bar Hadaya from instituting a stringent requirement regarding the writing of bills of divorce in order not to cast aspersions on the earlier bills.[83] Rabbi Eliyahu ibn Chaim (Maharnach) wrote[84] that this prohibition applies only to marriage regulations, where a previous error would have resulted in *mamzeruth* (bastardy). Several other authorities[85] agree with him. On the other hand, Rosh did not shrink from "casting aspersions," even in connection with a bill of divorce.

It appears, however, that most authorities apply this reason to other mitzvoth as well. Thus, for example, we find it applied to *'eiruvey chatzeroth*, *tereifoth*, *kil-ey hakerem*, *mikvaoth*, *tefilin*, Yom Kippur, Sukoth, *tevilah* and the recitation of *Akdamoth*.[86] Maharsham adduces proof for this position[87] from the *Tosefta*, which shows clearly that we should avoid the appearance of casting aspersions on the actions of previous generations—even regarding areas other than marital laws.

Terumath HaDeshen points out[88] that nonetheless we find many *chumroth* instituted by later generations without regard to such appearances. He concludes that if there are valid and cogent reasons for acting stringently, it is proper to do so; it is more important, he says, not to open a present divorce to possible challenges than to avoid possible aspersions on earlier divorces. However, in matters which are clearly permitted, we do not permit someone to act more stringently and be unduly careful, to prevent casting a bad light on previous generations.

A decision of Rashba[89] clearly indicates that we may ignore such considerations when the *chumra* is not noticeable. Similarly, R. Yosef ben Lev (Maharybal)[90] wrote that we should be cautious in this regard only if positive action is involved; when the *chumra* takes the form of inaction, however, we need not be concerned. *Taharath Mayim* writes[91] that any one of the three foregoing conditions—rational basis, imperceptibility, or lack of positive action—is sufficient to remove the suspicion of casting aspersions on previous generations.

When some authorities wanted to increase the minimum size acceptable for the *ethrog*, disqualifying fruits that had previously been considered fit, the "Chatham Sofer" took them to task for their boldness in innovating, saying "The new is forbidden by the Torah."[92] Presumably he objected to their arrogance which let them feel that they knew better than the early authorities, who had permitted these *ethrogim*.

Several authorities have discussed this concern at length, and similar considerations have been applied to the Jewish people as a whole, lest we imply that they are careless in mitzvah performance. In such cases, the authorities like to cite: "Let Israel be; if they are not themselves prophets, they certainly are the sons of prophets."[93].

7. Heretical *Chumroth* and Those Warranting Capital Punishment or Excommunication

"Do not add to His word lest He rebuke you and you be found false." This verse was explained by the Sages[94]—in connection with the sin of Adam—to mean that one should not make the "fence" (safeguards) higher than that which it is meant to protect, "lest it fall and cause destruction." They explain that it was because of excessive caution that Adam sinned and death was decreed on mankind.

The Mishnah[95] reports that R. Tarfon, while on a journey, read the evening Shema' in a reclining position, as required by Beth Shammai, and thereby brought himself into mortal danger from robbers. His associates told him that he actually deserved falling into the hands of the robbers, as punishment for ignoring the words of Beth Hillel (who do not require that the evening Shema' be read while reclining). In the Talmudic commentary on this Mishnah, Rav Yosef is quoted as saying that one who acts in accordance with Beth Shammai takes meaningless action; Rav Nachman bar Yitzchak says that one who does so is guilty of a capital offense; R. Yechezkel, on the other hand, permits this kind of behavior. The Jerusalem Talmud classifies R. Tarfon's stringent behavior as "tearing down the fences." The later authorities apparently adopt the opinion that actions such as those of R. Tarfon are improper. Rambam, in his commentary to this Mishnah, explains that in chiding him, R. Tarfon's associates are telling him that he was guilty of a capital offense.

Concerning persons who insist on standing to read the Shema', Rav 'Amram Gaon wrote:[96] "They are in error and stray from the path, and it is boorish, primitive and nonsensical... and he who does it is called a transgressor." Others, alluding to the incident of R. Tarfon, add[97] that such a person deserves death.

The incident involving R. Tarfon also appears to be the source of the comment by R. Meir of Rothenburg[98] that in his younger days he considered it heretical for people to adopt the *chumra* not to eat meat after cheese, as they thus appear to deny the validity of the Talmud, which permits this—and challenging the words of the Sages is heresy. Maharshal[99] permits the adoption of this particular *chumra* only to one who had inadvertently eaten cheese with meat because some cheese had remained between his teeth; otherwise, he too considers the stringent view as heretical. The halakhah, however, has adopted this particular *chumra*.[100]

Soleth LaMinchah, quoting an earlier authority,[101] says that those, who do not avail themselves of explicit leniencies of the Amoraim and act stringently in matters such as ignoring a negligible amount (less than 1.7%) of forbidden food accidently mixed with permitted food, or permission to heat food on the Sabbath in a vessel to which hot water was transferred, are heretics. So too, "anyone who does not eat warmed food on Shabbath should be investigated for possible heresy."[102] Rambam[103] comments about those who act stringently and avoid marital contact for forty days after the birth of a son and for eighty days after the birth of a daughter. He writes that this is not a custom, but merely an error on their part, a heretical practice learned from the Sadducees. Regarding the prohibition on oil obtained from a non-Jew, which was later rescinded, Rambam wrote:[104] "And he who forbids it is a great sinner, for he rebels against the court which permitted it." Here Rambam is alluding to a Talmudic passage reporting that the Amora Shemuel accepted the abolition of the prohibition, whereas Rav did not. Thereupon Shemuel told Rav "Eat! Otherwise I will proclaim you to be a 'rebellious elder.'"[105]

The *Ba'alei Tosafoth* were also very emphatic in their disapproval of *chumroth* which go beyond those mentioned by the Sages.[106] After forbidding bowing at the end of each of the Nineteen Benedictions, they write: "Do not ask what it matters—this overturns the words of the Sages, and people should not say that anyone may act stringently whenever he pleases." Some speculate[107] that the reason for this emphatic prohibition of private *chumroth* in general is that eventually such behavior might lead to the impression that these practices are actually required by halakhah. Rashi[108] compares these practices to the Torah-based prohibition against adding new laws to the Torah.

The early authorities wrote that those who act according to rejected opinions deserve excommunication. This was stated by Rosh, and also by R. Yosef Karo,[109] who likened a particular scholar to a "rebellious elder" and wrote: "Now, one scholar comes along and wants to appear especially pious by acting contrary to the generally accepted custom and tithing fruit which grew on land owned by non-Jews... until the scholars of that city had no other choice but to meet in session and excommunicate him." Similarly, the scholars of Safed, headed by Maharashdam, excommunicated those who, because of some uncertainty, would have observed additional sabbatical years, besides those generally observed according to Rambam's calculations.[110]

Mabit[111] bitterly deplores the actions of those who are unnecessarily stringent in matters of food, and concludes: "Because these *chumroth* resulted in strife concerning ceremonial meals [with some people not participating in meals served by others, thereby disrupting social ties—L.L.] as well as in domestic discord... we have already for several years issued a ban on [those who] levy *terumoth* and tithes when Rambam does not require it... and even if there was some doubt in the mind of these ascetic scholars, the ban is certain and a mere doubt cannot override it."

On what basis was such punishment meted out? Apparently—as seen from the above-cited incident involving R. Yehudah ben Kenusa—the reason for the severe punishment was a suspicion of arrogance. However, from the above words of the Jerusalem Talmud, Rambam, and R. Karo,[112] it appears that they likened him to the "rebellious elder."[113] On the other hand, the decision by the scholars of Safed, as quoted by Maharashdam, apparently intended to prevent future generations from erroneously accepting this opinion as halakhah. Any of the above reasons (except the first) would suffice to explain why R. Tarfon was judged so harshly.

In apparent contradiction to the above, there is a case of two disciples,[114] one of whom acted according to a stringent opinion of Beth Shammai (declaring that one must return to the place where one ate to recite the blessings after the meal) and found a purse filled with gold. This would seem to indicate that it is proper to act stringently—in accordance with Beth Shammai, rather than in accordance with Beth Hillel. But both the Tosafoth and Rosh agree that in this particular instance, Beth Hillel would concur with Beth Shammai that it is proper to take the stringent course, even though Beth Hillel did not require it. Elsewhere,[115] however, the Tosafoth offer a different explanation; they write in the name of R. 'Amram Gaon that in that case the halakhah is actually according to Beth Shammai.

Earlier, we noted that one who adopts an unnecessary *chumra* is considered a boor. This, too, may be because of his evident disagreement with the Sages. It would thus not apply to one acting stringently as a matter of caution.[116]

We consider one final case which, although only partly relevant to the present issue, is illuminating nonetheless. The Sages have warned us[117] not to associate with an evildoer; furthermore, Scripture admonishes us: "The fear of God is to hate evil."[118] One may be tempted to act so stringently in this matter that he will not say his prayers when evildoers are present. Yet this would come dangerously close to heresy. The Mishnah[119] states: "One who says [in his prayer] 'Let the good ones bless You' is guilty of following the way of the heretics." This is explained[120] to mean that "Jews must associate with transgressors in their fast-day prayer assemblies." Meiri explains why heresy is considered to be involved: "Because he does not believe that God wants the repentance of the evildoers."

8.   "The Fool Walks in Darkness"

The Sages censured those who act stringently not only in matters not mentioned by the Talmud but also those which are the subject of Talmudic dispute. Concerning a person who acts according to the stringent view of each of two mutually contradictory opinions, the Talmud says: "The fool walks in darkness"[121] — because his conduct is consistent with neither opinion. The Tosafoth explain that this applies "**even** if he knows according to which opinion the halakhah is decided, and nevertheless acts stringently." This shows that if he acts thus out of ignorance, he is certainly thought of as foolish.

How is one to act when he is confronted by two conflicting opinions and does not know according to which to decide the halakhah? At least in questions of Torah law, he must decide according to the more stringent view — and since each of the two mutually exclusive opinions is tenable, he must decide according to the more stringent implications of each. Perhaps the opprobrium of foolishness is applied to him although he is obligated to act that way, because he does not resolve the problem. And if he is presently unable to resolve it, then he is, in fact, a fool and must exert himself further to clarify the halakhah. Ritba[122] writes that the fault of one in such a position lies in his not clarifying the issue by studying it. This view resembles a passage in the Jerusalem Talmud in which a student is called foolish if he cannot decide the halakhah because of his indolence in Torah study[123] so that he has to act stringently. On the other hand, we find a later authority who writes[124] that he is called foolish because he does not have the intellectual ability to reach a conclusion.

Maharsha[125] lauds the lenient one (because his ability to be lenient implies that he is knowledgeable) and applies to him the verse: "When you eat the fruit of your labor, you are blessed, and all is well with you." — We thus see that if one toiled and, as a result, found the halakhah to be lenient, so that he can eat the once-questionable meat before him, he has an additional advantage and the best of both worlds. This is also the interpretation of Shelah,[126] who adds that the pious approach would be to act stringently for himself — if there is sufficient reason to act stringently. However, if there is no good reason to do so and his behavior results solely from lack of knowledge of the subject, he is called a pious fool, since, if he had taken the time and trouble to clarify the matter, he would have found that there is no reason to act stringently.

9. Conclusions

We have seen, on the one hand, just how important *chumroth* can be, and that occasionally one can even be punished for not acting stringently.

On the other hand, we have also seen how very careful one must be to determine just where and how to act stringently. If one acts stringently without previous examination of his *chumra*, the loss may exceed the benefit: he may be called a fool or a boor — or even a heretic, render himself liable to excommunication or even forfeit his life.

One broad general rule in adopting *chumroth*: follow the stringencies of our ancestors only and do not innovate any on your own. A second rule calls for exercising extreme caution not to establish a *chumra* which is not practiced by the public as a whole, unless we can do so in a totally unobtrusive manner. Furthermore, regarding doubt resulting from a difference of opinion, we are obligated to clarify the halakhah and act accordingly, whether leniently or stringently. Only if the doubt cannot be resolved by any means whatsoever are we permitted — and obliged — to act according to the *chumroth* of each of two mutually contradictory opinions.

We have already mentioned that, according to the Midrash, Adam's sin and the consequent decree of death on mankind were caused by his excessive precaution. We conclude by noting that the Exile, too, resulted from similar behavior. The Talmud[127] recounts the immediate cause of the destruction of the Temple as follows: A Jerusalem notable, bar Kamtza, was publicly insulted by another Jerusalemite in the presence of the rabbis, who did not intervene. Their silence prompted bar Kamtza to avenge himself on the Jewish people as a whole. He approached the Roman emperor to slander the Jews, saying that they were rebelling. When the emperor demanded evidence, bar Kamtza suggested that as a test of their loyalty, he send an animal to be sacrificed in the Holy Temple. The emperor did so; but on the way to Jerusalem, bar Kamtza cut the lip of the sacrificial calf, rendering it unfit as a sacrifice in the Temple. When the delegation bringing the sacrifice arrived in Jerusalem, the rabbis were in a quandary. On the one hand, the calf was halakhically unfit as a sacrifice and, on the other hand, they sensed the enormous danger inherent in their refusal to accept it. They therefore wanted to bring the sacrifice anyhow—for the sake of national safety. R. Zekhariah ben Avkulas objected: "People will say that defective animals may be sacrificed." The rabbis then suggested that bar Kamtza be killed. Again R. Zekhariah countered: "They will say that [in general] one who damages a sacrificial animal is to be killed." As a result of this caution, bar Kamtza's plot succeeded, bringing the Exile upon the Jewish people. The Talmud then concludes: "R. Yochanan said: 'The modesty of R. Zekhariah ben Avkulas destroyed our Temple, burned our Sanctuary, and caused us to be exiled from our land.'"

PART THREE

TEACHING TORAH AND REACHING OUT TO THE ESTRANGED

Having probed the subject matter of Torah study, we proceed to explore the mitzvah of talmud Torah itself: is this commandment principally fulfilled by studying or teaching? The Talmud derives this mitzvah primarily from a Scriptural verse which enjoins us to teach—and even the term talmud itself may imply teaching rather than learning.

Today, as unfamiliarity with Torah has reached abysmal depths, this emphasis on teaching is of particular significance. Those who are well-versed in Torah have a special obligation to instruct those who are not. Below, we investigate this responsibility and the urgent need to introduce Judaism to those estranged from it.

135

1

The Importance of Teaching Torah

Our Sages have repeatedly stressed the importance of teaching others over self-study. They adduced the commandment to study Torah from the verse[1] "and you shall teach them to your sons."[2] They considered personal Torah study as only a minor fulfillment of this obligation, but teaching Torah to many its major manifestation.[3] The Mishnah [4] also lauds only persons who study with the purpose of teaching others, and not those who have no such intent or who do not study in order to practice what they learn. Furthermore, R. Meir[5] states that one who studies but does not teach treats the Torah contemptuously and deserves *kareth*—"cutting off". (The precise meaning of *kareth* is not clear; perhaps it signifies a total spiritual estrangement from God.)

This topic assumes a special urgency in our time. For centuries, Torah Judaism has insulated itself against the onslaught of the various religions, the Reform, the Haskalah, socialism, and other such movements. Self-protection became a primary objective and the preferred method consisted of walling ourselves in. This conforms with the dictum of Hillel the Elder,[6] "If you see a generation which does not admire Torah, withdraw." Meanwhile, the Haskalah has virtually died out, while Reform Judaism and socialism have grown spiritually bankrupt; many of their erstwhile adherents now thirst for truth, perceiving no future in their present course. The time seems to be ripe for great accomplishments on the part of the Torah community, thereby sanctifying the Divine Name, restoring God's nation to Him, and perhaps even meriting redemption.

However, there is a precondition to this accomplishment, as specified by Hillel: "If you see a generation that admires the Torah, disperse." Once we recognize that interest in Torah is on the upswing, we are obligated to disseminate our knowledge. In the United States, R. Mosheh Feinstein has ruled that only Torah students are genuinely prepared to tackle the delicate task of attracting the estranged. Consequently, they should curtail their studies somewhat to meet this challenge. R. Feinstein recommended that they devote a tenth of their time[7] to such activity. In Eretz Yisrael as well, such leading personalities as R. Chayim Shmuelewitz[8] and R. El'azar Menachem Shakh[9] have called on yeshiva students to participate in this endeavor.

We proceed to investigate the multiple significance of teaching Torah to others — especially those who had no previous opportunity to study — as reflected in the words of our sages throughout history. Teaching Torah, a great mitzvah in itself, also enables fulfillment of at least five additional obligations: to perform acts of kindness; to assume responsibility for one's fellow Jew; to admonish a transgressor; to love God; and to strengthen Torah observance. We commence with an examination of the kindness inherent in teaching Torah.

2

The Kindness of Teaching Torah

Analyzing the verse[1] "Torah of kindness is on her tongue," the Talmud asks[1] whether there are two Torahs—one kindly and the other not. Its response is an affirmative one: "Torah of kindness" refers to Torah which is studied to be imparted to others. Moreover, one who teaches Torah to another man's son is considered as if he himself had fathered that child.[2] Can there be any greater kindness? Shelah[3] explicitly bases the superiority of teaching over learning on the fact that the teacher gives life to the pupil. The Mishnah[4] likewise indicates that one's Torah teacher (who has given him life in the next world) takes precedence over one's father (who has given him life only in this world).

Conversely, one who withholds a halakhah from a disciple is severely censured.[5] Our Sages declared[6] that causing another to transgress is worse than murder, implying that preserving his moral integrity is more important than saving his life. Maharashdam[7] and *Minchath Chinukh*[8] express this conclusion explicitly, saying that the obligation to save one's fellow man from moral danger is even greater than that of saving him from a physical threat.

According to Shakh,[9] the commandment to restore a lost object to its rightful owner includes "the **absolute obligation** to restore a sinful soul by exhortation." Similarly, R. Menachem HaBavli declared:[10] "If the Torah obligates you to restore the money your neighbor has lost, then you are certainly obligated to restore his soul when he is about to lose it... You must constantly seek ways of moving your fellow man to repent... because redemption depends [on it] and is delayed by this [delay in his] return to the proper path, 'and you may not withhold your help.'"[11]

By teaching Torah, we also fulfill the commandment[12] to love our fellow man, which forbids us to withhold benefit from him.[13] Can there be any greater benefit than Torah? Ramban,[14] commenting on the passage "You shall love your neighbor as yourself," noted that "one should endeavor to enrich his fellow man with wealth, property, honor, **knowledge** and wisdom." The "Chafetz Chayim"[15] puts it thus: "He who is poor in knowledge is the most destitute of all. ... Because he is ignorant in intellectual matters, he has strayed from the proper path and has become an evil-doer. One must think of a suitable approach to encourage him to repent and return him to the path of truth. He who accomplishes this has earned great reward indeed... And all this is part of the commandment to 'love your fellow man as yourself,' as Rambam has written."[16]

This commandment, to love your fellow man as yourself, is one of the great principles of the Torah.[17] Lest one think that the word "fellow" indicates a like-minded observant Jew, not a transgressor, the Talmud cites this verse repeatedly in connection with one who has committed a capital offense,[18] as emphasized by Remah.[19] Furthermore, the Talmud[20] records a dispute between R. Yehudah and R. Meir regarding the status of Jewish idolators: R. Yehudah contends that they cannot be considered children of God because they do not conduct themselves as such; R. Meir, however, maintains that regardless of their actions, they are still God's children. Both Rashba[21] and the Gaon of Vilna[22] endorse R. Meir, whose opinion is also quoted in the *Selichoth* prayers:[23] "Even though they are slothful and lax regarding Your laws... they are still [Your] children."[24]

Incidentally, love of one's fellow man is not only a reason for the commandment to teach the estranged, but also a vehicle for its fulfillment; love is not only the motivation behind our efforts, it is also a condition for their success. Hillel said:[25] "Be a disciple of Aaron, loving peace and pursuing peace, loving all creatures and drawing them to the Torah." Our Sages explain:[26] "How did he draw people to the Torah? When he discovered that a person had sinned, he would associate with him and show him a friendly countenance. The person would become ashamed and say to himself, 'If this pious man knew of my transgressions, he would keep far away from me.' Thus he would repent. This is indicated by a verse,[27] 'In peace and righteousness he walked with Me, and a multitude he brought back from transgression.'" This Mishnah obligates us to draw all human beings close and shows us the best way to do so: by expressing our love for them and by presuming that they have enough good in them to merit our good will and to rise to a higher level.

3

The Mutual Responsibility of All Jews

The Torah enjoins all Jews to accept responsibility for one another and commands us to admonish our fellow Jew. These obligations clearly overlap to some extent, although they also differ in certain ways. For example, admonishing also applies after a transgression has been committed, although it is then restricted to talking to the transgressor. On the other hand, mutual responsibility obligates us to take any appropriate step—even force, on occasion, if one has the appropriate authority—to prevent a transgression. Both these duties may obligate us to teach Torah to our fellow Jew. Below, we discuss the obligation entailed by this mutual responsibility and, in the next chapter, consider the injunctions implicit in the commandment to admonish.

From the verse[1] "And they shall stumble, one because of the other," the Talmud[2] derives that all Jews are responsible for one another. In fulfilling the Torah, they are like one body: any individual transgression implicates the nation as a whole and each of its members. This mutual responsibility not only imposes accountability for every person's misdeeds, but also entails specific halakhic ramifications. For example, the ruling that one not obligated to recite a benediction may fulfill another's obligation to recite it, is based on this principle.[3] As long as one's fellow man has not fulfilled his duty, one likewise remains under obligation. (The Talmud[4] even discusses whether this principle can be applied to itself.) Consequently, everyone must take action to return to the fold all those who have strayed—perhaps through no fault of their own. For, when an individual Jew strays, all Israel strays.

Today, the chief cause of estrangement from the Torah is the abysmal ignorance rampant among our people. The remedy, therefore, must be to teach Torah to those in need of it. Indeed, from the verse "If you extract preciousness from what is worthless, you shall be like My mouth," the Talmud[5] deduces the importance of teaching Torah to the son of an ignorant father. Furthermore, *Sefer Chasidim*[6] advises that it is better to teach someone less knowledgeable than to associate with equals. If this is true of someone who is merely somewhat less learned than oneself, it is surely even more applicable to a completely ignorant pupil.

Mutual accountability imposes an obligation, but it also promises a reward. Consider, for example, Daniel's vision of the end of days: "And those who turn many to righteousness [will shine] like the stars for ever and ever." Or, as our Sages put it,[7] this action can annul God's evil decree. Moreover,[8] "Anyone who brings merit to the many — no transgression will come his way." *Chovoth HaLevavoth*,[9] too, explains that the merit of one who puts another on the proper path, and turns an evil person into a good one, is many times greater even than that of one who has reached an almost angelic level of self-perfection.

The serious consequences of neglecting our mutual responsibility (when a transgression could have been prevented[10]) are elaborated in God's word to the Prophet Ezekiel:[11]

> And you, son of man, I have made you a sentinel for the house of Israel. ... You shall hear a word from My mouth and warn them in My name that I have said to the evil-doer, "Evil-doer, you shall surely die." If you have not spoken out to warn him, he shall die through his sin, and I shall seek his blood from your hand. But if you have warned the evil-doer of his [evil] ways — to turn from them — yet he does not turn from them, he shall die through his sin, but you have saved yourself.

These words, concerning the duty of a Prophet, bind us as well, obligating us to admonish whenever we can.[12] If we fail to do so, we are held accountable for the transgression which is committed, as stated explicitly by the Talmud.[13]

The same message is brought home to us by the Talmudic account of the prelude to the destruction of Jerusalem:[14]

> God said to [the angel] Gabriel, "Mark the foreheads of the righteous with a *thaw* in ink, so the angels of destruction will have no power over them, and mark the foreheads of the evil-doers with a *thaw* of blood, so the angels of destruction will have power over them." Thereupon Justice said to God, "Mas-

ter of the universe, how do they differ from one another?" God
replied, "These are perfectly righteous, while those are perfectly
evil." [Justice] replied, "But Master of the universe, [the righte-
ous] could have admonished [the evil-doers], but did not."

God accepts the argument, and the devastation begins with the
destruction of the elders of the Sanhedrin, illustrating that he who has
the power to rebuke, but neglects to do so, is punished together with the
evil-doer.[15]

Mutual responsibility imposes no specific duty to reprimand, but
rather an obligation to prevent the transgression. This implies that a *pro
forma* admonition has no merit. Instead, we must use all our God-given
wisdom and understanding to effect a change of heart in the transgressor.[16] If we fail despite all our efforts, there is no further obligation—or
reason—to reproach, as implied by God's instruction to Ezekiel and
also by the continuation of the above-cited Talmudic passage: "[God]
replied [to Justice], I know that if they had admonished, they would not
have been heeded." Came the response, "Master of the universe, You
know; but did they know?" implying that had they known that they
would not be heeded, they would not have been punished. Thus Tosafoth infer that if one's rebuke will be in vain, he need not utter it.[17]

Indeed, futile reprimands may actually be forbidden, as indicated in
Sefer Yere'im:[18] "[From the Tamudic dictum] 'Let them be. Better [they
transgress] unwittingly than knowingly,' we see that it is better not to
increase the measure of punishment." Furthermore, based on the verse,
"Do not admonish a scoffer, lest he hate you," Semag[19] concludes that
when one knows he will not be heeded, he should keep silent, even in the
face of intentional transgression. This is explicitly stated in the Talmud,[20] "A person is obligated not to utter something that will not be
heeded." (We discuss this in greater detail in the next chapter, in conjunction with the obligation to admonish.)

Furthermore, since the purpose of admonition is to influence the
listener, "one should not speak harshly or insultingly."[21] Likewise,
when the Mishnah requires one to remind his household of preparations
to be made before the Sabbath, the Talmud advises that this be done
gently, to assure compliance.[22]

This advice is particularly relevant to our generation. In the words of
Minchath Shemuel:[23] "I have learned from my teachers, especially R.
Chaim of Volozhin, that nowadays harsh words are not accepted, only

gentle and pleasant ones. . . . If one's nature does not permit him to speak gently and he will lose his temper with wrong-doers—whereupon they will not listen to him—he is exempt from the commandment to admonish." This point is emphasized also by the "Chafetz Chayim" in his letters[24] as well as by the "Chazon Ish" in his commentaries.[25]

Incidentally, the obligation to rebuke extends well beyond teaching. Rambam[26] writes that if the gentle approach fails, one must resort to more forceful means, to the point of shaming the transgressor in public, insulting him, and even cursing him, as all the prophets have done. This seems strange; if he does not respond to friendly persuasion, he will certainly not heed harsh speech. This apparent dilemma is resolved by an examination of the scriptural basis[27] of Rambam's statement. Rambam is evidently referring to people in position of authority, such as judges, who can enforce compliance (as explained in chapter 6).

4

The Mitzvah of Admonishing

The Torah says:[1] "Do not hate your brother in your heart; you shall surely admonish your fellow man and not load transgression upon him." Malbim explains that the term "admonition" denotes a cogent argument. The proper way to fulfill the mitzvah is, therefore, to clarify to the transgressor what the Torah expects in that particular case. Accordingly, admonition is essentially a form of teaching Torah.

Rambam stresses that this admonishing should be performed in a gentle manner, and that one must be careful not to offend the listener. However, only the mitzvah of admonishing is thus limited; the concept of mutual accountability requires us to go beyond the demand of the mitzvah to reproach; if all else fails, the transgressor should be convinced to change his ways by all means, even if this involves stern reprimands or public humiliation [by those responsible for the maintenance of public morality].[2]

What is the basis of the mitzvah of admonition if it is indeed distinct from the concept of mutual responsibility? From the context—"Do not hate... admonish your fellow man..."—it would appear that the purpose of this precept is to eliminate mutual animosity. This is stated explicitly in Sefer HaChinukh:[3] "If one person has harmed another and he admonishes him in private, [the offender] is likely to apologize and... they will make up. But if he does not admonish him, [the offended party] will bear a grudge and eventually harm him." (At first glance, this does not seem to cover mitzvoth between man and God; however, as we are commanded to despise evil, such admonition too may contribute to peace.)

This mitzvah is thus apparently an extension of the commandment to love one's neighbor. However, there are some fundamental distinctions between these two obligations. For example, unlike loving one's neighbor, admonition does not apply to an evil person:[4]

"You shall surely admonish your fellow man" — I might have thought that even when you know him to be evil and your enemy, you must admonish him — [this is not so, for] the Torah says, "You shall surely admonish your fellow man" — you are obligated to admonish the fellow who is with you in [the fulfillment of] Torah and mitzvoth, but not an evil person who hates you. Beyond this, you are not permitted to admonish him, as it is written: "He who admonishes a scoffer gets himself abuse... Do not admonish a scoffer, lest he hate you."[5]

We might ask why the scoffer's hatred ought to deter us? Perhaps the answer is that by provoking such enmity, we are causing him to transgress another prohibition and are ourselves guilty of "placing a stumbling block before the blind."[6] We will, in effect, be fostering more hatred by our admonition, whose avowed purpose is to eliminate hatred. This is in addition to the possible harm he may do to us.

However, another Talmudic passage[7] states that the mitzvah of admonishing must be carried out insistently and repeatedly, until the listener resorts to verbal or even physical abuse. This would seem to contradict what we have said above.[8] Rishonim resolve this discrepancy by distinguishing between admonishing a stranger or casual acquaintance and reprimanding a close friend or relative. In the former case, we are obligated to admonish only until we are sure that we will not be heeded. In the latter case, however, any anger on the listener's part will only be temporary; hence we must go much farther in carrying out this difficult commandment.[9]

According to Shulchan Arukh, we are required to rebuke every wrong-doer at least once, because he might heed us.[10] But this applies only if he is an occasional trangressor, not a deliberate or spiteful one.[11]

The obligation to remain silent on encountering an unresponsive transgressor also appears to be contradicted by a Talmudic statement which enjoins us to admonish even a hundred times if necessary.[12] In fact, however, this injunction refers to a person who accepts the admonishment, but later forgets himself or weakens in his resolve.[13] We are not allowed to give up hope regarding such a person.

The mitzvah of admonishing is not one that we are required to seek out.[14] However, heads of households and community leaders are obligated to pursue its fulfillment within their own spheres of influence.[15]

5

Love of God and Strengthening the Torah

The commandment to love God, which bears on all mitzvoth, obligates us to promote this love among all mankind. As Rambam states:[1]

> We have explained that this mitzvah also includes our summoning all others to serve Him and believe in Him. By way of example, if you had great love for a certain person, you would tell others about it, expound on his many good qualities and call on them to love him as well. So, too, if you truly love Him and begin to fully understand His truth, you will surely appeal to the ignorant and foolish to share in your knowledge... As the *Sifrey* says, "'And you shall love God'—Make Him beloved among His creatures, like your forefather Abraham, of whom it says... 'and the souls he made in Charan.'" This means that because of his great love for God... he urged others to feel the same. Similarly you should love Him so much that you call on others to do the same.

By interpreting the phrase "And you shall love God" to mean "make Him beloved among others," our Sages may have intimated that by expressing our love for Him by outward action, we are strengthening our inner love as well, reinforcing our own emotions. Thus, making God beloved by others is both an expression of love and a means of increasing our own love for Him. This is accomplished by teaching Torah, thereby acquainting others with God's greatness and wisdom.[2]

We are also obligated to strengthen our fellow man's observance of mitzvoth. The Sages understood the verse [3] "Accursed is he who will not uphold the words of this Torah" as referring to one who can strengthen Torah study and mitzvah fulfillment, but fails to do so. Such a person is cursed, even though he himself learns, teaches and practices.[4] Certainly the best way to encourage observance among the ignorant is to teach them the details of Torah and the mitzvoth.

6

Attitudes Towards Evil-Doers and Our Errant Brothers

We have shown that the obligation to love and take responsibility for our fellow Jews applies even to the wicked and the misled, according to several authorities. However, numerous statements also indicate that we should shun and despise such people.[1]

This issue takes on special importance in these days of rampant *minuth* and *epikorsuth* (heresy).[2] Our Sages have repeatedly stressed the need to keep one's distance from these aberrations—even more than from idolatry.[3] Specifically, we are enjoined to accept only a suitable disciple for Torah study.[4] How, then, are we to observe these commandments *vis-a-vis* the evil-doer and the errant?

Rambam and later authorities explain that those who were raised in ignorance of the Torah cannot be considered evil. Rather, they have the halakhic status of "a child raised by gentile captors," who cannot be held accountable for his transgressions.[5] Amid mass indifference to religious statutes, even a person who is aware of the mitzvoth but does not believe in them should be dealt with sympathetically.[6] This view, which prevailed during the 19th century, is even more applicable in our own day, as ignorance of Jewish law has become truly abysmal.

The "Chafetz Chayim" even maintains that, if we encounter a person who sins because of social pressure rather than malice, it is a great mitzvah for us—and especially the scholars and leaders among us[7]—to pity him and show him the correct path.

The "Chatham Sofer"[8] offers another reason for treating present-day heretics leniently. "The text... refers to a conscientious heretic, or one who believes in idolatry. However, those of our own day embrace their beliefs only for selfish reasons, and even though they have transgressed, they are Jews."

Similarly, the "Chazon Ish"[9] declares that the laws requiring harsh treatment for transgressors were applicable only when righteousness

was all-pervasive, Divine Providence was evident to all, and only perverted individuals would occasionally succumb to licentiousness and
hedonism. Under such circumstances, unless these deviants were dealt
with firmly, they would provoke God's wrath and cause misfortune.
Today, however, when faith is lacking and God's presence is concealed,
this approach would appear destructive and violent and would merely
arouse opposition and increase iniquity. Since our purpose is only to
improve the situation, these regulations are counter-productive and
consequently inapplicable. Instead, we must reach out to these transgressors through friendship and kindness wherever possible.

Furthermore, according to several major authorities,[10] we need
spurn only those sinners who have been properly admonished. As no
one truly knows how to rebuke today, no one can be considered properly admonished. The errant thus fall into the category of those who
transgress unwittingly.[11]

Showing transgressors kindness and love is so important that the
Midrash castigates our forefather Jacob for refusing to give his daughter
Dinah in marriage to the evil Esau — as she might have led him to mend
his ways. As punishment for this lack of concern, the Midrash says, the
tragedy in Shekhem befell Jacob.[12]

Today, most non-religious Jews are of the type termed "ignorant"
by our Sages. Consequently, it is a mitzvah to attract them. This
obligation is so overriding that the Sages allow one to risk defiling the
Sanctuary for its fulfillment.[13] One Amora even exclaimed: "They permitted the eating of untithed food, just to preserve the peace." Concerned lest one might withhold love and kindness from the "ignorant,"
the Sages occasionally even permitted facilitating possible transgression
on their part (see review at the end of Part 2).[14] It could even be argued
that by excluding transgressors from our places of worship, we may be
guilty of a form of heresy (ibid., Section 7).

Considering the above observations, one might inquire why Torah
leaders shun contact with the Reform and Conservative Movements, for
example, or with Zionism, of which R. A.Y. Kook wrote that "On its
forehead is inscribed the mark of Cain: 'Zionism has no connection with
religion'"?[15] Aren't most subscribers to these views halakhically considered as "children raised by gentile captors"? How can we reconcile
such divisive practices with our obligation to love these errant brothers?

To resolve this discrepancy, we must make two distinctions:

1. Despite the obligation to love our errant brothers, even when they attack the Torah, we may not abandon the souls of other Jews to their enticements. We are explicitly urged to counter any move to weaken the Torah—through legislation, for example—peacefully at first, but subsequently via any necessary means at hand.[16]

2. In his letters,[17] R. Samson Raphael Hirsch forbids associating with Reform-dominated communities, even if they permit Torah-observant members to hold their own prayer services and fulfill all other "religious" requirements. He declared them to be congregations of *minuth* and *epikorsuth*, which are worse than idolatry.[18] He then addresses our issue and writes:

> Some try to confuse the matter by claiming that this is dissociation from people whose beliefs differ from ours. It is not so, however... The issue is merely one of shunning any organization dedicated to *minuth* and *epikorsuth*. ... Today, thank God, we no longer find *minim* and *epikorsim* in the classic sense. All we have learned—that "non-Jews outside Eretz Yisrael are not idolators" and that "there are no *minim* among the nations; ... rather, they follow the customs of their forefathers"—also applies to contemporary Jews who have accepted the principles of *minuth* and *epikorsuth* and are two or three generations removed from those who originated these aberrations and promulgated them. Rambam's ruling regarding the *epikorsim* and Karaites of his day is wholly applicable to these later generations as well.[19]

> But just as we are obligated to act neighborly and peacefully towards [individual] fellow Jews who were raised on *minuth* and *epikorsuth*, and just as we must live a Torah-true life and [by example] kindle a desire for Torah values in their hearts, so too are we firmly enjoined to distance ourselves from [institutionalized] *minuth* and *epikorsuth*.

R. Hirsch writes of attracting only individuals—to whom the distinction between purposeful and inadvertent transgressions applies. However, the concept of "unwitting transgression" cannot apply to an organization. Consequently, we are commanded to separate ourselves totally from such an organization, while seeking to attract each of its unfortunate members, who are "like children raised by gentile captors."

Thus R. S.R. Hirsch has taught us a basic distinction which serves as the key to solving the problems in our attitude toward the errant. Most such persons, after all, are unwitting or inadvertent trangressors; hence we are duty-bound to invite them into our society and to love them. But their organizations, which are dedicated to *epikorsuth* can expect no such forbearance; neither are we enjoined to love them. In fact, we must keep as far from them as possible.

Another rule appears evident; it is better for us to invite such individuals into our own homes and acquaint them with their heritage than for us to enter their homes. This rule is implied by Rambam's observation[20] that one's thoughts and deeds are influenced by one's friends and associates. Therefore, it is better to bring the errant into a God-fearing environment than to join them in their own, as R. Eliyahu Dessler advises:[21] "The proper way to influence others is not to settle in places far removed from Torah, but rather to stay where you are and attract others, enlightening them with your learning. In one's own Torah environment, there is less danger of being influenced by others." (Presumably, settlement by a group of observant Jews would be exempted from this warning, as this would create a new Torah-true environment.)

There is another benefit to be gained from this approach: We effectively minimize the danger of exposing ourselves to the influence of the non-observant by working primarily with those who wish to be attracted —as evidenced by their willingness to come to us, rather than insisting that we come to them. Nevertheless, when the most effective results can be secured by approaching the errant in their own homes, doing so may be considered an act of great kindness.[22]

In light of the above analysis, we return to the question of why the Patriarch Jacob was punished for withholding his daughter from his evil brother. Should he have endangered her by letting her enter into such a union? It may be that marriage constitutes a special case, as "it is a man's way to follow [the direction] of his wife."[23] On the other hand, the Sages also teach us that marrying one's daughter off to an ignorant person is like binding her and surrendering her to a lion.[24] It appears, therefore, that a father's decision must depend on the particular circumstances prevailing; each case requires careful judgment.

Our children's education, and especially their attitudes towards the segment of our society estranged from Torah, demand very serious reflection. On the one hand, we must protect our children from destructive influences, yet on the other, we must educate them to love their neighbor. This is a genuine challenge—we dare not ignore it.

Our Sages labored to find the middle ground between these looming dangers: The rules governing the sale of agricultural tools to the uneducated Jew in the sabbatical year provide a good illustration of their efforts. Such a transaction may constitute "placing a stumbling block before the blind," as it enables the buyers to desecrate the sabbatical year. On the other hand, a total sales boycott would arouse hatred among the ignorant toward us, which is no less a transgression. Hence the Sages mapped out a delicately-refined compromise on this issue. Consider the enlightening words of the "Chazon Ish;" see above, the review to Part 2 (Section 3).

7

Epilogue

Today, many of those whose fathers were misled regarding Torah — and who in turn misled their own children — are developing a thirst for the word of God. Whoever teaches them Torah merits manifold reward:

1. He fulfills the mitzvah of teaching Torah to others, through which he will learn more than he learned from his teachers and extract preciousness from that which is worthless. Because of his efforts, he will be privileged to join the "Heavenly yeshivah."[1]
2. He saves many Jewish souls from oblivion and disgrace and fulfills the mitzvoth of not standing idly by in his fellow man's hour of need, rescuing his lost body and soul and loving his neighbor.
3. He will be rewarded for admonishing his neighbor.
4. Because he brings merit to the multitude, no transgression will come his way.
5. He saves himself and all his brethren from the punishment meted out to those who could have successfully remonstrated with transgressors.
6. He avoids the malediction, "Accursed is he who will not uphold the words of this Torah."
7. He fulfills the mitzvah of loving God by making Him beloved, perhaps hastening the coming of the Messiah, may he arrive speedily in our days.
   Herewith the words of R. Avraham bar Chiyah:[2]

Four advantages accrue to him who teaches Torah to the masses and disseminates words of wisdom:

... he spends a limited time teaching, and God repays him with eternity.

... when the fertile orchard produces fruits and beautiful

plants, it loses none of its fertility... Thus is he who irrigates with the waters of Torah and plants the seeds of wisdom: he acts in truth and kindness toward those who thirst and hunger for it—and his own waters of Torah wisdom flow and increase.

He who disseminates Torah and teaches it to the masses rebuilds ruins... The foundation laid in this generation will stand in the next.

As it is written: "And you will be called 'repairer of the breach.'"

PART FOUR

THE PURPOSE OF TORAH STUDY

In the civilized world, academic study has an aura of prestige. Especially in the present Age of Science, there is a strong tendency to idolize such studies for their own sake. Not surprisingly, people tend to perceive Torah study in this light as well. This conception, however, embodies a fundamental error.

We have shown that the world was created to serve as a means to translate Torah into reality. Clearly, then, Torah study is no mere academic pursuit, but rather the source of guidance for life.

Below, we investigate how this perception is reflected in rabbinic literature, the extent to which Torah study must be for the sake of obtaining guidance. We also discuss at length the relationship between such guidance and the concept of talmud Torah lishmah.

1

The Commandment to
Study Torah

Note:

The present subject is *talmud Torah* which, properly translated, most probably means "teaching Torah." In popular practice, however, the term is applied primarily to studying Torah; hence we translate it as "Torah study" here as well. At the same time, the reader should be aware that the term, as used here, does encompass teaching as well as studying Torah.

The Talmud derives the mitzvah of *talmud Torah* as follows:

What is the source of the commandment to study Torah? It is written: "And you shall teach them to your sons." However, if one's father neglected to teach him, he is obligated to teach himself, as the verse declares: "and you shall learn them [to be careful to fulfill them]."[1]

Rambam writes at the beginning of *Hilkhoth Talmud Torah*: "A father is obligated to teach his small son Torah... It is an obligation for every sage in Israel to teach every student... If one's father has failed to teach him, one is obligated to teach himself when he becomes aware." Semag's derivation is similar.[2]

When *talmud Torah* is presented primarily as an obligation to teach rather than study, it becomes an interpersonal obligation, which Judaism considers especially important.[3]

2

What is Meant by Torah Study *Lishmah*

1. Motivation for Torah Study

The mitzvah of studying Torah *lishmah* — literally: for its sake — is great indeed, and he who fulfills it is richly rewarded.[1] Our Sages teach:[2] "One verse indicates that God's kindness is as high as the heavens, while another states that His kindness is higher than the heavens. How can we explain this discrepancy? By assuming that the latter verse refers to one who practices [e.g. studies] *lishmah*, while the former alludes to one who has an ulterior motive — *shelo lishmah*." They also say:[3] "For one who studies the Torah *lishmah*, it becomes an elixir of life; but for one who learns *shelo lishmah*, it becomes a deadly potion." To clarify the concept of motivation for Torah study, we proceed to define the concepts *lishmah* and *shelo lishmah*.

Note that we examine here only the intent with which a Jew should approach Torah study. God's "intent" in commanding us to study Torah is another matter entirely and will not be considered here. Nor do we discuss here the many benefits conferred by Torah study which include: life and longevity; enjoyment and happiness in this world and the next; God's love and closeness; protection from our evil inclinations and from tribulations; and the perpetuation of the world.

In general, the proper performance of a mitzvah requires the intent to fulfill the commandment of the Creator. The mitzvah of Torah study also requires this intent, as it is a mitzvah in its own right and not merely a means of fulfilling other commandments.[4] Moreover, like other mitzvoth, it is fulfilled *lishmah* when performed without regard for reward or other advantage, but only out of love of Him who commanded it.[5]

On the other hand, we are taught: "Do things [i.e., mitzvoth] for the sake of their Creator and study them [the laws pertaining to their observance] for their own sake."[6] Hence, whereas a mitzvah must be fulfilled for the sake of God, its Torah regulations must be studied for the sake of knowledge. Consequently, it would appear that for Torah study, the intent to understand may replace the intent to fulfill the will of God, as expressed by R. Chaim of Volozhin:[7] "*lishmah* means... in general [mitzvah observance], for the sake of God... in the case of Torah study, for the sake of the Torah."

In reality, rather than contradicting each other, these definitions may simply be highlighting two aspects of the term *lishmah* in reference to Torah study: Love of God, which *talmud Torah* shares with all other mitzvoth as the ideal motivation, and intent to acquire knowledge, which is specific to *talmud Torah*; if this intent is missing, the fulfillment itself is deficient, or even void. According to this suggestion, the intent to obtain guidance is required for the study to be classified as *talmud Torah*, whereas love of God is necessary as motivation to render the study "*lishmah*." Consequently, both motivations are required for the study to be *talmud Torah lishmah*. This assumption eliminates several ostensible contradictions, as indicated below. The intent to obtain guidance, which is specific to *talmud Torah* and vital to its fulfillment, is discussed at length in the remainder of this chapter.

The term "Torah" itself, which literally means "guidance," teaches us that the purpose of Torah study must be to derive guidance and direction.[8] It is also alluded to in the verse that defines study *lishmah*: "As the Lord, my God, has commanded me **to do**"[9] and is stressed as well by the authorities. Rabbeinu Chananel wrote: "He who occupies himself with the Torah but not with [the fulfillment of] the commandments... [nor studies it] to clarify the law and establish the proper halakhah, is as if he lacks Torah itself."[10] Similarly, the Mishnah[11] praises only those who study to practice what they have learned (and, according to some readings, also those who study to teach). Several commentaries deduce that studying for the sake of theoretical and academic knowledge alone is not considered "Torah study." Rabbeinu Yonah declares: "Heaven forbid that this [praise] should refer to one who learns in order to teach but not to fulfill, for such a person will not be able to accomplish either."[12] Rambam's ruling[13] that children and other novices should be taught Torah to **serve** out of fear, or for reward, again implies that teaching should lead to action.

R. Shemuel Primo states:[14] "When they said that one may originally study Torah *shelo lishmah*, they meant that although it is not done with pure intent, the study is accompanied by the fulfillment of mitzvoth and hence engenders purification of one's character. It is this purification that leads from *shelo lishmah* to *lishmah*," again implying that study, even *shelo lishmah*, must at least lead to practice.

On this same Mishnah, Meiri writes: "One should not research [the Torah] pointlessly, but rather [do so] to fulfill its dictates and influence others [to do so], for that is the goal of perfection." Maharal adds: "For the intention of these two [he who learns to teach and he who learns to fulfill] is for the sake of Heaven, which is not so with one who learns for the sake of wisdom." R. Ya'akov Emden concurs: "One must at least intend to teach; otherwise, there is no reward for his study and he will not be able to accomplish anything, for this is not in the category [of Torah study]." **Studying Torah without the intent to practice is not considered *talmud Torah* at all.**[15]

The centrality of the intent to practice has interesting practical implications for proper fulfillment of the commandment to teach. In a personal communication, R. Simchah Wasserman noted that when he taught students who were not yet committed to the practice of Torah, he started with the commandments regulating social intercourse, for these would obviously be studied with the intent to practice. Only when these students were somewhat firmer in their faith and were acting on their resolve, did he teach them the mitzvoth concerning the relationship between man and God.

In other commandments, too, we find specific intent as an essential component of fulfillment. If one counts the '*omer* without realizing that he is counting, e.g., counting in a language he does not understand, he has not fulfilled the commandment,[16] even if he intended to carry out his obligation in general terms and was inspired by a great love of God at the time. Likewise, if one does not read the first verse of Shema' with proper intent, he has not accepted the Divine yoke and has not fulfilled the commandment.

Having concluded that the commandment of Torah study *lishmah* requires two kinds of intent — love of God and intent to practice — we may also explain the apparent contradiction in the Sages' view of one who learns *shelo lishmah*, as we elaborate in the following section.

2. Torah Study *Shelo Lishmah*

Let us summarize the Sages' comments concerning those who study or practice *shelo lishmah*.

1. In describing God's reward to those who do His will, one verse indicates that God's kindness is as high as the heavens, while another states that His kindness is higher than the heavens. How can we explain this discrepancy? By assuming that the latter verse refers to one who practices *lishmah*, while the former applies to one who practices *shelo lishmah*.[17]

2. Generally, one should occupy himself with Torah and the commandments even *shelo lishmah*, for through *shelo lishmah* he will come to *lishmah*.[18]

3. a) Anyone who reads [the Torah] *shelo lishmah* would have been better off had his afterbirth been thrust back on him [i.e. had he not been born].[19] b) Anyone who practices *shelo lishmah* would have been better off had he never been created.[20]

4. For one who studies the Torah *lishmah*, it becomes an elixir of life, but for one who learns *shelo lishmah*, it becomes a deadly potion.[21]

At first sight, there appears to be a difference of opinion among the Tanaim. [Indeed, when R. Meir states, "Whoever studies Torah *lishmah* merits many things," the Talmud concludes that he disputes R. Yochanan's dictum: "In general, a person should occupy himself with Torah, even *shelo lishmah*, for through *shelo lishmah* he will come to *lishmah*," and agrees with R. Akiva, who censured Torah *shelo lishmah* severely (Statement 3b).] Some Sages even seem to contradict themselves. For instance, Rava states that anyone who studies *shelo lishmah* would have been better off had he never been created,[22] but elsewhere[23] he maintains that of such a person it is said: "for [God's] kindness is as high as the heavens," "for he has, after all, fulfilled a commandment." Similarly, R. Yochanan himself, one of the authors of Statement 2, recommending *shelo lishmah*, is also responsible for Statement 3a according to which such a person would have been better off had he never been born.[24]

The Rishonim endeavored to reconcile these contradictions. We commence by examining the words of Rashi.

(a) The expression *shelo lishmah* of "God's kindness is as high as the heavens..." (Statement 1) refers to "one who practices to be honored."[25]

(b) The Talmudic statement indicating that it would have been better for such a person not to have been created (Statement 3) refers to "one who learns not to practice but to dispute."[26]

(c) the "deadly potion" (Statement 4) refers to one who studies to achieve the title "rabbi."[27]

On first sight, coveting the title "rabbi," which turns Torah into a deadly potion, would appear to be the same as wanting "to be honored" which is rewarded with "kindness as high as the heavens." However, a closer examination reveals that there is no contradiction at all. In Comment (a), Rashi carefully applied the reward "as high as the heaven" to one "who **practices** to be honored," i.e. one who studies in order to practice, which, after all, constitutes proper fulfillment of the commandment of Torah study. Only through practice does he seek honor. One who studies to be called "rabbi," however, is fashioning the Torah into a crown of self-aggrandizement. Such a person, "who exploits the crown [Torah] will fade away."[28] In other words, he makes the Torah itself into an instrument of self-destruction — a deadly potion. The Talmud adds:[29] "Do not make them into a crown of self-aggrandizement, nor into a hoe with which to dig. This can be derived from [the case of] Belshazzar, who was removed from the world for using the Temple vessels after they had already been profaned; this is all the more [applicable] to one who uses the holy Torah itself."[30]

Rashi's second comment relates to an intermediate situation, addressing the case of one who occupies himself with Torah solely for academic interest. He thus misses the goal of Torah study, namely practice.[31] Hence he fulfills no commandment at all and his life is of no value.[32] On the other hand, he has not abused the Torah either; hence it does not become a deadly potion.

It now remains for us to clarify Rashi's perception of the correct intention for "occupying oneself with Torah and the commandments, even *shelo lishmah*" [Statement 2]. The Talmud in *Pesachim* treats this recommendation as equivalent to the *shelo lishmah* that earns God's kindness. Hence it is reasonable to assume that Rashi would also consider them equal; both refer to a person studying with the intent to practice but motivated by selfish intentions. This is supported by the fact that the Talmud, when recommending *shelo lishmah*, lumps together Torah study and practice, implying that the only missing element is their common motivation — love of God.

In the same vein, the Tosafoth in *Sotah*[33] explain: "The *shelo lishmah* that is encouraged refers to one who occupies himself [with Torah] out of fear of punishment, or love of reward; he acts not purely to perform the will of his Creator, Who commanded him, but for his own benefit... However, when they speak of *shelo lishmah* in general [which makes the Torah a deadly potion, etc.], they indicate that such persons do not occupy themselves with the Torah to practice it, neither out of love nor out of fear." As Tosafoth reserve the severest censure for one who studies without intent to practice what he learned, the acceptable *shelo lishmah* refers to one who does study with such intent; only the element "for the sake of heaven" is missing in the permitted *shelo lishmah*. Since the essential element of the obligation — the intention to practice — is present; a commandment is fulfilled.[34]

Similarly, Rambam interprets *shelo lishmah* as motivated by love of reward and fear of punishment, i.e., not "the sake of Heaven." He does not mention the motivation of being honored,[35] although he does quote the Mishnah[36] condemning use of the Torah for self-aggrandizement, which is the same as the quest for honor.[37] Furthermore, Ritba[38] writes: "'A deadly potion' — if he learns for self-aggrandizement." *Yesod Ha'Avodah* follows suit.

Another opinion cited by Tosafoth is that of Ry,[39] who restricts the evil *shelo lishmah* to "one who studies to be haughty, to dispute and to overcome his colleague in halakhah, and not to practice." He, too, implies that the intent to practice is essential to render the *shelo lishmah* acceptable.

A Midrash[40] relevant to the issue at hand states: "It is written:[41] 'They abandoned Me, and did not guard My Torah' — [which we interpret as] 'would that they had abandoned Me but observed My Torah; for in occupying themselves with it, its inherent light would have brought them back to goodness.'" Here, "they abandoned Me" presumably refers to not heeding the commandments, and "they did not guard My Torah," to not studying. How, then, could God expressly wish they had studied even without intent to practice, when we have learned that such study makes the student better off had he not been born? We must therefore equate "they abandoned Me" with forsaking the love of God and fulfilling the commandments *shelo lishmah*. Consequently, "guard My Torah" refers to the fulfillment of the commandments together with Torah study, even *shelo lishmah*.[42] Accordingly, this Midrash would bear out Tosafoth's interpretation of the tolerable *shelo lishmah*.

So far, all authorities, including Tosafoth, agreed that Torah study without intent to obtain guidance has no value at all. Elsewhere,[43] however, Tosafoth maintain that even he who learns for his own benefit ("to gain honor"; "to be called 'Rabbi'"; "to be vainglorious and make a name for himself") should concentrate on studying, "for through *shelo lishmah* he will come to *lishmah*." Here, they do not specify that the recommended *shelo lishmah* must involve the intent to practice what is learned. On the other hand, we may avoid positing a disagreement among the Ba'aley HaTosafoth by claiming that they may simply have assumed it to be self-understood that he intends to practice what he learns, in addition to the benefit that he aspires to.

We find the same ambiguity in *Menorath HaMaor* who writes:[44] "A person should only occupy himself with Torah *lishmah* and should not benefit therefrom in this world any more than the Torah permits. Nevertheless, it is good and proper for him to learn even *shelo lishmah*, for after he understands the truth, he will...study *lishmah*." Acharonim such as Shakh[45] and *Chayey Adam*[46] express similar views. *Birkey Yosef*[47] contends that Rambam, too, sides with Tosafoth.

According to the simple interpretation, their opinion is that one should study under any circumstances — perhaps even learning without any intention of practicing. Although there is no merit in it, there is hope that he will repent before he abuses the "crown of Torah" and thus escape extirpation from the world. According to this view, "Would that they had forsaken Me, but observed My Torah" may be taken literally, and only one who learns in order to be haughty,[48] to argue or overcome others is excluded from the principle of "through *shelo lishmah* he will come to *lishmah*," for his study not only fails to fulfill the commandments but even contravenes them.

The above opinions are somewhat ambiguous regarding the merits of learning without intent to practice. R. Sheneor Zalman, however, permits this explicitly:[49]

> If one does not apply what he learns, he is an evil-doer, "And to the evil-doer, God said, 'Who are you to speak of My dictates...' Every scholar who takes the commandments lightly and does not respect Heaven is like the least in the community and worse than an ignoramus... As the Sages said: "If he is not worthy, his learning becomes a deadly potion for him."[50] Others say a person should nevertheless occupy himself with Torah,

for through *shelo lishmah* he may come to *lishmah*, to learning
in order to observe and practice, for its inherent light will bring
him back to goodness, as our Sages have said... "Would that
they had forsaken Me but observed My Torah..."

R. Ya'akov Emden[51] and R. Mosheh Chaim Luzzatto[52] share this
view.

How can a given act be "poisonous" and yet be recommended? R.
Chaim bar Betzalel of Friedburg (Maharal's brother) notes that just as
medicine can cure or kill, depending on the dosage, Torah study *shelo
lishmah*, which our Sages considered a deadly potion — is beneficial only
in limited quantities and only to one who is spiritually "sick."[53]

In sum, there appears to be a controversy regarding the applicability
of the principle of learning even *shelo lishmah* to one who lacks intention
of practicing, in the hope that it will eventually lead him to study
lishmah.

While all authorities apparently agree that Torah study *lishmah* does
include such intent, some indicate that the explicit goal of learning is
knowledge. Is this indeed a difference of opinion, or do they concur that
the ultimate purpose of learning is practice, whereas knowledge is only
an intermediary goal? We study this issue in the next chapter.

3

The Goal of Torah Study

Post-Talmudic literature records three goals for Torah study: to practice, to know, and to approach God. Below, we review these goals and examine their relationships with one another.

1. Learning with Intent to Practice

The Mishnah states: "The main object is not study but deed."[1] Similarly: "He who learns in order to teach will be enabled to learn and to teach; he who learns in order to practice will be enabled to learn and to teach, to observe and to practice."[2] In other words, the goal of studying the Torah is primarily to fulfill it and secondarily to teach it. R. David, Rambam's grandson, writes:[3] "This [learning in order to practice] is the highest level: It is achieved by one who studies the Torah with the aim of revealing its principles and viewing its mysteries, so that he may walk in its paths and fulfill its commandments." *Kesef Mishneh*[4] amplifies this idea: "If one learns in order to teach, his learning is not *lishmah*... but learning in order to practice is learning *lishmah*."

Rabbeinu Yonah[5] posits two levels of "studying in order to practice":

1. Studying with the intent to fulfill any halakhah one happens to learn, but without searching for guidance. This merely removes one from the category of those who study with "the intention of not fulfilling," which would void the mitzvah of Torah study entirely.
2. Learning with the intention of fathoming every detail of what one is supposed to do. Such study, says the Mishnah, enables one "to learn and to teach, to observe and to practice."

Perhaps, in all this, the words "in order to practice" should not be taken too literally—i.e. to carry out the halakhah as written—but rather interpreted more profoundly: Through intensive study of the **letter of the law,** we can increase our comprehension of the Lawgiver's intent and go beyond the letter to the **spirit of the law.** Even study of the opinions rejected by the Talmud is important for a complete understanding of the halakhah. As this deeper understanding affects fulfillment of the commandments, it is included in the concept of learning in order to practice.

The Midrash, too, avers that the primary purpose of Torah study is practice:[6] "Before learning, Moses would say: 'Blessed be God Who desires those who practice [the Torah].' He did not mention those who toil in it or those who immerse themselves in its study, but those who practice it—those who fulfill the words of the Torah."[7] Similarly Meiri:[8] "The only purpose of study is to foster practice."

When the Mishnah states:[9] "The main object is not study but deed," Rabbeinu Bachyay comments:

> That is to say, the purpose of knowledge and toil in the Torah is not that one study hard, but that one should come to practice...
> for the aim of learning is only that he should practice. Thus have our Sages interpreted the verse "Good understanding comes to all who practice them"—not "to all who study them" but "to all who practice them."

This Biblical interpretation was a favorite expression of Rava[10] to prove that "the goal of [Torah] wisdom is repentance and good deeds." *Sefer Chasidim* also quotes this verse:[11] "It is fundamental to the Torah that a person know what to do in all cases, as it says, 'good understanding comes to all who practice them'—not 'to all who study them'... One should learn in order to teach, observe, and practice—that is Torah *lishmah.*"

Similarly Rashi[12] implies that "one who acts with an ulterior motive" is one who "does not learn in order to practice." Rambam likewise states:[13] "...and his only goal in studying wisdom should be knowledge... and the goal of knowing it is practicing it." Adds Ran:[14] "It is well-known that the intent of Torah [study] is to instill reverence for God, not to acquire wisdom... We are commanded to learn Torah primarily so that we may be able to practice it, for one who does not know the details of a mitzvah cannot fulfill it... But the ultimate objective is to attain reverence for God." Accordingly, the immediate goal of the mitzvah of Torah study is the fulfillment of the mitzvoth, the purpose of which is the attainment of reverence for God — which is thus the ultimate goal.

Most Acharonim, too, agree that the goal of Torah study is practice, and learning to this end is *lishmah*. Says Shelah:[15]

> *Lishmah* means occupying oneself with Torah to practice what God has commanded us, "and you shall learn them." One should consider the Torah a royal edict issued to His subjects so that they know what to do and what not to do... When one opens a book [of Torah], he should say, "I wish to learn so that my learning will lead to practice, upright character traits and to knowledge of the Torah"... that is what *lishmah* means... It has already been shown that the ultimate goal of study *lishmah* includes practice.

Thus, the desire to both know and practice are part of study *lishmah*; but he concludes: "the true goal is practice."

The following is a brief list of later authorities who consider Torah study for the purpose of practice — or for knowing the details of practice — to be study *lishmah*:

> *Reishith Chokhmah* (Introduction): "For the fundamental aim of occupying oneself with Torah is to bring it to fruition... The object of studying Torah *lishmah* is undoubtedly to know it in order to practice its commandments."
>
> *Midrash Shemuel*:[16] "However, one learns *lishmah* if he learns in order to practice."
>
> R. Ya'akov Emden:[17] "This is Torah *lishmah*: in order to fulfill it."
>
> R. Sheneor Zalman of L'ady:[18] "To achieve *lishmah* is to learn in order to guard and do."
>
> The "Chafetz Chaim":[19] "As is written in the holy books, the essence of Torah study *lishmah* is knowing the halakhah [i.e. practice] clearly in every field of the Talmud."

The following state that the ultimate goal of Torah study is practice:

R. Yosef Ya'betz:[20] "They did not reach the ultimate goal of Torah, which is [good] deeds and piety, [nor] even knowledge of everyday commandments."

R. Mosheh Alshikh:[21] "The object is not study but deed; that is, exposition is nothing unless it leads to deed."

The Gaon of Vilna:[22] "For the goal and primary purpose of occupying oneself with Torah is to find the smooth, straight path of serving God."

R. Chaim of Volozhin:[23] "This is the entire fruition of learning Talmud: to extract from it practical rules of law." And elsewhere:[24] "Don't think study is the object—deed is."

The "Chatham Sofer":[25] "He who learns Torah to know it is very meritorious, but he will not succeed in his learning as well as he would if his purpose were to learn in order to teach... The ultimate goal, however, is to fulfill the commandments of God and refrain from that which is forbidden. Therefore, we should approach Torah study with the intention of understanding the practice of its commandments, for that is the basic goal."

Chayey Adam (Introduction): "It is well-known that Torah study is [undertaken] primarily to know the commandments in detail." Elsewhere[26] he testifies about his departed son: "His learning was perfect, for I can attest that his study was for the purpose of practicing."

R. Samson Raphael Hirsch:[27] "You must study for life —that is the highest principle of the Torah." And in his commentary on *Avoth*: "The supreme goal of studying Torah is to practice it, to fulfill it in truth... this purpose... is also best suited to helping one reach perfection in Torah study."

R. Yisrael of Salant: "The goal of the mitzvah of knowing the Torah is to know its regulations and laws in detail, so that one may have a clear understanding of the halakhah in all cases—how to observe and practice the whole Torah and all the mitzvoth."[28]

Why is the intention to practice so important in Torah study? Perhaps because, from the outset, the world was meant to serve the implementation of the Torah.[29] Consequently, one who studies in the presence of a corpse "mocks the destitute,"[30] because for the departed, even though his soul may still be studying the Torah in the "heavenly Yeshiva," its study no longer has practical significance for him.

2. Learning for the Sake of Knowledge

"Torah study *lishmah*" literally means "Torah study for its sake." The Hebrew possessive suffix concluding the word *lishmah* is feminine, as is the word Torah, implying that the term means "for the Torah's sake." If it had meant "for the sake of learning" or "for the sake of Heaven,"[31] the masculine form would have been used. This interpretation of *lishmah* is supported by Rambam:[32] "His only goal in learning the wisdom [Torah] should be to know it." Rosh concurs:[33] " 'And speak of them'—for their own sake—all your speaking and discussion of the words of the Torah should be for the sake of the Torah—to know, to understand, to increase learning and acuity." And R. Avraham of Montpellier writes:[34] "The commandment to learn concerns the mental grasp and knowledge of truth; the main object of the commandment is to acquire the truth and enjoy the knowledge that gladdens man's heart and mind."[35]

We find similar ideas among the Acharonim. As stated, Shelah maintains[36] that Torah study *lishmah* includes the idea "that learning will bring me to fulfill, and to good character traits, and to knowledge of the Torah." R. Chaim of Volozhin observes:[37] "*Lishmah* means for the sake of Torah... In connection with practice, it means for the sake of God... and in connection with study, for the sake of the Torah." In his commentary on *Avoth*,[38] he notes: "The object of study is not only to grow closer [to God], but also to grasp the general and detailed meaning of the commandments and laws through the Torah."

These opinions do not necessarily contradict the above-noted views indicating that the main objective of Torah study is practice. On the contrary, the knowledge perceived as the goal may well mean knowledge of the proper action. This interpretation is stated explicitly by Rambam (as quoted earlier): "His only goal in learning the wisdom should be to know it [the Torah]... and the goal of knowing it is to practice it." In addition, some of the Acharonim cited herein, who define Torah study *lishmah* as learning in order to know, also define it as learning in order to practice. Evidently, they believe that these are merely two aspects of a single motivation: study for the sake of knowledge, where the knowledge is for the sake of fulfilling the mitzvoth.

Furthermore, Maharal writes that one who learns in order to acquire knowledge for himself, without the objective of using it to serve his Maker, does not study *lishmah*:[39] "He who learns in order to teach, or to practice, learns for the sake of Heaven. But one who learns in order to acquire knowledge... does not necessarily do so for the sake of Heaven, for the honor of God—because everyone [naturally] wants to understand and know and everyone yearns for wisdom."

For other approaches relating the two aspects of Torah study—a means of fulfilling mitzvoth and a mitzvah itself—see Chapter 6.

3. Learning to Achieve Closeness to God

Acharonim cite an additional purpose for learning: to influence our spirit, uplift our soul and bring us closer to God. In the words of Bach:[40] "It appears that God's intent was always that we should occupy ourselves with the Torah so that our soul should realize itself with fulfillment, spirituality, and the sanctity of Him Who brought forth the Torah... So that our soul and our body—with all its 248 members and 365 ligaments—should cling to the 248 positive and 365 negative commandments of the Torah. If they study the Torah for this purpose, they become a chariot and edifice for the Divine Presence... [but now, that they learn for selfish reasons,] it is not *lishmah*."

This is also implied by *Chawoth Ya-ir* (no. 124): "[for all learning is beneficial] in accomplishing **the goal, which is perfection of character**... Therefore, [study of *Orach Chayim*] is optimal, as our Sages have taught: 'He who studies for the purpose of practicing is enabled to study...'"

Although this purpose is apparently not mentioned by the Rishonim, the Sages do allude to it:[41] "When the Torah commands, 'And you shall love the Lord, your God, with all your heart,' I do not know what this means. But when it continues, 'And these words shall be...,' [I can deduce that by studying His words] one recognizes and cleaves to His ways." In other words, Torah study leads to recognition and emulation of God.

Similarly, Torah study is considered service of God:[42] "'To serve Him'—that refers to study... Just as offering sacrifices is called service, so is study."

Some Chassidic authorities also state that Torah study *lishmah* is designed to achieve closeness to God.[43] For example, R. Shneor Zalman of L'ady states:[44] "[Torah study] *lishmah* means binding one's soul to God through understanding the Torah, each one according to his mental capacity."

R. Chaim of Volozhin[45] opposes this approach because it would lead people to concentrate on studying songs of praise, especially Psalms, rather than halakhah. This, he feels, is a mistake, for according to the Midrash, King David asks that God value his singing as highly as strictly halakhic Talmudic study, which shows that learning is greater than singing praises. Furthermore, he points out, there is no evidence that God acceded to his request. Nevertheless, R. Chaim himself considered a desire for closeness to God an important motive in Torah study.[46]

However, the role of closeness requires further clarification, in the light of the *Baraitha*[47] which states that the laws regarding the rebellious son can never be applied. The Talmud then asks why they are written, and answers: "Study them and receive reward." If the purpose of study is to achieve closeness to God, this question is baseless — obviously, they were written to reveal God's will in such a hypothetical case to help us come closer to Him. The answer may be that the "reward" here is precisely this closeness and the *Baraitha* is merely stressing that it should be our goal in Torah study.[48]

4

The Benediction Over Torah Study

Even the benediction we pronounce over Torah study alludes to its purpose. Most Rishonim render the blessing[1] "... Who has sanctified us through His commandments and commanded us regarding the words of Torah." Some, however, have the reading "... Who has sanctified us through His commandments and commanded us to **occupy ourselves** with the words of Torah." The latter version appears in most siddurim today.[2]

In parallel to this disagreement, there is also a difference of opinion regarding the essence of "occupying oneself with Torah."

Beth Yosef quotes ibn Yarchi as declaring that "occupying oneself with words of Torah" means simply reading them,[3] whereas Ra-avyah maintains[4] that reading the Torah in public does not constitute occupying oneself with it, as it is too superficial. *Orchoth Chayim*[5] goes even further, indicating that occupying oneself includes fulfillment of the commandments in addition to study. Support for this statement can be found in the words of the Sages, who refer to the fulfillment of mitzvoth as "occupying oneself with the Torah."[6] Rishonim like ibn Yarchi and Abudirham (as quoted in *Beth Yosef*) agree that the benediction covers deed as well as study.

Bahag (as quoted in *Pardes HaGadol*[7]) notes that the wording used in Rome, Spain and Lombardy is "regarding words of Torah," because it encompasses all aspects of Torah study—learning, teaching, guarding and doing. Apparently, all Rishonim who cite that text concur that it incorporates both deed and study. Rashi also includes both in the benediction,[8] although his rendition of the text is uncertain. *Or Zarua*[9] disagrees with Rashi and contends that study alone warrants the benediction—a view shared by *Beth Yosef.*

Some Acharonim[10] suggest that a deeper delving itself is called "occupying oneself with the words of the Torah." However, in the absence of support from Rishonim, this position is somewhat difficult to maintain, especially as such activity is not explicitly commanded.[11]

5

The Scope of the Commandment to Study Torah

The Mishnah states[1] that the commandment to study Torah has no measure. The Jerusalem Talmud explains this to mean that there is neither a maximum nor a minimum.

Note:

The following is a brief review of the discussion examined at length in Part 1, Chapter 2. It is summarized here for completeness' sake.

In the Babylonian Talmud,[2] R. Yishma'el contends that the commandment inherent in the verse "This book of the Torah shall not depart from your mouth... and you shall delve into it day and night" applies constantly. But from the same verse, R. Shim'on ben Yochai deduces that one fulfills the mitzvah simply by reading the Shema' in the morning and evening; this latter view is endorsed by Rava and consequently became halakhah.[3]

The same Tanaim differ in *Berakhoth*,[4] examining the phrase "and you shall gather in your harvest." R. Yishma'el adduces that one must devote himself to his livelihood in conjunction with his Torah study, while R. Shim'on objects: "Should a man sow at the time of sowing, plow at the time of plowing... winnow when there is wind? What will become of Torah?" Here, the halakhah is according to R. Yishma'el,[5] as both Abbayey and Rava follow it. Yet the words of R. Shim'on in these two passages appear to contradict each other. R. Yehudah HeChasid resolves the difficulty as follows: when R. Shim'on considers the commandment to study Torah to be unceasing, he means that it is always meritorious and should not be neglected; but only the reading of the Shema' is required absolutely. *Tosfoth HaRosh* offer a similar interpretation.[6] In *Nedarim*, too, the Talmud[7] implies that the obligation to study Torah is fulfilled by reading the Shema' twice a day. Ran, however, notes that the verse "You shall inculate them in your sons" means[8] that one should become so conversant with the Torah that "if asked about it, one need not hesitate, but answer immediately" — "and for this, reading the Shema' morning and evening is not sufficient." Rather, Ran considers it a Scriptural obligation to study Torah incessantly.

Radbaz counters that all of the other commentators disagree with this opinion, contending that incessant study is not a requirement. To support his claim, he cites Rashi, *Sefer Yere-im*, Rabbeinu Yonah, Rashba, Ritba, and Rosh, all of whom disagree with Ran.[9]

Besides considering the amount of time to be devoted to Torah study, the Torah authorities also address the issue of the quantity and quality of knowledge required.

Concerning the verse "You shall inculcate them...," *Orchoth Tzadikim* explains that the aforementioned fluency in Torah, as cited by Ran, refers only to Talmudic times, when study primarily involved repetition. This implies that fluency, rather than extent, of knowledge is intended.

Similarly, R. Sheneor Zalman of L'ady[10] states: "One's learning should be so orderly and fluent that if asked about anything **he has studied**, one can immediately answer 'permitted' or 'forbidden.'" Thus, the above derivation establishes the quality of learning and not the quantity.

However, R. Baruch Ber Leibowitz writes[11] that this derivation imposes "an obligation on each and every Jew to see to it that his sons and grandsons are scholars and geonim [complete masters] of Torah." This implies a demand for total grasp of Torah, total both quantitatively and qualitatively.

On the other hand, the "Chafetz Chayim" argues that "it is almost impossible for anyone to know all of the Talmud by heart... except for individuals, the geonim of the period... Therefore, I said to myself ...God commanded this to all Israel... [so] such a difficult task cannot have been intended."[12]

6
Two Aspects of Torah Study

The words of the Sages reflect apparent contradictions regarding Torah study. We are not allowed to speak of anything but Torah;[1] yet one paragraph morning and evening satisfies the requirement;[2] some statements indicate that Torah study is a means towards practice, while others deem Torah study a commandment in itself. To resolve these conflicts, some authorities ascribe two aspects to the commandment of Torah study, as presented in the following.

Torah study indeed involves several mitzvoth, as implied by *Sifrey*:[3] "If a person teaches Torah, he has one commandment to his credit; if he teaches and guards, he has two; if he teaches, guards and practices —there is nothing greater."

We have already noted that Ran postulates two mitzvoth of Torah study.[4] One of these — "speak of them... when you lie down and when you rise" — is satisfied by reading the Shema' mornings and evenings, whereas the other — "that the words of Torah be fluent in your mouth" — requires constant study.

R. Sheneor Zalman of L'ady formulates[5] two commandments of Torah study: to know the whole Torah and to delve into it (day and night). He develops a highly original theory based on this distinction and applies it to resolve several Talmudic difficulties, including the means-versus-end dilemma cited at the beginning of this Chapter.

R. Mosheh Chaim Luzzatto writes:[6] "The study of Torah is essential, for without it one cannot ever fulfill it. How can one fulfill his obligations without knowing what they are? Aside from this, however, the Torah also contributes greatly to personal perfection" — through reasoning and study, i.e., effort, and through intelligence, i.e., understanding. Thus, he explains why Torah study is a mitzvah in itself, besides a preparatory measure and prerequisite for proper mitzvah fulfillment.

Similarly, *Beth HaLevi*'s preface ascribes two parts to this mitzvah: fulfilling the specific commandment to study Torah and preparing oneself to fulfill other commandments. In his introduction to *Chayey Adam*, the author stresses this duality: part is fulfilled by pure study, regardless of applicability, while the other—which is primary and dearer in God's eyes—requires study of mitzvoth as needed for practice.

R. Yechezkel Sarna[7] writes that one aspect is study itself, to gain full knowledge of the Torah and familiarity with its halakhoth. The other is toiling in the Talmud—reviewing its words again and again, not necessarily to increase one's understanding but to make them part of him; this, too, facilitates fulfillment. In other words, both objective knowledge and emotional involvement are part of Torah study.

Along a somewhat different line, R. Yisrael of Salant[8] posits two distinct commandments: one, based on the phrase "you shall delve into it," requires the learning of Torah; the other, based on the phrase "and you shall teach them," requires knowledge of Torah. However, his derivation may not have been meant literally, as the first verse is from the Prophets and therefore may only clarify a commandment and not originate one. *'Eynayim LaMishpat*[9] also derives two aspects from two verses.

LeOr HaHalkhah[10] writes that ignorance in Torah matters involves the transgression of two commandments: a positive one, based on "You shall inculcate them"; and a negative one, based on "Guard [yourself well lest you forget]."

PART FIVE

FORMULATING A TORAH-STUDY PROGRAM

The Torah can be studied in many ways. One may ponder it slowly and thoroughly, or skim through it quickly and eagerly before commencing in-depth analysis. One student may want to begin by familiarizing himself with general, fundamental concepts, devoting much of his time to Scripture, while another will be impatient to get to the "meat and potatoes" — the Talmud— at once. Even Talmud study has its variations: One person may prefer learning sequentially, following the order in which R. Yehudah the Prince arranged the Mishnah, while another may start with a selected topic of immediate interest. Again, we ask whether Torah study should be limited to what the Sages have passed on to us or is there room for chidush (innovation)? And how should we divide our valuable—and limited—learning time between theory and the study of practical applications?

These are crucial issues for every serious Torah student, and there are no hard and fast rules governing them. But our Sages have provided us with numerous guidelines, enabling each student, in consultation with his mentor, to chart an appropriate course of study. Below, we survey the rich literature concerning these issues.

1

Introduction

Before examining the matter in detail, we survey the relevant parameters. There are two modes of study: extensive — to amass knowledge, and intensive — to deepen one's comprehension. It should be clear to the student, in a given learning situation, which mode he intends to adopt.

There are two aspects to intensive study:

1. Rigorous examination of the subject matter, deducing positive from negative and *vice versa*; drawing inferences from what was omitted and from ostensibly superfluous material. This is called **pilpul** (dialectics).
2. Discovering the reason behind the halakhah, which enables us to compare and contrast different cases. This is called **sevara** (theoretics).

Only through these methods can we determine halakhoth left unspecified by the Talmud. Thus R. Sheneor Zalman of L'ady[1] explains the Mishnah[2] "... at age twenty, to pursue..." as follows: "Applying pilpul to the Talmud" and "fathoming reasons and derivations — to deduce one matter from another and arrive at new halakhoth."

Yet it is possible to occupy oneself with the Torah, both intensively and extensively, and still remain ignorant of one's duties in this world. For both pilpul and sevara can be pursued out of academic interest, clarifying various approaches without reaching any decisive conclusion. Is such inquiry laudable in itself, or should studies be geared solely towards establishing halakhic conclusions?

Moreover, insofar as intensive learning is concerned, is it sufficient for us to fathom the basic intent of the classical commentaries, or should we also try to discover new interpretations?

Many people maintain definite opinions on these issues. Some may have developed these without sufficient deliberation. Below, we present a collection of guidelines culled from the writings of our Sages and generations of spiritual leaders.

2

Extensive Learning

1. Who is Preferable: The "Master of Sinai" or the "Uprooter of Mountains"

One major question facing the Torah student is: Which is more important, extensive or intensive study? In other words, should one cover much material without going into too much detail, or should one study in depth and apply dialectic principles, even at the expense of diminishing the extent of Torah learned?

The Talmud[1] expresses this dilemma through a parable. It likens the pilpul specialist to a rich banker, sought out constantly by the public, whose assets thereby constantly increase, whereas the knowledgeable elder, familiar with the halakhoth, corresponds to one who owns much produce. The Amoraim of Eretz Yisrael conclude that the "master of Sinai" (who learns extensively) is preferable to the "uprooter of mountains" (who learns intensively), "for everyone needs the wheat owner."[2] Rivash cites this observation as halakhah and R. Chaim Or Zarua' deplored pupils who "study intensively but not broadly."[3]

Shiyarey Keneseth HaGedolah[4] concludes that a scholar who resolves halakhic questions is called to the Torah before one who learns dialectically but does not decide such questions. This view is shared by Eliyah Rabbah and Peri Megadim,[5] the latter explicitly basing his conclusion on the Talmudic decision that the master of Sinai is preferred.

It has been argued that in our day, when the abundance and ready availability of books offer easy access to broad knowledge, this dictum is no longer applicable.[6] In contrast, it has also been pointed out that today's pilpul is unreliable and useless, so that extensive knowledge remains preferable to intensive analysis.[7]

All the above refers to Torah study in general. Concerning halakhic decision-making, however, broad knowledge is clearly essential. Indeed, in his introduction to Rav Pe'alim, "Ish Chay" emphasizes the importance of familiarity with the writings of even the very latest Acharonim.

2. Which Takes Precedence: Extensive Knowledge or Intensive Study?

Although the "master of Sinai" is preferable to the "uprooter of mountains," breadth of knowledge must obviously be supplemented by intensive study. Thus we are faced with another question in planning a study program: which should take precedence? Our Sages have provided a clear answer:[8] "Generally, one should learn the text of the Torah [first] and then meditate on it." They also teach:[9] "Who is [successful] in the battle of Torah? He who masters many Mishnayoth." Rashi explains:

'The battle of Torah'—Its teaching and reduction to essentials and principles. [This battle can] not [be waged] by a sharp-witted person who analyzes and dissects, nor by one who is a master of theory, but never learned many Mishnayoth or *Baraithoth*—for whence would he discover the truth? Rather, this refers to one who masters many Mishnayoth, so that, if he seeks a reason for one [Mishnah], he can deduce it from another; if two statements seem contradictory, he will understand that one is the opinion of another Tana who is known to differ.

This, perhaps, is what Rava meant when he said:[10] "The reward for extensive knowledge is sevara," implying that the ability to formulate sound theories derives from the extent of one's knowledge.

This restriction on pilpul without the support of extensive knowledge stems from the fact that such dialectic almost inevitably leads to error.[11] One should, therefore, not venture into pilpul unless he is properly armed with broad knowledge and close contact with Torah scholars. In other words, one should discourage students from pilpul until they have had their fill of Talmud. Thus *Orchoth Tzadikim* writes: "One should learn simply, even though he will forget and does not fully understand," for the Sages advise that one learn first and then theorize. Nowadays, he notes, everyone wants to learn only the Tosafoth, novellae, and novellae on the novellae, before understanding the basic Talmud. But how, *Orchoth Tzadikim* asks, could such a person succeed if he does the opposite of what the Sages recommend? *Yosif Ometz* explains[13] that there is no dispute about pilpul at all: both those who criticize pilpul and those who defend it agree that it is proper for those who are thoroughly prepared for it, but that for beginners, broad knowledge is more important. Maharshal[14] bemoans the fact that the scholars of his day covered too little of the Talmud, "spending day and night on one page, and the day after it is forgotten... They are guilty of diminishing the Torah and its students."

R. Sheneor Zalman of L'ady[15] also hinted at this distinction: "[After age fifteen,] one should spend five years on the Talmud, to learn the origin of and reasons for the halakhoth **in brief**... and after that, everyone should spend his time on Talmudic pilpul... according to his mental capabilities."

Similarly, R. Shemuel Mahlzahn[16] quotes the Gaon of Vilna: "First, he must get his fill of Scripture, Mishnah, and Talmud... with all the *Baraithoth*, and after that engage in pilpul with his companions... But if he reverses the order and first learns how to engage in pilpul without knowing even one Mishnah properly, he will lose even the little Torah he learned in his youth." R. Chaim Soloveichik of Brisk is quoted[17] as having said that, whoever indulges in pilpul before having memorized the entire Talmud together with Rashi's commentary, indulges in empty sophistry.

R. Menachem Mendel Kargau writes that one who must pursue a livelihood, rather than devoting his entire day to Torah study, must be especially wary of pilpul:[18] "Such a person should choose the proper course of study carefully, [selecting one] that will pursue the truth and lead quickly to the goal: to acquire broad knowledge of the Talmud, the poskim and the paths of halakhah."

R. Chaim of Zanz[19] defends the level of Torah study among the Chasidim of Poland as follows:

> They busy themselves day and night studying the simple halak-hoth, stated in the Talmud, Shulchan Arukh, and ethical works. It is not the custom of the Polish community to engage in pilpul, nor to innovate, except among its [spiritual] leaders or those rabbinical students ready to become such leaders. The others who study occupy themselves with Torah, Talmud, and poskim, to gain better understanding, and they toil over the novellae of Maharsha or the explanations of *Magen Avraham* in order to grasp them fully. It never enters their minds to innovate, for they know their own capabilities and they understand that it is not in their power to innovate properly and truly. This is not the

case in other communities, in which they engage in vain pilpul and anyone who knows just one Talmudic dictum immediately produces novellae.

3. Repetition

However, we must not cover a large amount of material without ensuring that it was really absorbed. Our Sages teach[20] that if one learns much at one time without going over it repeatedly, his learning will decrease; but if he studies with deliberation, it will increase. As a deeper understanding is not important for beginners, "deliberation" here refers to constant repetition of the material. Indeed, R. Yehoshua' ben Karchah[21] compares one who learns Torah without reviewing it to one who sows but does not reap. Such a person is very foolish, for he not only forgoes all profit from his work, but also loses whatever he expended in sowing. This statement of R. Yehoshua' is an interpretation of the verse "...for he has treated God's word with contempt; he will surely be cut off [from God's presence]." From this, Maharal[22] deduces that one who studies without reviewing belongs in this category, just as one who sows without reaping shows the ultimate comtempt for the seed.

Orchoth Tzadikim writes:[23] "In France, they labored hard and long, sitting in one place learning the entire Talmud and going over it time after time. The words of Torah were constantly on their lips, and they emulated the Rishonim. One should learn even if the material he learns is not clear to him, for we say that a person should first learn and then theorize. But all this is not what we do today."

R. Sheneor Zalman of L'ady[24] takes an extreme position on this point: "Anyone who forgets a single [Torah] matter for lack of adequate review is as if he has forfeited his life. Furthermore, he transgresses a commandment of the Torah."

4. Study Customs Established by Torah Leaders

Based on the words of the Sages, Torah leaders have established various practices to guide Torah study. Two such practices are discussed below:

1. Setting aside one period of time every day for extensive study and another for intensive study.
2. Learning an entire tractate with Rashi's commentary only, before learning it again intensively with the Tosafoth.
    Rash Sodilo writes in the name of R. Yitzchak di Leon:[25]

> Thus was the practice of the yeshivoth of Spain: Two days a week they would examine two short halakhoth to the fullest possible extent — for the time would not suffice to examine long halakhoth adequately. The rest of the week they would amass knowledge. This way, they succeeded in both intensive and extensive learning. This is good advice for students, to work on a short halakhah two days a week — because pilpul requires a teacher, for it is not written in books, but broad knowledge does not. It was the way of my teacher, R. Yitzchak di Leon, that on Monday and Thursday he taught pilpul in short halakhoth from other tractates, while the other four days he would learn a long halakhah with an abbreviated pilpul, and he would study Rashi's entire commentary simply, without pilpul or analysis. This method is of great use in acquiring both pilpul and broad knowledge.

Shelah reports similarly:[26] "Many consummate Torah scholars customarily study two tractates each day. From one they learn much, quickly, without analysis. From the other they learn a little, but with close analysis, pilpul, and dialectics." Similarly, Chida observes:[27] "The Rishonim had the custom of learning Talmud for a set period, merely to amass knowledge, while at other times they would devote themselves to pilpul and deep analysis of the halakhah." Also R. Ya'akov of Lissa [28] (author of *Nethivoth Mishpat*): "If you are privileged to learn [Torah], set aside a period each day for simple study, to cover not less than a folio of the Talmud, sequentially, besides a study period for intensive learning; this should be a hard and fast rule for you." Furthermore, R. Mordekhai M. Epstein[29] writes that as soon as one can learn Talmud with the Tosafoth on his own, he should set aside two study periods: one for intensive study of Talmud and the Tosafoth and another, lasting half the day, for reviewing Talmud without the Tosafoth, to acquire broad knowledge.

This custom of assigning separate times for straightforward learning and for pilpul apparently dates back to the Rishonim.[30] The author of *Beth Hillel,* citing his teacher,[31] reports that for one semester, the yeshivoth studied a tractate without the Tosafoth, but with much repetition, until they were fluent in it; the following semester, they studied the same tractate very intensively with the Tosafoth.

Many later authorities supported these practices. The "Chatham Sofer," instructed his son, the author of *Kethav Sofer,* to "learn much Talmud with Rashi, and whenever Rashi cites a second version, skip it."[32] Similar advice is given by R. Yitzchak Confanton:[33] "When you start studying [a *sugya*—(Talmudic theme)] you should first go over the entire subject, to understand its intent and obtain an overview of it; afterwards, go over it again to understand every detail."

3

Pilpul

1. The Advantages of Pilpul

Pilpul is essential for clarification of halakhah. The Talmud[1] likens the pilpul expert to one who is "rich in capital, rich in liquidity"; Rashi explains that he is constantly earning more, as he can add new halakhic clarifications through pilpul. Indeed, our Sages say[2] that through pilpul, 'Othniel ben Kenaz restored the halakhoth forgotten during the period of mourning for Moses. It therefore comes as no surprise that when we eventually face the Heavenly Tribunal, we will be asked not only "Did you set aside fixed periods for Torah study?" but also "Did you apply pilpul to wisdom?"[3] Shelah comments that "[by means of true pilpul] a person can discover many new explanations."

Furthermore, the pilpul of disciples is one of the forty-eight ways by which the Torah is acquired;[4] from here we can deduce that without it, the Torah cannot be fully acquired.[5] Thus, Maharil laments:[6] "And I live in the lands of the south, a desolate place, devoid of the pilpul of disciples, and new questions assail me constantly," implying that because of the lack of pilpul, he could not clarify the halakhah.

Yosif Ometz explains[7] that when the early authorities nevertheless decried the proliferation of pilpul, they only referred to students who should "learn extensively before they begin to theorize, so they will amass broad knowledge. But the scholars filled with [knowledge of] the Talmud and poskim obviously should delve constantly into the depths of halakhah, to understand and teach the essence of the fundamentals of the laws, which is impossible without pilpul."

We have already quoted R. Sheneor Zalman's description of the progression of study: Scripture, Mishnah, Talmud, pilpul, sevara, and innovation of halakhoth. Each of these stages is evidently a precondition for the next.

Apparently, in the Gaonic era, pilpul had fallen out of vogue, as is evident from the following responsum:[8] "Most people prefer final halakhoth and question the necessity for resolving discrepancies in, or applying pilpul to, the Talmud. They do not conduct themselves correctly, and it is forbidden to act thus." Similarly, a significant number of Acharonim[9] protested the learning of the final halakhah, such as *Mishneh Torah* or Shulchan Arukh, without first learning the relevant Talmudic passages. Maharsha writes,[10] "No one can fully comprehend a subject without a teacher who teaches him pilpul." R. Chaim,[11] Maharal's brother, disparages the rendering of decisions by anyone unfamiliar with pilpul. And Taz[12] goes even farther: "The Torah will never be properly absorbed unless one gives his life for it, i.e., involves himself in pilpul and [Talmudic] discussions of the Torah, as the Sages explained: 'You shall walk in my statutes...' meaning 'you should toil in the Torah.'"

Besides helping one understand the subject at hand, clarify what he has learned, and implant it in his mind, pilpul prepares one for better future application thereof; the more one practices, the greater his ability. This is the keenness the Sages lauded when they said:[13] "God grants success to two scholars who practice their keenness of mind in demonstrating the proper halakhah to each other." The Sages themselves employed it in teaching their disciples.[14] Shulchan Arukh rules[15] that a teacher should occasionally mislead his pupils to sharpen their wit. Among the later Acharonim, *Tif-ereth Yisrael*[16] says that "if one does not sift his learning with pilpul" the result will be like bread full of chaff. R. Yisrael of Salant confessed a strong personal penchant for pilpul and felt that indulging it was within the guidelines set by the Sages. He emphasized the importance of pilpul, even if it leads to a break with the truth.[17]

2. The Limitations of Pilpul

Although pilpul is a very useful tool in learning Torah, it must be used with great caution lest it do more harm than good (see Section 3). In fact, R. Elchanan Wasserman writes[18] that even outstanding students should spend no more than half an hour a day on it.

(1) Pilpul Alone Does Not Establish the Halakhah
Pilpul alone does not suffice for establishing the halakhah, even

when it is based on Talmud.[19] The Jerusalem Talmud states: "These matters are useful in understanding Talmudic discussion — but to apply them in practice is forbidden." Elsewhere, R. Yochanan is quoted: "Because we derive it from the halakhah, should we now act on it?"

The poskim continue in this vein. Rivash, for instance, remarks[20] that pilpul is not paramount in establishing the halakhah, since the Talmud declares[21] that Beth Shammai have no standing when they contradict Beth Hillel, even though Beth Shammai had the keener minds.[22] R. Ya'akov Weil writes[23] that when we apply pilpul, as they did in the era of the *ba'aley haTosafoth*, we become used to dealing with fine analyses and minute differences, which can "pull an elephant through the eye of a needle." But when it comes to making a practical decision, or to permitting that which seems forbidden, we should do so only on the strength of clear, tried, and true proof based on simple premises. Other authorities make this point as well.[24]

Paradoxically, the limitations of pilpul are best demonstrated by its ability to prove both sides of an argument. Thus the Talmud observes:[25] "It is well-known to God that there was no other like R. Meir in his generation. Then why did they not establish the halakhah according to his view? Because his companions could not fathom his final opinion — for he would prove the pure impure, and the impure pure."

Similarly, quoting Maharshal, R. Yonathan Eybeschutz[26] laments that in his generation, because of the proliferation of pilpul, not a single halakhic question can be answered clearly without some sort of doubt cast on it, and every proof is always refuted.

(2) Pilpul is Prone to Error

Apparently, the limitations of pilpul stem from its vulnerability to error. Consider the Talmudic adage:[27] "Errors occur in direct proportion to keenness." Rashi, too, comments:[28] "This is the erroneous interpretation of a keen-minded person who applies pilpul." And in the aforementioned responsum, Rivash writes: "We have seen several keen-minded scholars, able to apply pilpul, who 'pull an elephant through the eye of a needle,' raise a multitude of questions and heap fine distinctions on each jot and tittle, yet they cannot establish the halakhah. Instead, they permit the forbidden and forbid the permitted." In another context,[29] he warns: "Everyone capable of pilpul and keen of mind must be extremely careful... lest his pilpul and keenness lead him astray." *Sha-agath Aryeh* laments:[30]

I do not engage in pilpulim and fine distinctions like these, for this is not the way of the Torah — and neither did the early great rabbis take this path. [These are] only feeble subtleties invented by the later generations to sharpen students' minds after their hearts [i.e., reasoning powers] had been diminished and the gates of understanding closed. They accustomed themselves to this practice until it became second nature, and [now] they use it to derive laws and determine the halakhah. Thus, the honor of Torah has been lost and everyone who is wise in his own eyes — even though he does not know the Talmud — writes books of responsa and law. One should rend one's garments over this situation, just as one does when a Sefer Torah is burned, for the Torah shrouds herself in sackcloth for them. May the good Lord atone for them.

The "Chazon Ish" warned emphatically and repeatedly of this danger and enumerated many safeguards:[31]

Just as the Talmud's editors plumbed the depths of the halakhoth, they were very careful in their choice of words and in presenting these matters to future generations, which is the way of wisdom and wise men. It is inconceivable that they would leave a subject incomprehensible, and it is even more certain that they would not say one thing and mean another. If, occasionally, their words must be explained by deeper reasoning, this is the nature of wisdom and it can be understood by the researcher. But one must be extremely cautious in doing so, for if we read too much into their words, nothing will remain with us.

(3) Pilpul Should Not Be Recorded

Pilpul is not meant to be put on paper. Bach declares:[32] "If the *rosh yeshivah* was permitted to sharpen the minds of his students and fan the flames that burn in their hearts — just as Rabbah occasionally said something to sharpen Abayey's mind — it is only allowed in the yeshiva and only orally; likewise, [applications of this technique] must not be far-fetched, but close to the truth and readily discernible. However, [even] these matters must not be written in books, in ink — and certainly not printed." In a like manner, *Sha'agath Aryeh*, in his introduction, explains why he did not commit the result of his pilpulim to writing [see below, Section 3(2)].

3. Censured Forms of Pilpul

(1) Vain Pilpul

So far, we have only addressed the kind of pilpul meant to elicit the truth. But when pilpul becomes an end in itself, perhaps it is no longer *talmud Torah* at all. We proceed to examine the words of spiritual leaders throughout history on this subject.

Orchoth Tzadikim writes[33] that by investing so much effort in "pilpul chatter," students don't accomplish any learning of Torah or anything else.

The author of *Terumath HaDeshen* is quoted as follows:[34] "One cannot properly recite the blessing over Torah study on pilpul." Therefore, after his afternoon nap, he read a psalm after uttering this benediction. Maharal's[35] opposition to pilpul is also well-known: "They spend their days on matters that do not further their learning... Even in their youth they abandon the true Torah for such pursuits, for it is man's nature to desire these things, just as he prefers games and silliness... Better they should engage in a trade that requires skill, such as carpentry, etc., while claiming that it is their purpose to analyze Torah." Adds *Chawoth Ya-ir*:[36] "Let him not waste his time with such matters as vain casuistry and seeking minute differences, which, to our shame, have become common practice, [even though] we find no such thing among the early authorities... We should bewail the amount of time wasted on this."

Once matters came to such a state, that the Torah authorities had to issue a formal decree to prohibit such pilpul. *Zera' Beireikh* reports in the introduction: "The students did not seek the true interpretation and, instead, followed false sophistication. Therefore the sages of the generation met in session and issued decrees against this [form of study] and condemned it."

On going to Eretz Yisrael, R. Ze'ira tried to forget the Torah knowledge he had acquired in Babylon. In an effort to explain this, Maharsha writes:[37] "Perhaps the Babylonian Torah scholars engaged in pilpul much like our generation; anyone who can outdo the other in spurious pilpul is considered praiseworthy. And each one tries to refute the arguments of the other... Thus, they never reach any conclusion regarding the proper halakhah... Such pilpul only leads a person away from the truth."

Similarly, R. Ya'akov of Lissa comments:[38] "The purpose of your learning should be to find the halakhah, not the pilpul, which, to our disgrace, is so prevalent in this generation." R. Samson Raphael Hirsch laments:[39] "A new spirit is abroad: that of totally abstract thought, without any connection to the world. They do not learn to fulfill their purpose in life, to understand the world and the commandments. Research is made into an end in itself, rather than a means to an end." He especially warned not to succumb to the temptation to compete with one's fellow students,[40] which leads one into the trap of pilpul. Thus he writes:[41] "You should learn by the light of truth and in the warmth and loftiness of life. Do not worry about what others say; do not fret if, in the straightforwardness of your spirit, you cannot shine in the pilpulim of the great analytic minds, whose purpose is neither truth nor practice; do not despair if you cannot excel in the arts that, to you, are only auxiliary techniques."

The "Chazon Ish"[42] also urges: "Please do not endeavor to imitate the casuists... [learn] to hate the pilpulim of the hasty ones (whose foundation is carelessness, superficiality, and indolence); rather, direct all your energy toward a proper understanding of the subject, using healthy logic and straightforward intellect to comprehend the true Torah."

(2) False Pilpul

When pilpul departs not only from the halakhah but also from the truth, as when the speaker knows he is saying things that are false, it is even worse than vain pilpul. Our early teachers denounced the evils of this kind of obfuscation:

R. Yehudah HeChasid[43] writes: "Even when the evil-doers have the sharper minds, let the righteous sit in judgment... Do not think that the evil-doer will render a just verdict simply because he has the sharper mind. On the contrary, he will pervert it all the more." A pilpulist who makes false propositions appear true is comparable, according to *Orchoth Tzadikim*,[44] to a counterfeiter who makes copper look so much like gold that only an expert, with great difficulty, can discover the truth. *Yosif Ometz* quotes his words, bemoaning the fact that matters are even worse in his days. Maharik states[45] that anyone who conveys the simple halakhah truthfully and straightforwardly deserves the respect accorded to one's teacher. But whoever instructs students in intricate casuistry, irrespective of its veracity, is no teacher at all. This has been codified by Rema as halakhah in the Shulchan Arukh.[46]

Similarly, *Levush*[47] notes that:

> One need honor his teacher only if he set him on the path of truth and straightforwardness according to the halakhah, which excludes most of the learning of our times. Nowadays, the teacher does not intend to study the truth with the student, nor do students want to arrive at the truth. The whole intent of both teacher and student is to learn pilpul, which they call *chilukim*. Such a teacher is not called "his teacher," nor is the student called "his student," for this will not bring him closer to everlasting life. Would that they refrained from this.

Maharal,[48] too, bewailed the customary use of pilpul for false purposes:

> Today no scholarship, rule, or decision is possible without a search. The root of this great corruption is the falsehood at the outset, which causes crookedness in the end. They engage in inane pilpul about the halakhah, knowing that their talk is untrue, and they read into the Torah things that are not there, claiming that they are sharpening their minds. God forbid that such things should happen among the Jewish People, that one should sharpen his mind with lies and waste his time with deceit, for the Torah is the teaching of truth... If this idiotic false pilpul were at all comparable to true pilpul, one could say that, after all, this false pilpul might eventually lead to the true one; but this is not so... It is better for one to learn carpentry or some other trade, or a game which sharpens the mind or involves strategy... [than] reading things into the Torah which are not there, conceiving of falsehood and giving birth to lies. Because if one accustoms himself to lies... all his actions will follow his falsehoods, and he will remain false in deed... whereas a love of straightness, which means distancing oneself from lies, is one of the forty-eight prerequisites to the acquisition of the Torah, as enumerated by the Sages.

Likewise, Shelah castigated pilpulists unconcerned with the truth:[49] "The entire subject of *chilukim* should be null and void. Would that it did not exist. Even if the expounder claims to be explaining the simple meaning, and discourses on many truths, just one untruth renders everything else unfit for consumption. And who can assess the gravity of perverting the word of God, the Torah of Truth?"

In a similar vein, *Sha-agath Aryeh* contains no pilpul because, as the author explains in his introduction, "the wind will scatter it all, and it is nothing but vanity and striving after wind. And even though I have been as careful as I could to align the basis of my pilpul with the truth of the Torah, it is impossible to avoid untruth."

R. Shelomoh Efrayim Luntschitz[50] writes: "... and when he advances in years and deserves to sit among the wise, the tenor of his teaching will be casuistry and inane pilpul, which they call *chiluk*. Be appalled, Heavens, at this... Is there anything in the world as ugly as one who deceives himself and others?"

R. Moshe Shim'on Bacharach[51] adds: "Lately, some upstarts have come along, and for the past century or so they have not focused on learning the Torah of truth. Rather, their main endeavor and pursuit is to indulge in keenness, and some of them have said false *chilukim*, obfuscating the halakhah."

Indeed, *Peri Chadash* denounced the *Kneseth HaGedolah* for something he wrote by way of pilpul:[52] "The most recent authors of our time tend to equate things that differ from one another and to differentiate things that are equal, all through *chilukim*, be they true or not." The Gaon of Vilna writes:[53] "Whoever propounds beautiful explanations that are not in accord with the truth of the Torah will be severely punished." He advises:[54] "Don't walk along crooked paths that lead off the beaten track, with assumptions, farfetched innovations, and explanations far removed from the simple ones. Any interpretation that is close to the simple one is also close to the truth."

(3) False Pilpul to Sharpen the Mind

Certain proponents of pilpul argued that their purpose was to sharpen their minds, as the Sages did. But according to the authorities we have quoted, this argument is not strong enough to justify falsehoods.

Maharal[55] characterizes this method of pilpul as utter nonsense, designed to leave its practitioner bereft of Torah. Shelah[56] writes along the same lines: "There is a group of deranged people who say that the *chiluk* sharpens the mind; whoever says this is fit to be excommunicated... True pilpul increases keenness... but only true pilpul, which enables a person to work wonders in establishing each halakhah."

R. S.E. Luntschitz[57] accuses these proponents of preventing the multitude from studying Torah:

> We have seen what mischief this creates, especially among young men; for anyone with no reputation for this vapidity is considered worthless and perforce stops learning. But if studies were to concentrate on Scripture, Talmud, and poskim, he, too, would be counted. The yeshiva scholars do this for their own aggrandizement... In any case, I hope to God that my own pilpul is close to the simple explanation and to the truth, and one need not distance oneself from such pilpul to such an extent, for it may serve some purpose. Nevertheless, it is preferable not to teach it at all, because everyone claims that his is true—therefore, it is best to abolish it altogether.

The Talmud makes it clear that the Sages did not engage in false or vain pilpul at all; they merely tested their students with erroneous statements, presumably correcting the error immediately if it was not detected. Says Shulchan Arukh:[58] "A teacher should mislead his students, with questions and actions, to increase their keenness and determine whether they remember what they learned." Apparently, this practice is considered neither false nor vain pilpul if the error is immediately revealed.

(4) The Causes Underlying Improper Pilpul

Generations of Torah authorities have sought to explain the proliferation of pilpul irrelevant to the halakhah. Evidently, the main cause is a desire for honor. Although a generation that considers Torah knowledge the highest honor seems praiseworthy, the Prophets proclaimed otherwise:[59] "Let not the wise man glory in his wisdom..." "It is the fear of God that is his treasure." One must be extremely careful lest his precious respect for the Torah cause him to deviate from its path. And woe to him whose defender becomes his prosecutor!

R. Yehudah HeChasid[60] taught that one who wishes to support scholars should select those who fear God and study in order to fulfill the mitzvoth — not those who expound difficulties only to display their keen minds. Many other great authorities concurred that the learning of their days was more concerned with agility than with establishing the halakhah.

Shelah writes:[61] "I have heard the vain remarks by the scholars of this generation, stating that 'were it not for the *chiluk*, how would [I be] outstanding? A great many would come to establish yeshivoth.' One must rend one's garments on hearing such words — to increase one's own glory at the expense of the honor of Heaven!"

Maharal[62] evidently sought to alleviate the situation somewhat by stressing the study of Mishnah, but he concludes: "The teaching of the Mishnah is always thwarted by people who sin and would have others do likewise and whose only motivation is arrogance." He is especially critical of those who would lead schoolchildren astray: "And if one would ask the boy's father to teach his son the halakhah before teaching him the Tosafoth, it would be like asking him not to teach him at all, for the father is only interested in prestige... and anyone who supports this attitude, which is a painful thorn and a ruinous sting in the side of the Torah of Moses, is clearly counted among those who read things into the Torah which are not there, and he will not be among those who are remembered in the next world." R. S.E. Luntschitz[63] also condemns those who perpetuate pilpul in the education of their children for their own aggrandizement, therefore lowering the Torah by convincing others that pilpul is its quintessence.

The author of *Sefer Keytzad Seder HaMishnah*,[64] himself a schoolteacher, sums up by saying that we must observe tradition and not follow those who in their arrogance would teach casuistry to children unequipped for it, in the hope that they will then study everything on their own.

On the other hand, R. Yisrael of Salant defends pilpul, even if it is false.[65]

4

Sevara

New circumstances arise constantly, raising new halakhic questions. To these we must respond on the basis of earlier decisions. However, unless we understand the foundations of the earlier decisions, we cannot know which of these is analogous to our own situation.[1] Therefore it is not enough to analyze the discussion and the final decision; pilpul must be followed by sevara — discovering the underlying reason.

When God presented us with the Torah, He instructed us to seek such clarification:[2] "'And these are the ordinances that you shall set before them' — God said to Moses, 'Do not think that you will repeat the chapter and the halakhah for them two or three times, until they know it fluently, without troubling to explain the reasons for the [law] and its interpretation.' Hence the wording 'set before them' — like a table set for a meal." It is no wonder, as R. Chaim of Volozhin wrote to his grandson, that "all the greatest Rishonim and Acharonim were praised only for their straight sevara — the more straight the sevara, the greater the man... The important thing is to cling to a straightforward approach, while distancing yourself from that which is not straightforward in the light of Torah truth."[3]

Ramban[4] notes that it is impossible to clarify a subject by pilpul alone, without reference to a reasonable approach, for Talmud study is not like a mathematical proof: "Don't think that I consider all my arguments against R. Zerachyah HaLevi totally rigorous and compelling... for everyone who studies Talmud knows that among its commentators there is no such thing as absolute proof... For in this discipline there is no such clear proof as there is in geometry or in arithmetic."

Nevertheless, if broad learning and deep pilpul did not precede reasoning, it would never be dependable, because it would emanate not from the words of the Sages, but from a person himself, resulting in what is known unflatteringly as "gut reasoning." Toiling in Torah — that is, pilpul[5]—therefore requires great devotion and diligence, lest indolence diminish pilpul and increase sevara. This phenomenon is what led R. Avraham Bornstein of Sochaczov to write:[6] "It has come to my attention that nowadays young students are preoccupied with sevara and not with the simple explanation and clarification of the issues—which are also essential in halakhah." Similarly, the "Chazon Ish"[7] counsels: "One must be careful not to spend too much time expanding on sevara; rather, spend this time on the Talmud, investigating the simple explanation and clarifying its conclusions."

Pilpul is associated with wisdom and sevara with insight, i.e., the ability to infer one matter from another and contrast different things.[8] R. Samson Raphael Hirsch[9] comments that the Hebrew word for wisdom (*chokhmah*) is used in the active form (*kal*—chakham) because, like pilpul, it requires much effort and care, lest we err. In contrast, the Hebrew word for insight (*binah*) is in the passive form (*nif'al*—navon) because it demands that a matter be crystal-clear and nearly self-evident.

5

Arriving at a Halakhic Decision

When studying the Torah, our basic intent must be to fulfill its commandments—we should study "in order to do." This intent should shape our method of learning. Therefore, in all our studies we must keep in mind that our purpose is to arrive at a clear final decision and that all the tools employed in this endeavor—pilpul, sevara, application of extensive knowledge—are merely means to this end. If we do not attempt to reach a decision, when applicable, we show that our study is not for the sake of fulfilling the commandments. Thus the Sages teach[1] that "it is not study that is the main object, but deed," on which R. 'Ovadiah of Bartinoro comments: "The main reward is only for the deed."

The Talmud[2] interprets the verse "When you walk, it will lead you..." by citing the parable of a person traveling in the dark of night, fearing all manner of imminent dangers. When he reaches a crossroads [and finds the proper highway], he is saved from all of them. Mar Zutra explains that "this refers to a Torah scholar who arrives at a correct halakhic decision," which is the ultimate objective. Furthermore, the Sages expound:[3] "'And you shall inculcate them in your sons'—If someone asks you something, don't stammer; answer him immediately." This again refers to the required clarity of the conclusion. Hence R. Sheneor Zalman deduces:[4] "His learning should be so well-ordered, and he should know it so fluently, that if anyone asks him about any matter he has studied, he should be able to answer, immediately and without stammering, [indicating] whether something is forbidden or permitted."

This is consistent with the conclusion[5] that study is great "because it leads to deed,"—i.e., studying is great when it leads to a clear decision. Similarly, *Chawoth Ya-ir* comments: "The fruit of all learning is action, even though Torah study is itself greater than any other action."[6] Thus, when one's inability to resolve difficulties forces him to take a stringent position on both sides of a question, the Sages call him "the fool who walks in darkness."[7] Says Rabbeinu Chananel:[8] "Anyone who occupies himself with the Torah and fails to devote himself to mitzvoth, or [at least] to reaching a clear decision, is as if he lacks even Torah."

R. Yehudah HeChasid[9] points out that Scripture refers to man's fulfilling the commandments in the superlative, while it omits this superlative when it talks of his studies. He concludes that the basic purpose must be study *lishmah*, with all the clarification necessary to fulfill the commandments properly. Moreover, he states, better to determine a few halakhoth clearly than to raise and answer numerous theoretical questions.

Rabbeinu Yonah[10] writes that it is proper for one to spend days and even years resolving a small point so he can establish the truth and act accordingly. Semak of Zurich[11] maintains that it is not enough for a person to learn one or two halakhoth [i.e. Talmudic passages] every day unless he is also familiar with all the relevant conclusions. He adds that many people ignore this requirement; furthermore, they frequently forget what they have learned. Therefore, he recommends that everyone pay special attention to works that render final decisions, such as those of Rambam. Otherwise, one may easily make the wrong decision and even mislead others as well. In his ethical testament, R. Ya'akov *Ba'al HaTurim* also warns against the prolonged study of academic refinements rather than halakhic conclusions in depth.

Rivash contends[12] that even decision-makers need not be familiar with all the metamorphoses of the halakhah, but only with the final outcomes. Meiri explains[13] that the purpose of the Torah is to teach us to perform the commandments properly; consequently, the entire value and glory of Torah study lies in its leading to this performance. And Rema writes[14] that a "teacher" is one who teaches decisions and sets his pupils on a straightforward path of learning, and that this title, and the privileges that come with it, do not apply to one who teaches pilpul and *chilukim*, as was common in his time. Maharal[15] also sharply criticized those who neglected to teach the final decision.

Therefore, we must not abandon the study of the conclusions reached by the great authorities of old. According to R. Yosef ibn Migash, this learning qualifies one to render decisions better than Talmud study itself. Even one who has never learned halakhah [i.e., Talmud] with a teacher, only Gaonic responsa, is better equipped than "many of those who, in our days present themselves as decisors... Today no one is capable of studying the Talmud well enough to make decisions based upon it."[16]

According to R. Sheneor Zalman of L'ady, the purpose of Mishnaic study is to learn final decisions. Nevertheless, as he explains in his Shulchan Arukh,[17] "one-third [of one's time should be devoted] to Talmud, which presents the reasons for the halakhoth in the Mishnayoth, *Baraithoth* and pronouncements of the Amoraim. In our day, this includes the works of the early poskim, which outline the reasons for the final outcomes... For if one does not know the reasons for the halakhoth, he cannot understand the halakhoth themselves." Thus, even the Talmud is learned to clarify the halakhah.

Magen Avraham teaches[18] that the third Sabbath meal may be forgone for a discourse on "the laws and teachings of the Torah, to fill [people's] hearts with reverence for God, which is not usually [true of the discourses] in our day." Again, the purpose of learning is to acquire knowledge of the commandments. The Gaon of Vilna writes:[19] "Better to learn a little, review it constantly, and know it clearly, than to amass much [information] without knowing the law." Furthermore,[20] "This is what it means to toil in the Torah: to extract the clear halakhah." His disciple, R. Chaim of Volozhin, calls this extraction "the entire fruit of study,"[21] implying that learning without reaching a conclusion is like working the soil and planting trees without reaping the fruits.

We have already quoted R. Ya'akov of Lissa's view that the purpose of study must be to establish the halakhah, not to engage in pilpul. R. Mendel Kargau asserts[22] that a full-time student can afford to indulge in some pilpul, but one who has limited study time must choose a curriculum designed to impart broad knowledge of Talmud, poskim, and halakhic decisions. R. Samson Raphael Hirsch writes:[23] "Guide him toward the sources of Torah wisdom—Mishnah and Talmud. But his ultimate goal should always be life and the knowledge of the obligations and the life of Israel. Only then will his Torah life become strong and shining."

In the introduction to *Mirkeveth HaMishneh*, the author describes three kinds of students: The first studies only to gain knowledge of the text, without any analysis, while the second concentrates only on analysis, finding imaginary differences and neglecting the truth. Such students "do not know the ins and outs of the Talmud or the scholars... as they lack a historical perspective." He reserves his praise for the third type of student, who "deals with the subject matter to arrive at the halakhah... Cling to this [method] and do not be diverted from it."

R. Yisrael of Salant concurs:[24] "The highest level of Torah study is the ability to render true, proper decisions in Israel, based on the Talmud and the poskim, without having to search through the decisions of the later Acharonim."

In fact, the "Chafetz Chayim"[25] authored works specifically to help people draw conclusions from their Talmud studies "to know the essence of the halakhah that derives from the discussion—which is the goal of Torah study."

6

Chidush (Innovation)

The Oral Torah, in its entirety, was handed down from Mount Sinai, but in unfinished form,[1] leaving room for new interpretations and applications in its halakhic and agadic parts alike.

Innovation in agadah, says Rashbam[2] is an ongoing process. Regarding his grandfather Rashi, he wrote: "He admitted to me that had he had the time, he would have composed other commentaries according to the new interpretations that arise daily." In his introduction to *Horeb*, R. Samson Raphael Hirsch describes agadah as emanating from "the spiritual light within each individual. [Halakhah] was sealed with the completion of the Talmud. The domain of agadah, however, is free and accessible to enlargement by all generations."

However, halakhah too allows for *chidush* (innovation) in various ways; but these must be carefully defined and strictly limited and therefore require the highest level of scholarship. Only a scholar with a thorough grasp of the full Oral Torah is qualified for this.

1. When a new problem arises, we must arrive at a decision by drawing analogies, comparing the case under study to previous, similar cases in which the decisions are known. (During the period of the Tanaim and Amoraim, such decisions were based on reasoning and standard principles for interpretation of Scripture.[3])
2. While researching the basis of a given halakhah, we may occasionally discover a novel explanation, leading to a new halakhic decision on a question that had previously been undecided.
3. Sometimes, in studying the Talmud, new interpretations of the text present themselves, permitting the derivation of new halakhic decisions, as above.

The Midrash states[4] that whoever innovates a concept is considered to have been advised by God Himself: "Build me an edifice," and "his reward is great."

Chidush is also praised by Rishonim like R. Yehudah HeChasid,[5] who declares: "Anyone to whom God reveals a [novel] word [of Torah] and does not write it down—robs Him Who revealed it to him." Elsewhere, he writes: "Any scholar who occupies himself with the Torah and innovates, makes it his own." In Shevet HaMussar[6] we read: "One should find new interpretations of the Torah... for just as a person is required to procreate his kind, he must procreate in Torah... and let his chidush... not appear insignificant to him. Even if it is a minor chidush, let him not treat it contemptuously; rather, let him expand on it and consider it important, for this will cause him to toil further in order to innovate more, until he innovates great and weighty matters."

Later authorities echo these sentiments. For example, R. Sheneor Zalman of L'ady explains[7] that after age twenty, "all one's days... [should be spent] understanding matters by analogy, to innovate halakhoth and derivations from the poskim, regarding which it is said:[8] '... at age forty—creative insight (binah).'" Similar views are expressed by later authorities as well.[9]

To what extent is this kind of innovation laudable and to what extent is it dangerous? R. Eli'ezer[10] never said anything he had not heard from his teacher, even when practical halakhah was sought. He felt[11] that by teaching conclusions one has not learned from his teacher, one causes the Divine Presence to depart from Israel.[12] He was hailed[13] as "a well-calked cistern, from which not a drop is lost."

In contrast, R. El'azar ben 'Arakh was "an ever-increasing wellspring," producing new ideas all the time. There is a difference of opinion in the Mishnah as to which of these Sages was the most important in his generation.[14] In view of all the above evidence for the importance of innovation, why was R. Eli'ezer proud of his fidelity to his teacher, to the point of refusing to innovate at all? Perhaps he feared he might misinterpret the Torah, a transgression described as follows:[15] "Even though he [the transgressor] has Torah and good deeds to his credit, he will not have a share in the next world."

Consequently, some Acharonim discourage new interpretations. The "Chatham Sofer" writes[16] that one should not modify accepted halakhoth based on new theories, even to make them more stringent, for "Chadash asur min haTorah—The new is forbidden by the Torah." His

son, R. Avraham Shemuel Sofer (*Kethav Sofer*),[17] complaining about
the situation in his day, notes that responsa generally do not "respond"
at all—they only offer new theories, which erode the well-established
practices of the Rishonim. Furthermore, he adds, if one teaches the
simple halakhah—answering a question as the Rishonim did—he is
derided for not being innovative. Thus, the modern poskim have buried
the old interpretations under the avalanche of their own hypotheses
—whereas the pride of the early generations was their loyalty to their
teachers.

Similarly, the later authorities consider it "difficult to accept *chilukim* that are not mentioned in the Talmud or by the early poskim."[18] As
one of them indicates:[19] "The stature attained by one who succeeds in
presenting a new interpretation of the Torah is cited by the *Zohar* in
several places... but pay close attention to [the terrible things] the
Zohar says about those who derive false interpretations, based on vain
pilpul."

Rabbi S.R. Hirsch found[20] in Hebrew grammar an indication of the
caution required in attempting innovation by means of *binah* [insight,
deducing one matter from another]. He points out that most people
consider *chokhmah* [wisdom and knowledge] a passive matter but consider themselves active when their insight enables them to arrive at new
conclusions. In Hebrew, however, the verb for knowledge (*chakhamti*) is
used in the active voice, while the verb for innovative thinking (*navonti*)
is in the passive voice. He explains that Hebrew thereby implies that
proper knowledge requires much effort; without this, it will be clearly
misleading. On the other hand, innovation must be based on such
thorough knowledge, that the conclusion becomes self-evident and we
are essentially passive in arriving at it. He concludes: Only the strictest
self-discipline enables one to avoid the above pitfalls. Even more than
wisdom depends on insight, insight depends on wisdom. Thus, in general, Scripture lists wisdom before insight.

Perhaps today, the originality of the Talmud student must express
itself in clarifying the material handed down to us by the earlier authorities. Thus, according to *Kethav Sofer*,[21] the purpose of all our endeavors
is to expound the words of the Rishonim. Similarly, R. Chaim of
Volozhin[22] believes that in view of all the effort required in discovering
the true meaning of the Talmud, he who does so can be considered an
innovator. Said the "Chazon Ish"[23] of himself: "By nature, I shrink
from innovation, for the simple explanation is always the truth."

7

Curricula Recommended by Torah Authorities

One's choice of texts and commentaries fundamentally shapes his Torah study. Therefore, one should heed the recommendations of Torah authorities concerning this choice. These will not only guide the course of study but also aid in defining one's goal in learning.

1. Grammar

Authorities throughout the ages agree that grammar is basic to understanding the Torah, but also that one need not study it too deeply. In the words of R. Avraham ibn 'Ezra:[1] "It is beneficial for the intelligent person to acquire [knowledge] of this discipline, but not to spend all his time on it." *Chawoth Ya-ir* shares this view.[2] R. Pripot Duran (Ha-Afudi)[3] speaks at length about the importance of learning grammar. Similarly, R. Shabthai Sofer writes[4] that everyone is obligated to study it, adducing proof from Torah, logic, Midrash, Mishnah, *Targum, Sefer HaYetzirah*, and *Zohar*, among other sources. Furthermore, in their approbationary letters to the author of *Eim HaYeled*, both Maharal and *Levush* address the importance of a knowledge of grammar.

Shelah[5] considers it advisable to learn grammar while one is young, so that it will be remembered. R. Ya'akov Emden[6] concurs, adding that this knowledge "is a great necessity, for even if one has learned the entire Torah [without grammar], he cannot guard against occasional misinterpretation, which can lead, God forbid, to sacrilege... [Grammar] is a tool that serves the entire body of our holy Torah. Therefore its study takes priority in the order of learning. Nevertheless, it is beneficial only when limited in extent — too much would waste time without compensatory benefit."

The Gaon of Vilna, as quoted by his sons,[7] teaches in a similar vein: "He cautioned... to first become well-versed in the twenty-four books [of Scripture], with their vocalization and cantillation... including the study of grammar." And R. Menachem Mendel Kargau declares:[8] "It is unseemly for a person of stature to be devoid of any knowledge of science, especially the science of grammar, lest he speak faultily."

2. Scripture

The importance of Scripture (as well as Mishnah), as a prerequisite for the study of Talmud, is discussed in the next chapter. Here, we limit ourselves to quoting several texts which stress its importance and appropriate study methods.

R. Avraham Horowitz, brother of the Shelah,[9] states:

Certainly, study of the Bible is a primary and basic requirement for any aspiring *ben Torah*. Furthermore, how can we possibly justify ourselves before God if we reject His pride, the Holy Torah, which issued first from His mouth?

In my opinion, this obligation is also included in the verse "and you shall heed his voice," which our Sages interpreted as the voice of the Prophets... It makes no difference whether the Prophets are alive and we heed their voice or whether it is [only] their words that are alive and present... If you do not learn them, know them, and become well-versed in them, how can you heed their voice and fulfill them? And even for one whose only occupation is Torah study—no study in the world is entirely comparable to that of the Bible, that is, to Torah, Prophets, and *Kethuvim*, from start to finish, and one should become well-versed in them. Therefore, there is no valid objection or excuse by which a person can free himself from this obligation...

They say that a person should divide his time into three equal parts: one-third of the day for Scripture, one-third for Mishnah and one-third for Talmud. Rabbeinu Tam comments that one who has sated himself with Scripture and is thoroughly versed in the twenty-four sacred books... need not devote one-third of the day to them, for the Babylonian Talmud is permeated with them. But to neglect Scripture to the point where one is not completely familiar with the twenty-four bridal adornments [books of the *Tanakh*] — Heaven forfend... [is] to cast off the yoke of the Torah!

R. Pinchas of Polotzk, a disciple of the Gaon of Vilna, writes:[10]

The method of studying Scripture should be thus: study one [book] of the Prophets with Rashi's commentary. Then, if you have a good memory, go over it a few times without Rashi, until you are fluent in it. Thereafter, if you occasionally review it again with Rashi's commentary, don't fix the derivations and Midrashim that Rashi quotes... too firmly in your memory. The basic purpose is to analyze the parts necessary for the understanding of the simple text — this is what you should fix in your memory. Remember that you want to learn the verses, not the Midrashim. And if you wish to learn the Midrashim, do so separately — for what similarity is there between Midrash and the simple verse? Our people have erred, and because of the Midrashim they do not know the verses... If you ask someone about a verse, he will probably tell you the Midrash, but he will not know or understand the plain interpretation. Neither will he know which Prophet said it, nor to whom, nor under what circumstances, nor on which exile or for which consolation — all because the derivations confuse his mind and make him neglect the plain meaning.

R. Chaim of Volozhin advised[11] that Scripture be studied only with the simple standard commentaries, lest students be lured into explanations that might do more harm than good.

Netziv learned the weekly Torah portion with his students in the yeshiva of Volozhin every day.[12]

3. Mishnah

Maharal cites[13] the words of R. Nathan, who states that whoever neglects the Mishnah "has treated God's word with contempt." Maharal explains that the Talmud's current popularity is rooted in natural

curiosity and not in a desire to become acquainted with the commandments themselves, as taught by the Mishnah, which is God's word in a
more original form. *Chawoth Ya-ir*[14] writes that even when a boy is ready
for Talmud, his father should make sure he learns a chapter of Mishnayoth every day. This will prove highly beneficial in his later learning,
"especially nowadays," he continues, "when we have the advantage of
the commentary of R. 'Ovadiah of Bartinoro, which is like the Talmud
itself." Here, he merely echoes the words of Shelah:[15]

> Regarding the question of which should be given priority in
> apportioning one's time—Mishnah or Talmud—the Talmud
> says:[16] "In general, run towards the Mishnah more than the
> Talmud"... especially nowadays, when we have the benefit of
> the commentaries of Rambam and R. 'Ovadiah of Bartinoro,
> who explain the Mishnah according to the outcome of the
> [discussion in the] Talmud, and state the halakhoth, making the
> [study of] Mishnah of great value... Therefore, most of one's
> effort should go into Mishnah, studying and repeating it count-
> less times, without interruption.

Additionally, R. Chaim of Volozhin[17] considers the study of Mishnah especially suited for encouraging continual learning and the understanding of the basic meaning of Torah text. He suggests that everyone
learn eighteen chapters each day, reviewing them two or three times
until he knows them by heart. He adds that it is better to be thoroughly
familiar with one tractate than superficially acquainted with many.

4. Talmud and Halakhah

After learning Mishnah, one continues with Talmud. As the Sages
say:[18] "If one studies Scripture [primarily], it is of limited value; if he
studies Mishnah, it is of some value and is rewarded; but if he studies
Talmud, there is nothing more valuable." Shulchan Arukh declares:[19]

> A person must divide his study into three periods: one-third for
> Scripture... one-third for Mishnah... and one-third for Tal-
> mud... but only when he is beginning his studies. As he grows
> in Torah... he should set aside only certain times for the study

of the Written and the Oral Torah, lest he forget part of the laws
of the Torah. But he should devote all [the remainder of] his
time to studying Talmud, to whatever extent he is capable.
[Gloss by Rema:] Some say that by studying the Babylonian
Talmud—which comprises all three areas—one has fulfilled
his entire obligation.

Wawey Ha'Amudim writes: "[Learning] Talmud with Rashi and
Tosafoth is a [daily(?)] obligation like putting on *tefillin*."

Indeed, if one is unfamiliar with the Talmud, he cannot apply the
words of the poskim in rendering his own decisions. As Rosh declared:[20]
"Those who base their decisions on Rambam and are not conversant
with the Talmud, so that they do not know how Rambam reached his
conclusions—are likely to err... They think they understand, but they
do not; for if one is not well-versed in the Talmud, he cannot grasp a
subject correctly." Meiri[21] bewails this phenomenon at length and
Rivash[22] classifies those who decide halakhoth in this manner among
"those who render decisions frivolously." Maharal[23] goes even further,
branding them "destroyers of the world." He explains that if one has not
plumbed the reasons behind a Mishnah, his study cannot be considered
Torah. Since the world is based on Torah, such a person has crippled the
basis of the world:

> [Even worse are] those who base themselves on the codifiers
> alone, who only wrote their works for practical application in
> specific instances... It is much more appropriate to base one's
> decisions on the Talmud. For even though he may then miss the
> true path, failing to clarify the law properly... [this is not so
> bad] because a scholar can only follow the dictates of his own
> intelligence in interpreting the Talmud. If he is misled by his
> understanding and scholarship, he is nevertheless more beloved
> by God... than one who bases his conclusions on another's
> work without understanding the background.

This idea is repeated by Maharsha[24] and many other authorities,[25]
one of whom states: "People say that reading decisions without the
necessary Talmudic background is like eating fish without spices; I,
however, say that it is like eating spices without fish."

Which commentators and codifiers should be studied in conjunction
with the Talmud?

(1) Rashi

Rashi reigns supreme among Talmudic commentators. The Gaon of Vilna recommended[26] that students pay close attention to his words. The "Chatham Sofer" advised his son[27] to learn much Talmud with the commentary of Rashi. Interestingly, he advises him to ignore even Rashi's own occasional alternative explanations, until he reviews the whole subject again in greater detail.

(2) Alfasi, Rambam, and Rosh

Second to Rashi, according to Torah leaders throughout the generations, are the Talmudic poskim: Alfasi ("Rif"), Rambam, Rosh, *Tur* and others. Maharal laments that young men who have not yet mastered the Oral Torah[28] engross themselves in pilpul, "All because the Tosafoth are printed next to the text of the Talmud; had the decisions of Rosh been printed [there]... everyone would study to clarify halakhah."

Shelah[29] also urges everyone to study both the Talmud and the halakhic summaries, such as Alfasi, as well as Rambam and his commentators. This will clarify much that seems obscure in the words of Rashi or even the Tosafoth. His son, R. Sheftel, author of *Wawey Ha'Amudim*, writes in his ethical testament:[30] "I need not urge you to study Alfasi and the *Turim*, since you already know [their importance] for anyone who wishes to promulgate the Torah in Israel... Study once with *Tur* and *Beth Yosef* and once with Rif and *Mordekhai*.

Here is how Chawoth Ya-ir described his own training:[31]

[My father] studied with me and my comrades, outstanding students, Alfasi with some of his novellae, [which] helps one attain the objective better than any other study. This was also the way of the great early teachers... and it succeeded; for one will be able to complete [the study of Alfasi] easily in three years. And if he absorbs it and becomes well-versed in it, the gates of wisdom to all sections of the *Turim* will open up before him, after he also learns Rosh, who is to Alfasi as an abridged version of the Tosafoth is to the Talmud... No study is as proper and fitting as the study of Rosh.

Similar sentiments are expressed by *Yosif Ometz*:[32] "No study in the world is as successful for young men as the study of Alfasi, which is all-encompassing—[offering an] introduction and key to all the poskim." And by Sema':[33] "Let him take pride in knowing well the books of those who render decisions, such as Alfasi, Mordekhai, Rosh et al., for these are the basis of our Torah, and one in no way satisfies his obligation by learning Talmud with [only] the Tosafoth."

This is also the opinion of the Gaon of Vilna:[34]

> Let him get used to Alfasi... and if he is privileged, he will master it, together with Rashi, in two years. Afterwards, he should learn Rambam on the three orders I have mentioned [*Mo'ed, Nashim, Nezikin*]—[studying] his text only, without commentaries. I guarantee that this text will be as easy as if you had already learned it... Take note of any new law Rambam mentions but Alfasi does not bring; in such a case, look into [*Kesef Mishneh*] and *Magid Mishneh*, who will enlighten you. After constantly going over these three orders with Rambam for a year, you will certainly become thoroughly versed in them. Then go on to *Tur* on these three orders, which you will learn as easily as if you had already studied it. And for every new law mentioned by *Tur* but not familiar to you from Alfasi or Rambam, check *Beth Yosef*, which will enlighten you. I promise that if you learn Shulchan Arukh, your mind will be so quick that you will recognize, after one reading, all the words of the Acharonim... whose opinion is represented by every halakhah.

The "Chafetz Chayim" counsels[36] that since it is almost impossible to acquire knowledge of the entire Talmud, one "should attempt to gain extensive knowledge of at least the basic halakhoth of the Talmud. That is, he should learn Alfasi on the Talmud... with only Rashi's commentary... which was actually the practice for hundreds of years... This piece of advice is found in *Ma'aseh Rav* in the name of the Gaon of Vilna." Learning based on the Rosh is also endorsed by the Rabbi of Rogoczov.[36]

Similarly, R. Elchanan Wasserman writes in a letter: "It is difficult to learn all the Rishonim. However, it is proper that [one] learn the novellae of Ramban and Rashba. If even this is too taxing for him, let him study only Rashba... In tractates which have the halakhic summaries of Rif and Ran, he should learn those as well."

(3) *Tur* and Shulchan Arukh

As we have seen from *Chawoth Ya-ir* and will subsequently observe in the words of other Acharonim, the study of *Tur* and Shulchan Arukh was very widespread in previous generations. Thus, the "Chatham Sofer" advised his son: "Learn much Shulchan Arukh, *Choshen Mishpat* with the commentary of Sema'—and with that of Shakh only when you wish to study the halakhah in depth."[37]

So, too writes R. Sheftel Horowitz in his ethical testament: "Review Shulchan Arukh until you become so familiar with it that you can find whatever you seek. Then check the original sources." R. Ya'akov of Lissa[38] follows suit in his testament: "Learn a page or folio of Shulchan Arukh, *Orach Chayim* every day." R. Chaim of Volozhin[39] is also said to have told a student to "go over *Mo'ed*, covering five folios—or at least three—every day, and review the text of the Talmud twice and Rosh's commentary eight times. Then he should learn the text of Shulchan Arukh by heart. He need not study all the Tosafoth and Acharonim."

Similarly the "Chafetz Chayim" states:[40] "See Shulchan Arukh, *Yoreh De'ah* (par. 246), where Shakh quotes *Perishah* to the effect that everyone must learn halakhoth every day, so his learning will lead to practice... It therefore seems clear that first priority should be given to *Orach Chayim*—even though all four parts of Shulchan Arukh are necessary for proper practice—because knowledge of it is required every day of one's life to uphold the commandments of the Torah, and without it no one in Israel could make a move."

Nevertheless, it must be recalled that studying the final halakhah without knowing the underlying sources is certainly not sufficient. In the words of R. Chaim of Volozhin,[41] "it is like eating spices without fish."

(4) The Precedence of Tractates With Practical Application

The Talmud[42] relates that Rabbah bar Abuha was once astonished to find Elijah the prophet, a *kohen*, in a non-Jewish cemetery. Asked to explain himself, Elijah responded: "Haven't you learned the Order *Taharoth*?" Rabbah replied that he had studied only those four Mishnaic orders applicable in his day, but not the remaining two. Evidently some Amoraim adhered to this curriculum, as did the yeshivoth of Babylon; consequently, the orders *Zera'im* and *Taharoth* are represented in the Babylonian Talmud by only one tractate each: *Berakhoth* and *Nidah*, respectively. Even the great poskim—Alfasi and Rosh—followed this pattern. A disciple of the Gaon of Vilna[43] deduced from the incident with Rabbah—and from Rashi's commentary thereon—that if the early scholars neglected Mishnayoth inapplicable to them, so too should

our generation, which is so far inferior to them. He notes further that
Alfasi commented mainly on the three basic orders, whereas he only
collected a few relevant halakhoth from the others.

R. Yehudah HeChasid states:[44] "First learn what is constantly applicable... and in localities where there are business disputes, it is necessary
to study *Nezikin*." R. Sheftel Horowitz writes in his ethical testament:[45]
"It would be well if you could learn Talmud, for this is the goal of all
goals. Beloved sons, see that you are well-versed in *Berakhoth*—which
has great subject matter, *Shabbath*—which has magnificent subject
matter, *Kethuboth*—which encompasses the entire Talmud, and *Chulin*,
'Avodah Zarah, and *Nidah*—which enumerate basic rules. These tractates are almost obligatory—do not deviate from them." The Gaon of
Vilna is also very clear:[46] "Don't be foolish, laboring over Mishnayoth
that apply in messianic times but not in our day, and ignoring the most
important parts [i.e. those applicable today]." The "Chafetz Chayim" is
similarly specific:[47] "Although the commandment to study Torah is
fulfilled even by learning *Kodashim* and *Taharoth*, one's main study
must... lead to performance of the mitzvoth."

(5) Acharonim

In the name of his father-in-law,[48] the author of *Egley Tal* writes, as
does the "Chazon Ish,"[49] that the glosses of Maharsha are falling into
neglect, and that from the day they were abandoned, the simple explanation was lost.

Levush Mordekhai recommended:[50] "One should devote one hour a
day to studying *Ketzoth* [*HaChoshen*] with a clear-thinking comrade."

(6) Conclusions

Readers who find their study habits at odds with those recommended by the authorities will presumably protest that nowadays we
have different, more appropriate books to learn from; that human
nature has changed, demanding a different curriculum to maintain
interest; that the later generations have grown weaker intellectually and
emotionally, etc. There is certainly some truth to these protestations,
but do they suffice to justify the extent of the aberration? Everyone must
resolve this question to his own satisfaction—according to his teachers'
guidance, his own judgment and his sincerity.

8

The Course of Study

The Sages stipulated detailed rules regarding the course of Torah study, but over the centuries, the public has departed from them. Below, we review this course and the many ardent attempts to reinstate it.

1. **Mishnah**[1]: At age five [one is ready] for Scripture; at ten, for Mishnah; at thirteen for mitzvoth; at fifteen, for Talmud...

2. **Tractate Sofrim**[2]: One who toils in the Talmud will progress. But one should not pass over Scripture and Mishnah to concentrate on the Talmud; rather, he should study Scripture and Mishnah in order to reach Talmud.

   Rather than jumping from Scripture to Midrash to Talmud, one should learn Scripture [completely], then Mishnah, then Talmud. (Rosh[3])

   One should learn all of Scripture, then the entire Mishnah, then Talmud. (R. Yomtov Lipman Heller[4])

3. **Talmud**[5]: If you see a student whose studies are very difficult for him, it is because his Mishnah is not well-ordered, as Scripture says:[6] "... and he did not sharpen the edge."

4. **Ibid**[7]: "Prepare your work outside"[8] — that is Scripture. "And get it ready in the field" — that is the Mishnah. "Thereafter: build your house" — that is the Talmud.

5. **Ibid**[9]: Who [is successful] in the battle of Torah?[10] He who masters many Mishnayoth. (Rashi: 'The battle of Torah' — Its teaching, and reduction to essentials and principles; [this battle can] not [be waged] by a sharp-witted person who analyzes and dissects, nor by one who is a master of theory, but never learned many Mishnayoth...; for whence would he discover the truth? Rather this refers to one who masters many Mishnayoth, so that, if he seeks a reason for one [Mishnah], he can deduce it from another.)

6. **Midrash**[11]: Just as the bride is adorned with twenty-four ornaments, the scholar must be diligent in the twenty-four books [of Scripture].

7. **Sefer Chasidim**[12]: "Educate the youth according to his way; even when he grows old he will not deviate from it."[13] If he excels in Scripture but not in Talmud, don't pressure him to study Talmud. If he understands Talmud, don't pressure him to study Scripture. [Primarily]—educate him in what he knows. If a person sees that his son is incapable of Talmud, he should teach him *Halakhoth Gedoloth*, Midrashim, and *keriah* [=Scripture(?)].

8. **R. Yitzchak Abarbanel**[14]: The ages mentioned in the Mishnah regarding learning are all starting times, not finishing times. For surely one should not occupy himself with Biblical learning only until he turns five, as the Ashkenazim do today. Rather, when he reaches age five, instruction in Scripture should begin... and when he turns ten, he is ready for the Mishnah...

9. **Maharal**[15]: The Rishonim, Tanaim, Amoraim, Geonim, and Acharonim all learned in a set order—first Scripture, then Mishnah, then Talmud. But in this generation they begin with the Talmud: they educate youngsters in the Talmud at age six or seven and only at the end do they advance them to Mishnah—not to study it, but only to seek out specific halakhoth... Now, one has nothing left—no Talmud, no rule, and no decisions, unless he searches for them.

10. **Idem**[16]: Earlier generations set time limits on "educating the youth according to his way:" at age five, Scripture; at age ten, Mishnah; at fifteen, Talmud—adjusting the burden to what he can bear; for the youth will accept that which he can bear... And when he completes his study of the Mishnah, the great foundation and pillar of the entire Torah, and approaches the sacred study of the Talmud, he will be able to build a tower reaching Heaven, and not a pebble of it will fall. All this is possible because of the existing firm basis, i.e., the Mishnah... And afterwards, if he must fight the battle of Torah, then his hands will be well-prepared, laden with the armaments of Torah, which serve him as arrows in the hand of a warrior, striking their mark without fail; and these will forsake him neither when he lies down nor when he rises.

It is incumbent on the shepherds who guide the flock not to pressure or exhaust them with deceptive shortcuts—which are really the long route—not because it is lengthy, but because they will die before they reach the realm of Torah.

11. **Idem**[17]: First, one should acquire [knowledge of] Scripture, which is the root and the beginning. Afterwards, the Mishnah, for the Written Torah, by itself, is like the root of a tree and cannot reach the goal which is to convey the quality and substance of the mitzvoth. That is why they arranged for the Mishnah to follow, for it will help one grasp this quality and substance... But in the current generation, this arrangement has been disturbed to the greatest possible extent. Thus, when a youngster reaches age eight or nine, he starts with the Talmud. Does he really have the mental capacity for it? Surely no one can retain what is beyond his intellectual capacity.

   Idem[18]: He must also follow the learning schedule we have outlined—first, Mishnah; afterwards, Talmud; and he must constantly review everything. The same applies to small school children—first teach them the entire Scripture, in sequence, from beginning to end, and repeat it with them until they are fluent in it; thereafter, let them go on to Mishnah. This is the path trodden by the Rishonim and Acharonim.

12. **R. Yesha'yah Horowitz (Shelah)**[19]: Even though the obligation to learn Torah is fulfilled by studying the Babylonian Talmud... a person must study [Scripture] as well as Mishnah and Talmud; and he should learn the Torah, Prophets and *Kethuvim* in sequence, one after the other. After that, the Oral Torah, in the order of the Mishnah... And he should study [the Mishnayoth] enough times to become fluent in them and learn them by heart. And [one should learn] halakhah from the Talmud every day, fulfilling the requirement to divide one's day into three, etc.

   Teach your sons according to this program: Once the youngster begins learning Scripture, he should not stop until he has studied it all thoroughly. He should not skip from section to section every week; rather, he should learn it in sequence, without leaving any passage until he knows its translation and context, that is, its full interpretation. It is also advisable for him to study grammar while he is still young, for then it is engraved on the tablets of his heart and will always be remembered. After this, he should learn all six orders of Mishnayoth by heart. Afterwards, he should study the length and breadth of the Talmud, and the poskim. Then the world will be filled with knowledge.

13. **R. Avraham Horowitz**, brother of Shelah[20]: They say one should divide his life into three equal parts: one-third of the day for

Scripture, one-third for Mishnah, and one-third for Talmud. Rabbeinu Tam comments that one who has sated himself with Scripture and is well-versed in the twenty-four sacred books... need not devote a third of his day to them, for the Babylonian Talmud is permeated with them. But to neglect Scripture [altogether], Heaven forfend that one should entertain such a thought and cast off the yoke of Torah...

In addition, I wish to admonish and charge you that, besides the rest of the Talmud, you should learn Mishnayoth every day, until completing the six orders in all their glory. And every day of your life, review Scripture and Mishnah so you will not forget any of it.

14. **R. Sheftel**, son of Shelah[21]: I passed through the Amsterdam community. There I found distinguished men, many of them scholars, and I visited their study halls; each of them has his own domain. I saw that the young children learn Scripture from the beginning of Genesis to the end of Deuteronomy, and after that the [rest of] Scripture, and then all the Mishnayoth. And when they come of age, they start to study Talmud with the Tosafoth. They grow and thrive and produce fruit. And I wept — why cannot this system be followed in this country? Would that this custom spread throughout the Jewish world. What harm can there be in filling one with Scripture and Mishnah until thirteen, and [only] afterwards starting the study of the Talmud? For certainly, in one year he will reach the goal and, with God's help, [gain] a deeper understanding of the Talmud than our style of learning grants him in several years. ...

The method of raising one's children is thus: first Leviticus, then from Genesis to the end [of the Pentateuch]. In the Mishnayoth, *Mo'ed* and *Nezikin*; then they will be ready to study Talmud... and then the Torah "will never leave your mouth nor that of your descendants"... Also, learn grammar with them, so they will know [the difference between] the second and third person, plural and singular, masculine and feminine.[22]

15. **Maharsha**[23]: The *beith* [in the word *Bavel* (Babylon), as the second letter of the Hebrew alphabet] implies that there are two Toroth — the written and the oral... which the [Bablyonian Jews], in their arrogance, studied out of order: at age five they should have learned Scripture, but they learned Mishnah; at age ten they should have studied Mishnah, but they studied Talmud; in their youth they learned Mishnah and Talmud together, because of their arrogance.

This is the situation about which R. Yirmiyah invoked the verse: "He made me dwell in gloom."

16. **Idem**[24]: "... which bears its fruit at the proper time and its leaves do not wither."[25] If one teaches with his student's age in mind, his leaves will not wither; otherwise, the verse says of both student and teacher: "but not so the evil-doers, who are as chaff blown about by the wind."

17. **R. Yosef Yosfa Hahn**[26]: Afterwards, he should learn all of Scripture, not as they do in our generation, when many rabbis have never seen the [whole of] Scripture.

    He should immerse himself in Scripture until he is entirely familiar with it, before he starts Mishnah and Talmud... and when he turns ten, he should be taught Mishnah even if he lacks understanding.

18. **R. Yomtov Lipman Heller**[27]: When they say that one should not skip from Scripture to [Mishnah], this means that he should not advance to the corresponding Mishnah before completing all of Scripture. He should not learn one section of Scripture, then leave the rest and skip to the corresponding [Mishnah] and thence to Talmud. Rather, he should finish studying Scripture in its entirety, then the entire Mishnah and then the Talmud.

19. **R. Ya-ir Chaim Bacharach**[28]: [Our forefathers] certainly did not start out by learning the inferences and minutiae of the Mishnayoth... until they had learned all or most of the Mishanyoth. This is evident from the five years they spent studying Scripture, which they learned completely before they started on Mishnah. My own great father studied one chapter of Mishnayoth with me every day—in addition to what I learned from my teacher—until I matured, whereupon I studied Talmud with the Tosafoth.

20. **R. Shelomoh Efrayim Luntschitz**[29]: The proper sequence is to teach him the translation of the entire Pentateuch first... After he has learned all of Scripture and is familiar with God's commandments, one should teach him Mishnayoth—first those that are applicable nowadays and later even those that are not... After he has taught him all this, he can also teach him Talmud.

    Avoth teaches that "at age five, [one is ready] for Scripture; at age ten, for the Mishnah; at age fifteen, for the Talmud." It would seem that even an intelligent student should not start learning Talmud before completing [memorizing] the six orders of the Mishnah... but this is not necessarily so. In their day, the words of the Mishnah were not written down and it was forbidden to record them... Therefore, they needed much time to learn [memorize] Mishnah. Nevertheless, people certainly did not delve into the minutiae—which can be derived through critical examination —until they had learned all, or at least most, of the Mishnayoth.

21. **R. Yoel Sirkes (Bach)**[30]: A person is obligated to [teach his son] the Written Torah, including the Prophets and *Kethuvim*... Therefore the public is wrong not to pay money to teach their sons these subjects.

22. **R. Shabbethay HaKohen (Shakh)**[31] (regarding the above statement): But I maintain that the practices of Israel are like Torah; for have not the Tosafoth [Rabbeinu Tam] written[32], as has Semag[33]... that we can find support for our custom in the Talmudic statement[34] that the Babylonian Talmud... is a mixture of Scripture, Mishnah, and Talmud, so he need not allocate a third of his time to Scripture if he studies the Talmud.

23. Regarding **Chakham Tzevi**[35]: In matters of Torah education, too, [Chakham Tzevi] took up the task of righting the widespread wrong: the disruption of the learning schedule. They generally did not study Scripture at all, to such an extent that there were ordained rabbis who had never read Scripture and knew no Mishnah... He noted this and made it a major rule to establish the curriculum as specified in the Mishnah: "at age five, Scripture," i.e., one should first know the twenty-four books [of Scripture] together with the main commentaries, and then the thirteen syllogisms by which the Torah is interpreted... After that, he must know the Talmud.

24. **R. Ya'akov Emden**[36]: He should teach him all of Scripture, that is, the entire *Tanakh*. In this regard, the Sephardim have the advantage over the Ashkenazim, who invert the order. They want the youngster to learn the entire Torah while standing on one foot, and to look up the halakhah before he even knows the language properly. What sense does it make to enter the Torah's inner sanctum, where the Oral Torah is revealed, if one has not been given the outer keys, the requisite simple explanations of Scripture? This order has already been established at the end of the fifth chapter of *Avoth*. And the righteous Shelah and his righteous sons deplored this [deviation], as has Bach. (The words of Shakh on this subject are not at all convincing, although his honor remains intact.[37])...

If [the teacher] treats [his pupil] in this manner, he will build him a solid foundation on which the edifice of the desired learning can stand firm and straight. Talmud study will be easy for him; he will reach his goals faster, and whatever time was expended learning Scripture will be more than compensated for by the time saved when studying Talmud, the Tosafoth, and all the other great works. But those who disrupt the order lose [the time spent on] both. It is not necessary to expand on this, as any intelligent person knows it; but it is difficult for someone to change his habits and to swim against the tide of his environment. Even the Sages said that the "teachers knew this, but ignored it." What more can I say?

25. **Idem**[38]: [The father] brings [his son] to the teacher to read the Torah. Nowadays, they start with Leviticus. They learn the entire day, until they have completed all of Scripture many, many times—until he turns ten. One must review with him numerous times those sections of the Torah that contain mitzvoth explained in the Talmud, and those verses, words, and letters that the Talmud frequently discusses.

Then, for five years, he learns Mishnayoth by heart—plus the final halakhah, without any derivations. Thereafter, he studies Talmud for five years, learning the derivations of the laws and their sources in Scripture by means of the thirteen syllogisms, as well as the other derivations and rules used by the Sages, including the safeguards they established. Then each one, according to his intellect and ability, spends all his days understanding the minutiae of the Talmud, resolving difficulties, and plumbing the depths of the reasons and derivations. He learns to derive many new laws by analogy and to understand the words of the Sages and their riddles based on Scripture—which are called agadoth.

26. **R. Yosef Te-omim**,[39] author of *Peri Megadim* and in his youth a teacher of young children: As for those students who are ashamed to learn a section of the Pentateuch with Rashi or a chapter of Prophets or *Kethuvim*—if they were at all wise, they would learn this first of all...

[Be not] like those who learn Talmud with the Tosafoth and, if they can ask an appropriate question or resolve a difficulty, are immediately called "wise" and "rabbi," although they have no knowledge of Scripture, and the Language of Holiness [Hebrew] lies abandoned in a corner. I myself have little knowledge of these

matters but I am a victim of circumstance, for I had no one to teach
me or urge me on, and no books. But through God's mercy, I
realized what was necessary and, with God's help, learned what
little I could with students.

27. Regarding the **Gaon of Vilna**[40]: He cautioned... to first become
well-versed in the twenty-four books, with their vocalization and
cantillation, all in proper order, including the study of grammar...
Thereafter he demanded that the six orders of the Mishnah be
familiar to them—together with the better-known rules and explanations—starting with the Mishnayoth applicable today.

28. **Idem**[41]: He should start by filling him with [knowledge of] Scripture,
Mishnah, the Babylonian and Jerusalem Talmudim, etc. But one
who changes the order of learning... will lose even the little Torah
he heard in his youth.

29. **R. Pinchas of Polotzk**,[42] a disciple of the Gaon of Vilna: This is the
proper sequence, as we have said: Scripture must precede Mishnah
and Mishnah must precede Talmud—whoever reverses them is a
boor.

30. **R. Yechezkel Feivel of Vilna**,[43] a frequent visitor with the Gaon of
Vilna: If Israel's youngsters were well-versed in the Written Torah
from the beginning of their studies, it would undoubtedly be much
easier for them to follow the reasoning of the Mishnah and Talmud.
Not so nowadays—when the children come to school, almost the
entire Written Torah remains a hidden treasure, and when they
learn Mishnah and Talmud it is extremely difficult for them because
all the subject matter is foreign to them.

31. **R. Sheneor Zalman of L'ady**[44]: At age six or seven, depending on
[one's son's] robustness and capability, one brings him to a teacher
to read the Torah the whole day, until he has read the entire Written
Torah, together with the Prophets and *Kethuvim*, many times over,
until he turns ten... After this, five years of memorizing the Mishnah, which is, essentially, decided halakhoth without derivations.
After this, five years of the Talmud, so that he will know these
derivations briefly... And after this, for the rest of his life, each
according to his ability and proficiency, he should engage in Talmudic pilpul.

Nowadays, it is no longer customary to teach children the whole
of Scripture—merely the Pentateuch, for they rely on the child to
learn [the rest] on his own, when he grows up... In any case, he must

review all sections of the Torah numerous times, for they contain all the laws and commandments explained in the Talmud.[45]

32. **Zera' Emeth**[46]: We cannot close our eyes to the order of learning. The Sages in the Mishnah have specified: "at five, Scripture; at ten, the Mishnah; at fifteen, the Talmud," and their words are divinely inspired... It is quite clear that we should not encourage the unfortunate modern custom of teaching small boys Talmud, for which they seek support from the mighty oak, Rabbeinu Tam... based on the derivation of the word *Bavli* [=Babylonian—from the word *balul*=mixed], because the Babylonian Talmud is a mixture of Scripture, Mishnah and Talmud... for this refers not to the proper education of children but of adults, after they have become Torah scholars.

33. **R. Ya'akov of Lissa**, author of *Nethivoth HaMishpat*[47]: Maintain a daily study period for Scripture and Mishnah. For the Talmudic declaration, that the Babylonian Talmud contains all, applies to those who have already sated themselves with Scripture and Mishnah. Furthermore, the evil urge to study for ulterior motives is absent when learning Scripture and Mishnah.

34. **R. Samson Raphael Hirsch**[48]: After spending ten years on Scripture and five years on Mishnah—in this sequence—the youth will have acquired a basic understanding of the truths of the Torah and its commandments. It will then be easy for him to go on to the explanations and analysis of the Talmud, which perfects Torah study. After five years of studying Mishnah, no subject discussed by the Talmud will be strange to him and he will comprehend its discussions and conclusions in depth... When will our people return to the study program our forefathers have taught us?

35. **Idem**[49]: This way is in accord with nature and fosters the attainment of truth and life, as the Mishnah has taught us from the earliest time: "at age five, Scripture"—that is, start to read Scripture, equipped with knowledge of the language and subject matter. "At age ten, Mishnah"—start to learn the mitzvoth by studying the fundamentals of the Oral Torah. "At age thirteen, mitzvoth." "At age fifteen, Talmud"—that is, study the wisdom of the Torah in depth. Why did they abandon this path? Why did they pervert it? By misunderstanding one dictum of the Sages,[50] they have caused much straying.

36. **R. Yisrael of Salant**[51]: For us today, the Talmud is as Scripture was in the days of the Sages and the study of Scripture is as the alphabet

was in their days, enabling us to study the Talmud. And the works of the poskim—Rishonim and Acharonim—are as the Mishnah was... After becoming thoroughly versed in the Talmud (Babylonian and Jerusalem), the greatest of the poskim, etc., and the Tosafoth, one can study the "Talmud"... [referred to in the Mishnah cited above (1)], [having acquired] the proper insight to develop the foundations of the Talmud in detail from various sources and to understand and teach properly.

We conclude with a complete study program recommended by R. Mosheh Chaim Luzzatto,[52] who enumerates the topics of study in this order: Scripture (with commentaries); the thirteen syllogisms by which the Torah is interpreted; Talmudic methodology; the entire Talmud [including Mishnah] (with a simple understanding of its topics); Rambam's *Mishneh Torah* (with commentaries); Shulchan Arukh (wherever it differs with Rambam, *Beth Yosef* is to be consulted) and all the early Midrashim, plus a brief survey of logic, rhetoric, poetry, geometry, arithmetic, astronomy, etc.

9
Conclusions in Brief

The words of the Torah authorities throughout the generations reveal many important perspectives on the correct course of study.

1. The proper way to study the Oral Torah is to start with a simple reading designed to amass knowledge. Then, one progresses to intensive study, beginning with pilpul — that is, clarifying the meaning of the text in detail. This leads to sevara — that is, ascertaining the reasons for the halakhah. With this knowledge, one can discover new halakhoth and resolve novel questions that arise.

2. All learning should lead to clarifying the halakhoth. Therefore:

   One should be careful not to study in order to accumulate theoretical knowledge divorced from reality, as if the Torah were just another science. On the contrary, all learning must lead to appropriate halakhic conclusions.

   Since one may be tempted to engage in pilpul for his own pleasure, he should be especially careful to employ it only to clarify the halakhah. One Acharon justifies false pilpul as a means of sharpening the mind, but it appears that most poskim forbid it.

   One should review the poskim thoroughly after learning the Talmud.

3. One should gain extensive knowledge of topics that are applicable today before studying those that are not.

4. One should study Scripture and Mishnah before Talmud. According to most authorities, the Babylonian Talmud's status as "a combination of all three" elements may be exploited only after attaining proficiency in the first two.

PART SIX

TORAH STUDY VERSUS TORAH LIVING

Judaism involves studying the Torah and practicing what it teaches us. Which of these is more important? The Sages seem to be sending us conflicting signals. One Mishnah states: The main object is "not study but practice." Yet another Mishnah, discussing several practical mitzvoth, concludes: "but Torah study counterbalances them all," implying that study is worthier than practice. Similarly, one Amora goes so far as to proclaim that "all the mitzvoth of the Torah do not equal one word of the Torah," suggesting that Torah study is incomparably more valuable than practice. Yet when it comes to interrupting the performance of one mitzvah for another, more pressing one, Torah study is set aside more readily than any other commandment.

We find this tension between study and practice throughout the generations, and a proper evaluation of their relative roles requires that we analyze these and other passages in depth.

1

Which is Greater — Study or Practice?

1. The Talmudic Passage in *Kidushin*

Note:

The term "study" is used here as a translation of the Hebrew word *talmud* which subsumes teaching as well.

The Talmud in *Kidushin*[1] relates that at a gathering of Tanaim, the question was raised: "Which is greater, Torah study or Torah practice? R. Tarfon declared that the practice of the Torah is greater. R. 'Akiva declared study is greater. They all declared that study is great(er), because study leads to practice."

This conclusion seems self-contradictory: study is greater, because it leads to practice, because it is a means to practice. Logically, however, the means to an end is subservient and inferior to that end; hence it follows that study is the lesser of the two.[2]

There are four parts to this statement, each of which may be interpreted in different ways to resolve the paradox: (1) There are two types of study; (2) there are two types of greatness; (3) there are two types of practice; (4) there are two meanings to the words "leads to." The paradox may thus be resolved in four different ways, all of which are used by the commentators.

(1) According to Tosafoth, the "study" considered greater than practice is the teaching of others, while the "study" which is only a means for practice is self-study.[3]

(2) Alternatively, Tosafoth and others[4] interpret the term "great" to mean that study assumes (chronological) precedence over practice,[5] but practice is certainly more important.

(3) Hafla-ah[6] explains that study is greater than the practice of mitzvoth requiring no study, such as charity. It is greater since it leads to the performance of **all** mitzvoth.

(4) Another commentator[7] explains that according to R. Tarfon, study is simply a means to practice, in which case practice is greater. According to R. 'Akiva, however, study is a cause and practice is its effect, in which case study is greater, as the cause is primary to the effect (just as God is called the Prime Cause, for example). Therefore, "they all declared" refers to the two scholars, each of whom cited the phrase in defense of his own view. Accordingly, there is no paradox here either, neither for R. Tarfon nor for R. 'Akiva. R. Tarfon comprehends that the greatness of Torah stems from its leading to practice—which is even greater. R. 'Akiva, on the other hand, interprets "study leads to practice" as implying only a cause-and-effect relationship, without implying that practice is therefore greater than study.

Based on this interpretation, we may suggest that R. Tarfon and R. 'Akiva both believe that study has elements of both cause and means, and that study and practice each has an advantage one over the other. R. Tarfon is simply relating to the purpose aspect and R. 'Akiva to the cause-and-effect aspect, so that they do not necessarily disagree at all.

Another way of resolving the paradox is used by Ritba. Study is greater, according to him, because it is a mitzvah in itself and, in addition, leads to practice. We discuss this approach below.

2. The Talmudic Passage in *Bava Kama*

This issue is also explored in *Bava Kama*. There, the Talmud[8] relates that at King Hezekiah's funeral a Torah scroll was placed on his bier and he was praised as follows: "He practiced what is written herein." The Talmud adds that nowadays, however, we do not eulogize in this manner. When asked about this by Rabbah Bar Bar Chanah, R. Yochanan delays his response to put on *tefilin*. He then explains that even if we do eulogize in this manner, we only mention practice, but do not say: What is written here, he **taught**. According to Rashi, this implies that study is greater than practice. It is then noted that R. Yochanan states elsewhere that Torah learning is great because it leads to practice (which implies—according to Rashi—that practice is greater). The Talmud answers that the second statement speaks of learning for oneself, whereas the first, which makes *talmud Torah* superior, refers to teaching others.

Thus, based on Rashi, study is accorded superiority when it means teaching others, but when one learns for himself, practice is more important. The Tosafoth arrive at the same conclusion, although their interpretation of the passage differs from Rashi's.

Accordingly, the conclusion in *Kidushin* that "study is greater" refers to teaching others, which is considered superior to individual practice because it leads many to do so.[9] Thus, mass practice is preferred to mass instruction (see Fig. 1).

On the other hand, Ritba explains that R. Yochanan was not referring to contemporary practice — as Rashi assumes — but to Hezekiah's eulogy, implying that practice is in fact greater. The Talmud then challenges this implication with a statement, cited elsewhere, indicating that "study is greater," to which it replies that learning for oneself is indeed greater than practice, but practice is greater than teaching others.[10]

This clearly indicates that learning for oneself is more important than teaching others (see Fig. 2). This interpretation is based on a textual variant that deletes the words "even if" from R. Yochanan's response. Other authorities[11] seem to use this version as well, arriving at the same conclusion.

She-iltoth,[12] by R. Achai Gaon, contains a version that omits R. Yochanan's response to the query. The point is simply that R. Yochanan put on *tefilin* before responding, suggesting that practice takes precedence over "study." The Talmud then challenges this from the passage in *Kidushin*, which concluded that study has priority. According to the Gaon, the dispute and conclusion there concern only what takes precedence in time: in the case of R. Yochanan, where teaching was involved, practice takes priority, whereas in *Kidushin*, the reference is to self-study, which takes precedence over practice (see Fig. 3).

Meiri's words on this subject[13] are puzzling, on first sight. On the one hand, he writes: "One who encounters a mitzvah and [the opportunity for] Torah study, should — if the mitzvah can only be performed immediately — first attend to the mitzvah and then study. But if the mitzvah can be delayed, he should do as follows: If he needs to study, let him do so — for study beautifies and perfects practice, because a mitzvah is more exquisite if performed by one who understands its intent. But if he is knowledgeable and need not study — even though he wishes to

Fig. 1
ORDER OF SUPERIORITY
(Rashi & Tosafoth)

Practice of the many

Teaching the many

Practice oneself

Study oneself

Fig. 2
ORDER OF SUPERIORITY
(Ritba)

Learning oneself

Practice oneself

Teaching others

Fig. 3. TEMPORAL SEQUENCE (She-eltoth)

Learning ⟶ practice ⟶ teaching

teach—he should not postpone the mitzvah to instruct others."
Accordingly, practice takes precedence over teaching.

On the other hand, he writes: "[In eulogizing someone] we do not
laud him for having perfected [i.e. taught] others, for this is the epitome
of perfection, which has eluded most Sages, and we must eulogize a
person according to his actual achievements."

This comment favors the interpretation of Rashi and Tosafoth,
stating that teaching others is greater than practice. Yet according to
Meiri's first statement, practice takes precedence over teaching others
—and only when one learns for himself does study take precedence
over practice. How can we resolve this apparent contradiction and
whence does Meiri draw this conclusion?

Meiri appears to be raising a subtle point: according to Rashi and
Tosafoth, by delaying his response to put on *tefilin*, R. Yochanan seems
to ignore his dictum that teaching others is greater than personal practice. Instead, he must have meant that even though teaching others is
more important, practice takes chronological precedence.

Here, then, is the Meiri's conclusion: Chronologically, individual
learning precedes individual practice, as evidenced by the passage in

Kidushin,[14] but individual practice precedes teaching others, as indicated by the delay in R. Yochanan's response (as in Fig. 3). In order of importance, however, teaching others precedes individual practice, and individual practice precedes individual study (see Fig. 1).

3. The Views of the Rishonim

According to the version of Rashi and Tosafoth, which appears in all editions of the Talmud, practice is greater than individual study, but teaching others is greater than practice. Why should this be so? If, as Ritba contends, study is a mitzvah in itself and also leads to practice,[15] why should practice alone be more important? Perhaps this is so because study does not involve any concrete action; therefore any mitzvah which does, would take precedence over it. Even the fact that study eventually leads to practice cannot outweigh a mitzvah involving immediate, concrete action. (The Torah considers concrete action to be more significant than mere speech.)

Why, then, is teaching others greater than practice? According to Maharsha,[16] it leads to mass action, which supersedes the individual practice of the teacher. This interpretation dovetails with another Talmudic conclusion:[17] "Torah study [of many] is greater than the daily sacrifices... but private Torah study is less important."

According to *She-iltoth* (as well as Rabbeinu Chananel, 'Arukh and Ritba) individual study supersedes individual action and individual action supersedes teaching others. This can be understood from the fact that the priority addressed in *She-iltoth* is a chronological one: "His learning precedes his action... His action precedes teaching others." This may also be the conclusion intended by Rabbeinu Chananel and 'Arukh.

How are we to understand this order of precedence in time, which is the reverse of the order of importance? The temporal precedence of individual action over teaching others can be understood from the fact that teaching, like Torah study, involves no concrete action. Perhaps this order also teaches an important pedagogical lesson: since actions speak louder than words, one should not begin teaching until his conduct is in order. This idea is borne out by the Talmudic statement that observing a teacher is more important than studying his words and that "words are fitting when they emanate from the mouth of those who practice them."[18]

Netziv[19] explains that "here, teaching means simply encouraging others to learn, but actual teaching would take precedence over everything because, when one teaches others, he also learns." This point is similar to a remark by Shelah.[20]

Unfortunately, in interpreting Ritba, we cannot assume that action is superior to self-study, as Ritba states explicitly that "study comprises both: it is in itself a form of practice, for it is a mitzvah [and] it leads to action." But if so, why is not the same true of teaching others?[21]

This question may be answered as follows: Torah study is a mitzvah which does not involve concrete action; it is only elevated to this status because it does lead the student to action. Teaching, however, does not, because a pupil's actions are not an extension of the teacher's.[22]

Nevertheless, teaching ought to subsume individual study because, as Netziv notes,[23] one learns while teaching. At the very least, it should be covered by the Talmudic dictum[24] that one who repeats his learning 101 times is qualitatively different from one who repeats it 100 times. A possible answer: Ritba is referring to a teacher who is not about to forget. Consequently, his teaching will not lead him to any additional practice; hence it is inferior to action.

Nevertheless, Ritba's insistence on the primacy of individual study remains difficult. He claims that it is greater than teaching others (the grammatical construction used implies "many others") and yet King Hezekiah (from whose eulogy the inferiority is learned) is praised for teaching others, presumably many others. R. Yasha'yah points out that there is much evidence that guiding the masses outweighs self-study.[25] Other authorities have raised similar questions.[26]

Rabbeinu Chananel and 'Arukh, however, also seem to maintain that learning from one's teacher (if this is still warranted) is preferable to teaching others. To quote the Mishnah,[27] better "to be the tail among lions than the head among foxes."

2

Study Versus Practice
in the Mishnah

A Mishnah in *Avoth*[2]—evidently undisputed—teaches: "It is not learning that is primary, but doing." The commentators[2] stress that this Mishnah is consonant with the aforementioned Talmudic passage: "They all declared: 'Study is great because it leads to practice.'"

This fits in well with all the authorities quoted above, who believe that the greatness of *talmud Torah* signifies only chronological precedence, or refers only to public teaching. The only remaining difficulty involves Ritba's interpretation that individual Torah study is greater than practice.[3]

We suggest that he differentiates between the term "great" in the debate of study vs. practice and the term "primary" of the Mishnah in *Avoth*. To better understand this distinction, we examine another Mishnah which bears on the subject at hand.

The first Mishnah in *Peiah* states:[4] "These are the matters whose dividends are enjoyed in this world, but whose principal remains in the next world: honoring one's father and mother, performing acts of kindness, and making peace between one's fellow men; but Torah study counterbalances them all." The Jerusalem Talmud cites the following discussion concerning this Mishnah: "R. Berakhyah and R. Chiya of Kefar Techumin: One says that the entire world is not equal to one word of the Torah, and one says that even all the mitzvoth of the Torah are not equal to one word of the Torah. In the name of R. Acha: One verse states 'And all precious things are not equal to it,' and another verse says, 'And all **your** precious things are not equal to it' — 'precious things' refers to gems and pearls; 'your precious things' refers to the words of the Torah [i.e. its mitzvoth]."[5]

This passage is difficult. All commentaries note the unanimous conclusion of both Talmudim[6] that one interrupts Torah study for the sake of a mitzvah no one else can perform. How, then, can one say that all the mitzvoth of the Torah do not equal even one word of it? Some scholars[7] suggest that the superiority of the Torah is asserted only for those mitzvoth that another can indeed perform. But the wording of the Talmud, which is entirely general in nature, does not seem to support that explanation.

Yafeh Mar-eh offers a solution based on Rambam's commentary on this Mishnah. All the mitzvoth of the Torah together do not equal one word of the Torah insofar as the dividends we earn from them are concerned. In general, there is no reward for mitzvoth in this world, except the interpersonal mitzvoth enumerated by the Mishnah. Torah study, however, is different. By learning, the student discovers what to do in this world to enter the next world — and this may be considered the most valuable dividend of all.[8] In this way, Torah study is greater than any other mitzvah. Nevertheless, everyone agrees that practice is primary and Torah study must defer to any mitzvah that cannot be performed by another.

This may also be what Ritba means when he maintains that study is greater: in terms of the dividends in this world (to which he alludes by noting that study leads to other mitzvoth), it is indeed greater; however, generally speaking, action is certainly primary. Hence, as R. Ya'akov Emden[9] indicated: "It is doubtful whether Torah study that does not lead to action can be included in this dictum [that Torah study counterbalances them all], for such study is not even as great as action... in my opinion, this is rather obvious from the context."

3

Does Torah Study Exempt the Student
From Other Mitzvoth?

The Talmud reports:[1] "[The Sages] decided, in the loft of Aris in Lod, that study takes precedence over practice. The rabbis of Caesarea said: 'That statement applies when there is another who can perform [this mitzvah]; but if there is no other, practice takes precedence over study.'"

The same conclusion can be drawn from other Talmudic passages, e.g.: "Thus did Rabi teach: Action takes precedence over study" and[2] "'All your precious things are not equal to it' — Therefore, you should forfeit all that is precious to you [i.e. mitzvoth that can be fulfilled by another] to occupy yourself with the Torah. But things precious to Heaven are equal to it — that is, if you must occupy yourself with a mitzvah [which cannot be fulfilled by another], you should forfeit Torah study to do so."

But what if one is already engaged in Torah study when the mitzvah confronts him? In this case as well, the Talmud[3] teaches that one should interrupt his learning to bury the dead, to bring a bride to the wedding canopy, and to recite the Shema' and other prayers [i.e. mitzvoth that cannot be fulfilled by others to the required extent].[4] This rule applies even to someone who is in the middle of teaching.[5]

How do we reconcile this with the general principle that one who is engaged in the performance of one mitzvah need not perform another,[6] even if the second mitzvah cannot be fulfilled by another, such as sitting in a *sukah*, reciting the Shema' and the *tefilah*, and putting on *tefilin*?[7] Why should we interrupt Torah study when, under similar circumstances, we would not be bidden to abandon any of the other mitzvoth? *Talmud Torah* would thus appear inferior to other mitzvoth.

The Rishonim explain that this simply affirms the principle that it is not study but practice which is primary, as Meiri noted: "One might ask why the Torah was more lenient regarding Torah study than it was concerning any other mitzvah... For example, a scribe need not interrupt his work [to perform a mitzvah, whereas one studying Torah must do so]... The answer is that the sole purpose of study is action. How, then, could a student forgo this action?" This is also explicitly stated by Chida[8], quoting Ran and Rosh.[10]

R. Ya'akov Kanievsky[11] adds that what makes Torah study so important and dear is that it leads to action. Hence if one studies without intending to implement what he learns, his mitzvah of Torah study is flawed. It follows that he must interrupt his study for all other mitzvoth, lest he mar his learning. Moreover, says R. Kanievsky, since the Torah does not state how much learning is required, one must be expected to learn only as much as he can. However, as the other mitzvoth are delineated more precisely, he must fulfill them first.

We have learned,[12] "Sometimes one [actually] establishes the Torah by neglecting it." Rashi interprets this as follows: "For example, when he neglects the Torah for the sake of attending a funeral or bringing a bride under the bridal canopy — 'he establishes it', that is to say, he receives reward as if he sits, establishes, and occupies himself with [Torah]." Maharal queries Rashi's explanation, as it does not clarify how the study process is fulfilled by neglecting it. Perhaps this paradox can be resolved on the basis of the above comment by R. Kanievsky: failure to completely fulfill a mitzvah constitutes a concomitant failure to completely fulfill the mitzvah of Torah study. Conversely, performance of a mitzvah constitutes the completion and fruition of the mitzvah of Torah study — in other words, its establishment.[13]

Meiri, as cited above, indicated[14] that "one who encounters a mitzvah and [the opportunity for] the study of Torah should — if the mitzvah can only be performed immediately — first attend to the mitzvah and then study. But if the mitzvah can be delayed he should first study, if he needs [the information]." Note that Meiri adds another requirement to the Talmudic one: not only must the mitzvah be one that cannot be performed by another person,[15] but it must also be transitory — one which cannot be fulfilled at all unless it is performed at once. This can be derived from the Talmudic law[16] that one should study Torah and marry only afterwards, for as the Gaon of Vilna[17] points out, if one may neglect a mitzvah that can be performed by another, he may certainly neglect one that he himself can perform later.

From all the above, we can deduce that one need not interrupt his learning to perform acts of kindness, unless they can only be carried out by him. Therefore, one could conceivably spend all his time studying Torah without ever performing any kindness. Perhaps it is to guard against such a situation that R. Huna[18] warned: "One who only studies Torah is like one who has no God ['to protect him' — Rashi]." Indeed, R. Chanina ben Teradyon was not spared a cruel death — despite his enormous self-sacrifice for the sake of Torah study — because he did not perform enough acts of kindness.

PART SEVEN

SECULAR STUDIES — THE TORAH VIEW

We began this work by discussing the relationship between Torah and the physical world, showing them to be part of one divinely created system, in which the Torah embodies the goal and the world the means of attaining it. We conclude by analyzing the Torah's attitude towards the study of the physical world and secular studies in general.

We should not expect Judaism to view all areas of secular studies as one homogeneous entity. Some secular subjects wrestle with issues such as the purpose of the world or the meaning of life, ethics and morality; they clearly compete with Torah. Others endeavor to explore the physical world and the laws which appear to govern it — these aid and support the Torah. Below, we investigate the Torah's attitude towards each of these two categories. To test our findings against actual halakhic decisions, we conclude with summaries of four responsa by outstanding authorities of the last generation, dealing with the question of university studies.

1

Introduction

The Sages and later authorities frequently reiterated the importance of studying the sciences. However, a closer examination of their opinions reveals an unusual phenomenon—apparent blatant and extreme contradictions. On the one hand, they obligate us in no uncertain terms to study the sciences:

* Ponder His works, for this will lead you to recognize the Creator. (*Baraitha*)[1]
* It is a mitzvah to calculate the seasons and the zodiac... Of him who is able... but fails to do so, Scripture says, "They do not regard the work of God and do not see the deed of His hands." (Talmud)[2]
* When a person reflects upon and recognizes all creation, and sees the wisdom of God in everything that exists, it increases his love of God. (Rambam)[3]
* We are duty-bound to study creation and to derive proof of the Creator's wisdom. (*Chovoth HaLevavoth*)[4]
* All the sciences are necessary for the study of Torah, for they form a ladder which leads to the knowledge of God. (Rabbeinu Bachyay)[5]
* The other sciences form a ladder which leads to the wisdom of Torah. (Maharal)[6]
* Each of the seven sciences is praiseworthy in the eyes of our Sages, who embraced them wholeheartedly. Nowhere—neither in the Talmud Bavli, nor Yerushalmi, nor in any Midrash—do they disparage any science. (R. Ya'akov Provencali)[7]
* When a person lacks knowledge of other wisdoms, he consequentially lacks a hundred times that in Torah wisdom. (Gaon of Vilna)[8]
* All the sciences are portals to the Torah. (Chatham Sofer)[9]

On the other hand, we find equally definitive expressions deprecating secular studies:

* He who reads "alien" books has no share in the next world. (Talmud)[10]
* Accursed is he who teaches his son wisdom of Greek. (Talmud)[11]
* Keep your children away from [the study of] logic. (Talmud)[12]
* "To walk in [the words of the Torah]"—Make them primary, not secondary: engage only in them; combine them with nothing else; do not say "I have learned the wisdom of Israel, now I will learn the wisdom of the other nations." (Midrash)[13]
* Study of Mishnah and Talmud strengthens the body and promotes proper behavior... If one turns his heart away from this and occupies himself with [philosophy], he will cast off the yoke of Torah, lose his fear of God... and rid himself of all words of Torah. (Rav Hai Gaon)[14]
* [Scripture asks:] "Why do you weigh out silver for [something which is] not bread, and toil unsatiated?" This teaches us that one should not occupy himself with other disciplines, but only with the primary one—our Torah. (R. Bachyay)[15]

We might assume that these two enumerations simply represent two divergent opinions. Just as the Sages and later authorities were divided on other matters, so too did they differ regarding this one. However, on examining the individual statements in context, we find no explicit dispute and no conflicting points of view. In fact, some of their authors actually appear to contradict themselves! For example, R. Hai Gaon denounces the study of philosophy, but also wrote a poem which counsels "Know arithmetic and understand books of medicine."[16] The Gaon of Vilna praises science study but bemoans Rambam's attraction to "the accursed philosophy."[17] Moreover, statements by Rabbeinu Bachyay appear in both of the above lists. Could these authorities have experienced such a radical change of heart?

The solution to this ostensible dilemma is actually rather straightforward. Although the other nations of the ancient world did not differentiate between the natural and speculative sciences or humanities—all were called "philosophy" (literally, "love of wisdom")—our Sages did distinguish between them. They deemed the natural sciences the province of all nations, while the speculative sciences were to be learned only from Israel, based on the Torah. Whatever we need to know of the speculative sciences is to be found in the Torah, whereas the natural sciences were left for us to discover. This is sound advice, as there is no way of testing hypotheses in the speculative sciences; only in the natural sciences can we test our theories and establish the truth. Thus, in the words of our Sages,[18] "If someone tells you that there is wisdom among the other nations, believe him; but if he says there is Torah among the other nations, do not believe him." Here, "Torah" clearly refers to speculative science and "wisdom" to natural science.

This distinction is also recognized in halakhah:[19] "If one sees a scholar of the other nations **who is wise in the natural sciences**, one recites: 'Blessed be You... Who gave of His wisdom to flesh and blood.'" In other words, the blessing applies only to experts in the natural sciences—and not to theologians.[20] Similarly, in the above citations, all approbation concerns the natural sciences, whereas disapproval focuses almost exclusively on the speculative ones (with two exceptions, to be discussed in the next chapter).

2

The Study of the Natural Sciences: The Obligation

God has presented us with two creations — the Torah and the world. The first teaches us the will of the Creator, while the second provides us with the tools for fulfilling it.

Just as an artisan must know not only his art but also his materials, so too must a Jew familiarize himself with the world to lead a Torah life. Therefore, worldly wisdom has always occupied a lofty position in Judaism.

On the other hand, the sole purpose of this knowledge is to be the promotion and perfection of Torah life. Consequently, its study is always subservient to Torah study. Regarding the passage "You shall guard my statutes, to walk in them," the *Sifra* states:[1] "Make them primary, not secondary." R. Samson Raphael Hirsch points out that although the *Sifra* forbids considering scientific study as important as Torah study, the expression "make [the words of the Torah] primary, not secondary" implies that the sciences do have their place — even if only a secondary one.[2] Under these conditions, study of the sciences becomes an adjunct of Torah Study.[3] Here, R. Hirsch follows in the footsteps of R. Avraham ibn 'Ezra, who writes:[4] "The other wisdoms and sciences are but handmaidens to the Torah, and Heaven forbid that we should be preoccupied with the means and never reach the goal itself." Similarly, Rambam states poetically:[5] "For before I was created in the womb, the Torah knew me...; it is she who is the object of my love, the wife of my youth... And though many gentile women became her rivals... God knows that, from the outset, they were only taken in as spicers, cooks, and bakers, to show the world the beauty of their mistress." So too in the writings of Rabbeinu Bachyay:[6] "The other wisdoms should be employed by an accomplished scholar only as spicers, cooks and bakers."

In the words of R. Yonathan Eybeschutz:[7]

What is meant by the expression [regarding the lighting of the candelabrum in the Sanctuary]: "From the [westernmost lamp] he started and with it he ended?" Wisdom is referred to as a light, for "a man's wisdom lights up his countenance." The seven lights [of the candelabrum] therefore represent the seven wisdoms, and the westernmost light symbolizes the wisdom of our holy Torah—the "Divine Presence is in the West." All the other wisdoms derive from our Torah... and thence will they return, for they are all handmaidens to the queen; or, as Rambam writes, they are spicers and cooks necessary for our Torah.

Many other authorities[8] concur that the sciences are subordinate to the Torah. Therefore we must sate ourselves with Torah before approaching them in earnest, even though we must study science to some degree before learning halakhah in depth.[9] In sum, as stated succinctly by R. Ya'akov Provencali (cited in the previous chapter), the Sages never opposed study of the sciences but only questioned the extent to which it is to be carried out. On the contrary, anyone who disparages Torah scholars who study science not only "denigrates Torah scholars," but also attacks "the departed holy ones; for he defames the savants and early sages who studied science."[10]

1. Specific Mitzvoth

The purpose of mitzvoth is to establish proper behavioral norms in this world. Hence they all demand some familiarity with the world. Some, in fact, require considerable knowledge.

The "Chazon Ish"[11] writes that errors occur far more frequently in assessing a situation than in mastering a theoretical halakhah: "Clarification of a law's application to a given situation involves two elements: separating the wheat from the chaff—insofar as Torah law is concerned—and analyzing the specific case, assessing its positive and negative aspects and evaluating its details for application of the appropriate halakhah. The danger of drawing a false analogy is more common than that of misinterpreting the law." He is speaking in general terms and certainly does not exclude natural phenomena from his remarks.

The Kuzari writes:[12]

The members of the Sanhedrin were obligated to know all the true and speculative sciences, as well as those based on convention... Could there always be 70 wise sages among the people if these sciences were not widespread and well-established among the people? They obviously were, these sciences being necessary for fulfillment of mitzvoth. The Jew needs sciences for the mitzvoth related to agriculture... and then knowledge of *terei-foth*, which involves distinctions finer than those mentioned by Aristotle... and then knowledge of the physical defects disqualifying *kohanim* from service, as well as those disqualifying sacrificial animals, and finally the distinctions among various bodily discharges...

He adds that the details of these issues would be unfathomable without divine assistance.

We find an even more extensive listing in a sermon of R. Yonathan Eybeshutz.[13]

Similarly, *kashruth* may require a detailed knowledge of science. For instance, one may have to study ichthyology to establish the permissibility of a given fish, as fish which have fins and scales, even if only temporarily, may be eaten.[16] Hence one may have to know a fish's life cycle to establish its status.

To establish the permissibility of firstborn animals,[17] the Amora Rav spent eighteen months with herdsmen learning which blemishes are transitory and which are permanent. Had he been able to deduce this information from Scripture, or by reliable tradition, he certainly would have done so rather than spend so much time away from his Torah studies.[18] The Talmud relates[19] that R. Yehudah once sought to declare a chicken, which had lost its feathers, as unfit for consumption (*treifah*) because it could not have survived. However, R. Shim'on ben Chalafta placed such a chicken in an oven and covered it with a scrap of leather, whereupon it grew stronger feathers than it had before. Here we have an example of a scientific experiment performed to clarify the halakhah. Similarly, to clarify a halakhic question, R. Yishma'el's disciples performed a post-mortem examination on a woman who had been executed.[20] On occasion, the Sages actually favored the opinions of non-Jewish scientists over those of the Jewish ones.[21] We even find a halakhic dispute in which R. Yishma'el's opinion is based on a Scriptural derivation, while the Sages' view is based on the research of gentile scientists.[22]

In the Jerusalem Talmud,[23] the Amoraim appear divided regarding the permissibility of learning science from gentiles for the purpose of clarifying the halakhah. According to the authoritative Babylonian Talmud, however, it is unequivocally permitted.[24] The "Chatham Sofer"[25] deduces from this passage that "the Sages relied on the early naturalists in many Torah matters." Indeed, many later authorities cite scientific data from non-Jewish sources to clarify the halakhah.[26] *Chelkath Ya'akov*[27] writes that Rambam and other Torah scholars who were physicians surely did not acquire their knowledge by divine revelation alone, with no recourse to normal anatomical research.[28] After explaining at length the importance of the study and practice of medicine, *Kaftor WaFerach*[29] adds explicitly: "Presumably, thorough acquaintance with this science necessitates familiarity with the works of gentile authors."

Discussing the use of mechanical devices in the performance of mitzvoth, R. Ya'akov Ettlinger (*'Arukh LeNer*) writes[30] that, while innovations in Torah [halakhah] are entirely improper, one may accept the results of research in the natural sciences when they further the observance of mitzvoth. The "Rogaczover" voices a similar opinion.[31]

Obviously, familiarity with specific aspects of science is a prerequisite for understanding certain halakhoth. But there are also some basic, all-encompassing mitzvoth which are closely connected with science. Thus, Torah demands a theoretical knowledge of nature to enable one to love and fear God, study Torah, and sanctify God's Name, as well as practical knowledge to "subdue the world,"[32] preserve our lives, and earn a livelihood.

2. Love, Fear, and Knowledge of God

Love and fear of God are perhaps the most basic mitzvoth. (Belief in God would be even more basic, but the early authorities disagree whether it is a mitzvah in its own right or merely the basis of other mitzvoth.[33]) "What does the Lord your God demand of you, other than that you fear the Lord your God?"[34]

The Sages have shown us how to come to love God:[35] "After the Torah says 'You shall love the Lord your God with all your heart,' I still do not know how to do so. Therefore, it continues: 'And these words ... shall be upon your heart;' this will lead you to recognize God and cling to His ways." Alternatively:[36] "Observe His works, for this will lead you to recognize the Creator." Thus, the study of both Torah and creation are needed to enable us to love God.

As we cannot love that which we do not know, recognition of the Creator is clearly a prerequisite for the love and fear of God. There are only two ways of achieving such recognition, for God revealed Himself to us by only two phenomena: His Torah and His world. Of the two, the Torah is a far more direct and profound revelation; therefore its study takes precedence. But if we neglected entirely the study of the world, we would perforce limit our knowledge of God and consequently our love and fear of Him as well.

This idea appears repeatedly in Scripture,[37] especially in the Psalms. For example: "The heavens proclaim the dignity of God" or "The voice of God is in glory." The Prophet Isaiah exhorts us: "Lift your eyes on high and see Who created these [heavenly bodies], Who parades their hosts by number, calling each by name, by the greatness of His might and the strength of His power; not one is missing." We have already noted his warning: "They do not regard the work of God and do not see the deed of His hands; therefore My nation was exiled, for lack of knowledge," which is quoted by the Talmud[38] as a reprimand to those who are able to perform astronomical calculations but fail to do so. The Amora Shemuel took this to heart, declaring:[39] "The paths of the heavens are as clear to me as the paths of [my native] Naharde'a." R. Asi earned the title "Experimenter" because he conducted experiments to confirm verses attesting to God's greatness.[40] The great post-Talmudic authorities continued on this path. Herewith the words of R. Bachyay ibn Pakudah:[41]

Contemplation of creation, as proof of the wisdom of the Creator, is an obligation for us, based on reason, Scripture, and tradition. On reason, because it teaches us that man is superior to animals only insofar as he apprehends the basic wisdom evident in all of existence. As the Poet says, "He teaches us by means of the beasts of the earth and enlightens us through the fowl of the heavens." When a person uses his mind and his intelligence in discovering the foundations of science and examining its phenomena, he demonstrates his superiority over the animals. But if he is negligent in this, he is not only like the animals, but even lower than they.

Rambam inquired:[42] "Which path should be taken to love and fear of God? When a person contemplates His wondrous and great works and creatures and deduces His limitless and infinite wisdom, he will immediately love...

Assuming that recognition of God as the Creator is part of Sabbath observance, Rambam's son, Avraham, states:[43] "There is a special way [of observing the Sabbath]... by contemplating the world as a whole and its discernible details—from the surface of the Earth until the outermost heavenly sphere—and meditating on the wisdom of the Creator in the creation of the world."

Rabbeinu Yonah interprets Scripture in a similar vein:[44] "'A balance and scales of justice' teaches us to probe the works of the Creator, as [the Psalmist] has said, 'When I see Your heavens, the work of Your fingers' —for this is the way to develop love and fear of God."

Elsewhere,[45] discussing the importance of settling the earth, he notes that "certain types of nourishment and pharmaceuticals are peculiar to certain places. In addition, the science of astronomy—**which serves as a ladder leading to divine knowledge**—would not be known [without such widespread settling of the earth]."

Yakhin UVo'az, too, elaborates on the importance of the sciences in developing love of God.[46]

Although science has apparently always had overly cautious opponents, R. Sa'adyah Gaon attributes such opposition to ignorance:[47] "If a person asks 'How can we accept the study of science?... Is it not so, that people denigrate this occupation and believe it leads to heresy?' I say that this is only the opinion of the unlearned." This view is echoed by *Mirkeveth HaMishneh*, who writes in his introduction: "Those who wish to disparage science study are uttering only nonsense."

Many additional authorities throughout the ages emphasized the importance of science study to the attainment of reverence for God. For example, Rema states:[48] "They did not forbid the study of either the words of the scientists or their research into the nature of things. On the contrary, through these we can know the greatness of the Prime Mover." R. Ya'akov Emden, who disparaged systematic secular study, nevertheless writes:[49] "However, natural science is different; for it is certainly a permitted and praiseworthy science, necessary for the appreciation of

God's great, awe-inspiring works and deeds." Tosfoth Yom Tov[50] explains that "[studying] the seasons and the zodiac... draws a man's heart to the highest of wisdoms—divine wisdom; for through knowledge of the celestial cycles, he will know and recognize the Creator." The usefulness of scientific knowledge for intensifying our faith is shown also by the "Chazon Ish,"[51] who details the wonders of nature in modern scientific terms, in support of faith in God.

On the other hand, he writes in a private letter:[52] "Even though the basic principles of faith and knowledge, which have been handed down and established for us, are founded on the profoundest wisdom and scientific investigation, the straightforward path before us is to walk in simpleness and to believe with complete and pure faith. We must refrain from investigation, but plant firmly in our hearts the simple truths familiar to all, scholar and simpleton alike."

Just as the "Chazon Ish" used science as a means of strengthening faith, so did the "Chafetz Chayim" use technology.[53]

3. Torah Study

"God contemplated the Torah and created the world"[54]—that is, the world was created to enable us to fulfill the Torah. Therefore, the Torah effectively constitutes the operating instructions for the world. If one is studying the instructions for operating a particular device, he should be acquainted with the device itself. Similarly, students of the Torah, to be fully successful, must become familiar with the world.

A cursory knowledge, which everyone can acquire effortlessly, almost subconsciously, is generally sufficient; but a deeper understanding of the Torah requires a more intensive comprehension of the world, as Rambam states:[55] "It is utterly impossible for anyone to attain perfection without becoming versed in logic, then in mathematics, then nature, and then theology [Torah]." Maharal is even more explicit:[56] "One should study the wisdom of the nations... which stems from God... for this wisdom is like a ladder leading to the wisdom of the Torah."

His source appears to be R. Bachyay, who writes:[57] "The seven wisdoms are a ladder leading to the wisdom of the divine," elaborating on this extensively. Elsewhere, however, R. Bachyay states:[58] "One should not occupy himself with other disciplines, but only with the primary one—our Torah." And in a third place, he adds:[59] "When one's primary occupation is the wisdom of the Torah, he makes it a basic foundation; he is then permitted to build an edifice of the other wisdoms upon this foundation." How are we to resolve this ostensible disparity? Apparently, this is a classic case of "two verses which contradict each other, until a third verse decides between them." The third statement offers a key to understanding the first two: The other wisdoms can serve as a ladder to attain the heights of divine wisdom—but only if a Torah foundation has been prepared first. The statement forbidding the study of other wisdoms seems to apply only to disciplines which do not contribute to divine wisdom.

Maharsha[60] characterizes the sciences as an introduction to Torah study: "Other sciences are similar to fine flour: Just as fine flour is only a prerequisite for bread, together with water and other substances, sciences such as astronomy... and mathematics... are a preamble to our Torah; the water of Torah turns them into spiritual bread and nourishment."

The necessity of such wisdom for reaching the heights of Torah knowledge was expressed even more emphatically by the Gaon of Vilna:[61] "When a person lacks knowledge of other wisdoms, he lacks a hundred times that in Torah wisdom, for the Torah and the sciences go together." He therefore asked R. Barukh of Sklov to translate into Hebrew whatever scientific works he could, "so that the masses will be able to absorb it and their knowledge will increase." R. Barukh complied, and rendered the works of Euclid into Hebrew.

R. Hillel of Sklov, too, quotes the Gaon:[62] "To gain a deeper understanding of the wisdom of the Torah, which is part of divine wisdom, it is important to learn the seven wisdoms inherent in our world, the natural world." Similar remarks are ascribed to the Gaon by R. Yisrael of Sklov (author of *Pe-ath HaShulchan*):[63]

[The Gaon of Vilna] said that all areas of wisdom are necessary for our holy Torah and are incorporated therein. He said he knew them all thoroughly, enumerating algebra, trigonometry, geometry and music... He also explained the nature of all the sciences and said he understood them all. He knew the science of medicine, anatomy and their related fields. He had wanted to learn pharmacology from contemporary physicians, but his righteous father had forbidden it, lest he neglect his Torah studies during the time he would have to save lives. He also knew the art of sorcery... but lacked knowlege of herbology and its final stages, because that information was in the hands of heretical gentiles and his fastidiousness did not allow him to learn from them. He said he had studied philosophy thoroughly, but had found only two good things in it.

The first part of these remarks could be interpreted to mean that one can learn all disciplines from the Torah, but the second part makes it clear that the Gaon learned them from gentile experts.[64] Herewith the words of the Gaon's grandson, R. Ya'akov Mosheh:[65] "One can only ascend to the higher wisdom as one ascends a ladder... starting at the lowest rung, namely, the wisdom of the mundane world."

R. Yomtov Lipman Heller writes:[66] "Knowledge of the natural sciences, while not on the same level as Torah knowledge, is essential for mankind. It precedes one's Torah wisdom, both chronologically and logically."

Outlining a course of study for aspiring scholars, R. Mosheh Chaim Luzzatto recommends[68] that after one completes the entire Talmud, all of the Rambam, the Shulchan Arukh and the early Midrashim, he should study basic geometry, mathematics, and astronomy. Similarly, Netziv states[69] that by studying Talmud and agadah, "one can soar, attain fine character traits... and accomplish great things in Israel. But the grand foundation of it all is the Talmud, which is like rain. Afterwards, the agadah—which is like dew—is also beneficial. And after all this, let him gain further strength by studying other wisdoms—which are like the sun."

The "Chatham Sofer" likewise writes:[70] "For all the other wisdoms are spicers and cooks for the Torah, and portals to it." He continues by explaining why Torah study must be accorded preference nonetheless. Elsewhere, he comments:[71] "And the other wisdoms, which are necessary as spicers and cooks... he will find them all in the Torah."

In several instances, Talmudic sages apply a knowledge of nature to understand the Torah. R. Yishma'el[72] finds a connection between the gestation period and the duration of the mother's postpartum impurity. Although the Talmud also quotes opinions differing regarding this matter and even challenges the reliability of the experiments he cites, the approach is clear: through knowledge of nature we can gain a deeper understanding of the Torah's commandments. Similarly, R. Shim'on

ben Chalafta conducted experiments to confirm King Solomon's statement[73] that ants have no ruler. This earned him the title "Experimenter." R. Yisrael Lipshutz of Danzig (*Tif-ereth Yisrael*) sets another
important example[74] by using the paleontological findings of his time to
explain the Midrash which states that before creating our world, God
created other worlds and destroyed them:

> And now, my dear brothers, come and see the basis of the
> foundations of our Torah. For this enigma, revealed to us
> centuries ago by our forefathers and teachers, has been disco-
> vered in nature and demonstrated before our eyes. Man's
> yearning spirit, which seeks to discover all mysteries worthy of
> investigation, revealed four strata in the bowels of the earth,
> superimposed on one another, each of a different composition.
> Between these strata lie the fossilized remains of creatures
> — which indicates that the earth has been in upheaval four
> times... And we can see the perfection and beauty of creation
> increasing in each succeeding layer... The tradition handed
> down to us by the kabalists for hundreds of years — that four
> worlds were destroyed, each closer to perfection than its prede-
> cessor — has now been demonstrated clearly and accepted
> universally.

He explains the opening verses of the Torah as follows: "In the
beginning [many thousands of millennia ago], God created Heaven and
Earth. And [five thousand seven hundred fifty years ago] the earth was
formless and void."[75] Between these two events, God created worlds and
destroyed them.

The importance of science study in conjunction with *talmud Torah* is
challenged by Bach,[76] who states: "It is inappropriate to group the
request for both these wisdoms [Torah and secular] into one prayer
[recited at the conclusion of the Sabbath]... for they are as different as
light and darkness and there is no connection between them; one is holy
and the other profane, and it is offensive to combine them in one
prayer."

4. Sanctification of God's Name

The concept of Israel's serving as a guide and a living example for the
peoples of the world — as a "prophet to the nations,"[76] is found exten-

sively in the words of the Prophets and is implied in the Torah itself. On appointing Abraham for his mission, God tells him that He would make him into a nation whose mission would be: "to be a blessing,"[77] which the Sages interpreted to mean[78] that he should draw the estranged to God. And, when the Children of Israel were given the Torah, they were told[79] to become "a nation of Kohanim," i.e. "messengers of God."[80]

If this is indeed the mission of Israel, then the commandment to sanctify God's name — by affirming its sanctity among others — is our most basic national mitzvah. Because God's name is associated with us, our esteem in the eyes of the other nations is critical. The Talmud repeatedly stresses the importance of inspiring respect among the gentiles. Although the mitzvah to sanctify God's name applies with full gravity only in the presence of ten Jews,[81] the Talmud also applies it regarding non-Jews: we must not cause a gentile to suspect us of transgression.

The Torah states:[82] "For this is your wisdom and your insight in the eyes of the nations." The Sages deduce: "What wisdom is apparent to the nations? The calculation of the seasons and the zodiac." Hence our obligation to perform this calculation ("especially its non-halakhic aspects"—Maharsha). Both Rif and Rosh cite this injunction as an explicit halakhah.

This obligation also serves as the basis for the words of Rabbi Eliyahu, the Gaon of Vilna, as quoted by R. Hillel of Sklov:[83]

> It is well-known that the eminent R. Eliyahu occupied himself extensively with natural phenomena and mundane investigations to gain a better understanding of the wisdom of the Torah, to sanctify God's name in the eyes of the nations and to hasten the final redemption. Even in his youth, he excelled in all seven wisdoms and sought ever more knowledge. He also ordered his disciples to learn whatever they could about the seven wisdoms by which the world is investigated, so that the science of Israel —in conjunction with the wisdom of the Torah—would achieve great recognition in the eyes of the nations, as it is written: "For this is your wisdom and your insight in the eyes of the nations." Thus, Israel would achieve spiritual superiority, as Scripture states: "To exalt you above all the nations, which He did for praise, for fame, and for glory." He often asked us rhetorically: how are the contemporary Torah figures sanctifying God's name, as many of the earlier authorities did, by their

great knowledge of the secrets of nature and the wonders of the Creator? Many righteous gentiles also extolled the wisdom of Israel, possessed by the Torah scholars, the members of the Sanhedrin, the Tanaim and Amoraim, etc. In later generations, there were such giants as our teacher, Rambam, R. Yomtov Lipman Heller, and others who sanctified God's name abundantly in the eyes of the nations through their knowledge of secular research.

R. M.C. Luzzatto advises:[84] "A person who must mingle with gentile scholars should learn that which will earn him their respect; thus God's name will be sanctified through him." Netziv voices a similar recommendation.[85]

Although we are told to be "firm as a leopard"[86] and not allow public opinion to divert us from the true course, we must not permit our dignity to diminish in the eyes of the gentiles, nor desecrate God's name before them. We must not cause them to treat our holy Torah disrespectfully. It is not enough for us to show them how to serve God; in all substantive matters, we must not appear inferior to them. Thus we are bidden by the Mishnah to "know how to answer the heretic."[87] Here, the use of the term "heretic," rather than "heresy," implies that we must attempt not only to refute heretical arguments, but also to influence their proponents. In fact, the Sages[88] apply this Mishnah only to a gentile heretic, for a Jewish one is likely to become more stubborn when contradicted.

From this Mishnah, Rashbatz[89] derives permission to study science. *Midrash Shemuel* comments: "Although [according to the wording of the Mishnah] it appears that acquisition of the knowledge needed to answer a heretic is a matter of choice [left to the individual], it is as important to God as studying Torah and fulfilling the commandments. Therefore, [the Mishnah] mentions it in context [with Torah study and mitzvah fulfillment]." Furthermore, in the name of R. Yisrael, he explains why Torah study is mentioned first: "They have taught us the course of study: you should study Torah first and foremost, with its commentaries, until it is fully absorbed into your mental make-up and you know every detail... Thereafter, you should study the other sciences to be able to answer [the heretic's] questions."

Based on this Mishnah, Maharal[90] permits the study of the works of gentile authors if it is done with the proper intent, supporting his decision with the argument: "If he does not know their words, how can he answer them?"

Among those unfit to testify in court are "those who eat abominations,"[91] i.e., "those who accept charity from the gentiles, for this is a desecration of God's name." If we become dependent on the gentiles for scientific knowledge, are we not "eating abominations" on the national level?

A similar point is made by the "Chatham Sofer":[92] "And you shall [interrupt your Torah study to] gather your grain—because of the mitzvah of settling Eretz Yisrael... And not only agriculture but all crafts should be studied for the sake of settling and dignifying Eretz Yisrael, lest it be said that there is no cobbler, construction worker, or the like in all of Eretz Yisrael, and they must be brought from far away."

5. "Fill the Earth and Subdue It"

When God told the first man and his wife:[93] "Be fruitful and multiply, fill the earth and subdue it, and master the fish of the sea, the birds in the sky, and every living thing," this may have been a commandment as well as a blessing.[94] Either way, it is an expression of God's will, and once God's will is revealed to us, we are obliged to carry it out, even without a direct commandment.[95] Hence we are to subdue the world and acquire its wealth in the service of God.

To assist us in this endeavor, God imposed laws on nature, without which we would have no control over events. Without the laws of inertia, we could not maintain our position; without the laws of chemistry and biochemistry, we could not control our limbs. We would be entirely passive, unable to achieve any goals. Thus, to be fit for responsible action, we require dependable laws of nature which we can use to attain our objectives. God tells us through the Prophet Jeremiah:[96] "Were it not for my covenant day and night, I would not have established the laws of Heaven and Earth"—not merely Heaven and Earth, but their laws as well, the laws of nature, are prerequisites to moral, religious law.

Obviously we must understand natural laws to make use of them. The ability to achieve our goals depends on this knowledge. For example, when we develop a new alloy, we can construct a better *shechitah* knife, or build a faster airplane which will shorten the time required to bring help to the sick, thereby adding precious years to a life devoted to God's service. Technological developments — in such varied fields as printing, medicine and automation — can contribute much, directly or indirectly, to the observance of many commandments, including such basic mitzvoth as Torah study, preservation of life, acts of kindness and Sabbath observance.

The obligation to subdue the earth implies that we must use the means nature provides. We are commanded[97] to be "cunning with the mitzvoth." By developing modern machinery and modes of transportation, we may indeed become "stronger than lions" and "swifter than eagles."

6. Preservation of Life

The Torah imposes strict obligations regarding health. Thus, "we are commanded to remove any obstacle that can lead to loss of life ... as the Torah states: 'Be cautious and guard yourself.'"[98] Even a cursory scanning of the Talmud reveals how important these obligations were to our Sages. One work,[99] devoted to medicine in Judaism, spans 735 pages, citing approximately two thousand passages dealing with healing and health, culled from the Talmud alone. R. Yehudah HeChasid compared the refusal to study medicine to manslaughter.[100] Rambam was a world-renowned physician whose works on medicine were of great importance to the development of medical science. Even his *Mishneh Torah* devotes three entire chapters[101] to matters of health and personal safety. Furthermore, when Rashba issued[102] a fifty-year ban on the study of the Greek classics by young people, he specifically exempted medical texts. In a responsum cited earlier, R. Ya'akov Emden recommends the study of nature:

> Especially that part which deals with medicine, because it is concerned with healing, and the Torah has testified to its validity and commanded its application. This knowledge seems to have been lost to the world and its very bases have been corrupted; every day, new opinions arise, and their conclusions are equally dubious. Nevertheless, even if a researcher discovers only a little about medicine, it can lead to great results, comparable to major discoveries in other disciplines, especially if it can

be substantiated by experimentation. Certainly, his reward will be great, and if the opportunity presents itself, he should exert himself to pursue it.

The obligation to take care of our health demands that we acquaint ourselves — at least superficially — with the latest developments in physiology and medicine. Not everyone can become an expert in these fields, but basic knowledge is clearly required — if only to know when to call the doctor. Hygiene also demands more than following instructions blindly, even if they originate in the Talmud or in Rambam's writings, especially now that human physiology has apparently changed.[103]

7. Earning a Livelihood By Means of a Profession

A father is obligated to teach his son a trade.[104] According to the Sages,[105] this obligation is alluded to in the verse "See life [i.e. a profession] with the wife you love." Essentially, the son himself is enjoined to learn a trade and the father's obligation to teach him is derived from the son's responsibility. In the Jerusalem Talmud, this obligation is deduced from the Biblical command, "choose life."[106] Rambam simply writes:[107] "It is the way of intelligent men to provide themselves with work which supports them." *Tur* and Shulchan Arukh, citing a Mishnah, state:[108] "Then [after his Torah studies] he goes about his business, for 'All Torah that is not combined with work will end in failure and cause sin.'" According to halakhah,[109] teaching one's son a trade is a "matter of divine concern." Therefore, such instruction may be arranged even on the Sabbath.

When choosing a vocation, the primary concern should be that it will not be harmful spiritually or physically. Thus, the Sages advise:[110] "Above all, a man should teach his son a clean and easy trade." Furthermore, because "[Torah] is not across the ocean," they deduce[111] that "you will not find [the Torah] among merchants or traders." They also discourage[112] a father from training his son to be a donkey or camel driver, barber, boatsman, herdsman, or shopkeeper — all trades associated with various deceptions or encroachments. Discounting all such professions — and their modern equivalents — someone seeking a "clean and easy trade" nowadays might well choose one of the sciences

or technologies. Science study would then contribute to another important mitzvah — "choose life."

Both *Kaftor WaFerach* and Tashbatz[113] demonstrate at length how
much the Sages toiled to fulfill this mitzvah. R. Ya'akov Provencali
writes:[114] "One who studies medicine to gain money and honor — thereby to perfect himself and become wiser — will have blessings bestowed
upon him, for it is praiseworthy in the eyes of God and man."

According to R. Mosheh Chaim Luzzatto:[115] "One who chooses a
profession to gain a livelihood will certainly have to acquire all the
knowledge it requires." In the broadest sense, this includes familiarity
with the language and culture of one's society. Thus, the Talmud compares the requirement to learn Greek with the obligation to learn a
trade.[116] Furthermore, the house of Rabban Gamliel was permitted to
study the forbidden "wisdom of Greek" because that family frequented
the royal court.[117]

8. Summary

*   Both the Torah and the world derive from the same source and were
    created to enable us to serve God. Therefore, familiarity with the
    world is important to Torah life.
*   This requisite scientific knowledge occasionally far exceeds what
    one absorbs in everyday life.
*   Some of the most fundamental mitzvoth require much scientific
    knowledge for their proper fulfillment.

On the other hand, this knowledge is always secondary to Torah
study, as elaborated in the following chapter.

3

The Study of the Natural Sciences: Limits

Although the study of the sciences is important, it must be somewhat limited, as it might otherwise lead us astray, causing us to lose our faith, forsake the Torah, or neglect its study.

1. The Danger of Heresy

The study of science generally involves reading books authored by gentiles—and occasionally by heretics. We must clarify to what extent such study is permitted when these texts contain heresy. The problem of heresy *per se* is discussed in the next chapter;[1] here, we consider this issue only as it relates to study of the natural sciences.

The Mishnah[2] which enumerates those who will not share in the next world adds, in the name of R. 'Akiva, "those who read alien books." The Talmud[3] explains this to mean the books of the Sadducees (according to one opinion[4] even the works of ben Sira are forbidden). On this basis, Rivash prohibited[5] the reading of science books which challenge the basic tenets of Judaism.

Furthermore the Talmud rules,[6] "He who learns even Torah from a *magus* has forfeited his life," where *magus* refers to a "devoutly idolatrous heretic who constantly blasphemes God and incites others to idolatry." This rule has been codified in the Shulchan Arukh.[7]

R. Ya'akov Emden counseled a student attending a university far from any Jewish community:[8]

> Therefore, it is proper to toil [in the study of medicine, but] not to such an extent that one would neglect, God forbid, the beautiful and sacred studies because of it. Blessed is he who can

grasp one and not forsake the other, to do as they ["Rambam, Ramban and many other leaders of various generations"] have done. But to journey to their study hall is improper, even if it is not tantamount to learning from a *magus*. Nevertheless, "do not approach the entrance of her house" and do not seek to join them in their domiciles in order to learn their customs and their manners.

Here, R. Emden refers to social intercourse with gentiles. However, similar circumspection is obviously required when dealing with Jews who are apt to lead us astray.

Putting aside the need to "know what to answer the heretic," there is some difference of opinion concerning the acquisition of knowledge from heretical books (as distinct from learning from a heretic personally). In one responsum[10] on a question of *tereifoth*, Rema bases his argument, in part, on Aristotle. Greatly disturbed by this, Maharshal[11] responded by quoting the above responsum of Rivash and the words of the Sages,[12] " 'Keep your course far from her'—This refers to heresy." Regarding Aristotle, he added: "There is no heresy and ruin like that of their scholars." He also relates that he found the prayer of Aristotle in the young people's prayer books, blaming this on Rema's attitude. The latter answered him, raising several significant points:[13]

1   The study of the works of heretics is the subject of an old debate.[14] Rashba forbade such study only for young people, who had not yet learned the wisdom of the Talmud.
2   The reservations of the early authorities referred only to works of philosophy, "but they did not outlaw the study... of the nature of things; on the contrary, through it, we may realize the greatness of the Creator." (Maharshal apparently did not differ with him regarding this issue.)
3   These reservations applied, at most, only to the original texts, where forbidden ideas are admixed. But translations, which entail no such problems, are permitted. (It is not clear whether Maharshal concurred with Rema on this point.)

A responsum by Chawoth Ya-ir[15] is also interesting in this connection. It opens as follows: "The greatest of the Greek philosophers wrote, 'Love Socrates, love Plato—love only the truth more.' " It continues with a long list of great Torah authorities, throughout the generations, who quoted this aphorism.

One important safeguard against exposure to heretical ideas is surely a thorough familiarity with Torah. Regarding the importance of studying Torah before science in general, Redak writes:[16] " 'This book of the Torah shall not depart from your mouth...' It appears that this commandment was addressed to Joshua as well as to everyone else, until they knew the Torah; thereafter, they were to learn the sciences." R. Yitzchak of 'Akko, a disciple of Ramban, remarks:[17] "For our teachers were well-versed, and engrossed, in the natural sciences — after they had sated themselves with wine and meat [i.e. the Torah]."[18]

2. The Danger of Forsaking the Ways of the Torah

Ascribing too much importance to the study of science can lead to an additional danger. At certain times in our history, Jews gravitated toward scientific works and revered them as if they were part of the Torah. In Rashba's day, for example, several of the scholars of Provence interpreted the history of Creation as a parable, deemed the *Urim WeThumim* merely an astrolabe, and declared nature immutable, thereby denying the creation of the world and the miracles God performed. They also considered the sciences their main area of study, with Torah study only an adjunct. Eventually, Rashba and his court declared a fifty-year ban on the study of Greek writings for anyone below age twenty-five[19] (on the basis of this age limit, Rema defended his citing Aristotle in a responsum, as noted above).

A similar situation apparently prevailed at the time of the expulsion from Spain, when many preferred scientific study to Torah study. R. Y. Ya'avetz (himself a Spanish exile) even attributed the expulsion to this sorry state.[20] He compared such people to one who aspired to learn the art of "fashioning the royal robes, whose intricate embroidery requires considerable skill. At first, he saw a mallet, needle and linen thread. He went to the smithy to learn how to make mallets and needles, and then set out to master the women's art of spinning linen thread. He spent all his time on this and never accomplished his original goal of learning this precious art. The poor soul never realized that this was not part of the artisan's craft. He could have purchased mallet, needle, and thread easily and inexpensively. Similarly, these worthless people have expended all their time on alien wisdom . . . and they are devoid of God's Torah and its mitzvoth."[21]

According to this parable, one should not remain ignorant of the sciences. However, one should build on the scientific achievements of others, rather than innovating in this field (unless, presumably, such innovation is the source of his livelihood).

3. Neglecting Torah Study

The Talmud warns against neglecting Torah study,[22] and the danger of such neglect must further limit the study of science.

God commanded us through Joshua:[23] "This book of Torah shall not depart from your mouth, and you shall meditate in it day and night." How, then, can we justify the study of other knowledge? The answer is that science study is permissible when it is in the service of the Torah —even if only indirectly. As noted,[24] R. Samson Raphael Hirsch points out that as long as we study the sciences as an aid to Torah study, we are not forsaking it. The Jerusalem Talmud illustrates this in an interesting passage:[25]

R. Yehoshua' was asked about teaching one's son [wisdom of] Greek. Based on the verse in Joshua, he responded that it is permissible only "when it is neither day nor night." Thereupon the Talmud asks, if this verse is meant literally, how could R. Yishma'el maintain that a Jew must learn a trade? The answer: "[Wisdom of Greek was prohibited only] because of the informers" (familiarity with "wisdom of Greek" would draw these Jews into the social circle of the royal court until, eventually, they would identify with the court more than with their own people and inform on them). The implication of this passage is that both learning a trade and "wisdom of Greek" are, in principle, compatible with "meditating in Torah day and night"—if they are studied with the proper motivation. This confirms the above derivation by R. Hirsch and is also similar to Maharal's position, as cited below.

Note:
The meaning of the term "wisdom of Greek" is discussed in the next chapter.

A similar discussion is found in the Babylonian Talmud:[26] "Ben Dama, the nephew of R. Yishma'el, asked him, 'Having learned the entire Torah, may I study wisdom of Greek?' R. Yishma'el quoted him the verse '[the words of Torah] shall not leave [your mouth]... day and night' [and continued] 'Go seek a time that is neither day nor night and learn wisdom of Greek then.'" But the Talmud continues: "And he disagrees with R. Shemuel bar Nachmani, who said in the name of R. Yonathan that this verse is neither an obligation nor a mitzvah, but a divine blessing." Earlier, the Talmud quotes yet a third opinion: "R. Yochanan said in the name of R. Shim'on ben Yochai, 'Even if a person has merely read the Shema' morning and evening, he has fulfilled the requirements of this verse—but it is forbidden to proclaim this to the unlearned.' Rava said, 'It is a mitzvah to proclaim this to the unlearned.'" Since Rava sides with R. Shim'on, this became halakhah.[27] In the Shulchan Arukh, Rema permits science study, but, to ensure the supremacy of Torah study, on an incidental basis only.

According to Maharal,[28] the other wisdoms are "a ladder that leads to the wisdom of the Torah"—and one in no way neglects the Torah by studying them. However, he himself challenges this position:

> The following Midrash[29] presents some difficulty: ["'The Torah] is not in the heavens'—Shemuel said, 'The Torah will not be found among the astrologers, who deal with the heavens.' They said to him, 'But you are an astrologer, and yet you are great in Torah!' He replied, 'I only studied astrology when I was exempt from Torah [study], when I entered the privy.'" Accordingly, a person is only permitted these studies when he is otherwise exempt and cannot study Torah at all... We must say that this wisdom refers to stargazing [i.e. investigating the influence of stars on a person's destiny], which does not involve the order of the universe. But the study of the orbits of the stars and constellations is certainly required.

Maharal proceeds to support his view from the Talmudic passage which commands us "to calculate the seasons and the zodiac."[30] Clearly, he too holds that only study which contributes nothing to the service of God is excluded by the commandment to "meditate in the Torah day and night."

In the words of a more recent Torah authority:[31]

> It is an educational mistake, bordering on the criminal, to teach

our children that all science and craft, not entirely derived from the Torah, is despicable. Such an outlook is founded on falsehood and ignorance. Anyone who thinks that by this means he can protect his children, and guard them against the harmful effects of contact with scientific aspirations that contradict Torah views, will have to bear responsibility for the results of his error... It is forbidden to use deceit to strengthen the recognition of the truth. It is forbidden to despise something the Sages honored, and for which they instituted a special blessing."

4

The Study of the Humanities

As we have demonstrated in Chapter 1, the Sages and later authorities decried the study of any alien wisdom, except for natural science. To elucidate their rulings, we first clarify the terms they use in discussing this issue.

1. Definition of Concepts

(1) The Seven Wisdoms

The seven wisdoms are enumerated by Rabbeinu Bachyay:[1] logic, arithmetic, mensuration, nature, astronomy, music, and divinity. He defines logic as linguistics (a branch of philosophy).

Here, we use the term "philosophy" in the modern sense, including the humanities and speculative and untestable disciplines.

(2) Wisdom of Greek

The Mishnah[2] states: "During the wars against Titus, they decreed... that brides were not to wear a diadem and that no one was to teach his son [wisdom of] Greek[3]." The Talmud adds:[4] "Accursed is one who teaches his son wisdom of Greek." Rivash[5] was asked whether the prohibited "wisdom of Greek" includes the famous books of physics and metaphysics. He answered by citing the Talmudic passage on the above Mishnah, from which it is evident that "wisdom of Greek" is a language:

When Jerusalem was under siege... one old man there knew "wisdom of Greek," and spoke to the city's attackers in wisdom of Greek... Thereupon they said, "Accursed is one who raises pigs and one who teaches his son wisdom of Greek." The question was then raised: "Did not the master teach... In Eretz Yisrael—speak either Hebrew or Greek!" [implying that Greek is permitted]? The answer given was: "The Greek language is one thing, and wisdom of Greek is another." From this distinction, it appears that these books [of physics and metaphysics] are not included in this prohibition; for, although they are written in Greek, that language was not forbidden... And as far as the wisdom itself is concerned, what was it that the old man said to them? Therefore, it appears to me that wisdom of Greek refers to speaking Greek in riddles and ambiguities which the general public does not understand.

Rashi's explanation is similiar: "Wisdom of Greek: A subtle language used by the courtiers, which other people do not understand." Elsewhere[6] he merely defines it as "allusions," as do other commentators.[7]

R. Yitzchak of 'Akko also explains it as a means of communication:[9] "Wisdom of Greek is not natural science, for in this the Sages excelled over the Greeks, who—like the other nations—only derived it from Israel. Rather, the 'wisdom' the Sages warned us about is that which the Greeks made up, and anyone who follows it will cast off the yoke of the Torah. This wisdom involves symbols and allusions by which one can communicate with another."

Apparently only one Rishon, R. Meir HaLevi (Remah),[10] disagrees with this definition, and he, too, does not include science in this term.

(3) Alien Books (*Sefarim Chitzonim*)

As stated in the opening chapter of this part, alien books may rob their reader of his share in the next world.[11] According to the Talmud[12] this refers to books of the Sadducees[13] or to Bible commentaries which are not based on the scholarship of the Sages[14]—"For in them some heresy will be found." R. Yosef adds that even the Book of Ben Sira is forbidden.

Note:

The Book of Ben Sira is similar to Proverbs, but was not included in the *Tanakh*. According to Maharil (*Likutim*, begining), ben Sira was the son of the prophet Jeremiah.

The Jerusalem Talmud[15] explains: "Alien books...such as the Books of Ben Sira and Ben La'anah; however, [reading] the books of Homer and those who succeeded him is merely like reading a letter. Why?[This is explained in Scripture:] 'Beyond these, my son, beware...'— these were meant for perusal but not for intensive study." The question "Why?" apparently refers to why the books of Homer are permissible. Scholars wonder why our Sages would be more stringent regarding the Book of ben Sira than those of the idolator Homer. One commentator[16] feels that the reading in the Jerusalem Talmud's version erroneously reverses what is prohibited and what is permitted. Others[17] speculate that only the works written close to the time of the canonical books are forbidden, for fear that they might be accorded equal status. This is similar to R. Bloch's[18] theory that the Sages are speaking of the books the Christians added to the Bible; these are especially dangerous, as they might be equated with the books of the *Tanakh*, which were written with divine inspiration.

However, Ritba explains:[19] "Even though the Talmud refers to '*Sefer Ben Sira*' as 'alien books,' we can deduce that they only prohibited its regular study. But it is permissible to review it occasionally for wisdom and instruction, unlike real heresy." According to this interpretation, the question "Why?" refers to the restrictions on reading the Books of Ben Sira and Ben La'anah, which, consequently, are permitted for perusal. This resolves several difficulties inherent in the previous interpretation.[20]

Rashbatz evidently equates "alien books" with nonsensical writings[21] and "books by heretics, which contain no wisdom and are merely a waste of time... But books which have a reasonable foundation are not included in this [prohibition]."

(4) Books of Idolatry and Heresy

Reading books of idolatry is forbidden:[22] "Many books have been written by idolators regarding their beliefs, practices and worship, and

God has commanded us not to read them." This is based on the verse: "Do not learn to imitate the abominations of these nations."

Books of heresy are those that deny God's omnipotence or His Torah;[23] here, the ban on contact with heresy is also based on a verse, and is even stricter because heresy is more attractive.[24] Said R. Tarfon of such books,[25] "If they got into my hand, I would burn them together with all the [sacred] Names they contain, for one who is pursued by a killer or a serpent may even take refuge in a house of idolatry, but not in a house of [heresy], for they know the truth, but deny it."

R. Elchanan Wasserman explains[26] that the loss of one's share in the next world for reading heretical books is not a punishment for transgressing a prohibition, but a consequence of reading; such reading leads to heresy, which causes the loss of his share. Note that the prohibition against heresy is derived from a verse: "'Do not explore after your heart'—This refers to heresy."

(5) The "Magus"

In the first section of Chapter 3, we discussed the prohibition of learning anything, even Torah, from a "magus"—"a heretic who draws one to idolatry."[27] The Talmud debates whether a magus is a heretic or a magician; the above ruling, however, applies only to a heretic.[28]

2. Reasons for the Prohibitions

(1) The Danger of Studying Philosophy

As quoted in Chapter 1, R. Hai Gaon maintains that one who neglects Torah study to explore philosophy will eventually abandon the yoke of Torah and lose all reverence for God. R. Y. Ya'abetz[29] details how the study of foreign wisdoms can undermine the best of us. In *Sefer HaYashar*,[30] we find: "Certain wisdoms destroy one's faith, such as the alien wisdoms, the wisdom of the heretics, and philosophy; from all these ... one should distance himself as much as possible, for he will lose his faith before gaining any use from them... Imperceptibly, the study of philosophy will slowly but surely estrange him [from the Torah]... unless he has a well-versed and pious teacher to guide him and watch over him in matters that might weaken his faith; [only] thus will he save himself from the dangers of philosophy and yet reach the desired goal [of benefiting from its study]."

Rivash writes[31] that philosophy caused even some of the greatest of the early authorities to stray slightly: "Hence... even these two great [authorities] could not keep to a straight path... How can we, who never experienced the proper illumination?"

(2) The Lack of Benefit from Such Study

As Rashbatz[32] equates "alien books" with nonsense, he apparently derives the prohibition against them from a Talmudic dictum: "And you shall speak of [Torah]—but not of other things [which simply are not worthy of one's time]." From the context, it appears that these "other things" include *higayon* (logic).

When the disciples of R. Elie'zer asked him to teach them the proper way of life, "he said to them, '...and keep your children from *higayon.*'"[33] *Nimukey Yosef*[34] offers the following interpretation of the term *higayon*:

> R. Sa'adyah Gaon translated the term as *almanask*, which the Christians call "logic"—[it is disparaged] because it distracts people [from more important studies]. R. Hai agrees and explains that it is intriguing and may cause someone to become so involved that he abandons the Torah and forgets what he has learned. It is even forbidden to set aside certain times to study this, even if one has already learned the entire Torah... Everyone should cherish the words of the Torah and not abandon them to pursue vanities that will not help, but will only waste one's time.

Incidentally, Rashi explains the above statement of R. Eli'ezer: "Do not allow them to become overly involved with Scripture, because it is attractive. Another interpretation: [keep your children] from childish chatter." Thus, according to Rashi, the statement is irrelevant to the present issue.

R. Ya'akov Emden writes similarly:[35] "My son! Who permitted you to attend their schools, learn their manners, pursue vanities and errors, and waste time on logic which is entirely theoretical, and which our Sages never used? Simply put, that is what our Sages meant when they said, 'Keep your children from logic'—and you will not find any Sage who wasted his time on it."

R. Shelomoh Efrayim Luntschitz[36] describes the study of logic as follows: "One person built a skyscraper, basing it on his mental conjectures; suddenly, another thrust [the foundation] aside, and its walls collapsed... 'Its builders have toiled over it in vain.'" About using philosophical concepts in halakhic analysis, the "Chatham Sofer" declares:[36] "Anyone who admixes Kabala with halakhoth transgresses the prohibition of planting different species together [kil-ayim]... On the other hand, one who admixes logic and Torah is guilty of 'plowing with an ox and a donkey.'"

The Mishnah says:[39] "Turn [the Torah] over again and again, for all is contained therein." Tosfoth Yom Tov comments: "Don't say that by studying wisdom of Greek you will also acquire knowledge of sociology, proper conduct and good character traits—all [these things] are arranged and contained in [the Torah]." R. Avraham Yitzchak Bloch[40] puts it this way: "All study of belles-lettres... and all the popular studies that have no useful application are certainly not worth the time."

(3) "An Assemblage of Scoffers" and Arousal of the Evil Impulse
In the Tosafoth we find:[41] "Reading stories in the vernacular appears to R. Yehudah to be forbidden [on the Sabbath]. And even on weekdays, R. Yitzchak wonders who permitted it, as it is akin to joining 'an assemblage of scoffers.'"

Rosh—citing Rabbeinu Yonah[42] and codified in Shulchan Arukh[43] —adds: "Poetic writings and parables of mundane matters and romances, such as the *Book of Emanuel*, and war stories, may not be read on the Sabbath, or even on weekdays, because they fall under the prohibition of 'an assemblage of scoffers'... and romances violate the additional prohibition against arousing the evil impulse."

3. Permitted Aspects

Despite all these prohibitions, some aspects of humanistic study are permitted nonetheless:

(1) Wisdom of Greek
Wisdom of Greek was permitted to those close to the court,[44] as the Talmud confirms in the name of R. Shim'on ben Gamliel: "There were a thousand children in my father's house; five hundred learned Torah and five hundred learned wisdom of Greek." Apparently, for them such study was akin to learning a trade. Meiri comments on this passage that

the royalty expected courtiers to be thoroughly versed in this art.[45] This juxtaposition of wisdom of Greek and knowledge of a trade is corroborated by another Talmudic passage.[46] Furthermore, knowledge of wisdom of Greek enabled them to use their political influence to save lives.[47]

One was also allowed to teach his daughter this art, for through it she would curry favor with the noble matrons.

(2) Heretical and Idolatrous Books

Under certain conditions, one may even study books of a heretical nature or similar works, primarily to enable one to refute heretical arguments. Thus, the Midrash[48] derives: "'Do not learn [the abominations of the nations] in order to do'—Learning to do is forbidden, but learning to understand and guide is not." Rashi explains that such study is permitted if it helps in the performance of a mitzvah. Meiri[49] explicitly links this passage and the Mishnah that prohibits the reading of alien books: "What is forbidden is to read these books in order to embrace their faith; but [to read them] to understand and to guide others is not [forbidden]."

Though he forbids the reading of idolatrous books in general,[50] Rambam, too, allows[51] one to learn "the opinions of the gentiles in order to answer the heretic." Later authorities concur that to perform a mitzvah, such as responding to challenges to Torah, such studies are permitted.[52] Regarding the obligation to be prepared to answer the heretic, R. Ya'akov Emden states:[53] "You should be aware of the need to know these matters, as our Sages ordained. What is forbidden is only to study them in depth, as one studies the Torah, or to make them primary. Yet their study is necessary, and the Torah personality should not lack knowledge of these matters. One who believes [in the Torah] will not be harmed by the noxious fumes." R. Avraham Yitzchak Bloch adds[54] that they are occasionally necessary "...to warn others, as well as oneself, not to be misled by their false ways."

Concerning books which mingle valuable material with heretical concepts, the author of *Zekan Aharon* writes[55] that a person resistant to corruption might be permitted to read them: "Even though [they] contain errors regarding divine providence, some of which contradict the fundamentals of the Torah, this is insufficient reason to denigrate one who has studied them, for their subject matter depends not on faith, but on evidence... and anyone who accepts the word of God will cull from their words whatever agrees with our faith, just as 'one eats the fruit and discards the parings,' as did R. Meir [who learned from the heretical Acher in this fashion], and he will use them as 'spicers and cooks.'" R. Ya'akov Emden[56] testifies that his father, the Chakham Tzvi, spent some of his spare time perusing alien books and amassing general knowledge.

In addition to the prohibition of reading heretical books as such, there is another, forbidding one to learn anything from a "magus." Concerning this, Maharal writes[57] that the obligation to study science "needs investigation, as learning from an unfit teacher is prohibited." He concludes: "This refers to learning from him directly... [but not] to reading his works." Later authorities shared this opinion.[59] This leniency is evidently based on the views of many great authorities throughout the generations,[60] who often quote gentile—and presumably heretical—sources.

R. Ya'akov Emden taught[58] that studying at medical school is not considered learning from a "magus."

(3) History

As stated,[61] the Tosafoth and Shulchan Arukh compare the reading of war stories to joining "an assemblage of scoffers." But R. Yehudah Ashkenazi[62] permits reading *Yosifon* (Josephus Flavius, *The Antiquities of the Jews*), *Sefer Yuchasin*, and *Shevet Yehudah*, "for from these one can learn admonition and reverence." R. Ya'akov Emden allows reading the first part of *Yosifon* and *Sefer Yuchasin* on Shabbath.[63] Otherwise, he confines all such reading to weekdays, noting that most of it "deals with the chronicles of past gentile kings, knowledge of which is entirely useless. As we said, systematic reading is forbidden, except during periods of leisure, when one cannot concentrate on learning, on days when the academy is closed, or to learn correct, clear diction." He enumerates several reasons for permitting the occasional study of history:

a) A Talmud scholar should not be so ignorant of history and changing times that he cannot answer his questioners properly and is considered an ignoramus.

b) Occasionally, historical events are analogous to matters concerning our nation.

c) We may be able to gain experience in dealing with the world at large, especially in political action and in currying favor with royalty.

R. Samson Raphael Hirsch maintains[64] that we must listen to history with the ears of the Prophet Isaiah, and that both history and science serve an important function in knowing God. The "Chazon Ish" agrees:[65] "Chronicles and historical occurrences greatly help the Torah scholar in his pursuits, and he should base his wisdom on past developments."

But not only past history; it is also certainly an obligation to keep up with contemporary events, for not doing so is akin to walking a dangerous path with closed eyes. *'Arukh HaShulchan*[66] permits, when necessary, the reading of newspapers that report on world affairs. There is support for this opinion in Rava's reproof of R. Papa,[67] when the latter found it necessary to ask whether Rome or Persia was the greater power: "This man hides out in the woods all his life, so that he has not heard of the status of Rome."

Giduley Taharah[68] writes:

One should not neglect other knowledge, for an intelligent man should not be devoid of all knowledge of [those] sciences that are not misleading. R. Yosef Shelomoh, the physician [Yashar] of Candia, considered them "mundane, but in the realm of the sacred." In general, all the knowledge we acquire will enhance us and our spirit, aside from the benefits we will ultimately reap from it. The rabbis who preceded us were very knowledgeable in Torah. Yet, instead of expending much valuable time elucidating obscure Midrashim by means of spurious explanations, they would have done well to amass some [general] knowledge. Then we would not have to suffer from the "little foxes that destroy" the best we have.

(The author lived in Germany during the rise of the Reform movement. His complaint seems to concern the earlier rabbis' lack of awareness of the cultural environment and its demands.)

(4) Foreign Languages, Writing, Etc.

The study of foreign languages was apparently always accepted in Torah education. The Sages tell us that both Joseph and Mordekhai spoke seventy languages, as was also required of the members of the Sanhedrin.[69] Hence the Gaonic practice of teaching children foreign languages:[70] "It was said in the name of R. Hai Gaon, 'It is permitted to teach the children, along with their Torah studies, Arabic writing and arithmetic. But if this is not done in conjunction with Torah studies, it is improper.'" (Others, however, teach that, on the contrary, it must be done in a separate locale.[71]) Similarly, *Zera' Emeth*[73] links this custom to the Mishnah in *Avoth*, which recommends a combination of Torah study and mundane pursuits. R. 'Akiva Eger is like-minded:[73] "Torah together with secular studies is good, i.e., spending an hour or two each day teaching one's children writing and arithmetic, as we do with our children."

We have already noted a similar recommendation by R. M.C. Luzzatto.[74] R. Yechezkel Landau ("Noda' BiYehudah") fought vigorously against the innovations that threatened to undermine the supremacy of Torah. Nevertheless, he recognized the importance of learning the language of one's country:[75] "In Scripture, we were castigated for our ignorance of the language of each nation... For he who fears God will act intelligently and grasp both; although Torah is primary, one should also learn diction and proper manners."

R. Shemuel Landau — his son and successor to the rabbinate of Prague — followed suit:[76] "It is impossible to exist in these times, in this country, without a knowledge of spoken and written German. One who cannot read and write German will not be considered for any kind of work, and will not be successful; everyone must teach his son the language and customs of his host country."

Even the "Chatham Sofer" — who incessantly battled the corrosive infatuation with gentile culture, as manifest in the study of foreign languages — nevertheless recognized its potential benefits. In his approbation of Leopold Dukes' German translation of Rashi's commentary on the Torah, he states that "the author was raised on the knees of yeshiva scholars... and then turned to the vineyard of the scholars of other wisdoms and the languages of the nations... and I found my soul's desire, for he held fast to one but did not abandon the other (1 Cheshvan 5593 [October 25, 1832])."

When R. Samson Raphael Hirsch developed the curriculum for his school, he included general studies, such as language, mainly because every father must teach his son a trade from which he can earn a livelihood. He also urged that history be taught in conjunction with *Tanakh*, to infuse it with the spirit of the Prophets.[77]

R. Simchah Zisel Ziv, the principal disciple of R. Yisrael of Salant and a leader of the Mussar movement, incorporated language in his school's program in Kelm and Grobin. He writes: "We have also instilled in [the students'] heart a desire to learn writing and the language of the surrounding country, arithmetic and geography. All this, in order to uphold the Torah, not merely for curiosity's sake."[78]

The frequent use of foreign terms by Rashi and many other authorities also supports this approach.(R.L.)

However, this kind of learning is conditioned by time and place. It is well-known that the Yeshiva of Volozhin closed because of government efforts to introduce secular studies as a major part of the curriculum (see note at the end of this part). Also over the past century or so, the rabbis of Jerusalem have banned such subjects as foreign language and writing in the community Torah schools—whether taught in a separate building or at the Torah school itself. "Even though Torah law permits it," they perceived such study as a "gateway to idolatry."[79]

Similar considerations surfaced when the Russian rabbinate faced the Haskalah movement. The Russian government wanted to recognize the rabbinate as the official representative of the Jewish people, which meant that its members would have to be familiar with the Russian language and customs. At a rabbinical conference in Petrograd in 5670 (1910), Rabbis Meir Simchah of Dvinsk ("Or-Sameach"), Y. Rabinovicz (of Ponievicz), Chaim Ozer Grodzensky (of Vilna) and David Friedman (Karlin) favored a resolution which would obviate the need for the obnoxious "rabanuth mita'am" (government appointed and religiously unqualified rabbis), by allowing candidates for the rabbinate to study four subjects specified by the Russian government. R. Chaim Soloveichik and the "Chafetz Chayim" objected vehemently and carried the day.[80]

There was also bitter opposition to the use of Western languages in the orthodox communities of the Hungarian Lowland. We can gauge the ferocity of this opposition from a responsum of Maharam Schick,[81] who was inclined to permit sermons in German in emergencies and under specific circumstances, but nevertheless, in a case, that was brought before him regarding a candidate for a rabbinic position, concluded as follows:

> We know he is a God-fearing scholar. He lectures in this language, but his entire intent is to enlarge the realm of the sacred, to attract those with little knowledge and instill in them the Torah and the fear of God, and to wage God's war against the evil-doers... He aspires to benefit the community, and

"whoever benefits the community will not be the cause of sin"[82]... I see no reason to forbid him [to do so] if they only want to listen to German. If he does not speak this language they will surely hire someone less qualified than he... However, my colleagues disagree, and I must accept their decision with fear and trembling. Far be it from anyone to contradict them.

In another context,[83] he explains that the "Chatham Sofer" objected only to the "Germanists" who prided themselves on their knowledge of German; "but the master's words cannot apply to those who are forced to [speak German] because of this generation's low learning level or to attract those with little knowledge to Torah and divine service."

(5) Logic

Some authorities have praised the study of logic, while others have expressed reservations. Thus, R. Avraham ibn 'Ezra writes:[84] "It is also necessary for the intelligent student of the Talmud to have some knowledge of logic." Rambam is more emphatic:[85] "It is entirely impossible... for one to seek human perfection without learning logic." Commenting on the statement "Keep your children from logic," the editor of 'Ein Ya'akov avers:[86] "It is inconceivable that this logic is the logic of today, for the latter is a valuable wisdom in Torah study." Even R. Ya'akov Emden, when criticizing[87] the study of logic, said that "it is not good to be totally bereft of [secular studies]... A small amount will serve the Children of Israel well, arming them to defend themselves against verbal onslaughts and not to cede the field to the heretics... Nevertheless, too much of it is harmful and a waste of valuable time."

5

The Opinions of the Torah Leaders of the Past Generation

In the Introduction, we noted that R. Samson Raphael Hirsch regarded the study of science as a necessary adjunct to the fulfillment of Torah life. Elsewhere,[1] he explains himself at length, but does not detail the manner in which such study should be undertaken after elementary school. About sixty years ago, Jews began to question university study, which had been common among observant Jews in Western Europe (like his teacher, R. Ya'akov Ettlinger ['Arukh LeNer], R. Hirsch himself briefly attended university). Eastern European Jewry equated this practice with the then rampant Haskalah, which attempted to eradicate the "backward" Jewish Orthodoxy. Consequently, when young Shim'on Schwab came from Germany to Eastern Europe to study, he asked the Torah authorities of Lithuania and Poland for their opinion.

The Rabbi of Ger, R. Avraham Mordekhai Alter, refused to answer in detail, but R. Schwab quotes him thus: "It is certainly forbidden to study alien wisdom. But we must surely look out for the dignity of R. Hirsch, the saint of Frankfurt, who was a living *Mussar Sefer* (book of ethics)."

(On the other hand, R. P.M. Alter, R. Avraham Mordekhai's son, informed me that his father had not prohibited secular study entirely. He even allowed some people to study medicine in Berlin, giving them specific guidance; whoever followed these instructions came to no spiritual harm.)

One rabbi and three yeshiva deans responded at length: R. Avraham Yitzchak Bloch of Telshe, R. Elchanan Wasserman of Baranowicz, R. Barukh Ber Leibowitz of Slobodka-Kamenitz and R. Yosef Rozin of Rogoczov.[2]

In evaluating these responses, we should recall the impact of the Haskalah in Eastern Europe. Many yeshiva students were drawn away from the yeshiva, to the university, believing that a general education promised wealth and honor, in contrast to their peers' life of grueling poverty and deprivation. Ultimately, nearly every such university student abandoned Torah.

1. R. Avraham Yitzchak Bloch[3]

R. Bloch distinguishes four types of study:

(1) Heretical studies

He forbids academic disciplines tending toward heresy, such as the philosophy that is taught at universities nowadays, which is generally based on premises inimical to faith. Nevertheless, select individuals may study them to achieve one of three goals:

1   To learn to guard against them and caution others.
2   To know how to answer a heretic.
3   To pursue some other Torah objective.[4]

But even then, only if:

1   "They have perfected a Torah outlook and saturated themselves with Talmud."
2   They study them part-time only.
3   "They do not assimilate them into their mental make-up."

(2) Scientific studies mixed with some heresy

"True scientific matters, which have become mixed with heretical material, such as natural science, medicine, etc... are not prohibited, but one must separate the chaff from the wheat... and it would be very welcome if textbooks were written by God-fearing men involved with Torah." Here, too, certain conditions must be met:

1-2 A youth should be taught them "after he has already learned Torah and gained faith from the holy books." Yet one should "teach him the basics in his early youth, before Talmud study becomes obligatory at age fifteen,[5] for then he must channel all his thoughts and time into the Talmud, examining scientific works only occasionally, when he needs a respite from his Torah studies. [This restriction applies] unless he studies for the purpose of earning a livelihood."

3   "He should learn from a God-fearing teacher."

4   "One must not make these studies intrinsic to the curriculum; rather, they must be secondary."

(3) Religiously neutral studies

"Academic subjects that do not impinge on religious matters, such as mathematics, engineering, and foreign languages, are basically not prohibited, although they involve a neglect of Torah study." They are permitted only:

1   "For girls, who are exempt from the obligation to study Torah."

2   "For those whose position requires it."

3   "As a profession."

The conditions for such study are:

1   "Precedence — in both importance and time — must be given to Torah study, even for girls... These studies must not be considered to be on the same level with Torah study; rather, they are like learning a profession."

2   "Every father must aspire to raise his son to study Torah."

3   "No general education may be established [in these fields by the Jewish community], lest the world become devoid of Torah disciples."[6]

(4) Literature

"It is certainly improper to waste time studying and reading literature and all the useless popular studies, as one can learn proper conduct from our Torah. [This is] especially so because such literature contains erotic and [other] forbidden material."

2. R. Elchanan Wasserman[7]

Based on Rambam's prohibition of reading idolatrous texts, R. Wasserman forbids secular studies involving heretical works, since heresy is worse than idolatry.[8] Rambam actually read such books, but R. Wasserman assumes he did so only for the sake of a mitzvah, and "a mitzvah emissary is safe from harm."[9] He acknowledges that this principle cannot be invoked if the mission is especially dangerous, but maintains that Rambam, who was particularly pure and wise, surely prepared himself for his venture, thereby rendering it relatively safe. Nonetheless, such preparation cannot protect "inferior beings like us." In addition, if there is a danger of socializing with gentiles, it is forbidden.[10]

He continues:

> If he engages in secular studies to learn an occupation and gain a livelihood, there is no prohibition, for the learning of a trade is a mitzvah... But if one sees that his son yearns for Torah, and is gifted enough to become a Torah leader, in regard to such a son, R. Nehorai said: "I will neglect every occupation in the world and teach my son only Torah," although R. Nehorai did not dispute the obligation to teach one's son a trade.[11]
>
> But if one's profession does not require this study, and he only wants to amuse himself with it, this might be forbidden because it wastes time that should be devoted to Torah study... Aside from this, perhaps he should not study them regularly, lest they become as important to him as the Torah... For indeed, all science is necessary to maintain the world, but it is not the goal, only the means thereto... and one who makes secular studies his steady occupation seems to indicate that they are an end in themselves, which is contrary to the Torah.

3. R. Barukh Ber Leibowitz[12]

In contradiction to the preceding two *roshey yeshivah*, R. Leibowitz appears to oppose secular study entirely. He writes: "Once one tastes Torah, he understands how hateful secular studies are."

He also cites his teacher, who permitted one man to send his son to a place where Sabbath desecration would be required, in order to keep him out of the army (which, apparently, was life-threatening), but forbade another to send his son to the "Gymnasium" (high school) for the same purpose—for this involved heresy, which is forbidden even if one's life is threatened.

R. Leibowitz quotes Rema to the effect that all of one's time should be devoted to Torah subjects, and only occasionally may he learn secular subjects that do not involve heresy. From this, he deduces a ban on science study, even for the purpose of acquiring a profession, even though learning a trade, as such, is obligatory.

To explain this, he defines two kinds of Torah neglect:

a) Simple neglect, which results from any activity which will not compete with Torah in importance.

b) Active neglect, by studying matters designed to replace the Torah as the ultimate aspiration. These are completely prohibited.

To earn a living, one may engage in the former, but not the latter:

> As part of the obligation to study Torah, one must consider the Torah paramount and not believe, God forbid, that any other knowledge or human endeavor is comparable. Otherwise, God would have revealed it on Mount Sinai. Rather, every person should resolve that the Torah reigns supreme, and nothing else leads to human perfection—for [if it did,] it would make the Torah secondary. Furthermore, he must not combine any other matter with Torah. Although one spices food to enhance its flavor, mixing other disciplines with the sacred Torah would degrade it. Furthermore, if one learns something steadily and it is important to him to demonstrate his virtuosity, this is called "abandoning the Torah" ... and cannot be excused by the need to earn a livelihood.
>
> Lest those who engage in secular study declare that they ascribe no importance to it—that it is merely like a needle to a tailor or a pen to the scribe—Rema has already pointed out that one may learn these matters occasionally, but not regularly, for this would be [active] neglect of Torah.

According to R. Leibowitz, it is forbidden to study science on a steady basis, even for the sake of a livelihood or any other mitzvah, because studying it regularly equates it with the Torah, regardless of one's intent; he does not cite any basis for this ruling.

4. R. Yosef Rozin[13]

R. Rozin, "the Rogoczover," makes several novel points:

a) Knowledge of nature has fundamental halakhic importance; for whole categories of halakhah are determined by scientists.

b) According to Rambam, a father must teach his son not only Torah and a trade, but also "wisdom." Since astronomy, medicine and mensuration are in any case necessary for halakhah, and are therefore included in his duty to teach him Torah, R. Rozin concludes that "wisdom" must refer to other sciences, even the social ones.

c) "'You shall speak of them'—... You should not admix other things with them." From this passage in the *Sifrey*, he deduces that only admixture is forbidden, but studying secular subjects separately is permitted.

d) Every father may teach his son secular knowledge, but this permission does not extend to the community as such.

We proceed to examine these innovative observations in detail.

a) A knowledge of nature is undoubtedly necessary for the performance of many mitzvoth. However, it might be argued that this knowledge may be derived from the Torah itself. R. Rozin proves the opposite: A scholar's facility with veterinary physiology had to be certified before he was accredited to rule on the status of first-born animals. This accreditation, like all Torah-related certification, could be granted only by the *Nasi* (Prince) in Eretz Yisrael. However, certification of the prerequisite veterinary expertise itself could also be issued by the authorities in Babylonia, indicating that such knowledge is not Torah knowledge.[14]

   R. Rozin also implies that the physician's knowledge of the extent of a person's injuries—life-threatening or not—cannot be derived from the Torah, except for the rule that a wound inflicted by an iron instrument—no matter how small—can be fatal.[15] This ruling is the only medical-related issue which remains outside the physician's province.

b) The Rogoczover deduces from Rambam's wording that the requirement to teach one's son wisdom refers to science. This is somewhat difficult to reconcile with other facts. It is clear from the wording of the Talmud, which Rambam cites as his source,[16] that the wisdom mentioned refers to moral instruction, not science, as the duty to teach one's son "wisdom" is based on the Talmudic statement: "Even though he learns [Torah], he is performing a mitzvah [by chastising him to instill the proper personality traits]." This is also evident from Rambam's commentary on the Mishnah, in which he points out that one who accidentally causes his son's death is subject to exile, unless the accident occurred while he was teaching him Torah, a profession, or **good personality traits**.[17]

Indeed, good personality traits are termed "wisdom" elsewhere in Rambam's writings;[18] Rambam defines anyone who has achieved good and balanced personality traits as a "wise one." It is therefore difficult to understand the words of R. Rozin on this point.

c) R. Rozin's reasoning, based on the wording of the Midrash—that only the mixture of Torah and secular science is prohibited, but each by itself is permitted—is similar to R. Hirsch's reasoning based on the same Midrash: one may study sciences if they are considered secondary to the Torah.

d) In his commentary on the Torah,[19] R. Rozin emphasizes that community instruction in science would be prohibited by the Torah. His source for this prohibition seems somewhat obscure. However, others exhibit the same reluctance to introduce public secular education within the framework of Torah education. R. Chaim Berlin writes in his ethical will that "[Netziv] was ready to sacrifice his life to prevent secular studies from infiltrating the Yeshiva of Volozhin. Therefore the yeshiva was shut down [see note at end of the section—L.L.]... He ordered me not to agree to such a thing under any circumstances and not to articulate anything even approaching permission. He said that God Himself hinted at this in His Torah, which tells us 'to distinguish between the sacred and the profane.'" Similarly, the "Chazon Ish"[20] states: "In the councils of the great Torah authorities, it was decided not to permit yeshiva students to engage in secular studies while they are engaged in Torah study with their youthful fervor. They considered this a weakening of [the students'] defenses, which would cause them harm... Therefore, they declared this a *milchemeth mitzvah* ['holy war']."

Thus, while there is no reference to this halakhah in the Torah (the verse R. Berlin cites is evidently only an allusion), it is considered an emergency decision regarding a perceived clear and present danger. R. Rozin's words imply that this decision is absolute and based on the Torah. This requires further clarification, especially because we have seen that, at least since the time of the Gaonim, schools and "*chadarim*" have customarily taught arithmetic and the vernacular.[21]

Note:

Under heavy pressure from the Russian government, the spiritual leaders of Russian Jewry agreed reluctantly to introduce a modicum of secular studies into the Volozhin Yeshiva program. These classes were to be strictly supervised by the dean of the yeshiva, the "Netziv," and taught outside the yeshiva building.[22] Subsequently, the government insisted on the following conditions:

a. Secular studies must be conducted from 9:00 AM to 3:00 PM.

b. The yeshiva must close at sunset.

c. No one may study more than ten hours a day.

d. The head of the yeshiva and all teachers must hold academic diplomas.

Clearly, it was futile to maintain the yeshiva under these conditions.[23]

The following report by the author of *Torah Temimah* (and nephew of Netziv himself) concerning the level of secular knowledge at the yeshiva is of special interest:

It was obvious to all that there was broad academic knowledge of the sciences and languages at the Volozhin Yeshiva and that students interested in such knowledge could acquire it extensively. Quite a few students read daily, weekly, and monthly papers in various European languages. A spirit of aristocratic nobility and charm enveloped the Volozhin Yeshiva, to such an extent, that it became proverbial that there Torah and *derekh eretz* (i.e. general education) went hand in hand. When fathers discussed their sons' education with principals, one would tell the other: "If you wish to see your son become a man of stature, a man of Torah and *derekh eretz*, integrated into society and worldly as well, send him to Volozhin."[24]

It is interesting to note that even Netziv himself, under special circumstances, prefers secular studies organized by the community over such studies handled on an individual basis. He writes:

If by law they have to learn secular subjects also, this should be supervised by the Rabbi and the leadership, [to ensure] that the teacher be a God fearing man. This would be impossible if each father makes arrangements for his children... Thus perforce he avoids teaching his son secular subjects and that causes the son to rebel and find improper means to attain secular studies. But if the arrangements are in the hands of the community and its heads, they would not avoid these studies.[25]

It is obvious, however, that he proposed this only as a necessary evil; for he concludes: "Although there is no hope that, from such [limited] hours of [Torah] study, the student would become fit for the Rabbinate."

In Conclusion

Already in the introduction to this work we pointed out that, in a sense, *talmud Torah* is the very foundation of Judaism so that it behooves us to be meticulous in its performance — and just as in the fulfillment of other Torah commandments, here too the Torah itself guides us in the proper fulfillment of the mitzvah.

There is a tendency, among the more practical-minded of us, to be lax in the fulfillment of this mitzvah, which involves "mere" study, while the more intellectually inclined tend to stress it excessively. But deviation from the Torah-prescribed limits, in either direction, can seriously reduce the effectiveness of our study. Superficiality in Torah study leaves us unprepared to face the many challenges with which Torah life confronts us constantly, be they in the area of ethics or ritual — and leaves us totally unqualified to reach the higher levels of perfection (*chasiduth*). On the other hand, an exaggerated emphasis on study, at the expense of active involvement with this world, threatens to turn Torah study into a purely academic activity. The Torah's admonition not to deviate from G-d's commands "either right or left" (Deuter. 5:29) applies here no less than to other mitzvoth.

Many are the ways in which such "study for study's sake" can cancel the enormous potential benefits inherent in proper *talmud Torah*. Such academization may turn Torah study into a sterile intellectual exercise with little impact on our conduct; or, in our excessive preoccupation with individual "trees," it may cause us to lose sight of the "forest" as a whole. Again, it may seduce us into neglecting the development of the substrates necessary for the thriving of *talmud Torah*, and evidently such substrates, both economic and academic, are vital for successful Torah study. Here true love of Torah study may cause us to neglect the very means needed to nurture it as an effective force guiding our life.

In this work, we have surveyed in depth a number of issues bearing on these questions, as they are relevant to today's Torah student, collecting and organizing the pronouncements of Torah authorities throughout the ages with special emphasis on the opinions of the contemporary spiritual leadership. We have done this in an attempt to present objectively all that we have found on these issues. I hope that this work will help the reader to think intelligently and knowledgeably about his *talmud Torah* program. If so, I consider myself well compensated for my labors.

Bibliographic Information

NOTE: It is impossible to present, within the present framework, a full introduction to the rich Judaica literature. To provide a minimal bibliography, we list here, in Section 1, the major works of the Talmudic period (to about 450 CE) and in Section 2, those post-Talmudic works which are cited in the "Notes and References" without authors' names. Section 3 lists the frequently cited authorities, with their dates.

Halakhah (pl. halakhoth) comprises absolute rules governing the conduct of the observant Jew.

Agadah (pl. agadoth) comprises moral principles, biographical tradition, allegories, etc.

Abbreviations are explained under "Notes and References."

1. Talmudic Literature

Mishnah is a compendium of legal and religious rulings of the *Tanaim* (teachers of the Mishnah) and serves as the basis of the two Talmudim.

Mesekhtoth Ketanoth are collections of tanaic statements not codified in the Mishnah.

Tosefta is an additional compendium of such rulings.

Talmudim (Jerusalem and Babylonian Talmud) consist of discussions of the Mishnah and, in conjunction with this, of additional agadic material.

Targumin (Onkelos and Yonathan) are early interpretive translations of parts of the Bible into Aramaic.

Midrashim are additional tanaic compendia. Those cited in the "Notes and References" are presented below in alphabetical order, together with an indication of their principal character.

> *Mekhilta* (halakhic/agadic)
> *Midrash Rabbah* (agadic)
> *Midrash Rabbi Tanchuma* (agadic)
> *Midrash Shochar Tov* (agadic)
> *Mishnath Rabbi Eli'ezer* (agadic)
> *Pirkey Avoth*, Chapter 6 (*Perek Kinyan HaTorah*) (agadic)

Pirkey Rabbi Eli'ezer (agadic)
Sifra (halakhic)
Sifrey (halakhic/agadic)
Tana DeBey Eliyahu (agadic)
Yalkut Shim'oni (a medieval agadic-midrashic compendium)

2. Post-Talmudic Literature

Major post-Talmudic works cited without the name of the author are listed here, together with the name of the author and the type of work. For explanation of abbreviations, see below, heading "References." Books cited by acronym are listed under "Authorities Cited."

Agudah, Sefer — MaHaRZaKh — Halakhic compendium
Agur — Ashkenazi, Rabbi Ya'akov Barukh — Halakhic compendium
'Arukh — Nathan ben Yechiel of Rome, Rabbi — Talmudic dictionary
'Arukh HaShulchan — Epstein, Rabbi Yechiel Michel — Halakhic compendium
Avkath Rokhel — Karo, Rabbi Yosef — Responsa
Ba-er Heitev — Ashkenazi, Rabbi Yehudah — Glosses to SA
Beiur Halakhah — Kagan, Rabbi Yisrael Meir HaKohen — Glosses to SA
Beth HaLevi — Soloveitchik, Rabbi Yosef Dov — (a) Responsa, (b) Commentary on
    Pentateuch
Beth Yosef — Karo, Rabbi Yosef — Glosses to *Tur*
Birkey Yosef — ChYDA — Glosses to SA
Chafetz Chayim — Kagan, Rabbi Yisrael Meir HaKohen — Halakhic treatise on
    gossip and slander (*leshon hara'*)
Chasdey David — Pardo, Rabbi David — Commentary on Tosefta
Chatham Sofer — Sofer (Schreiber), Rabbi Mosheh — Responsa
Chawoth Ya-ir — Bacharach, Rabbi Yair Chaim — Responsa
Chayey Adam — Danzig, Rabbi Avraham — Halakhic compendium
Chazon Yechezkel — Abramsky, Rabbi Yechezkel — Commentary on Tosefta
Chelkath Mechokek — Mosheh of Brisk, Rabbi — Glosses to SA *Even Ha'Ezer*
Chelkath Ya'akov — Breisch, Rabbi Yaakov — Responsa
Chizkuni — Chizkiyahu bar Manoach, Rabbi — Commentary on Pentateuch
Chovoth HaLevavoth — Bachyay ibn Pakudah, Rabbi — Ethical treatise
Divrey Chayim — Chaim of Zans, Rabbi — Responsa
Eliyah Rabbah — Shapira, Rabbi Eliyah — Glosses to SA
'Eyn Ya'akov — Ya'akov ibn Chaviv, Rabbi — Compendium of the Agadoth of BT
Giduley Taharah — Kargau, Rabbi Mendel — Responsa
Hafla-ah — Horowitz, R. Pinchas HaLevi — Novellae on BT *Kethuboth*
Igroth Mosheh — Feinstein, Rabbi Mosheh — Responsa
Kaftor WaFerach — Ishtori HaParchi, Rabbi — Halakhic compendium concerning
    the Land of Israel
Keren Orah — Karlin, Rabbi Yitzchak — Novellae on BT

Kethav Sofer—Sofer, Rabbi Avraham Shemuel Binyamin--Responsa
Ketzoth HaChoshen—Heller, Rabbi Aryeh Leib—Glosses on SA *Choshen Mishpat*
Kol Bo—Medieval halakhic compendium
Korban Aharon—Aharon ibn Chaim, Rabbi—Commentary on *Sifra*
Korban Ha'Eidah—Frankel, Rabbi David—Commentary on JT
Kuzari—Yehuda HaLevi, Rabbi—Philosophical treatise
Lechem Mishneh—Buton, Rabbi Avraham di—Commentary on MT
Lechem Shamayim—Ya'AVeTz—commentary on Mishnah
Levush Malkhuth—Yafeh, Rabbi Mordekhai—Glosses to SA
Machzor Vitry—Simchah of Vitry, Rabbi—Prayer compendium
Magen Avraham—Gumbiner, Rabbi Avraham Aveli—Glosses to SA *Orach Chayim*
Magid Mishneh—Vidal, Rabbi Yomtov—Commentary on MT
Menorath HaMaor—Abuhav, Rabbi Yitzchak—Ethical treatise
Meshekh Chokhmah—Meir Simchah of Dvinsk, Rabbi—Commentary to Pentateuch
Midrash Shemuel—Ozido, Rabbi Shemuel di—Compendium of commentaries on M *Avoth*
Mikhtav MeEliyahu—Dessler, Rabbi Eliyah E.—Moral/philosophical compendium
Migdal 'Oz—Emden, Rabbi Ya'akov—Treatise on laws and customs
Minchath Chinukh—Babad, Rabbi Yosef—Glosses on *Sefer HaChinukh*
Minchath Kohen—Pimentil, Rabbi Avraham—Three halakhic treatises
Minchath Yitzchak—Weiss, Rabbi Yitzchak Ya'akov—Responsa
Mishnah Berurah—Kagan, Rabbi Yisrael Meir HaKohen—Glosses to SA *Orach Chayim*
Mishneh Torah—RaMBaM—Halakhic compendium
Mordekhai—Ashkenazi, Rabbi Mordekhai ben Hillel—Halakhic compendium on BT
Nimukey Yosef—Chaviva, Rabbi Yosef—Glosses to RYF
Orach Meysharim—Treves, Rabbi Menachem—Ethics compendium
Orchoth Tzadikim—Author unknown. Late XV century (cf. R. G. Zalieshinsky, Jerusalem 1988 edition)—Ethics compendium
Or Zarua'—Yitzchak of Vienna, Rabbi—Halakhic compendium [A responsa collection, by the same name, was written by his son R. Chaim.]
Pachad Yitzchak—Lampronti, Rabbi Chizkiyah—Talmudic encyclopedia
Peney Yehoshua'—Falk, Rabbi Ya'akov Yehoshua'—Novellae on BT
Peri Chadash—Silva, Rabbi Chizkiyah di—Glosses on SA
Peri Megadim—Te-umim, Rabbi Yosef—Glosses on SA
Perishah—SeMA'—Glosses on *Tur*
Rav Pe'alim—Yosef Chaim of Bagdad, Rabbi(*Ben Ish Chay*)—Responsa
Reshith Chokhmah—Vidas, Rabbi Eliyahu di—Ethical treatise
Sedey Chemed—Mediney, Rabbi Chaim Chizkiyahu—Halakhic encyclopedia
Sefath Emeth—Alter, Rabbi Yehudah Aryeh—Novellae on Pentateuch (and BT)
Sefer Charedim—Azkari, Rabbi El'azar—Enumeration of mitzvoth
Sefer Chasidim—Yehudah HeChasid, Rabbi—Ethical treatise

Sefer HaBerith—Pinchas Eliyahu, Rabbi—Scientific/moral compendium

Sefer HaChinukh—Aharon HaLevi of Barcelona, Rabbi—Halakhic/ethical compendium

Sefer HaEshkol—Avraham of Narbonne, Rabbi—Halakhic compendium

Sefer Ha'Ikarim—Albo, Rabbi Yosef—Philosophic treatise

Sefer Ha'Itur—Yitzchak of Marseilles, Rabbi—Halakhic compendium

Sefer HaMitzvoth—RaMBaM—Enumeration of mitzvoth

Sefer HaMiknah—Horowitz, Rabbi Pinchas—Novellae on BT *Kidushin*

Sefer HaYashar—Yonah Gerondi, Rabbeinu—Ethical compendium

Sefer HaTerumah—Barukh of Worms, Rabbi—Halakhic compendium

Sefer Yere-im—Eli'ezer of Metz, Rabbi—Enumeration of mitzvoth

Sefer Yuchsin—Zakuth, Rabbi Avraham—History

Seridey Eish—Weinberg, Rabbi Ya'akov Yechiel—Responsa

Sha-agath Aryeh—Ginsburg, Rabbi Aryeh Leib—Responsa

She-iltoth—Achai Gaon, Rabbi—Halakhic compendium

Shevet Yehudah—Virga, Rabbi Shelomoh ibn—History of Jewish persecutions

Shevet Yehudah—'Ayash, Rabbi Yehudah—Responsa

Shevuth Ya'akov—Reiser, Rabbi Ya'akov—Responsa

Shitah Mekubetzeth—Ashkenazi, Rabbi Betzalel—Medieval compendium of Talmudic novellae

Shulchan 'Arukh (SA)—Karo, Rabbi Yosef—Halakhic compendium. Glosses thereon by ReMA

SA HaRav—Sheneor Zalman of L'ady, Rabbi—Halakhic compendium

Terumath HaDeshen—MaHaRaY—Responsa

Toldoth Adam—Treves, Rabbi Mosheh David Avraham—Commentary on *Sifrey*

Torah Temimah—Epstein, Rabbi Barukh—Commentary on Pentateuch

Tosafoth—Medieval France and Germany—Glosses to BT

Tosfoth Yom Tov—Heller, Rabbi Yomtov Lipman—Commentary on Mishnah

Tur—Ya'akov ben Asher, Rabbi—Halakhic compendium

Tzitz Eli'ezer—Waldenberg, Rabbi Eli'ezer Yehudah—Responsa

Yalkut Shim'oni—Shim'on of Frankfurt, Rabbi—Midrashic compendium

Yam Shel Shelomoh—MaHaRShaL—Novellae on BT

Yechaweh Da'ath—Yosef, Rabbi 'Ovadyah—Responsa

Yefeh Mar-eh—Yafeh, Rabbi Shemuel—Commentary on MR

Yefeh Toar—Yafeh, Rabbi Shemuel—Commentary on JT agadoth

Yesod Ha'Avodah—Avraham of Slonim, Rabbi—Ethical treatise

Yosif Ometz—Neuerlingen, Rabbi Yosef Yuspa Hahn—Compendium of halakhoth and customs

Zekan Aharon—Eliyahu HaLevi, Rabbi—Responsa

3. Biographical Listing of Post-Talmudic Authorities Cited

NOTE: Authors known primarily by acronyms, or by the name of their major work, are listed accordingly. Contemporary authors are listed only if they fall into these categories.

Note that Hebrew acronyms (in their written form) consist only of consonants, with the necessary vowels supplied by the reader. Here we spell these with the essential consonants capitalized. The consonant *'ayin* is indicated by an apostrophe.

Abramsky, Rabbi Yechezkel (*Chazon Yechezkel*) (1886-1976)
Abudirham, Rabbi David (?-1340)
Abuhav, Rabbi Yitzchak (*Menorath HaMaor*) (1433-1493)
Achai Gaon, Rabbi (*She-iltoth*) (680-752)
Aharon Berekhyah of Modina, Rabbi (*Ma'avar Yabok*) (?-1639)
Aharon ibn Chaim, Rabbi (*Korban Aharon*) (ca. 1560-?)
Aharon HaLevi of Barcelona, Rabbi (*Sefer HaChinukh*) (ca. 1300)
Alashker, MaHaRaM, Rabbi Mosheh (ca. 1460-1542)
Albo, Rabbi Yosef (*Sefer Ha'Ikarim*) (1380-1444)
Alnakawa, Rabbi Efrayim (?-1442)
Alnakawa, Rabbi Yisrael (?-1391)
Alshikh, Rabbi Mosheh (1508-1591)
Alter, Rabbi Yehudah Aryeh of Ger (*Sefath Emeth*) (1847-1905)
'Amram Gaon, Rabbi (*Sidur*) (?-875)
Arieli, Rabbi Yitzchak (*'Eynayim LaMishpat*) (1898-1974)
ARY (Rabbi Yitzchak Lurya) (1534-1572)
Ashkenazi, Rabbi Betzalel (1520-1564)
Ashkenazi, R. Mordekhai ben Hillel ("Mordekhai") (ca. 1240-1298)
Ashkenazi, Rabbi Ya'akov Barukh (*HaAgur*) (?-1600)
Ashkenazi, Rabbi Yehudah (*Ba-er Heitev*, 1742)
Avraham ibn 'Ezra, Rabbi (1090-1164)
Avraham min HaHar, Rabbi (ca. 1240-?)
Avraham ben HaRaMBaM, Rabbi (1186-1237)
Avraham of Narbonne, Rabbi (*Sefer HaEshkol*) (1110-1189)
'Ayash, Rabbi Yehudah (*Shevet Yehudah*) (ca. 1700-1760)
Azkari, Rabbi El'azar (*Sefer Charedim*) (?-1600)
Babad, Rabbi Yosef (*Minchath Chinukh*) (1790-1874)
BaCh, Rabbi Yoel Sirkes (*Bayith Chadash*) (1561-1640)
Bacharach, Rabbi Yair Chayim (1628-1701)
Bachyay, Rabbeinu (?-ca. 1340)
Bachyay ibn Pakuda, Rabbi (*Chovoth HaLevavoth*) (?-1161)
BaHaG (*Ba'al Halakhoth Gedoloth*) Rabbi Shim'on Kayara or R. Yehudai Gaon (ca. 750)
Bamberger, Rabbi Yitzchak Dov, of Wurzburg (1807-1878)
Bartinora, Rabbi 'Ovadyah of (1445-1530)
Barukh of Worms, Rabbi (*Sefer HaTerumah*) (1202-?)
Benabeshti, Rabbi Chayim (*Kenesseth HaGedolah*) (1603-1673)
Berlin, Rabbi Yesha'yahu (1725-1799)
Berlin, Rabbi Naftali Tzvi Yehudah (NeTzYV) (1817-1893)
Bruna, Rabbi Yisrael (ca. 1400-1476-)
Buton, Rabbi Avraham di (*Lechem Mishneh*) (1545-1588)
Chafetz Chayim, see Kagan
Chaim *Or Zarua'*, Rabbi (son of R. Yitzchak of Vienna) (ca. 1260)

Chananel, Rabbeinu (980-1050)
Chatham Sofer, see Sofer
Chaviva, Rabbi Yosef (*Nimukey Yosef*) (ca. 1340-ca. 1400)
Chazon Ish (Rabbi Avraham Yesha'yahu Karelitz) (1879-1953)
Chizkiyahu bar Manoach, Rabbi (*Chizkuni*) (?-ca. 1270)
ChYDA (Rabbi Chayim Yosef David Azulai) (1727-1806)
Danzig, Rabbi Avraham (*Chayey Adam*) (1748-1821)
David HaLevi, Rabbi (*TaZ*) (1586-1667)
Dessler, Rabbi Eliyahu Eli'ezer (1891-1953)
Eger, Rabbi Akiva Ginz (1762-1838)
Eli'ezer of Metz, Rabbi (ReEM,*Sefer Yere-im*) (1115-1198)
Eliyahu HaLevi, Rabbi (Disciple of R. E. Mizrachi; *Zekan Aharon*) (ca. 1500)
Emden, Rabbi Ya'akov (Ya'AVeTz) (1698-1776)
Epstein, Rabbi Barukh (son of R,Y.M. Epstein, see follow.) (1860-1942)
Epstein, Rabbi Yechiel Michel (1829-1908)
Ettlinger, Rabbi Ya'akov (*'Arukh LeNer*) (1798-1871)
Eybeshitz, Rabbi Yonathan (1690-1764)
'Ezra, Rabbi Avraham ibn (1089-1164)
Falk, Rabbi Ya'akov Yehoshua' (*Peney Yehoshua'*) (1680-1756)
Falk, Rabbi Yehoshu'a (SeMA') (1550-1614)
Feinstein, Rabbi Mosheh (*Igroth Mosheh*) (1895-1986)
Frankel, Rabbi David (*Korban Ha'Eidah*) (1707-1762)
Gabirol, Rabbi Shelomoh ibn (1021-1060)
Gaon of Vilna, GeRA, see HaGeRA
Gershom, Rabbeinu (965-1040)
Ginsburg, Rabbi Aryeh Leib (*Sha-agath Aryeh*) (1696-1785)
Grodzinsky, Rabbi Avraham (ca. 1882-1942)
Gumbiner, Rabbi Avraham Aveli (*Magen Avraham*) (1637-1683)
HaGeRA (HaGaon Rabbi Eliyahu of Vilna) (1720-1798)
HaRav, Rabbi Sheneor Zalman of L'ady ("*Tanya*", SA HaRav) (1745-1813)
Heller, Rabbi Aryeh Leib (*Ketzoth HaChoshen*) (1745-1813)
Heller, Rabbi Yomtov Lipman (*Tosfoth YomTov*) (1579-1654)
Hirsch, Rabbi Samson Raphael (1808-1888)
Hoffman, Rabbi David Tzevi (*Melamed LeHo'il*) (1843-1921)
Horowitz, Rabbi Pinchas Eliyahu of Vilna (*Sefer HaBerith*, 1797)
Horowitz, Rabbi Pinchas HaLevi (1530-1605)
Horowitz, Rabbi Yesha'yahu (*SheLaH*) (1560-1630)
Hutner, Rabbi Yitzchak ("*Pachad Yitzchak*") (1906-1980)
Ishtori HaParchi, Rabbi (*Kaftor WaFerach*, 1322)
Kagan, Rabbi Yisrael Meir HaKohen ("Chafetz Chayim") (1839-1933)
Kamenecki, Rabbi Ya'akov (*'Iyunim BaMikra*) (1892-1986)
Kanievsky, Rabbi Ya'akov Yisrael ("The Steipler") (1899-1985)
Karelitz, Rabbi Avraham Yesha'yahu ("Chazon Ish") (1879-1953)
Kargau, Rabbi Mendel (*Giduley Taharah*, disciple of Rabbi Yechezkel Landau)
    (1722-1842)
Karlin, Rabbi Yitzchak (*Keren Orah*) (1788-1852)

Karo, Rabbi Yosef (*Kesef Mishneh, Beth Yosef*, Shulchan Arukh) (1488-1575)
Kook, Rabbi Avraham Yitzchak HaKohen (1865-1935)
Kotler, Rabbi Aharon (*Mishnath Rabbi Aharon*) (1892-1962)
Lampronti, Rabbi Chizkiyah (*Pachad Yitzchak*) (1679-1757)
Landau, Rabbi Yechezkel (*Noda' BiYehudah*) (1714-1793)
Luntshitz, Rabbi Shelomoh Ephraim (*Keley Yakar*) (?-1619)
Luzatto, Rabbi Mosheh Chaim (RaMChaL) (*Mesilath Yesharim*) (1707-1747)
MaBYT (Rabbi Mosheh di Trani) (1500-1580)
MaHaRaL (Rabbi Yehudah Liwa ben Betzalel, Rabbi Loeb of Prague) (1512-1609)
MaHaRaM of Lublin (Rabbi Meir ben Gedalyah) (1558-1616)
MaHaRaM of Rothenburg (Rabbi Meir ben Barukh) (1220-1293)
MaHaRaM Shik, (Rabbi Mosheh ben Yosef) (1807-1879)
MaHaRaShDaM (Rabbi Shemuel di Medina) (1506-1590)
MaHaRAY (Rabbi Yisrael Iserlein, *Trumath HaDeshen*) (1390-1460)
MaHaRShA (Rabbi Shemuel Eli'ezer HaLevi Edels) (1555-1631)
MaHaRShaL (Rabbi Shelomo Lurya) (1510-1573)
MaHaRShaM (Rabbi Shalom Mordekhai Schwadron) (1835-1911)
MaHaRYK (Rabbi Yosef Kolon) (1410-1480)
MaHaRYL (Rabbi Ya'akov HaLevi Mulin) (1355-1427)
MaHaRYT (Rabbi Yosef di Trani) (1569-1639)
MaHaRZaKh (Rabbi Alexander Zuslin HaKohen of Frankfurt, *Sefer Agudah*) (?-1348)
MaLBYM (Rabbi Meir Leibish bar Yechiel Michel) (1809-1879)
Margolioth, Rabbi Ephrayim Zalman (*Yad Ephrayim*, 1820)
Mediney, Rabbi Chayim Chizkiyah (*Sedey Chemed*) (1833-1905)
Meir Simchah of Dvinsk, Rabbi (*Meshekh Chokhmah*) (1843-1926)
Meiri, Rabbi Menachem (1249-1306)
Migash, Rabbi Yosef ibn (1077-1141)
Mizrachi, Rabbi Eliyahu (ca. 1435-1525)
Mordekhai, see Ashkenazi
Mosheh of Brisk, Rabbi (*Chelkath Mechokek*) (1605-1658)
Nathan ben Yechiel of Rome, Rabbi ('*Arukh*) (1035-1106)
Neuerlingen, Rabbi Yosef Yuspa Hahn (*Yosif Ometz*) (ca. 1570-1637)
NeTzYV (Rabbi Naftali Tzvi Yehudah Berlin) (1817-1893)
Orenstein, Rabbi Ya'akov Meshulam (*Yeshu'oth Ya'akov*) (1775-1839)
'Ovadyah, Rabbi—see Bartinoro
Ozido, Rabbi Shemuel di (*Midrash Shemuel*) (ca. 1540-ca. 1610)
Papo, Rabbi Eli'ezer (*Pele Yo'etz*, 1824)
Pardo, Rabbi David (*Chasdey David*) (1710-1792)
Pimentil, Rabbi Avraham (*Minchath Kohen*, 1668)
RAH (Rabbi Aharon HaLevi of Barcelona) (1235-1300)
RaLBaG (Rabbi Levi ben Gershom) (1288-1344)
RaDBaZ (Rabbi David ben Zimra) (1480-1574)
RaMBaM (Rabbi Moshe ben Maimon, Maimonides) (1135-1204)
RaMBaN (Rabbi Moshe ben Nachman, Nachmanides) (ca. 1194-ca. 1270)
RaN (Rabbi Nissim ben Reuven) (ca. 1320-ca. 1380)

RaSh (Rabbi Shimshon of Shanz (?-ca. 1230)
RaShBA (Rabbi Shelomoh ben Adereth) (1235-1310)
RaShBaM (Rabbi Shemuel ben Meir) (ca. 1085-ca. 1174)
RaShBaTz (Rabbi Shimshon ben Tzemach, *TaShBaTz*) (1361-1444)
Rashi (Rabbi Shelomoh Yitzchaki) (1040-1105)
RAVaD (Rabbi Avraham ben David) (1120-1198)
RAVaN (Rabbi Eli'ezer bar Nathan) (1090-1170)
RAVYaH (Rabbi Eli'ezer bar Yoel HaLevi) (1140-1225)
ReDaK (Rabbi David Kimchi) (1160-1235)
Reiser, Rabbi Ya'akov (*Shevuth Ya'akov*) (1670-1734)
ReMA (Rabbi Mosheh Isserles) (1530-1573)
ReMaH (Rabbi Meir HaLevi Abul'afia) (1170-1244)
"Rogoczover", see Rozin
ROSh (Rabbenu Asher) (1250-1328)
Rozin (Rabbi Yosef of Rogoczov) (1858-1936)
RYF (Rabbi Yitzchak AlFasi) (1031-1103)
RYVaSh (Rabbi Yitzchak ben Shesheth) (1326-1408)
RYTBA (Rabbi Yom Tov ben Avraham) (1250-1330)
SeMA' (*Sefer Me-irath 'Eynayim*), see Falk
SeMaG (*Sefer Mitzvoth Gadol*), Rabbi Mosheh of Coucy (ca. 1190-ca. 1260)
SeMaK (*Sefer Mitzvoth Katan*), Rabbi Yitzchak of Corbeil (?-1280)
SeMaK MiZurich (Glosses on above), Rabbi Mosheh ben Zusman of Zurich
    (ca. 1300-ca. 1385)
Sforno, Rabbi 'Ovadyah (1475-1550)
ShaKh (*Sifthey Kohen*, Rabbi Shabthay HaKohen), (1623-1663)
Shapira, Rabbi Eliyah (*Eliyah Rabah*) (1660-1712)
SheLaH (*Sheney Luchoth HaBerith*), Rabbi Yesha'yahu Horowitz (1560-1630)
Sheneor Zalman of L'ady, Rabbi (*Tanya*) (1747-1812)
Shim'on of Frankfurt, Rabbi (*Yalkut Shim'oni*) (?-1170[?])
Silva, Rabbi Chizkiyah di (*Peri Chadash*) (1659-1698)
Simchah of Vitry, Rabbi (*Machzor Vitry*) (?-1105)
Sirileo, Rabbi Shelomoh (ca. 1490-ca. 1558)
Sirkis, Rabbi Yoel (*BaCh*) (1561-1640)
Sofer (Schreiber), Rabbi Mosheh (*Chatham Sofer*) (1763-1840)
Sofer (Schreiber), Rabbi Avraham Shemuel Binyamin (*Kethav Sofer*) (1815-1872)
Soloveitchik, Rabbi Yosef Dov (1820-1892)
Tam, Rabbeinu Ya'akov (Tos.) (1100-1171)
TaShBaTz; see RaShBaTz
TaZ (*Turey Zahav*), Rabbi David HaLevi (1586-1667)
Te-umim, Rabbi Yosef (*Peri Megadim*) (1727-1792)
Trevis, Rabbi Mosheh David Avraham (*Toldoth Adam*) (ca. 1775)
Trani, R. Yesha'yah di (RYD) (1180-1250)
Vidal, Rabbi Yomtov (*Magid Mishneh*) (?-ca. 1390)
Vidas, Rabbi Eliyahu di (*Reshith Chokhmah*, 1575)
Virga, Rabbi Shelomoh ibn (*Shevet Yehudah*, 1551)
Waldenberg, Rabbi Eliezer Yehudah (*Tzitz Eli'ezer*, 1945-)

Weinberg, Rabbi Ya'akov Yechiel (*Seridey Eish*) (1892-1966)
Weiss, Rabbi Yitzchak Ya'akov (*Minchath Yitzchak*) (1901-1989)
Ya'abetz, Rabbi Yosef (*Or HaChayim*) (?-1507)
Ya'akov ben Asher, Rabbi (*Tur*) (1269-1343)
Ya'akov ibn Chaviv, Rabbi (*'Eyn Ya'akov*) (?-ca. 1516)
Ya'AVeTz, see Emden
Yafeh, Rabbi Mordekhai (*Levush*) (1530-1612)
Yehudah HeChasid, Rabbi (*Sefer Chasidim*) (1150-1217)
Yehudah HaLevi, Rabbi (*Kuzari*) (1074-1141)
Yisrael Iserlein, Rabbi (*Terumath HaDeshen*) (1390-1460)
Yisrael of Salant, Rabbi (founded Mussar movement) (1810-1883)
Yitzchak of Corbeil, Rabbi (*SeMaK*) (?-1280)
Yitzchak of Marseilles, Rabbi (*Sefer Ha'Itur*) (1122-1193)
Yitzchak of Vienna, Rabbi (*Or Zaru'a*) (1180-1250)
Yonah, Gerondi, Rabbeinu (1200-1264)
Yosef, Rabbi 'Ovadya (*Yechaweh Da'ath*, 1977-)
Yosef ben Mosheh, Rabbi (*Leket Yosher*) (ca. 1410-?)
Yosef Chayim of Bagdad, Rabbi ("Ben Ish Chay") (1835-1909)
Zakuth, Rabbi Avraham (*Sefer Yuchsin*) (ca. 1440-1550)
Zerachyah HaLevi, Rabbi (ReZaH, "Ba'al HaMaor") (1135-1186)
Zevin, Rabbi Shelomoh Yosef (1888-1978)
Ziv, Rabbi Simchah Zisel of Kelm (1824-1898)

4. Glossary of Types of Halakhic Authorities

Tana—teacher of the Mishnah
Amora—teacher of the Talmud
Rishon—medieval post-Talmudic authority
Acharon—later authority
Posek—Post-Talmudic authority, rendering halakhic decisions

Notes and References

Note the following abbreviations used:

M	Mishnah
MK	*Mesekhtoth Ketanoth*
MR	*Midrash Rabbah*
MRT	*Midrash Rabbi Tanchuma*
BT	Babylonian Talmud
JT	Jerusalem Talmud
MT	*Mishneh Torah* (of RaMBaM)
SA	Shulchan Arukh

Common abbreviations of author's names are also used. These are explained in the Biographical listings.

NOTES TO PART 1

NOTES TO CHAPTER 1

1. *Machzor Vitry, Avoth* 3:17.
2. RaMBaM, Commentary on the Mishnah, *Kidushin* 1, end.
3. *Midrash Shemuel* on *Avoth* 2:2.
4. This is evident from the words of R. Yishma'el in BT *Berakhoth* 35b, and the commentaries of Rashi, R. 'Ovadyah of Bartinoro, and Rabbeinu Yonah on *Avoth* 2:2.
5. R. S.R. Hirsch, *Sidur, Avoth* 2:2.
6. MR Leviticus 89:3, *Yalkut Shim'oni* on Genesis 34, end.
7. M *Avoth* 3:17.
8. MK *Avoth DeRabbi Nathan.* The latter is quoted by R. Yisrael Alnakawah in his *Menorath HaMaor,* in the beginning of the chapter on *derekh eretz,* and is printed at the end of *Reishith Chokhmah.*
9. *Orchoth Tzadikim* 9.
10. R. Ya'akov Emden, *Migdal 'Oz, 'Aliyath Derekh Eretz* chap. 8, beginning, based on BT *Berakhoth* 63a.
11. R. Ya'akov Yechiel Weinberg in *HaRav Shimshon Refael Hirsch, Mishnatho WeShitatho,* Yonah Emanuel, ed.; Jerusalem, 5722 (1962), p.192.
12. R. S.Z. Ziv, *"Lishmor eth Derek 'Etz HaChayim"* in *"Or RaShaZ,"* Genesis p. 51. Also in op. cit. (note 11 above), pp. 183-4. R. S.R. Hirsch frequently uses the expression "Mensch-Jisroel," by which he expresses the same idea, i.e. that a person must pass the stage of being a full human being ("Mensch"), before he can hope to be a full Jew.
13. *Ha'amek Davar,* Genesis 2:4.
14. *Lechem Shamayim, Avoth* 3:17.
15. MK *Avoth DeRabbi Nathan* 11:1; see also *Mekhilta DeRabbi Shim'on ben Yochai* on Exodus 20:9.
16. *Chovoth HaLevavoth, Sha'ar HaBitachon* 3, end.
17. *Yalkut Shim'oni* 22 cites two conflicting interpretations of the verse. We have interpreted it according to the first, as have apparently all the early Torah commentators (R. A. ibn 'Ezra, ReDaK, Chizkuni — all ad loc.; RaMBaN, Genesis 2:8). Thus, too, in the Midrash (MR Genesis 14, end): "He made Adam [before the sin] a slave to himself, who, if he did not toil, did not eat."
    According to the second interpretation in the Midrash, however, the verse refers to occupying oneself with Torah and mitzvoth.

18. MaLBYM, cited by R. David Cohen (*Ohel David* I, I Samuel 25:2).
19. *Beth HaLevi*, commentary on *Bereshith*, s.v. *wehinei amru kol hame'aneg*.
20. *Meshekh Chokhmah* on Deuteronomy 11:13. See also his words, and those of MaHaRaM Alashker, brought further at the end of part 6.
21. R. Shim'on ben El'azar at the end of BT *Kidushin*.
22. *Mishnath Rabbi Eli'ezer* 20.
23. M *Avoth* 3:5.
24. BT *Berakhoth* 32b.
25. BT *'Avodah Zarah* 19b.
26. RaMBaN on Levicitus 18:4. The only level higher than this, according to RaMBaN, is the forsaking of all wordly matters, as if one were disembodied, by which one merits eternal physical life, like Elijah and Enoch.
27. R. Bachyay, commentary on Leviticus 18:4.
28. *Moreh Nevuchim* 3:51.
29. R. Y. Hutner, *Pachad Yitzchak, Igroth UMikhtavim* 94.
30. Op. cit., note 12, above.
31. M *Avoth* 1:2.
32. Psalms 89:3.
33. R. Y. Abarbanel, *Nachalath Avoth, Avoth* 1:2.
34. BT *Berakhoth* 58a.
35. SeMA', SA *Choshen Mishpat* 264, note 19; *Perishah* ad loc., note 7.
36. *Mekhilta, Bo* chapter 18 (No. 124).
37. R. Yosef Rozin ("The Rogoczover"), in his responsum concerning the study of sciences, as cited in part 7, chapter 5, section 4b.
38. R. S.R. Hirsch, commentary on Genesis 48:3.
39. BT *Berakhoth* 32b.
40. II Samuel 10:13.
41. *Migdal 'Oz, Beth Midoth, 'Aliyath HaBinyan* section 11.
42. "Chatham Sofer," *Torath Mosheh, Shoftim*, s.v. *mi ha-ish*.
43. BT *Berakhoth* 16b.
44. BT *'Eiruvin* 86a and Rashi ad loc.
45. BT *Chagigah* 9b.
46. BT *Shabbath* 92a. See *Shemonah Perakim* (Introduction to his commentary on *Avoth*), chapter 7, where Rambam explains this in line with *Avoth* 5:1, "Who is rich? He who is satisfied with his lot." Also see *Derashoth HaRaN* 5, who disputes his position.
47. JT *Peiah* 1:1.
48. BT *Kidushin* 30b, based on Ecclesiastes 9:9.
49. BT *Bava Metzi'a* 30b. Cf. Rashi on BT *Bava Kama* 100a, where he interprets this expression as meaning Torah study. However, *Peney Yehoshua'* ad loc. and R. Ya'akov Emden (*Migdal 'Oz, Beth Midoth, 'Aliyath Melakhah* section 43) explain that Rashi's two interpretations mean the same thing. Also compare *HaRav Shimshon Refael Hirsch, Mishnatho WeShitatho*, Yonah Emanuel, ed.; Jerusalem, 5722 (1962), p.168.
50. RaShBaTz, *Magen Avoth* 1:10.
51. Mordekhai on BT *Shabbath* 1:258.

52. BT *Bava Metzi'a* 29b referring to Exodus 18:20.
53. Most authorities agree that not only the bare necessities, but also further acquisition of property is not only permitted, but may be considered part of the mitzvah (cf. RAVYaH, *Shabbath* 198; *Magen Avraham* on 248, note 19). One authority even maintains that the verse "six days you shall work" constitutes a positive Torah commandment (*Divrei Menachem* II, Notes on Sabbath Regulations 2, based on *Mekhilta DeRabbi Shim'on ben Yochai* on Exodus 20:9).
54. MT *De'oth* 5:11.
55. BT *Bava Bathra* 110a.
56. BT *Shabbath* 118a.
57. BT *Kethuboth* 50a.
58. MT *Shemitah WeYovel*, end.
59. M *Avoth* 4:5.
60. *Kiryath Melekh* to MT *Shemitah WeYovel*, end.
61. BT *'Avodah Zarah* 19b.
62. MT *Talmud Torah* 3:10.
63. R. Mosheh Feinstein, *Igroth Mosheh, Orach Chayim* II 111.
64. R. Mosheh Feinstein, "*Teshuvah Be'Inyan Shutafuth Yissakhar UZevulun*," in *Moriah* 133-6, p. 106.
65. *Derashoth UFerushey Rabbeinu Yonah, WaYelekh*, beginning.
66. Ibid., *BaMidbar*, beginning, citing Proverbs 22:29 and 24:27.
67. BT *Kidushin* 29a.
68. BT *Shabbath* 150a. *Tur* and SA *Orach Chayim* 306:6.
69. BT *Makoth* 8a,b. (Cf. also MT *De'oth* 6:10.)
70. BT *Kidushin* 29a.
71. *Magen Avraham* 156, end.
72. JT *Gitin* 5:8; *Bava Bathra* 10:5.
73. *Sefer HaBerith* II 12:10.
74. M *Kidushin* end. See later on (chap. 2, sect. 4) for a discussion of this quotation.
75. *Sedey Chemed, Kelalim, Ma'arekheth Aleph* 230.
76. Ibid., *Peiath HaSadeh* 160.
77. BT *Pesachim* 50a.
78. *Ahavath Tzion* 12 alluding to M *Avoth* 3:17.
79. R. Ya'akov Emden, *Migdal 'Oz* loc.cit. (note 49).
80. BT *Bava Metzi'a* 30b and Rashi ad loc.
81. BT *Shabbath* 33b.
82. *Lechem Shamayim, Avoth* 3:17, alluding to the passage cited below, note 84.
83. BT *Kethuboth* 50a, based on Psalms 110:3.
84. BT *'Eiruvin* 22a citing Song of Songs 5:11.
85. A wife's acquiescence can free her husband from his obligation (ROSh, *Kethuboth* 5:29). The reason cited is that, although the right to relief from distress generally cannot be waived, this principle applies only when such acquiescence is obtained by persuasion, implying that acquiescence on the wife's initiative is acceptable (*Birkey Yosef, Yoreh De'ah* 246:21).
86. M *Avoth* 1:10.
87. MK *Avoth DeRabbi Nathan* 11:1.

88. *Kaftor WaFerach* 44.

89. RaShBaTZ, *Magen Avoth, Avoth* 1:10.

90. *Tosfoth Yom Tov* ad loc.; Rabbeinu Yonah, R. 'Ovadiah of Bartinoro, Rabbeinu Bachyay, and RaShBA, based on BT *Kethuboth* 59b.

91. *Lechem Shamayim, Avoth* 1:10.

92. ChYDA, *Sefer Chasdey Avoth.*

93. MK *Avoth DeRabbi Nathan*, version II, 21.

94. MR Leviticus 25:3.

95. *Yefeh Toar,* ad loc.

96. BT *Berakhoth* 43b, and Rashi ad loc., s.v. *yafeh lo.*

97. *Mishnath Rabbi Eli'ezer* 20, based on Genesis 30:31; Exodus 2:1; Psalms 78:70; Amos 7:14-15.

98. R. Yisrael Alnakawah, *Menorath HaMaor* III, *Talmud Torah* fol. 300.

99. Compare *Kesef Mishneh* on MT *Talmud Torah* 3:10, which suggests that R. Yosi's praise of work is based on medical grounds, and that Hillel the Elder was a wood hewer only before becoming prince.

100. Rabbeinu Bachyay, *Avoth* 1:10.

101. JT *Ma'asroth* 2:4 (text of R. Shelomoh Sirileo).

102. *Derekh Chayim* on *Avoth* 1:10.

103. SA *Yoreh De'ah* 246:21, gloss.

104. BT *Berakhoth* 8a.

105. MaHaRShA on *Chulin* 44b and SheLaH (*Shavu'oth,* s.v. *takhlith ha-limud*) explain that "handiwork" refers to one who labors to clarify the halakhah in order to find the lenient view, while "one who fears Heaven" is one who takes the stringent view.

106. RaShBaTz, *Magen Avoth* 1:10.

107. *Ruach Chayim, Avoth* 1:10.

108. *Derekh Chayim, Avoth* 1:10.

109. MR Genesis 74:12.

110. MRT *WaYeitze* 13.

111. *Chovoth HaLevavoth, Sha'ar HaBitachon* 3, end.

112. R. 'Ovadiah Sforno, *Avoth* 2:1.

113. SheLaH, *Sha'ar HaOthioth, Derekh Eretz* folio 46b.

114. *Mekhilta DeRabbi Shim'on ben Yochai* on Exodus 20:9.

115. *Menorath HaMaor* 96.

116. See Rashi's commentary on *Kidushin* 30b, s.v. *'iska.*

117. See further, below, chapter 2, section 3.

118. R. D. Katz, *Tenu'ath HaMusar* II, p.24.

119. *Tosfoth Yom Tov* on *Avoth* 2:5.

120. *Sifra, Metzora'* 5:12 referring to Leviticus 14:33-47.
    Some sages even took the lenient view when doubt arose about a Scriptural commandment — even regarding a harmful substance — when loss of property was at stake (BT *Chulin* 49b; 77a). This is not surprising; for in some respects "property is treated more stringently than prohibitions." For instance, whereas forbidden food becomes nullified in an overwhelming majority of kosher food, this is not so when one's property becomes mingled with another's or when statistics point in

one direction(BT *Bava Kama* 27b, beginning). Property is even comparable to life itself; for a pauper is considered dead (BT *Nedarim* 64b).

121. BT *Yoma* 39a.

122. Ibid., 44a.

123. BT *Rosh HaShanah* 27a.

124. BT *Menachoth* 76b.

125. Ibid., 86b.

126. Ibid. 89a, according to one opinion.

127. BT *Chulin* 94a. This is deduced from the fact that Jacob went at night alone in the wilderness to fetch small earthenware jars he had forgotten.

128. BT *Chulin* 105a.

129. MT *Melakhim* 5:9.

130. Cf. Tosafoth on BT *'Avodah Zarah* 13b, s.v. *lilmod*, on whether these mitzvoth are more or less stringent than others.

131. *Magen Avraham* on SA *Orach Chayim* 248, note 19; also see ibid., 531:4 in the text.

132. *Yalkut Shim'oni, Pikudey* 502.

133. BT *Kethuboth* 67b.

134. Proverbs 1:19.

135. BT *Bava Kama* 119a, based on Proverbs 22:23. The importance of caring for one's physical well-being is discussed in the following section and in part 2 [chapter 2, section 8(1)].

136. BT *Pesachim* 64b.

137. BT *Pesachim* 8b.

138. BT *Kidushin* 39b.

139. BT *Berakhoth* 54a.

140. This is stated explicitly by the author of *Sha-agath Aryeh* (*Gevurath Ari, Ta'anith* 19a); also by R. Mosheh Feinstein (*Igroth Mosheh, Orach Chayim* II 111).

141. MR Ecclesiastes 9:18.

142. *Chovoth HaLevavoth, Sha'ar HaBitachon* 4:1.

143. MT *Yesodey HaTorah* 5:1.

144. BT *Kethuboth* 30a.

145. Tosafoth ad loc., s.v. *hakol biyedey*.

146. BT *Chagigah* 4b, 5a citing Proverbs 13:27.

147. BT *Bava Kama* 60a.

148. RaMBaM, Responsa (Mekize Nirdamim edition, Jerusalem, 5720, no. 436), also in *Shemonah Perakim* 8.

149. See Rashi to BT *Mo'ed Katan* 18b; RaN to RYF ad loc.; TaShBaTz II 1.

150. *Sifrey*, Deuteronomy 15:18.

151. *Tosefta, Berakhoth* 6:13.

152. MRT *WaYeitze*, end, citing Job 1:10.

153. *Chazon Ish, Shevi'ith* 18:4.

154. Jerusalem Talmud, quoted by Tosafoth on BT *Shabbath* 31a, s.v. *emunath*.

155. *Chovoth HaLevavoth, Sha'ar HaBitachon* 3, end.

156. M *Avoth* 2:2.

157. BT *Pesachim* 50b; Proverbs 10:4; 22:29; Ecclesiastes 10:18.

158. *Derashoth HaRaN*, 8 (ed. Feldman, pp. 129, 140).

159. BT *'Avodah Zarah* 54a.

160. *Meshekh Chokhmah, BeChukothay*, beginning.

161. Cf. L. Levi, *Torah and Science* (Feldheim, 1983), section 7.4.

162. RaMBaN on Genesis 12:10 and (following passage) Deuteronomy 20:9. Cf. also RaMBaN on Leviticus 26:3.

163. RaMBaN on Numbers 26:11, 13:2.

164. *Sefer Ha'Ikarim* IV 22.

165. BT *Berakhoth* 60a, end, citing Exodus 21:19.

166. *Torath HaAdam*, ed. R. C.D. Chavel, p. 42.

167. *Perishah, Tur Yoreh De'ah* 336, note 3.

168. *Tur* and SA loc. cit.

169. *Kaftor WaFerach* 44.

170. RaMBaN on Leviticus 26:11.

171. RaShBA, Responsa, I 413.

172. RaN on *Yoma* 82, s.v. *chutz*.

173. RaMBaM on M *Pesachim* 4, end.

174. *Shevet Yehudah*, quoted by *Tzitz Eli'ezer* V, *Ramoth Rachel* 20.

175. *Birkey Yosef, Yoreh De'ah* 336, note 2.

176. *Shevet Yehudah* on SA *Yoreh De'ah* 336.

177. *Igroth Chazon Ish* I 136.

178. BT *Yoma* 84b.

179. BT *'Avodah Zarah* 55a.

180. *Sefer Chasidim*, Mekize Nirdamim ed., no. 1469.
     Full quote, see below, part 2 [chapter 2, section 8(1)].

181. R. Prof. Abraham S. Abraham, *Lev Avraham* II 1:5.

182. *Shemonah Perakim* 8.

183. MR Genesis 89:3, citing Jeremiah 17:7.

184. "Chazon Ish," *Emunah UVitachon* 2:6.

185. MR Exodus 25:10.

186. Scripture (II Chronicles 16:12) itself denounces the ailing King Asa for not seeking God—only physicians. This would seem to have been his duty. But RaMBaN explains (on Leviticus 26:11) that, at the time of the prophets, the world was run along miraculous lines and therefore obligations were different. Others point out that the verse implies that he trusted in the physicians exclusively.

187. M *Avoth* 3:5.

188. BT *Berakhoth* 32b.

189. BT *'Avodah Zarah* 19b.

NOTES TO CHAPTER 2

1. Joshua 1:8.

2. JT *Peiah* 1:1, citing Deuteronomy 30:19.

3. We have followed (in brackets) the reading of RaSh (ad. loc.); *Or Zarua'* (*Alfa Betha* 19); commentary of R. Yitzchak ben Shelomoh of Toledo on *Avoth* (2:14); Tosefta as quoted by Rabbeinu Chananel (BT *'Avodah Zarah* 22a); and *Midrash Shochar Tov* [Psalms 1, s.v. *ki im* (last)]. Their reading seems preferable to formulating a new

prohibition against studying Greek — especially since the Greek language was favored by the sages (cf. M *Megilah* 1:8 and BT *Bava Kama* 82b-83a for a discussion of the difference between Greek and "the wisdom of Greek").

4. BT *Berakhoth* 35b, citing Deuteronomy 11:14.

5. *Tur* and SA *Orach Chayim* 155.

6. BT *Menachoth* 99b.

7. SA *Yoreh De'ah* 246:1. See the extensive discussion in *Sedey Chemed, Ma'arekheth Waw* 15. This leniency is really quite limited; see part 4, chapter 5.

8. *Tosfoth R. Yehudah HeChasid* on BT *Berakhoth* 35b.

9. *Tosfoth ROSh*, ad loc.

10. MT *Talmud Torah* 3:6.

11. This is the interpretation of *Chasdey David* on *Tosefta, 'Avodah Zarah* 1:3; R. Yesha'yah Berlin in *She-eilath Shalom* on *She-iltoth*, introduction to the addenda; R. Yehudah Shemuel Ashkenazi in *Gevul Ye-udah, Likutim, Menachoth*; R. Shelomoh Algazi in *Apirion Shelomoh, Menachoth* 99b; ChYDA, *Birkey Yosef, Yoreh De'ah* 246:1; R. Yechiel Michel of Glogau in *Nezer HaKodesh*, MR Genesis fol. 68d. *Chasdey David* explicitly permits the study of the wisdom of Greek if it is necessary for a livelihood.

12. *Tzapichith BiDevash* 60.

13. Rashi on BT *Shabbath* 33b. This is also the simple meaning of the verse, which continues, "and the sons of foreigners, your farmers and vintners," a clear reference to gentiles.

14. *Sefath Emeth* on *'Ekev*, s.v. *we-itha*.

15. See chapter 1, section 1.

16. *Ginath Bithan, Avoth* 3:17.

17. M *Avoth* 2:2.

18. We must clarify whether *derekh eretz* here means desirable character traits (as in "*derekh eretz* preceded the Torah") or earning a livelihood (as in "'You shall gather your grain' — live [Torah] according to *derekh eretz*"). All the well-known early commentaries (Rashi, RaMBaM, Rabbeinu Yonah) here opt for the latter meaning. This is supported by the latter part of the mishnah. It is also implied by MR Ecclesiastes 7:11 as well as by the commentators cited below. On the other hand, MR Numbers 13:15-16 suggests the former meaning.

19. Commenting on this mishnah, Rabbeinu Yonah details the many evils this may cause, remarking that instead of being rewarded for eking out a sparse livelihood, one may be severely punished for many sins. This resembles Rava's plea to the rabbis (BT *Yoma* 72b and Rashi ad loc.) not to sentence themselves to two forms of Hell — one in this world and one in the next. R. Y. Alnakawah's *Menorath HaMaor* (III, *Talmud Torah*) makes a similar point at length — because, "while his motives are good, his deeds are not."

20. M *Avoth* 3:21.

21. According to Maharsha, this concept is hinted at in the very verse from which the mitzvah of learning a trade is derived: "See life with the wife." The Sages interpreted this to mean: "Just as one is obligated to teach [his son] Torah [i.e. his spiritual spouse] he must teach him a trade [i.e. a living]." — "This precept is connected with the Torah, for even if one studies Torah constantly, he needs a trade."

22. MR Ecclesiastes 7:11.

23. MR Leviticus 35:6 regarding Genesis 3:24.
24. *Sidur Beth Ya'akov, Limud Achar HaTefilah* 7, fol. 96a.
25. *Tosafoth Yeshanim, Yoma* 85b, s.v. *teshuvah*; *Hagahoth Maimonioth*, MT *Talmud Torah* 3, note 2.
26. RaSh, M *Taharoth* 7:4, end.
27. ChYDA, *Zeroa' Yamin* on *Avoth* 2:2, s.v. *we-efshar.*
28. R. Mosheh Alshikh, *Avoth* 2:2.
29. A similar interpretation is given by *Midrash Shemuel* ad loc. and by BaCh, *Tur Yoreh De'ah* 156. ChYDA (on *Avoth* 2:2) offers a like explanation, but he divides the two groups addressed according to family size, economic conditions, etc.
30. R. Mosheh Alshikh, *Thazria'*, s.v. *we-hu ma-amareinu.*
31. *Nefesh HaChayim* 1:8.
32. *Hafla-ah, Pithcha Ze'irta* 35, end.
33. *Sefer Chasidim* 314.
34. R. Yisrael of Salant, quoted in *Mikhtav MeEliyahu* I, p. 34.
35. *Beth HaLevi* on *Yithro*, s.v. *we-zoth torath ha-adam.*
36. Above, chapter 1, section 1(2).
37. SA *Yoreh De'ah* 246:21, gloss.
38. MK *Avoth DeRabbi Nathan* 28, end.
39. MR Ecclesiastes 9:9.
40. MT *Talmud Torah* 1:12.
41. MT *Talmud Torah* 3:6.
42. M *Avoth* 3:5.
43. Cf. RaMBaM and Rabbeinu Yonah ad loc.
44. BT *Berakhoth* 35b. Especially interesting is the comment of MK *Avoth DeRabbi Nathan* 13:2 on *Avoth* 1:15 ("Make your Torah fixed"): "This teaches us that if one hears the words of a scholar in a study hall, he should make them not temporary but permanent." According to this interpretation, the mishnah concerns a different matter altogether. Rashi, however, interprets it like the passage in *Berakhoth.*
45. Rashi on *Avoth* 1:15, second explanation.
46. RaShBaTz, *Magen Avoth* ad loc.
47. Rashi on BT *Shabbath* 31a.
48. M *Avoth* 4:10.
49. *Pirkey Avoth* 6.
50. Cf. the words of R. Yisrael of Salant cited above, chapter 1, section 1(4), end.
51. *Sefer Chasidim* 951 and 952, perhaps based on BT *Menachoth* 99.
52. Ecclesiastes 7:8.
53. MaHaRaL, *Derekh Chayim* 6:4.
54. M *Avoth* 3:17. *Tosfoth Yom Tov*, citing *Midrash Shemuel*, which quotes *Lev Avoth.* Similarly MaHaRaL, *Derekh Chayim* ad loc.
55. In view of all this, the following words of R. Mosheh Feinstein (*Yoreh De'ah* III 82) require clarification: "Once they start to neglect Torah study and spend time studying secular subjects, [his inclination] will tell him to expend more time on the latter, because this is necessary for his livelihood. But even aside from this, it will be impossible for him to achieve stature in Torah knowledge or become even moderately learned or scholarly if he takes time out from expending his full energies on Torah study and learns secular subjects instead; rather than advancing,

he will decline steadily." His point may have been made in light of today's circumstances, just as several later authorities permitted remuneration for teaching Torah — as an emergency measure. (See chapter 3, section 2(3).) See *Igroth Mosheh, Orach Chaim* II 111: "For a man is not only permitted but obligated to engage in business or work in order to earn a livelihood"; and *Moriah* (133-6, p. 106), cited above, chap.1, sec.1(2).

56. *Pirkey Avoth* 6:4, also cited in MT *Talmud Torah* 3:6.

57. BT *Ta'anith* 21a. Our assumption that Ilfas and R. Yochanan had been supporting themselves by manual labor and wanted to turn to business activity, is supported by the commentary of MaHaRaL (above, note 53), that they incurred the wrath of the angels because they were planning to leave study permanently, while temporary interruptions were perfectly in order.

58. See above, chapter 1, section 1(4), end.

59. BT *Berakhoth* 16b.

60. BT *Shabbath* 11a.

61. Responsa ROSh, 15:8, as quoted by *Tur Yoreh De'ah* 243.

62. *Nimukey Yosef, Bava Bathra* 8, s.v. *belo*, quoting RaN, quoting R. Yosef ibn Migash in the name of his teacher, RYF.

63. Responsa of MaHaRaM Alashker 19, in the name of RaShBA.

64. *Korban Ha'Eidah*, JT *Sotah* 9:13, end.

65. ReDaK (*Sefer HaShorashim, Oman*, referring to Song of Songs 7:2) explains that an *uman* is dedicated to a particular trade. Furthermore, the connotations of *umanuth* are clear from its use in *Shevi'ith* 6:4, where trafficking in forbidden food is prohibited, if done on a steady basis. Cf. R. Shelomoh Sirileo's commentary, ad loc.

66. M *Kidushin* 4:14.

67. The evidence implicit in ROSh's decisions is cited in *Imrey Shefer* 52.

68. SA HaRav, *Hilkhoth Talmud Torah* 3, *Kunteras Acharon*, s.v. *we-hinei*.

69. MaHaRShA on BT *Kidushin*, end.

70. *Lechem Shamayim, Avoth* 3:17.

71. *Igroth Mosheh, Orach Chayim* II 111.

72. *Sefer HaMiknah* at the end of *Kidushin*.

73. ChYDA, *Kisei Rachamim*, on MK *Sofrim* 16.

74. See chapter 1, section 1(2).

75. *Nachal Eshkol* on *Sefer HaEshkol, Hilkhoth Pidyon HaBen*, II 2, p.137, attempts resolutions of this difficulty. *Bei-ur Halakhah* 306, note 6, considers this to be the subject of a tanaitic dispute, but does not relate to the views denying the existence of such a dispute and the evidence they cite.

76. *Chatham Sofer*, BT *Sukoth* 36b, s.v. *domeh lekushi*.

77. The "Chatham Sofer", in his commentary on the Torah (*Shoftim*, s.v. *mi ha-ish*) implies that the halakhah is according to R. Shim'on ben Yochai, which is difficult to maintain since both Abayey and Rava evidently side with R. Yishma'el. Furthermore, according to his interpretation both R. Shim'on ben Yochai and R. Nehorai addressed their remarks exclusively to those who live outside Eretz Yisrael, even though they both lived in Eretz Yisrael themselves and made their statements perfectly general.

78. "Chatham Sofer," commentary on BT *Bava Bathra* 21a, where the Talmud refers to

a teacher of gentile children. In contradiction to the Rishonim (see next note), the "Chatham Sofer" takes this literally.

79. RaMBaM (in his commentary on the Mishnah); Mordekhai; RYTBA; *Nimukey Yosef, Bava Bathra* 21a; *Beth Yosef* & SA *Choshen Mishpat* 156:1.

80. See Responsa *Chelkath Ya'akov* III 130; *Minchath Yitzchak* V 79; *Yechaweh Da'ath* III 75 and V 56.

NOTES TO CHAPTER 3

1. M *Avoth* 4:5.
2. BT *Nedarim* 62a.
3. M *Bekhoroth* 4:6 (BT, fol. 29a).
4. BT *Nedarim* 62a.
5. MT *Talmud Torah* 3:10; *Tur Yoreh De'ah* 246; SA ad loc., 21, gloss. Cf. RaMBaM and Rabbeinu Yonah on M *Avoth* 4:5.
6. BT *Shabbath* 22a.
7. TaShBaTz I 147; and *Midrash Shemuel* on M *Avoth* 4:5.
8. SA HaRav, *Hilkhoth Talmud Torah* 4:15.
9. See Part 4, Chapter 2, where this is discussed at length.
10. MT *Talmud Torah* 3:10; SA *Yoreh De'ah* 246:21, gloss.
11. RaMBaM on *Avoth* 4:5.
12. The various opinions regarding this are discussed in the next section.
13. MaHaRaL, *Derekh Chayim, Avoth* 1:10.
14. Ibid., 4:5.
15. *Seder HaYom, Seder 'Asakaw* fol. 16a.
16. *Keren Orah* on BT *Nedarim* 62a.
17. Responsa *Giduley Taharah* 7 (at the start of R. Avraham Sofer, *Sefer He'aroth WeHe-aroth.*
18. R. 'Ovadyah of Bartinoro, commentary to M *Bekhoroth* 4:6.
19. SA *Even Ha'ezer* 154:4.
20. Furthermore, commenting on M *Bekhoroth* 4:6, *Tosfoth Yom Tov* also disagrees with him at length. Compare RaMBaM on M *Avoth* 4:5, where he explains in great detail that it is forbidden to accept money, and TaShBaTZ I 142-148 and R. Ya'akov Emden (*Lechem Shamayim* ad loc.) who dispute him at length.
21. BT *Nedarim* 62a.
22. BT *Bava Metzi'a* 84b.
23. BT *Pesachim* 53b.
24. BT *Bava Bathra* 22a.
25. RaMBaM on *Avoth* 4:5.
26. JT *Ma'aser Sheni* 5:3.
27. BT *Yoma* 72b and Rashi ad loc.
28. BT *Shabbath* 114a and Rashi ad loc.; BT *Kidushin* 70a; and JT *Sanhedrin* 2:6 as quoted by *Hagahoth Maimonioth*, MT *Sanhedrin* 25, note 3. However cf. the authorities cited in the following note.
29. TaShBaTz I 148; and Meiri on BT *Nedarim* 62a.
30. BT *Kethuboth* 111b.

31. BT *Berakhoth* 10b.
32. BT *Yoma* 71a; *Kethuboth* 105b; *Berakhoth* 34b.
33. BT *Sanhedrin* 92a, and many others. See TaShBaTz I 144.
34. BT *Berakhoth* 10b.
35. *Tana Devey Eliyahu Rabba* 18, s.v. *ma'aseh bekohen*.
36. BT *Chulin* 134b.
37. TaShBaTz, (loc. cit. note 29, above) based on mishnah at the end of *Horayoth*.
38. SA HaRav, *Hilkhoth Talmud Torah* 4:16.
39. BT *Kethuboth* 105a.
40. M *Bekhoroth* 4:6.
41. Tosafoth on *Bekhoroth* 29a, s.v. *mah*.
42. SA HaRav, *Hilkhoth Talmud Torah* 1:4. Also see RaSHBaTz, *Magen Avoth, Avoth* 4:5; R. Yosef Chiyon, *Miley DeAvoth*; and R. 'Ovadyah Sforno, both ad loc.
43. MT *Shekalim* 4:7 and RaMBaM on *Avoth* 4:5. He does not cite the reason. However, see next sub-section where his position is analyzed.
44. Rabbeinu Yonah, *Derashoth UFerushim, BaMidbar*.
45. Cf. chapter 1, section 1(2). Perhaps the ruling is different here because he receives a fixed salary from the community.
46. *Kesef Mishneh*, MT *Talmud Torah* 3:10.
47. *Yam Shel Shelomoh, Chulin* 3:9.
48. SA *Yoreh De'ah* 246:21; gloss ad loc.; ShaKh, note 20.
49. Responsa *Devar Shemuel* 138.
50. *Nachalath Avoth* 4:5, based on BT *Temurah* 14b citing Psalms 119:126.
51. *Kesef Mishneh*, MT *Talmud Torah* 3:10. The formal basis for abolishing a halakhic restriction under emergency conditions is based on the verse (Psalms 119:126): "It is a time to accomplish for God—they void your Torah." Cf. M *Berakhoth*, end and BT, ibid. 63a.
52. This opinion is shared by ReMA on SA *Yoreh De'ah* 246:21.
53. *Yam Shel Shelomoh, Chulin* 3:9.
54. Chatham Sofer, Responsa, *Choshen Mishpat* 164.
55. *Igroth Mosheh, Yoreh De'ah* II 116, based on *Kesef Mishneh* and ShaKh on SA *Yoreh De'ah* 246:21.
56. *Igroth Mosheh, Yoreh De'ah* III 82.
57. SA HaRav, *Hilkhoth Talmud Torah* 4:16, quoting *Kesef Mishneh* and TaShBaTz.
58. *Birkey Yosef, Orach Chayim* 155, beginning.
59. BT *Nedarim* 37a.
60. SA *Yoreh De'ah* 246:21, gloss.
61. TaShBaTz I 142.
62. M *Horayoth* 3:8 (BT, fol. 13a).
63. BT *Megilah* 22a and *Gitin* 59b. Note that the obligation to "sanctify [the *Kohen*]" applies today as well; cf. SA *Orach Chayim* 201:2 and 167:14, gloss.
64. BT *Shabbath* 114a.
65. Rashi, BT *Shabbath* 114a.
66. RaShBaTz, *Magen Avoth, Avoth* 4:5 and in his responsa, I 147.
67. R. 'Ovadyah Sforno on M *Avoth* 4:5.
68. TaZ, SA *Yoreh De'ah* 246, note 7; *Yam Shel Shelomoh* on *Chulin* 3:9; BaCh, Responsa 52.

69. *Magen Avoth, Avoth* 4:5, end.
70. *Sifrey, Zoth HaBerakhah.*
71. MR Genesis 98:12.
72. MR Genesis 99:9.
73. Ibid., 72:5.
74. MRT *WaYechi* 11, based on Proverbs 3:18.
75. BT *Sotah* 21a.
76. Rabbeinu Yerucham, *Nethiv* 2, end.
77. BT *Sotah* 21a, citing Song of Songs 8:7.
78. *Tur* and SA *Yoreh De'ah* 246:1, gloss.
79. M *Avoth* 2:2.
80. See *Bei-ur Halakhah* on SA *Orach Chayim* 156.
81. HaGeRA on Proverbs 18:16.
82. R. Yosef Ya'abetz on M *Avoth* 4:6.
83. Responsa *Meishiv Davar* III 14, end.
84. Responsa *Avkath Rokhel* 2.
85. ShaKh, SA *Yoreh De'ah* 246, note 2.
86. *Kether Rosh* 64.
87. R. M. Feinstein, Responsum published in *Moriah*, Nisan 5743 (1983), no. 133-6, p. 103.
88. MR Song of Songs 8:10.
89. Commentary of R. Ze-ev Wolf Einhorn (MaHaRZU), ad loc.
90. *Hafla-ah, Kethuboth, Pithcha Ze'irta* 43.
91. Loc. cit., note 87.
92. MT *Teshuvah* 8:2-3.
93. MR Deuteronomy 4:3.
94. BT *Berakhoth* 17a (according to some readings. So, too in *'Ein Ya'akov* and the ms Munich), citing Psalms 111:10.
95. *Imrey Binah* I, end.
96. A responsum quoted in Responsa MaHaRaM Alashker 101.
97. Op. cit. (note 87), p. 99.
98. Brought above, subsection (4).
99. SA HaRav, *Hilkhoth Talmud Torah* 1:7.
100. Op. cit., 3:4.
101. *Sefer Chasidim* 957 (in Mekize Nirdamim edition, no. 778). Also see *Mekor Chesed* ad loc.
102. BT *Kidushin* 29a.
103. Deuteronomy 27:26.
104. JT *Sotah* 7:4.
105. Rashi and *Ba'al HaTurim*. See especially RaMBaN, ad loc.
106. *Sha'arey Teshuvah* 3:19.
107. MR Leviticus, 25, beginning.
108. Proverbs 3:18.
109. Deuteronomy 27:26.
110. Deuteronomy 33:18.
111. *Peney Mosheh; Korban Ha'Eidah* on JT *Sotah* 7:4; R. Yosef Chiyon, *Miley DeAvoth* 4:5; R. Yitzchak Elchanan Spektor, *'Etz Peri* 2.

112. MT *Talmud Torah* 1:4; *Tur* and SA *Yoreh De'ah* 245:2.

113. MT *Talmud Torah* 3:10.

114. Although from the Talmud (BT *Kidushin* 30a) it appears that he need teach him only Scripture, the halakhic authorities restricted this limitation to a father in financial straits (Rabbeinu Yerucham cited in *Tur* and SA *Yoreh De'ah* 245:6).

Compare, however, R. Sholom Dov, *Darkhey No'am* 1: "If one sees that another is mentally better equipped than himself and is able to achieve greater scholarship, then he may engage in labor or business in order to provide a livelihood for the other, and he will receive reward as if he himself had studied Torah." This suggests that the nation should best be divided into two parts: those who are better equipped for it would study Torah day and night, while the others would only work and provide for them.

R. Ya'akov Emden (*Sidur Beth Ya'akov, Limud Achar HaTefilah* 8, fol. 96a) goes even further, in regard to setting aside certain hours for learning: "But this is not appropriate to the nature of all people, for nowadays ignorance is rampant; in addition, some individuals are not naturally equipped for perfect Torah study. They were created to engage in a trade in order to provide food and drink for the servants of God who spend all their time studying Torah. These are not asked to set aside time for Torah study. ... And an ignorant person who studies causes his Creator to weep, for better he not be burdened with this unnatural load. He will accomplish nothing, except that he will not be able to do good for others... for neither he nor his fathers will have a share in it and no good will come of it."

115. RaMBaM on *Avoth* 4:5.

116. MR Leviticus 5:4. Similarly, JT *Horayoth* 3:4.

117. MRT *Re-eh* 18.

118. *Sefer Chasidim*, Mekize Nirdamim edition 1307, based on JT *Shekalim* 5:4. When one Amora said: "How much money my fathers invested in this [beautiful synagogue]," another corrected him: "You should say: 'How much humanity did they invest here. For were there no people toiling in Torah [who needed their support]?".

119. M *Ma'aser Sheini* 2:9. Also see JT *Peiah* 8:6.

120. Responsa *Nishmath Kol Chay, Yoreh De'ah* 56.

121. BT *Berakhoth* 5b.

NOTES TO CHAPTER 4

1. Cf. *Igroth Mosheh, Orach Chayim* II 111.

2. According to RaMBaN, there is an exception: in the days of the Prophets, the healing process was a normally miraculous intervention of God, so there was no need for physicians.

3. RaMBaM (MT *Talmud Torah* 3:10); MaHaRaL (*Avoth* 1:10); *Giduley Taharah* (Resp. 7); see chapter 3, section 1.

4. R. Yitzchak Abarbanel; *Kesef Mishneh*; MaHaRShaL; *Divrey Shemuel*; "Chatham Sofer"— all above, chapter 3, section 2(3).

NOTES TO REVIEW:
"...BY DAY AND BY NIGHT"

1. Joshua 1:8.
2. *She-iltoth, Wa-Ethchanan* 143.
3. ShaKh, SA *Yoreh De'ah* 246, note 1.
4. *Birkey Yosef* on *Yoreh De'ah* 246:1; also in *Shiyurey Berakhah* ad loc.
5. This is explained in greater detail in *Sedey Chemed, Ma'arekheth Waw* 15, s.v. *uve'ikar.*
6. BT *Nedarim* 8a.
7. SeMaG, pos. 12.
8. R. Zeev Wolf Boskowitz, *Seder Mishnah* on MT *Talmud Torah* 1:8.
9. *Sedey Chemed, Ma'arekheth Waw* 15, s.v. *we-li.*
10. BT *Shabbath* 33b.
11. *Keren Orah* on BT *Nedarim* 8a.
12. RaDBaZ, Responsa III 416. Note that Rashi's commentary to Nedarim, referred to here, is of doubtful authorship. (Cf. ChYDA, *Shem HaGedolim*, R. Shelomoh Yitzchaky, s.v. *peirush mes. Nedarim.*)
13. R. Yehudah Shemuel Ashkenazi, *Gevul Ye-udah, Likutim Nifradim, Menachoth* (fol. 28).
14. *Birkey Yosef* on SA *Yoreh De'ah* 246, note 1, s.v. *umitivutheih,* end.
15. R. Sholom Dov, *Darkhey No'am* 1; also see MaHaRaM Schick in his work on the 613 commandments, 421.

    R. Eliezer of Metz (*Shitah Mekubetzeth, Nedarim* 8b) connects the Talmudic passage in *Nedarim* with that in *Menachoth*, but says that "nevertheless, there is an additional mitzvah derived from 'and you shall instruct them' [which clearly goes beyond the reading of the Shema']." This explanation suffers from the same difficulty as the above. This was noted by R. Y.F. Perlow (*Sefer Mitzvoth LeRav Sa'adyah Gaon*, pos. 14, fol. 127b ff).
16. MaHaRaM Schick, commentary on the 613 commandments, 420.
17. *Toldoth Adam* on *Sifrey, 'Ekev* 42, note 5.
18. Concerning the superiority of teaching over studying, see part 6, chapter 1 at length.
19. SA HaRav, *Hilkhoth Talmud Torah* 3, *Kunteras Acharon* 1.
20. R. Yechiel Michel of Glogau, *Nezer HaKodesh*, MR Genesis, fol. 68d. Similarly in *Keren Orah, Menachoth* 99b.
21. *Nefesh HaChayim* 1:8.
22. MaHaRaM Schick, commentary on the 613 commandments, 421.
23. *Tzapichith BiDevash* 60.
24. BT *Bava Metzi'a* 29b.
25. *Darkhey Shalom*, fol. 124.
26. RaMBaN, Leviticus 26:11.
27. *Sha'agath Aryeh, Kunteras Acharon* 1, s.v. *amnam.*
28. *Birkey Yosef, Yoreh De'ah* 246, note 1.

29.   *Yefeh Mar-eh*, based on JT *Peiah* 1:1 and BT *Sotah*, end.
30.   *Sedey Chemed, Ma'arekheth Waw* 15, s.v. *uvemikhtav*, in the name of R. A.M. Chalfon.
31.   Introduction to *Sefer Divrey Nechemiah*, quoting *Birkey Yosef.*

NOTES TO PART 2

NOTES TO CHAPTER 1

1.   A Comment by R. Aharon Soloveichik:

In my opinion the expression "non-halakhic mitzvoth" is incorrect and self-contradictory. The meaning of halakhah, according to 'Arukh... is that which Israel follows... which means that all laws and mitzvoth of the Torah are included in the term "halakhah." To characterize the mitzvah "You shall be holy" or "And you shall do that which is good and just" as "non-halakhic" is to utter a contradiction in terms. Mitzvah is halakhah and halakhah is mitzvah. The Torah establishes general and specific regulations for the mitzvah of "You shall do that which is good and just," just as it establishes general and specific regulations for the laws of *tefilin* and Shabbath. All the mitzvoth of the Torah are halakhic mitzvoth. However, there is a difference between the commandment "You shall be holy"—which is based on the principle, as RaMBaN puts it, of "there can be vileness licensed by the Torah"—and the other mitzvoth, such as *tefilin*, honoring one's parents, eschewing theft, and the like, which are based on the principle "there can be vileness unlicensed by the Torah." What is the meaning of "there can be vileness licensed by the Torah"? To understand this concept, we must quote the words of RaMBaM in MT *Teshuvah* 7:3.

> Don't say there is *teshuvah* only for transgressions that involve an action, such as immorality, theft, and robbery; rather, just as a person must repent for these trangressions, he must examine his evil traits, and abandon his bad temper, his hatred, his jealousy, his mockery, his acquisitiveness, his gluttony and other sins like them. He must repent for all of them; and these sins are more serious than those that involve actions, for while one is involved with them it is difficult to desist from them, as suggested by the verse, (Isaiah 55:7) "Therefore shall the evil-doer forsake his way ..."

These words require explanation. Why does RaMBaM say that acquisitiveness and gluttony do not involve action, when both clearly do? Certainly, when RaMBaM refers to transgressions that do not involve action, he means those that involve no sinful action. RaMBaM here lists transgressions that involve the destruction of, or lack of, good character traits.

Actually, there is no interdiction in the Torah against gluttony or the quest for honor. If one is a glutton or seeks honor, he is regarded as a sinner because he does not travel the median path as explained by RaMBaM in MT *De'oth* 3:1:

> Perhaps a person will say, "Since jealousy, lust, honor and such like are evil and remove a person from the world, I will refrain from them altogether and distance myself from them to the furthest extreme," to the point where he will not eat meat or drink wine—one who walks this road is called a sinner.

Hence one who does not travel the median path is called a sinner, even though no commandment or interdict exists.

A person becomes a sinner without doing any sinful action. This is what is meant by "vileness licensed by the Torah." If one does not travel the median path—as, for instance, an alcoholic—he is called a sinner and degenerate licensed by the Torah, meaning, without any prohibition against alcoholism and without having taken any sinful action.

2. See part 4, especially chapter 3.

3. "*Beth Shammai bimekom Beth Hillel einah mishnah*," BT *Berakoth* 36b.

4. Regarding slander (*leshon hara'*) and related questions, this was true, at least, until *Chafetz Chayim* was published a hundred years ago—and even this revolutionary work is based primarily on deductions made from agadic material, rather than on explicit halakhic passages. RaMBaM devotes only part of one chapter to this (MT *De'oth* 7:1-6) and Shulchan Arukh does not treat it at all.

5. *Mekhilta*, Exodus 15:26.

6. *Sifrey, 'Ekev* 48, Deuteronomy 11:22.

7. R. Samson Raphael Hirsch, *Horeb*, Foreword (p. clvi, in Soncino edition, London 1962).

8. M *Avoth* 4:16.

9. R. S.R. Hirsch, *The Nineteen Letters*, no. 18.

10. R. Mosheh Chayim Luzzatto, *Ma-amar 'al HaAgadoth*.

11. M *Chagigah* 2:1.

12. R. S.R. Hirsch, loc. cit. It is interesting to note that Rabbi Hirsch used Kabala, and in particular the *Zohar*, extensively in writing his *Horeb*. See the list of sources in his preparatory notes to the Chapter on *Milah*, where most of the sources are from the *Zohar*. (R. J. Breuer, "Aus den Vorarbeiten zum *Horeb*," *Nachalath Zvi*, Vol. 5, pp. 142 ff; list reprinted in *HaRav Shimshon Rafael Hirsch: Mishnatho WeShitatho*; pp.339-341.)

13. "...these forbid and those permit, these disqualify and those declare fit. Hence you might ask: 'How, then, can I learn Torah?' Therefore Scripture says: 'Given by one Shepherd' [One God said all of them. None of the disputants brings evidence from another god's Torah, only from our God's Torah—Rashi, ad loc.]" (BT *Chagigah* 3b, citing Ecclesiastes 12:11).

14. BT *Berakhoth* 7b and MaHaRShA ad loc. based on II Kings 3:11.

15. R. M. Gurevich, personal communication. The words of R. A. Kotler, which we cite below (chapter 2, section 3) imply the same.

16. RaMBaN, introduction to his commentary on the Torah.

17. See the responsum, printed in the appendix to the Hebrew edition. It is discussed in part 7, chapter 5.

18. *Mishnath Rabbi Aharon* I, p. 201.

19. *Magid Mishneh* to MT *Shekheinim*, end. Similarly, *Sefer Ha'Ikarim* (III 23) explains the necessity for the "Thirteen Syllogisms by Which the Torah is Expounded": "Because it is impossible for God's Torah to be perfectly explicit in all details that develop in all eras and that are far too numerous to be contained in one book, they were transmitted to Moses on Mount Sinai as general principles only hinted at in the Torah; by applying these syllogisms, the sages of every generation can derive the details necessary for their time."

     So, too, SheLaH (*'Eser Ma-amaroth* 7:2): "There is good reason why the Torah did not warn against this explicitly. It is impossible to mention everything, for each person undergoes myriads of changes. Thus, everyone would require his own version of the Torah; and even this might be subject to change from one hour to the next," and, even more explicitly in *Torah Shebikhtav, Kedoshim*.

20. *Mesilath Yesharim*, chapter 13, end.

21. *Tur Orach Chayim* 625: "He commanded us to build *sukoth* so that we should remember His wonders and His greatness." BaCh comments on this that by these words *Tur* implies that one has not fulfilled the mitzvah of *sukah* properly unless he knows the simple intent of it. This requirement also applies to the mitzvoth of *tzitzith* and *tefilin*, unlike other mitzvoth.

NOTES TO CHAPTER 2

1. M *Peiah* 1:1.

2. *Chovoth HaLevavoth, Sha'ar 'Avodah* 1:4.

3. *Mishnath Rabbi Aharon* I, p. 207.

4. MR Deuteronomy 6:2. Also in other midrashim and commentaries.

5. *Sha'arey Teshuvah* 3:10.

6. BT *'Avodah Zarah* 17b.

7. M *Avoth* 2:6.

8. *Sefer Chasidim* 261.

9. *Sifrey*, Deuteronomy 306, and, in brackets, *Toldoth Adam* ad loc.

10. BT *Chulin* 24a and *Pesachim* 113a.

11. Also see R. Ya'akov Emden's comment about teaching Torah to an *'am ha-aretz* in part 1, chapter 3, section 2(6).

12. *Ha'amek Davar*, Numbers 15:41, referring to M *Avoth* 2:1.

13. HaGeRA, commentary on Proverbs 14:2.

14. *Or Same-ach, Talmud Torah* 1:2, s.v. *beyoma*.

15. BT *Shabbath* 11a.

16. BT *Berakhoth* 32b. They had only about three hours each day to spare. These had to be divided between working and Torah study.

17. BT *Bava Kama* 30a.

18. Leviticus 19:2.

19. BT *Berakhoth* 22a.

20. Isaiah 9:16.
21. See BT *Sukah* 28a; also cf. MT *De'oth* 2:4, and RaMBaM *Avoth* 1:16—referring to other personalities.
22. Deuteronomy 28:9.
23. BT *Sotah*, end of first chapter.
24. BT *Shabbath* 133b, citing Exodus 15:2.
25. MR Genesis 60:8.
26. R. A. Kotler, *Mishnath Rabbi Aharon* I, p. 132.
27. BT *Bava Metzi'a* 85a.
28. *Sha'arey Teshuvah* 3:172.
29. BT *Sotah* 42a.
30. Exodus 23:1 and Leviticus 19:16. Although lying is generally also not permitted, Leviticus 19:11, "You shall not lie ..." has been expounded by the Sages, in BT *Bava Kama* 105b, as referring to perjury. Thus, there is no explicit prohibition against lying outside the court unless fraud is involved. Compare R. Y.F. Perlow's commentary on R. Sa'adiah Gaon, *Sefer HaMitzvoth* I, pos. 22.
31. BT *Sotah* 4b, 5a.
32. BT *Bava Bathra* 10b.
33. BT *Yoma* 86a based on Deuteronomy 6:5.
34. MT *Yesodey HaTorah* 5:11.
35. BT *Sanhedrin* 74a&b.
36. Loc. cit., note 33.
37. M *Shekalim* 3:2.
38. BT *Pesachim* 13a.
39. BT *Yoma* 38a. For an extensive discussion of this obligation, see R. Menachem Treves, *Orach Meysharim* 14:5, gloss.
40. Thus R. Yochanan made efforts to avoid causing a Roman matron to suspect him of uttering a false oath—BT *'Avodah Zarah* 28a.
41. BT *Shabbath* 75a, based on Deuteronomy 4:6.
42. BT *Yoma* 86a; M *Avoth* 4:4 (literally "are alike," but cf. commentaries ad loc.).
43. As cited above, chapter 1, note 19.
44. BT *Bava Kama* 100a based on Exodus 18:20.
45. BT *Bava Metzi'a* 30b.
46. SeMaK, no. 49.
47. BT *Bava Metzi'a* 24b, 30b.
48. BT *Bava Kama* 99b.
49. BT *Kethuboth* 97a.
50. R. Yehudah of Orleans, Tosafoth on *Bava Kama* 100a, s.v. *lifnim*.
51. Deuteronomy 6:18.
52. Deuteronomy 6:18; BT *Bava Metzi'a* 108a; SA *Choshen Mishpat* 175:6.
53. BT *Bava Metzi'a* 16b.
54. BT *'Avodah Zarah* 25a based on above verse.
55. *Torah Temimah*, Deuteronomy 6:18, note 74; based on Joshua 10:13.
56. BT *Shabbath* 31a.
57. RaMBaN on Deuteronomy 6:18.
58. BT *Bava Metzi'a* 35a.
59. MT *Shekheinim* 12:5.

60. *Magid Mishneh*, MT *Shekheinim*, end.
61. BT *Bava Metzi'a* 83a, citing Proverbs 2:20.
62. BaCh, *Tur Choshen Mishpat* 12:4, at length.
    Also *Pithchey Teshuvah* ad loc., no. 6.
63. *Orach Meysharim* 1, note 9.
64. SA *Choshen Mishpat* 259:5, gloss. Also 62, above.
65. R. Yehonathan, *Shitah Mekubetzeth, Bava Metzi'a* 24b.
66. Proverbs 3:27.
67. BT *Bava Metzi'a* 76a.
68. BT *Yevamoth* 11b.
69. SeMaG, neg. 229, on the other hand, explains it as based on the prohibition against wastefulness. In the Talmud, though, it is quoted in connection with the levirate laws; from this it would appear that it is part of the rules regulating our love of neighbor.
70. BT *Bava Kama* 81b.
71. SA *Choshen Mishpat* 153:8; 154:3, gloss; 174:3; 264:4, gloss; 318:1. Also 363:6. Also see Responsa MaHaRYK 9, s.v. *wenachzor*.
72. BT *Bava Metzi'a* 58b, based on Leviticus 25:17.
73. M *Bava Metzi'a* 4:10; BT ibid. 58b.
74. MT *Mekhirah* 14:14.
75. Compare the wording of the Talmud in *Bava Metzi'a* 58b and Rashi, ad loc. It is evident there that the prohibition includes causing discomfort to a person when potential buyers are sent to him to ask for items he does not sell. *Sefer Yere-im* (51) also includes nonverbal insults such as unfriendly facial expressions. Similarly, *Sefer HaChinukh* (338) writes that this mitzvah includes the prohibition of paining another in any way.
76. *Sefer HaChinukh* 338.
77. *Tur* (*Choshen Mishpat* 378) states explicitly that it is forbidden to damage another's property. The source of this prohibition, however, is not specified there. Later authorities deduce it from other mitzvoth (cf. BaCh ad loc.). But that does not contradict our thesis, since both prohibitions may apply, depending on the circumstances. See also R. Y.Z. Gustman, *Kuntrasey Shey'urim, Bava Kama* 1:18.
78. BT *Chagigah* 5a; MK *Derekh Eretz Rabbah* 9; *Tur* and SA, *Orach Chayim* 170:15-16.
79. The Talmud recounts that in the Temple on Yom Kippur the High Priest recited one Scriptural passage by heart, rather than scrolling while the public waited—even though it is generally prohibited to recite Scripture by heart. See BT *Yoma* chapter 7, beginning. *Berakhoth* 27b, 31a; *Megilah* 22b.
80. SA *Orach Chayim* 114:3 and *Magen Avraham* ad loc., note 7.
81. R. Mosheh Feinstein prohibits smoking in public when people suffer from it (*Igroth Mosheh, Choshen Mishpat* II 18). For a collection of responsa and medical opinions on smoking, see *Assia* 37 (Kislev 5744), *Sefer Assia*, vol. 5, part 4 (1986), and *Nishmath Avraham* (*Choshen Mishpat* 155:2). Cf. also note 116, below.
82. R. Z.N. Goldberg speculates that this case may be similar to the Talmudic discussion of the right of way of two ships or two camels travelling in opposite directions. The comparison, however, is not obvious; these cases refer to the public domain and may assume that the license to use this domain depends on observing the established rules—implying that anyone who does use it while violating the

rules is misappropriating public property. This would not apply in our cases, since they are not dependent on the use of public property.

83. *Mishnath Rabbi Aharon* I, p.203.

84. R. Y.Y. Kanievsky ("The Steipler Rav"), *Karaina DeIgratha* 59.

85. BT *Shevu'oth* 30b, 31a.

86. See *Kesef Mishneh* on MT *Sanhedrin* 24:1.
    R. Chaim Kanievsky, *Kiryath Melekh* (ad loc.) quotes the following midrash on Proverbs 1: "When a person has been appointed judge, he must use his intellect to insure that the innocent gets his due and the guilty are punished." This is the halakhah, even today (SeMA', *Choshen Mishpat* 15:15).

87. Some illustrations: there is no accepted decision between conflicting authoritative opinions (BT *Bava Bathra* 62b); two conflicting contracts bear the same date (BT *Kethuboth* 94a); two people with the same name claim the same bequest (BT *Kethuboth* 85b). For other instances of *shuda de-dayana*, see BT *Kidushin* 74a.

88. Responsa RYVaSh, 299; *Nimukey Yosef* on BT *Yevamoth* 89b.

89. BT *Sanhedrin* 6b; SA *Choshen Mishpat* 12:2.

90. BT *Shabbath* 133b based on Exodus 15:2; *Bava Kama* 9b: "Up to one third."

91. RaMBaN, introduction to his commentary on the Torah.

92. BT *Shabbath* 31b, expounding Deuteronomy 10:12, "What does the Lord, your God, require of you but to fear the Lord, your God..." Furthermore, from the cantillation and the missing "and" we can deduce that what follows — "to walk in His ways, ... etc." — are only explanations, or results, of the mitzvah to fear God. This is explicit in the commentaries of R. S.R. Hirsch and *Torah Temimah* ad loc.

93. *Sifrey, Wa-Ethchanan* 33.

94. *Sifrey, 'Ekev* 49.

95. *Nefesh HaChayim* 4:9.

96. *Pirkey Avoth*, end.

97. M *Yoma* 3:11; BT *Yoma* 38a.

98. *Sefer HaMitzvoth*, pos. 1, on Exodus 20:2.

99. RaMBaN, glosses to *Sefer HaMitzvoth*, Additional pos. no. 7, based on Deuteronomy 18:13.

100. M *Avoth* 4:17.

101. BT *Yoma* 86b.

102. a. Exodus 20:8; b. Deuteronomy 16:3; c. Ibid. 4:9-10; d. Ibid. 25:17; e. Ibid. 9:7; f. Ibid. 24:9.

103. While the exact derivation of the commandment to safeguard one's health is by no means clear, the Poskim agree that this is a mitzvah. The verses generally cited as the source are, however, frequently interpreted differently by the Sages.

104. BT *Sanhedrin* 74a and *Yoma* 85a.

105. BT *Bava Metzi'a* 62a, based on Leviticus 25:36.

106. Proverbs 11:17 and RaLBaG's commentary ad loc.; MR Leviticus 34:3. Also see the special review at the end of this part, and Rashi's commentary on BT *Shabbath* 127a, where prayer is described as attending to one's this-worldly needs. (But contrast RaSh's comment thereon, at the beginning of his commentary on *Peiah*.)

107. BT *Gitin* 67b; Rashi, cited by *Kesef Mishneh* on MT *Talmud Torah* 3:10; *Moreh Nevukhim* 3:25; R. Ya'akov Emden's commentary on *Avoth* 1:10; *Sefer Chasidim* (Mekize Nirdamim edition, no. 1469); and many other Rishonim and Acharonim.

108. *Kesef Mishneh* to MT *Talmud Torah* 3:10.
109. *Moreh Nevukhim* III 25.
110. R. Y. Emden *Avoth* 1:10 and *Sidur* folio 113c.
111. *Sefer Chasidim* (Mekize Nirdamim edition) 1069.
112. BT *Shabbath* 82a.
113. MT *De'oth*, chapter 4.
114. *Yam Shel Shelomoh, Chulin* 8:12.
115. For an extensive survey see *Sha'arey Talmud Torah* III, chapter 2, section 8(1).
116. Loc. cit. above 81, citing J.M. Bragg, "Research on the effect of smoking and non-smoking on mortality and morbidity," *Amer. Lung Assoc. Bul.*, Sept.-Oct. 1982, pp.4-5.
117. BT *Shabbath* 118a.
118. BT *Kidushin* 29a; M *Kidushin* 4:14.
119. Here, too, it is unclear whether this is a genuine Torah commandment, and if so, whence we derive it. In BT *Kidushin* 30b, the obligation to learn a trade is based on Proverbs 9:9, while in JT *Peiah* 1:1, on Deuteronomy 30:19. In any event, we clearly have an obligation to acquire a profession.
120. Part 1, chapter 1, section 1(2).
121. *She-iltoth* 137, based on Leviticus 20:25.
122. *Ha'amek She-eilah* ad loc.
123. MR Genesis 19:3.

NOTES TO CHAPTER 3

1. *Sefer Chasidim* 153. In his commentary on Numbers 22:33, R. Yehudah HeChasid derived this from the fact that Balaam said, "I have sinned." See section 5, where we discuss that even a gentile is thus obligated. This idea is also found in SheLaH, *Torah Shebikhtav* at the end of *Balak* and the beginning of *Matoth*.
2. *Moreh Nevukhim* 3:17, s.v. *we-hada'ath ha-chamishith*.
3. *Chizkuni*, Genesis 7:21.
4. BT *Kidushin* 59a; BT *Sanhedrin* 58b; BT *Nedarim* 22a.
5. Psalms 5:5.
6. This can be derived from the nazirite, who is called "sinner" because he deprives himself of wine. See BT *Nedarim* 10a.
7. RaMBaM, MT *De'oth* 1:5 and *Shemonah Perakim* 4; Rabbeinu Yonah, *Avoth* 2:5; RaShBaTz, *Magen Avoth* ad loc.; Meiri ad loc.; ReDaK, Psalms 4:4 and *Shorashim*, s.v. *chesed*. Also see Rashi on BT *Rosh HaShanah* 17b, s.v. *chasid*.
R. Avraham ibn Ezra (Leviticus 20:17), RaMBaM (*Avoth* 5:7), and perhaps R. Sa'adyah Gaon derive the word *chasid* from a word indicating something beyond the normal, hyperbole. R. Samson R. Hirsch follows in their footsteps (commentary on Psalms 4:4) by interpreting it as one who has "perfect, selfless devotion."
Others, such as *Sefer Chasidim* (10) and R. Avraham, son of RaMBaM (*Sefer HaMaspik Le'Ovdey HaShem, Perek HaHalikhah BeChukoth HaTorah*), trace it to the word for "kindliness" and "love" — meaning that he performs things that are

not required of him. MaHaRaL (on *Avoth* 2:6)and R. Mosheh Chayim Luzzatto (*Mesilath Yesharim* 18) concur.

8. M *Avoth* 2:5.
9. BT *Shabbath* 120a.
10. BT *Berakhoth* 47b, and Rashi ad loc.
11. MT *Melakhim* 5:9.
12. JT *Terumoth* 8, end, where the following occurrence is recounted: 'Ula bar Koshav, who had been sentenced to death by the government, fled to Lod to seek shelter with R. Yehoshua' ben Levi. When the gentiles came and beleaguered the city, threatening to destroy it unless 'Ula was delivered to them, R. Yehoshua'—in accordance with an explicit *Baraitha* (Tosefta, *Terumoth* 7:23)—persuaded him to permit himself to be surrendered. Thereupon, Elijah the Prophet ceased to visit R. Yehoshua', as had been his wont—because this was not a "teaching of piety.' This seems very surprising. As TaZ (in SA *Yoreh De'ah* 157, note 7) puts it, "What sin caused Elijah to shun him? How should he have known not to follow an explicit mishnah? For if this is so [that he should not have followed it], every day we cannot know on what to rely ... [and furthermore,] how **should** he have practiced this piety? by letting all of Israel be killed, God forbid, because of piety?" This question can perhaps be answered on the basis of the midrash (MR Genesis 94, end) which indicates that R. Yehoshua' should not have acted personally, but should have permitted another to do the deed. Or as Meiri (BT *Sanhedrin* 72b) puts it, he was too quick about it, rather than waiting to see whether the threat would indeed be carried out.

The "Chazon Ish" (SA *Yoreh De'ah* 69) explains the words "Such a thing should have been done by someone else, not by you" as follows: "This is not a mishnah for the pious, i.e., God does not bring such a trial upon his pious ones." However, halakhically he was required to do what he did.

13. BT *Bava Kama* 30a and *Shitah Mekubetzeth* ad loc.
14. Rashi on BT *Shabbath* 120a.
15. MT *De'oth* 1:5.
16. BT *Shabbath* 121b.
17. JT *Berakhoth* 2, end.
18. BT *Shabbath* 21b.
19. BT *Chulin* 105a; Mordekhai on *Chulin* 8:687; *Yam Shel Shelomoh, Chulin* 8:6.
20. All of the following quote this rule: R. 'Amram Gaon; Rabbeinu Tam; RaMBaM; MaHaRaM of Rothenburg; ROSh; Or Zarua'; Mordekhai; RaMBaN; RaShBA; RYTBA; RaN; Rabbeinu Simchah; R. Ya'akov Weil (RIW); and MaHaRAY. Furthermore, I have found fifteen laws to which the Poskim apply this rule. For details, see the review ("Praiseworthy..."), which is appended to this part.
21. Meiri, *Shitah Mekubetzeth, Bava Kama* 87a.
22. M *Avoth* 1, end.
23. Psalms 34:15.
24. MR Genesis 38:6.
25. BT *Sanhedrin* 110a, based on the verse "and he shall not be like Korach and his congregation..." (Numbers 17:5). The Poskim are divided about whether this is a Torah commandment [e.g., *Sefer Charedim*, (neg. 4:42, in the name of R. S. ibn Gabriol, Rabbeinu Yonah, and RaShBaTz); *Sefer Yere-im* 345—357 in Goldblum

edition)] or merely a rabbinic interpretation [e.g., RaMBaM (*Sefer HaMitzvoth*, 8th principle)].

26. M *Avoth* 1:12.

27. Numbers 6:26.

28. JT *Sotah* 1:9; BT *Sukah* 53b.

29. BT *Yevamoth* 65b.

30. Job 23:2.

31. Judges 6:24; BT *Shabbath* 10b.

32. See MR Deuteronomy 5, end, where the sages expound at length how dear peace is to God.

33. Where Jews are concerned:

   a) The concept of '*Eiruvey Chatzeiroth* was established to insure social harmony; b) it is forbidden to change the place where the '*eiruv* is stored; c) a *Kohen* is called to the Torah first, etc. d) a *Kohen* may sprinkle the blood of an offering brought by one who has vowed not to benefit from him; f) the well nearest to the water channel is the first one to be filled; g) a woman may lend her dishes to a neighbor suspected of violating the laws of either the sabbatical year or ritual purity.

   Where non-Jews are concerned:

   a) One helps non-Jews during the sabbatical year and inquires after their well-being; b) one helps their poor; c) one visits their sick; d) one buries their dead; e) one eulogizes them; f) one comforts their mourners; g) one saves their possession from theft; h) in a Jewish city with non-Jewish residents, taxes are imposed on both and assistance is provided for both.

34. BT *Gitin* 59b, based on Proverbs 3:17.

35. M *Peiah* 1:1.

36. Deuteronomy 21:10-14 and BT *Kidushin* 21b.

37. BT *Kidushin* 21b, 22a.

38. BT *Kidushin* 29b.

39. M *Sotah* 3:4.

40. MT *Talmud Torah* 1:13.

41. *Sefer Chasidim* 313.

42. As quoted in *Torah Temimah* on Deuteronomy 11, no. 48.

43. *Perishah* on SA *Yoreh De'ah* 246, note 15.

44. TaZ, SA *Yoreh De'ah* 246, note 4.

45. R. A. Grodzensky, *Torath Avraham*, p.134.

46. *Likutey Halakhoth, Sotah*, fol. 11, note 3, citing Deuteronomy 32:7.

47. *HaRav Shimshon Refael Hirsch, Mishnatho WeShitatho*, Yonah Emanuel, ed.; Jerusalem, 5722 (1962), p. 159.

48. *Torath Yerucham* 1.

49. *Eshel Avraham, Peiroth HaNoshrim* on BT *Sotah* 20.

50. *Moznayim LaMishpat* 42, based on Genesis 12:8 and 13:3. He does not give a reason. It may be that faith is normally, and most readily, instilled at a young age, and this is when primarily the mother shapes the budding personality.

51. *Shem HaGedolim*, s.v. *rabanith*.

52. Tosefta, *Keilim, Bava Kama* 4:9.

53. Ibid. *Bava Metzi'a* 1:3.

54. TaShBaTz 3:78; introduction to *Perishah*, usually printed in the front of *Tur Yoreh De'ah*; R. Berakhyah Berakh, *Zera' Berakh*, vol. 3; and *Zikhron Ya'akov Yosef*, in his lectures.
55. Tosafoth, BT *Shabbath* 11b, s.v. *hai*.
56. ShaKh on SA *Yoreh De'ah* 326, note 4; introduction to *Chawoth Ya-ir*; *Panim Yafoth* on Leviticus 9:7; R. Y. Berlin, *Miney Targima* on Genesis 32:5.
57. Introduction to *Ma'avar Yabok*.
58. R. Yosef Chaim ("Ben Ish Chay"), *Rav Pe'alim* I, *Sod Yesharim* 9.
59. *Igroth Mosheh, Yoreh De'ah* III 87.
60. *Sifrey*, Numbers 178.
61. M *Avoth* 2:2.
62. JT *Berakhoth* 5:1 and *Peney Mosheh* ad loc.
63. MT *Keriath Shema'* 2:5 and *Kesef Mishneh*, ad loc.; SA *Orach Chayim* 70:4.
64. JT *Shevi'ith* 3, end.
65. MR Leviticus 9:2, based on Psalms 50:23.
66. *Derekh Chayim, Avoth* 2:2.
67. MT *Teshuvah* 3:6.
68. *Minuth*, however, is scripturally prohibited, as expounded in BT *Berakhoth* 12b, based on Numbers 15:39.
69. MT *Teshuvah* 3:11.
70. BT *Nidah* 13b, referring to Isaiah 1:15.
71. See Rashi on Genesis 38:7; BT *Yevamoth* 34b.
72. BT *Nidah* 13a, and Rashi ad loc., s.v. *ke-ilu*.
73. Even though BT *Nidah* derives the prohibition from "'You shall not commit adultery' — there shall be no adulterous action taken by you, neither by your hand nor by your foot", this is apparently not a rigorous derivation (Responsa *Peney Yehoshua', Even Ha'Ezer* 44, at length).

   The early authorities are also divided on whether lustful thoughts are forbidden by the Torah or the Rabbis. When the Talmud expounds (Deuteronomy 23:10), "And you shall guard yourself against all evil matters," to mean, "A person should not fantasize by day and [thus] come to impurity at night," many decisors conclude that this is a rigorous derivation (Tosafoth on BT *'Avodah Zarah* 20b; RaMBaN on BT *Chulin* 37b; RaN, *Chidushim* ad loc; *SeMaG*, neg. 126; *SeMaK* 25; Rabbeinu Yonah in *Igereth HaTeshuvah*, quoted in *Orchoth Chayim*, vol. 2, p. 113; Meiri, BT *Chulin* 37b). On the other hand, we find an opinion that this is only a rabbinic regulation (*Sefer Yere-im* [HaShalem] 25).
74. Moses — Exodus 4:1; Elijah — II Kings 19:10; Isaiah — Isaiah 6:5.
75. MR Song of Songs 1:6.
76. II Kings 7:2 as expounded in the Midrash, as quoted in *Sefer Charedim* and in SheLaH; see Ref. 79, below.
77. *Igereth HaShemad*. A critical edition of the complete text appears in the memorial volume for R. C. Shmuelewitz, Jerusalem, 5740 (1980), pp. 229-260.
78. BT *Pesachim* 87b, based on Proverbs 30:10, and Rashi ad loc.
79. *Sefer Charedim*, negative traditional mitzvoth 4:23: SheLaH, *Kedushath HaPeh WeHaKaneh* (*Sha'ar Ha-Othioth, Oth Koph*).
80. *Mesilath Yesharim* 19, end.
81. *Torath Avraham, Torath HaSekhel Ha-Enoshi*.

82. Genesis 6:12, 38:10; Ezekiel 16:49 (as explained by Rabbeinu Yonah in *Sha'arei Teshuvah* 3:15); Deuteronomy 23:5; Isaiah 10:5-19, 14:4-23; Amos 1:3.
83. R. Yehudah HeChasid, in his commentary on Numbers 22:33.
84. *Chizkuni*, Genesis 7:21, as quoted in paragraph 1 of this chapter.

NOTES TO CHAPTER 4

1. *Sifra, BeHar*, beginning. RaMBaM's introduction to Seder Zera'im explains the words "in detail and in general" to mean that all derivations employing the principle of "the general and particular" (*Kelal uferat*) were told to Moses at Sinai.
2. JT *Sanhedrin* 4:2.
3. BT *Bava Metzi'a* 86a.
4. *Derashoth HaRan*, 7, s.v. *'akhshaw*; also quoted in the introduction to *Ketzoth HaChoshen*.
5. BT *Menachoth* 29b.
6. Introduction to *Igroth Mosheh, Orach Chayim*.
7. BT *Temurah* 16a.
8. RaMBaM, introduction to *Seder Zera'im*.
9. RaMBaM states in MT *Mamrim* 2:1 that a court whose decision contradicts that of an earlier court should nevertheless follow its own judgement. Thus, not all laws are based on tradition, but they can all be derived by the rules of exegesis and by reason. Also see his statement in *Sefer HaMitzvoth*, principle 2; RaMBaN ad loc.; and MaLBYM in his introduction to Leviticus.
   But in *Doroth HaRishonim* part 1, vol. 5(3), chapters 7-25, pp. 467-573, R. Isaac Halevy goes to great lengths to prove that the Tanaim did not originate any laws by exegesis, and that all the laws were expounded on the basis of tradition—the exegesis only serving as support. But even he concedes (in chapter 16) that some laws were derived by the Sages.
10. BT *Bava Kama* 46b.
11. BT *Pesachim* 25b; BT *Sanhedrin* 74a.
12. See many other such mitzvoth, as enumerated by R. M. Kasher in *Kaw HaTaarikh HaYisraeli*, chapter 55. In addition, the laws the Torah entrusted to the Sages (the establishment of the calendar, for instance) are Torah-based, but left the logical interpretation to the Sages. See the articles by Y. Emanuel in *HaMa'ayan*, Teveth and Nisan 5735 (1975) and Nisan 5737 (1977).
13. BT *Kethuboth* 22a; *Bava Kama* 46b; *Nidah* 25a.
    Cf. also Tosafoth, *Shevu'oth* 22b, s.v. *iba'ith*.
14. MT, Introduction. *Kesef Mishneh* to MT (note 9, above). MaHaRShaL (*Yam Shel Shelomoh, Chulin*, Introduction) writes: "Since the days of Ravina and Rav Ashi [the editors of the Talmud] there is a tradition to decide according to any Gaon or later authority, only if his words are decisively proven to be based on the [Babylonian] Talmud—or on the Jerusalem Talmud and the Tosefta when the [Babylonian] Talmud is undecisive."
15. R. Mosheh ibn Chaviv, *Get Pashut* 1, based on *Beth Yosef* on SA *Choshen Mishpat* 13 and *Yoreh De'ah* 228. Also see *Sedey Chemed, Ma'arekheth Yud* 5.

16. *Chazon Ish*, letter printed at the beginning of *Hilkhoth Kil-ayim*. Introduction to *Igroth Mosheh, Orach Chayim*.

17. *Chazon Ish, Choshen Mishpat, Likutim* 1, beginning.

18. This is similar to the decision of ReMA, SA *Choshen Mishpat* 25:1.

19. *Igroth Chazon Ish* II 15.

20. Meiri, BT *Bava Bathra* 130a.

21. *Nethivoth 'Olam, Nethiv Torah* 15.

22. SA *Choshen Mishpat* 25:1, in the name of ROSh (*Sanhedrin* 4:6).

23. See further, part 5, chapter 7, section 4(3).

24. R. Avraham ben HaRaMBaM, Responsa, 97. Also no. 63 in the 5707 (1947) New York edition of *Mishneh Torah*.

25. Proverbs 3:17.

26. BT *Sukah* 32ab, and Rashi ad loc.

27. BT *Yevamoth* 87b, which declares that a widow whose son dies does not require *chalitzah* for the reason cited.

28. *Or Same-ach* on MT *Yibum We-Chalitzah* 5:23.

29. BT *Gitin* 59b. Perhaps this thesis is based on MR Genesis 1:1, according to which God looked into the Torah when He created the world. This implies that physically, and spiritually, the Torah helps us towards perfection. This use of the Torah as a blueprint for the world also gives us a valuable touchstone with which to clarify details of halakhah — **when they cannot be clarified otherwise**: does a given halakhah lead to peace and perfection in health and society?

30. BT *Bava Metzi'a* 115a and *Kidushin* 68b.

31. Concerning levirate marriage, see Tosafoth on BT *Yevamoth* 2a, s.v. *we-achoth*, and 17b, s.v. *esheth*. Regarding damage to others, see ROSh, Responsa 108:10, quoted by *Tur Choshen Mishpat* 155:21; also in MaHaRaShDaM, Responsa *Choshen Mishpat* 267. According to them, this is a Torah-based law.

32. Regarding the mitzvah of honoring one's parents, see RaDBaZ, Responsa 663. In connection with seriously injuring oneself to save another's life, see op. cit. 1052, where he also says "...the laws of our Torah should also conform to reason and logic."

    This verse is also cited regarding whether a woman requires *chalitzah* from an apostate; see the Responsa of R. Eliyahu Mizrachi (68) and Binyamin Ze-ev (70).

33. References for the verse and its classical applications: Exodus 23:2; BT *Yevamoth* 89b; BT *Sanhedrin* 2a. Application to community decisions: ROSh, Responsa 6:5; Responsa *Zekan Aharon* 143; R. Moshe Amarilo, *Devar Mosheh* II 52. In the sense that those who support the community cannot be overruled: MaHaRaShDaM, Responsa *Orach Chayim* 37.

    In connection with the validity of trade-union agreements, based on the right of the court to confiscate property (RYTBA, BT *Bava Bathra* 8b), the verse is cited in the responsa of the MaHaRYK (no. 181).

34. R. Ya'akov Ibn Tzur, *Mishpat UTzedakah BeYa'akov* 1:52. Concerning a store rented out for a year, with the owner unexpectedly needing it for himself earlier: RaDBaZ, Responsa 1214.

35. RaDBaZ, Responsa 412.

36. MT *Melakhim* 12, end.

37. Responsa *Beth Yosef, Diney Kethuboth* 5.

38. MaHaRaSHDaM, Responsa *Even Ha'Ezer* 120.
39. *Tur Choshen Mishpat* 275:4 and BaCh ad loc.
40. BT *Bava Metzi'a* 10a.
41. From a manuscript.
42. M *Kethuboth* 13:10.
43. *Tur Even Ha'Ezer* 82:7.
44. *Shufra DeYa'akov* I, *Even Ha'Ezer* 59.
45. Responsa *Noda' BiYehudah II, Even Ha'Ezer* 79.
46. RaDBaZ, Responsa 1049.
47. *Meshekh Chokhmah*, Genesis 9:7.
48. JT *'Eiruvin* 3:2.
49. MaHaRShA, BT *'Eiruvin*, end.
50. JT *Nedarim* 9:1.
     Similarly, BT *Ta'anith* 11a, cited by Rashi on Numbers 6:11.
51. JT *Kidushin*, end.
52. M *Sanhedrin* 4, end.

NOTES TO REVIEW "Praiseworthy ... Chumroth

1. *Shevuth Ya'akov* III, *Yoreh De'ah* 98.
2. BT *Yoma* 28b. *'Eiruv Tavshilin* is a rabbinic institution, established to permit cooking for Shabbath on a Yom Tov that falls on Friday.
3. MK *Avoth DeRabbi Nathan* 1 and 2.
4. Ezekiel 4:14 as interpreted in BT *Chulin* 37b.
5. See ShaKh on SA *Yoreh De'ah* 17, note 8, in the name of *Magid Mishneh* quoting RaMBaN and RaShBA.
6. BT *Chulin* 105a.
7. M *'Eiduyoth* 3:10. The permission to do so is apparently disputed among the Tanaim. See *Tosfoth Yom Tov* on *Avoth* 1:15; *Orach Meysharim* 34:17 at length.
8. Herewith a short list:
    R. Chiya paid for damage he had caused, even though he was exempt from compensation (BT *Bava Kama* 99b).
    R. Papa interrupted his meal to enable his son to participate in *birkath hazimun* where he need not have done so (BT *Berakhoth* 45b). He also returned to the original owner a field he had acquired (BT *Kethuboth* 97a).
    In general, sages returned lost properties (BT *Bava Metzi'a* 24b) and helped others with heavy loads (BT *Bava Metzi'a* 30b) in circumstances where they need not have. Similarly, throughout the Talmud (e.g., BT *Shabbath* 118b, 119a; BT *Ta'anith* 20b; BT *Megilah* 27b, 28a) we find mention of pious customs and *chumroth* practiced by the Sages.
9. BT *Ta'anith* 10b.
10. JT *Berakhoth* 2, end, and *Peney Mosheh* ad loc.
11. BT *Shabbath* 21b.
12. BT *Sukah* 26b. RaMBaM, MT *Sukah* 6:6. For an example of Tanaim acting stringently, see M *Sukah* 2:5.
13. BT *Kidushin* 31a; and RaN ad loc.; *Machatzith HaShekel* 17:1.

14. BT *Shabbath* 133b; BT *Bava Kama* 9b.

15. BT *Bava Kama* 78b; RaMBaN, quoted by ROSh, *Rosh HaShanah* 3:1; ReMA on SA *Orach Chayim* 673:1, citing *Mordekhai, Kol Bo* and MaHaRYL — based on *Rokeach* 226.

16. Numbers 10:9.

17. This is implied by the wording of Rabbeinu Bachyay's commentary on *Avoth* 1:1, "Build safeguards for the Torah": "**A person** should build safeguards for the mitzvoth of the Torah." Cf. also *Midrash Shemuel* loc. cit.,s.v. *we-'asa*.

18. For example, RaShBaTz, *Magen Avoth, Avoth* 1:1; NeTzYV, *Ha'amek She-eilah* 137, in connection with Leviticus 20:25. Also see our discussion of voluntary safeguards at the end of chapter 6, below, especially note 93.

19. BT *Ta'anith* 11b.

20. Proverbs 16:5 and both RaMBaM (MT *De'oth* 2:3) and ROSh (*Orchoth Chayim*, beginning) list arrogance first among the most odious traits. Also compare the commentaries of RaMBaM and Rabbeinu Yonah on M *Avoth* 4:4.

21. BT *Berakhoth* 16a. For a survey of the halakhic opinions, see *Sha'arey Talmud Torah* III, *Kuntras*, chapter 3, second note.

22. BT *Bava Kama* 80b-81a and Rashi ad loc. Further see MaHaRShaL, *Yam Shel Shelomoh, Bava Kama* 7:41.

23. *Magen Avraham* 63, note 2. See also Responsa MaHaRaShDaM, *Yoreh De'ah* 192, end and *Birkey Yosef, Orach Chayim* 32:2.

24. R. Y. Bruna, Responsa 96.

25. Responsa *Tzitz Eli'ezer* VIII, 3:5.

26. BT *Bava Kama* 59b.

27. RAVYaH cited in *Mordekhai, Berakhoth*, end of no. 1.

28. *Shevuth Ya'akov* II 44. See also *Me'il Shemuel* on RaMBaM, *Talmud Torah* 1:13. *Peirush Ba'al Sefer Chareidim* on JT *Berakhoth* 2, end.

29. *Tosfoth Yom Tov, Shabbath* 1:9. ChiDA, *Pethach 'Eynayim, Chulin* 37; *Pethach HaDevir* 38:4; *Zekhor LeAvraham* fol. 64b.

30. As related in the incident in JT *Shevi'ith* 9, end, in connection with R. Yehoshua' ben Levi. The bracketed phrase is derived in *Kav WeNaki*, ad loc., note 31.

31. *Chok Ya'akov*, SA *Orach Chayim* 472, note 10.

32. R. Chaim of Zans, Responsa *Divrey Chayim* II, *Orach Chayim* 6.

33. A man must not preen himself. This is in the category of feminine practices prohibited for men. SA *Yoreh De'ah* 156:2, gloss ad loc., and 182, end.

34. *Chazon Ish, Hilkhoth Shevi'ith* 12:9.

35. Rabbeinu Yonah, BT *Berakhoth* 8, end, s.v. *lo yiten*, quoted by ReMA, SA *Orach Chayim* 169:2, and TaZ ad loc., 3.

36. Cited in *Peri Megadim, Mishbetzoth* ad loc., note 3.

37. M *Demay* 4:2 and JT ad loc.

38. Cf. BT *Chagigah* 22a and Tosafoth ad loc. (re accepting the word of an ignoramus concerning the purity of sacrificial wine and oil.); Responsa *Shevuth Ya'akov* II *Yoreh De'ah* 58 (re the reliability of a ritual slaughterer); Responsa MaBYT 3:49 (re excessive concern for the beauty of an *ethrog*); and his words, below, section 7.

39. BT *Pesachim* 82a.

40. *Tur Yoreh De'ah* 352 and *Beth Yosef* ad loc.

41. Limits on wedding expenditure have been proclaimed by many rabbinates. Such limitations were already included almost 800 years ago in the "*Takanoth ShUM* (Speyer, Worms, Mainz)". See Responsa MaHaRaM Rothenberg [Prague 5368 (1608); fol. 158b ff]. For such regulations promulgated by the "Four-Country Synode," see Responsa MaHaRaM Mintz 102.

42. *Magen Avraham* on SA *Orach Chayim* 252, note 1, quoting *Tzemach Tzedek* 28.

43. Leviticus 12.

44. M *Kerithoth* 1:7.

45. Responsa *Tirosh WeYitzhar* 88; also compare a negative responsum there.

46. R. Z. Bing, quoted in *Birkhatha DeEliyahu*, London, 5742 (1982), p. 35.

47. BT *Sanhedrin* 29a.

48. Ecclesiastes 7:29.

49. Proverbs 4:27.

50. R. Z. Bing, ibid. (note 46), p. 38.

51. Oral communication, quoting R. Y.Z. Gustman.

52. JT *Terumoth* 5, end.

53. *'Aley Tamar* on JT *Berakhoth* 4:2, fol. 150b, quoting *Yalkut Shim'oni* on Malachi, no. 588.

54. MaHaRaL, *Be-eir HaGolah* II s.v. *amnam ma'aseh ov.*

55. ShaKh, *Kitzur BeHanhagath Hora-ath Isur WeHeter*, printed in SA *Yoreh De'ah*, after 242; no. 9.

56. JT *Berakhoth* 2, end; *Shabbath* 1:2. We follow the reading of R. Shelomoh Sirileo (RaShaS) in *Berakhoth*, which is similar to that in the printed editions of *Shabbath*. The text as printed in *Berakhoth* seems garbled.

57. Some authorites hold that the Babylonian and Jerusalem Talmudim differ on this question. We have sought an explanation that satisfies both. See *Sha'arey Talmud Torah*, footnote p. 124 (p. 111 in the earlier editions), for details.

58. References for the paragraphs indicated:

(1) *Sidur* of R. 'Amram Gaon, *Seder Keriath Shema' UVirkhotheyha* 21.

(2) R. 'Amram Gaon and Rabbeinu Ya'akov Tam (the latter throughout the Talmud, e.g. *Gitin* 6b, 17b and *Menachoth* 32b). Also other Rishonim quoting Rabbeinu Tam: Rosh (*Halakhoth Ketanoth, Sefer Torah* 7); Rabbeinu Yerucham (II 2); *Sefer HaTerumah, Sefer Torah* 196; *Or Zaru'a* I 543. *'Ittur* and others are quoted as invalidating *tefilin* written on scored parchment (cf. *Beth Yosef, Orach Chayim* 32, s.v. *we-eyn tzarikh*, end.

(3) Rabbeinu Simchah, *Hagahoth Maimoniyoth, Sukah* 6:3; SA *Orach Chayim* 639:7, gloss.

(4) MaHaRaM of (Nurnberg) [Rothenburg] cited by ROSh, *Berakhoth* 3:2; *Mordekhai, Mo'ed Katan* 930; *Tur Yoreh De'ah* 341.

(5) *Terumath HaDeshen* 101.

(6) MaHaRaM of Rothenburg, *Mordekhai, Chulin* 8:687; *Terumath HaDeshen* 101.

(7) RAVYaH, *Berakhoth*, beginning; *Mordekhai*, op. cit., 8:1, end.

(8) R. Yisrael of Bruna, Responsa 96.

(9) Challenged by *Shiltey Giborim, Hilkhoth Tzitzith*, beginning; and hypothetically by RaMBaN, *Chidushey Kidushin* 31; RYTBA, ibid.; *Meiri, Rosh HaShanah* 33.

(10) MaHaRYL, *Agur* 27.

(11) R. Yomtov Lipman Heller ("Tosfoth Yom Tov"), *Divrey Chamudoth* on *Berakhoth* 2:58; *Magen Avraham* 70, note 5.
(12) TaZ and MaHaRShaL in *Magen Avraham* 472:6.
(13) *Pethach HaDevir* 38:4.
(14) ROSh on *Shabbath* 2:18, end, lauded this action, even though it is not required; but *Be-er Sheva'* 21 asks why this is not boorishness.
(15) *Shevuth Ya'akov* II 44.

59. RaMBaM on M *Sotah* 3:3.
60. RaShBA, *Chidushey Sukah* 25a; RaN on RYF ad loc. Cf. also *Yam Shel Shelomoh, Chulin* 11:11.
61. RaMBaN, *Chidushey Kidushin* 31a.
62. RYTBA, ibid. See *Sha'arey Talmud Torah* for a detailed analysis of his statement and ChYDA, *Birkey Yosef, Yoreh De'ah* 333:1, and *Sha'ar Yosef* 8, for an extensive treatment of our issue.
63. Meiri, *Bava Kama* 87a.
64. *Sefer HaTerumah, Hilkhoth Sefer Torah* 196; *Beth Yosef, Orach Chayim* 32. But cf. *Ma'adaney Yom Tov* on ROSh, *Halakhoth Ketanoth, Sefer Torah* 7:3.
65. *Sha'ar Yosef* 8; *Ya'ir Ozen, "Peh"*, no. 13; *Pethach 'Eynayim, Bava Metzi'a* 30, s.v. *ulefi.*
66. *Pethach HaDevir* 146:4, fol. 161a.
67. *Ohaley Yehudah* 101; ChYDA in: *Pethach 'Eynayim, Bava Metzi'a* 20, s.v. *wekhol*; *Ya'ir Ozen, "Peh"*, no. 13. Also quoting him, *Meshek Beythi* 238. Cf. also *Be-er Sheva*, Responsa 21.
68. BT *Ta'anith* 11a, based on Numbers 6:11.
69. JT *Nedarim* 9:1.
70. See BT *Nedarim* 9b-10a.
71. *Tif-ereth Yonathan, Kedoshim*, beginning.
72. *Migdal 'Oz, Beth HaMidoth, Aliyah Derekh Eretz* 8.
73. Proverbs 11:17. See RaLBaG's extensive commentary there.
74. MR Leviticus 34:3.
75. MR Genesis 1:1.
76. Proverbs 3:17. See at length above (chapter 4, section 3).
77. JT *Kidushin*, end.
78. Loc. cit.; cf. *Korban Ha'Eidah* ad loc.
79. *'Aley Tamar* on JT *Berakhoth* 4:2, fol. 150b.
80. BT *Menachoth* 64a.
81. R. Aharon Kotler, *Mishnath R. Aharon* I, pp. 200-201.
82. *Terumath HaDeshen; Beth Yosef* (in *Avkath Rokhel*); *Levush*—all quoted later.
83. BT *Gitin* 5b.
84. R. Eliyahu ibn Chaim (HaRANaCh), Responsa II 11.
85. R. Ya'akov Castro, *'Erekh Lechem, Yoreh De'ah* 119 and 242, quoting RYVaSh. Also see R. Yechezkel Landau, Responsa *Noda' BiYehudah* II, *Yoreh De'ah* 139, end; R. Menasheh Sithhon, *Kenesiah Leshem Shamayim* 60b. In contrast: see ROSh, Responsa 43:6.
86. *Terumath HaDeshen* 74 (regarding *'eiruv*); *Avkath Rokhel* 210, s.v. *wehineni ba* (*treifah*); ReMA, Responsa 117 (grafted *ethrog*); MaHaRaShDaM, Responsa, *Yoreh De'ah* 193 (*kil-ayim*); *Levush, Yoreh De'ah* 198:31, and MaHaRaM Lublin,

Responsa 97, quoted by SHaKh ad loc., note 48 (*mikveh*); *Magen Avraham* 32, note 48 (*tefilin*); TaZ, SA *Orach Chayim* 161:6 and 614:1 (wearing shoes on Yom Kippur); Responsa *Chut HaShani* 56 (*tevilath nidah*); '*Afar Ya'akov*, quoted by *Pachad Yitzchak*, s.v. *keriath haTorah* (regarding *akdamoth* in the middle of the Torah reading).

87. MaHaRShaM, *Divrey Shalom*, end, note 36, quoting Tosefta, *Parah* 3:4.

88. *Terumath HaDeshen* 232.

89. RaShBA, Responsa 1190.

90. R. Yosef ibn Lev (MaHaRYBaL), Responsa II 13.

91. R. Avraham ben Menachem Hakohen, *Taharath HaMayim*, fol. 33, no. 20.

92. Responsa *Chatham Sofer, Orach Chayim* 181. See note 16 (Part 5, Chapter 6) for the source of the quote and the explanation of the play on words.

93. BT *Pesachim* 66b. See Meiri, *Magen Avoth*, Introduction, that our sages applied this principle even toward their colleagues. For additional authorities discussing this concern: See *Sedey Chemed, Ma'arekheth Lamed* 25; R. Y.D. Bamberger, Responsa *Yad HaLevi* 197.

94. MR Genesis 19:3 to Proverbs 30:6.

95. M *Berakhoth* 1:3 and BT *Berakhoth* 11a. It is interesting that, on another occasion and under entirely different circumstances, R. Tarfon got into similar difficulties (JT *Shevi'ith* 4:2, end).

96. R. 'Amram Gaon, *Sidur, Seder Keriath Shema' UVirkhotheyah* 21; also quoted by *Tur Orach Chayim* 63 and *Magen Avraham* ad loc., note 3.

97. *Peri Chadash, Orach Chayim* 63, note 2. MaHaRaShDaM, Responsa *Yoreh De'ah* 192; and MaHaRShal, Responsa 54. BaCh and TaZ on SA *Orach Chayim* 551, note 10, agree in principle and differ only in that instance.

98. *Mordekhai*, BT *Chulin* 8:687.

99. *Yam Shel Shelomoh, Chulin* 8:6.

100. See SA *Yoreh De'ah* 89:2, gloss and SHaKh, note 17.

101. Quoted by *Pithchey Teshuvah, Yoreh De'ah* 116, note 10, end, in the name of *Torath HaAsham*. But cf. R. Yonah Ashkenazi, *Issur WeHeter* (57, end) who holds that one may act stringently in such matters.

102. R. Zerachyah HaLevi (*Ba'al HaMaor*) on BT *Shabbath* 3, s.v. *we-im tish-al*; *Kol Bo* 32a, quoted in SA *Orach Chayim*, gloss at end of 257.

103. MT *Isurey Biah* 11:15; similarly, MT *Shabbath* 2:3.

104. MT *Ma-akhaloth Asuroth* 17:22.

105. Based on JT *Shabbath* 4:1, referring to Deuteronomy 17:8-13.

106. Tosafoth on BT *Berakhoth* 34a, s.v. *melamdim*.

107. MaHaRaShDaM, Responsa, *Yoreh De'ah* 192, end.

108. Rashi on '*Eiruvin* 96a, s.v. *we-lo michu*; *Rosh HaShanah* 33a, s.v. *ha-nashim*. See Tosafoth, '*Eiruvin* 96a, s.v. *mikhol shecholkim*, and MaHaRShA to *Rosh HaShanah* ad loc. *Terumath HaDeshen* (101) uses a similar expression.

109. ROSh, Responsa 21:8-9; *Kesef Mishneh* on MT *Terumah* 1:11, end.

110. MaHaRaShDaM, Responsa, *Yoreh De'ah* 192-193.

111. MaBYT, Responsa III 68.

112. Notes 104 and 105, above, and *Kesef Mishneh* on MT *Terumah* 1:11.

113. Deuteronomy 17:11 and *Sifrey* ad loc.

114. BT *Berakhoth* 53b.

115.   Tosafoth on BT *Sukah* 3a, s.v. *de-amar*.
116.   *Apey Zutra, Orach Chayim* 472, fol. 140b.
117.   M *Avoth* 1:7.
118.   Proverbs 8:13, cited in BT *Pesachim* 113b.
119.   M *Megilah* 4:9 (BT, fol. 24b-25a).
120.   R. 'Ovadiah of Bartinoro. Similarly, Rashi ad loc.
121.   Ecclesiastes 2:14; BT *'Eiruvin* 6b; *Rosh HaShanah* 14b and Tosafoth ad loc.
122.   RYTBA on BT *'Eiruvin* 7a.
123.   JT *Terumoth* 2:1 and R. Shelomoh Sirileo's commentary ad loc.
124.   R. Aryeh Leib of Metz, *Turey Even* to BT *Rosh HaShanah* 14b. Cf. also *Chazon Ish, Yoreh De'ah* 150:5.
125.   MaHaRShA to BT *Chulin* 44b s.v. *ha-ro-eh*, citing Psalms 128:2.
126.   SheLaH, *Shavu'oth*, s.v. *takhlith ha-limud*.
127.   BT *Gitin* 56a.

NOTES TO PART 3

NOTES TO CHAPTER 1

1.   Deuteronomy 11:19.
2.   BT *Kidushin* 29b.
3.   BT *Megilah* 3b.
4.   M *Avoth* 4:5.
5.   BT *Sanhedrin* 99a.
6.   BT *Berakhoth* 63b.
7.   Quoted in *The Jewish Observer*, Sivan 5733 (1973).
8.   Ibid., Tamuz 5740 (1980), p. 9.
9.   E.g., R. E.M. Shakh, letter, 5735 (1975) and *Moresheth Avoth*, Elul 5736 (1976).
10.   It appears from the end of the first chapter of *Bava Kama* that teaching others is more laudable even than practicing, which, in turn, is more laudible than learning for oneself. This is also evident from the commentaries of Rashi, Tosafoth and Meiri there. MaHaRShA (*Kidushin* 40b) says that teaching is considered greater than practicing because many others will be influenced by it. See NeTzYV, *Ha'amek She-eilah* (on *Lekh-Lekha* 7:5), who gives other cogent explanations. According to RYTBA, however, action is preferable to teaching others. According to *She-iltoth* (*Lekh-Lekha* 7), the Talmudic passage refers to chronological sequence rather than order of preference. See part 6, chapter 1, at length.

NOTES TO CHAPTER 2

1.   BT *Sukah* 49b.
2.   BT *Sanhedrin* 19b and 99b.
3.   SheLaH, *Shavu'oth, Perek Baruch Atah*, s.v. *kevar*.
4.   M *Bava Metzi'a* chapter 2, end.

5.   *Menorath HaMaor* 88.
6.   *Sifrey*, Deuteronomy, 252. See Rashi's comment on Deuteronomy 23:9.
7.   MaHaRaShDaM, Responsa, *Yoreh De'ah* 204.
8.   *Minchath Chinukh* on *Sefer HaChinukh* 239, note 4.
9.   ShaKh, *Po'el Tzedek* 220.
10. SheLaH, *Torah Shebikhtav, Ki Theitzei*, near end.
11. Hence spiritual rescue should take precedence over the laws of Shabbath, as many authorities hold under certain circumstances. See: ReMA on SA *Orach Chayim* 328:6; BaCh on *Tur Orach Chayim* 306, s.v. *kathav*, quoted by *Magen Avraham* ad loc. note 29, and TaZ, note 5.
12. Leviticus 19:18.
13. M *Nedarim* 9:4.
14. RaMBaN on Leviticus 19:17.
15. *Ahavath Chesed* 3:7.
16. MT *De'oth* 6:3.
17. JT *Nedarim* 9:4. This applies specifically when teaching Torah to others; for if personal safety is involved, the rule is that one's own life takes precedence over others (deduced by "Chatham Sofer" on *Kedoshim*, referring to BT *Bava Metzi'a* 62a).
18. BT *Pesachim* 75a; *Kethuboth* 37b; *Sotah* 8b; *Bava Kama* 51a; *Sanhedrin* 45a, 52a.
19. *Shitah Mekubetzeth, Kethuboth* 37b, s.v. *we-ahavta*. Another Talmudic passage (MK *Avoth DeRabbi Nathan* 16, end) reads: "If he conforms to the accepted norms of behavior, love him; but if not, do not love him." The author of this passage apparently disagrees with the Babylonian Talmud. Cf. also note 5 to chapter 6.
20. BT *Kidushin* 36a.
21. RaShBA, Responsa 194.
22. HaGeRA on SA *Yoreh De'ah* 159, note 3.
23. *Selichoth* for the first Monday of BaHaB, s.v. *Yisrael 'amkha*.
24. For an explanation of King David's exclamation (Psalms 139:21-2): "Those who incite hatred of You, O God, I will hate," as well as that of his son, King Solomon (Prov. 8:13): "Fear of God is [expressed by] hatred of evil"—see chapter 6.
25. M *Avoth* 1:12.
26. MK *Avoth DeRabbi Nathan*, quoted by R. 'Ovadyah of Bartinoro, ad loc.
27. Malachi 2:6.

NOTES TO CHAPTER 3

1.   BT *Shevu'oth* 39a.
2.   Leviticus 26:37.
3.   BT *Rosh HaShanah* 29a and Rashi, ad loc.
4.   BT *Sotah* 37b.
5.   BT *Bava Metzi'a* 85a, based on Jeremiah 15:19.
6.   *Sefer Chasidim* 946.
7.   BT *Bava Metzi'a* 85a and Daniel 12:3.
8.   M *Avoth* 5:18.
9.   *Chovoth HaLevavoth, Sha'ar Ahavath HaShem* 6.
10. "According to the Torah, coercion frees from punishment" (BT *Bava Kama* 28b).
11. Ezekiel 33.

12. See the words of RaMBaM at the end of this chapter, that here we derive the obligation of an ordinary individual from the action of the prophet.

13. BT *Shabbath* 54-55.

14. BT *Shabbath* 55a. Based on Ezekiel 9:6.

15. BT *Shabbath* 54b.

16. Elsewhere in the Talmud, we find a seemingly contradictory approach. M *Ma'aser Sheni* 5:1 calls upon field owners to mark trees under three years old, whose fruits are forbidden (*'orlah*). This is required only during the Sabbatical year, when all produce becomes public property. But otherwise, "feed the wicked one and let him die" (BT *Bava Kama* 69a). This seems to exclude from the demands of mutual responsibility a transgressor who remains a transgressor in one area (stealing in this case) even after we have stopped him in another. We even find an opinion that a willful transgressor need not be admonished. (See the commentary of R. Shelomoh Eiger, *Gilyon MaHaRShA, Yoreh De'ah* 151, on ShaKh, note 6, and R. Y. Landau, *Dagul MeRevavah*, ad loc.) Apparently we seek to prevent a transgression not for its own sake, but to reform the transgressor and if he remains a transgressor even afterwards, there is no point to prevent a specific sin. This is elaborated in my article in *Kovetz Chidushey Torah* II, Jerusalem College of Technology, Jerusalem 5749, pp. 135-9.

17. Tosafoth, *Shabbath* 55a, s.v. *af'al gav; Sefer Yere-im HaShalem* 223. Regarding the commandment "you shall surely admonish"—which according to some Rishonim, is a separate mitzvah—see chapter 4.

18. *Sefer Yere-im* 37.

19. SeMaG, pos. 11, referring to Proverbs 9:8.

20. BT *Yevamoth* 65b.

21. MT *De'oth* 6:8.

22. BT *Shabbath* 34a.

23. *Minchath Shemuel* 11.

24. "Chafetz Chayim", Letters, letter 26, quoted in *Mitzvoth HaShalom*, p. 295.

25. *Chazon Ish, Shemitah* 2:16.

26. MT *De'oth* 6:8.

27. Nehemiah 13:25 as interpreted in BT *Mo'ed Katan* 16a.

NOTES TO CHAPTER 4

1. Leviticus 19:17 and elaborated by MaLBYM ad loc. Also cf. Rashi on Genesis 20:16 and 24:44.

2. In MT *De'oth* 6:7, RaMBaM states that the admonishment should be gentle and kindly; but in halakhah 8 he writes that if this admonishment is ignored, one must use the strongest means possible—including public shaming—to try to bring about a change. MaHaRaM Schick (in his Responsa, *Orach Chayim* 303) resolves this difficulty by pointing out the duality of this mitzvah: while the commandment to admonish requires gentleness, the fact that we are responsible for others' actions leads us to use any means at our disposal.

3. *Sefer HaChinukh* 239.

4. *Tana Devei Eliyahu Rabba* 18, end.

5. BT *Yevamoth* 65b, based on Proverbs 9:8. This is accepted by Tosafoth (BT *Shabbath* 55a, s.v. *we-af 'al gav*); by *Sefer Yere-im* 37; by SeMaG (pos. 11), and by Rabbeinu Yonah in *Sha'ar HaTokhachah*.
6. Leviticus 19:14 as elaborated in BT *Pesachim* 22b.
7. BT *'Erkin* 16b.
8. *Nimukey Yosef* on BT *Yevamoth* 65b.
9. A careful reading of *Chidushey RYTBA* (*Yevamoth* 65b) leads to this interpretation. We find it explicitly in *Sefer Chasidim* 413 and in *Likutey Amarim*, chapter 32.

    However, note that ReMA (*Orach Chayim* 608:2) makes a distinction between public admonition, which is to be given only once, and private admonition, which should be carried on until the person admonished strikes or curses the admonisher. The reasoning underlying this distinction is, however, unclear (cf. *Birkey Yosef, Orach Chayim* 608, note 5).
10. ReMA on SA *Orach Chayim* 608:2.
11. *Bei-ur Halakhah*, loc. cit., s.v. *aval*, end.
12. BT *Bava Metzi'a* 31a.
13. MaHaRShaL to SeMaG, pos. 11.
14. Cf. *Sedey Chemed, Dinim, Ma'arekheth Heh* 2.
15. Responsa *Kethav Sofer, Even Ha'Ezer* 47, based on BT *Shabbath* 54b.

NOTES TO CHAPTER 5

1. *Sefer HaMitzvoth*, pos. 3.
2. *Toldoth Adam* on *Sifrey, Devarim* 32: "You shall love God—make him beloved by people: teaching others is greater than teaching oneself." Also cf. *Chovoth HaLevavoth* 10:6: "One character trait of those who fear God is to bring others to His service."
3. Deuteronomy 27:26.
4. JT *Sotah* 7:4.

NOTES TO CHAPTER 6

1. In II Chronicles 20:37 it is prophesied to Jehoshaphat, "Because you have joined Ahaziah, God has destroyed your work." Similarly, *Avoth* 1:7 counsels, "Do not join with an evil person." And in BT *Pesachim* 113b, the Sages refer to Proverbs 8:13 to show that it is an obligation to hate a person one has seen transgress. This is codified by RaMBaM (MT *Rotze-ach* 13:14) and in SA *Choshen Mishpat* 272:11.
2. The terms *minuth* and *epikorsuth* are used throughout this chapter and require some clarification. *Minuth* (its proponent is a *min*—plural *minim*) is the belief in concepts inimical to Jewish tradition—including apostasy; the early Christians were referred to as *minim*. *Epikorsuth* (its proponent is an *epikorus*—plural *epikorsim*) is, in the classical sense, the denial of the authority of the sages and rabbis; however, its meaning has popularly been extended to include anyone with heretical beliefs and it has become almost synonymous with *minuth*.

3. BT *'Avodah Zarah* 17a, citing Proverbs 5:8. Also *Shabbath* 116a, citing Psalms 139:21-2. Also BT *'Avodah Zarah* 27b: "*Minuth* is different, because it is attractive."

4. BT *Chulin* 133a: "Whoever teaches an unsuitable disciple is accounted as one who throws a stone for [i.e., serves the idolatrous statue of] Mercury and falls into Gehenna."

5. In MT *Mamrim* 3:3, RaMBaM writes: "To whom do these laws [that one must treat non-believers harshly] apply? To one who denies the Oral Torah in his mind and according to his own opinion. For he has followed his light-headedness and the stubbornness of his heart and denies the Oral Torah, like Tzadok [the founder of the Saducees] and Boethius [the founder of the Baithusim] and everyone who followed them in their error. But the children of these errant ones, and their children's children, who were led astray by their fathers and raised by the Karaites [the spiritual heirs of the Saducees, who were rampant in RaMBaM's time] in their own faith, are like children who are captive among them and are not anxious to accept the mitzvoth; they are like unwitting trangressors. And even if they hear later [that they are Jewish and become aware of their Judaism and its laws], they are considered unwitting, for they were raised in the errors of their parents. So, too, those of whom we spoke, who espouse the erroneous opinions of their Karaite fathers. Therefore, it is proper to encourage them to repent and to attract them with peaceful words until they return to the strength of the Torah."
   Similarly, on M *Chulin* 1:2, RaMBaM comments: "But those who were born into these beliefs, and were raised according to them, are like coerced transgressors and we apply to them the rules of 'children in captivity among the gentiles,' all of whose transgressions are considered inadvertent, as we have explained. But the first instigator — he is a deliberate trangressor, not inadvertent." (We have based this translation on that of R. Y. Kappach.) His words are cited in Responsa MaBYT (no. 37) and quoted by *Beth Yosef* in *Tur Orach Chayim* 385 and *Yoreh De'ah* 159 and are codified by ReMA, SA *Yoreh De'ah* 159:6.

6. R. Ya'akov Ettlinger ('*Arukh LeNer*) in his responsa *Binyan Tzion* II 23, end:
   Regarding the Jewish transgressors of our day — I do not know how to adjudge them; for, because of our many sins, the conflagration has spread to the masses, and the desecration of Shabbath is looked upon as if it were permitted. Perhaps we can adjudge them as "one who says: it is permitted," who is considered only "borderline deliberate," ... especially in the case of their children, who have never heard of the laws of Shabbath, and who are exactly like the Saducees, who are not considered heretics — even though they desecrate Shabbath — for they [merely] follow the customs of their fathers and are like children raised in captivity among gentiles, as explained (SA *Orach Chayim* 385).
   Also see R. David Tzvi Hoffmann in *Melamed Leho'il, Orach Chayim*, no. 29:
   The majority of Israel in our country [Germany] desecrate Shabbath; they do not intend, by this, to deny our basic beliefs. ... There is another mitigating circumstance in our day, in that their desecration cannot be considered "in public;" since the majority is doing the same ... the individual thinks that this is not such an important transgression and therefore he need not [bother to] do it in private.

7. "Chafetz Chayim," Letters, letter no. 26, quoted in *Mitzvoth HaShalom*, p. 295.

8. "Chatham Sofer", Responsa, *Even Ha'Ezer* II 60.

9. *Chazon Ish, Yoreh De'ah, Hilkhoth Shechitah* 2:16.

10. MaHaRaM Lublin, Responsa (no. 13), based on *Hagahoth Maimonioth* on MT *De'oth*. His words are elaborated, as brought in the text, by R. Yehonathan Walliner in *Marganitha Tava* (printed by the "Chafetz Chayim" at the end of his *Ahavath Chesed*) 17 and in *Chazon Ish, Shechitah* 2:28 and *Yibum* 118:6.

11. Based on BT *'Erkin* 16b, according to several outstanding authorities, as cited in the preceding note. For a brilliant explanation, see R. Ya'akov Kamenecki, *Iyunim BaMikra, WaYeitze* 29:4.

12. MR Genesis 76:9, quoted by Rashi on Genesis 32:23.

13. BT *Chagigah* 22a.

14. See chapter 3 of review at end of part 2.

15. R. A.Y. Kook, *Letters* II 571.

16. *Bei-ur Halakhah* on 1:1.

17. These letters were written, in German, to R. S.B. Bamberger and printed in *The Collected Writings of R. S.R. Hirsch* IV.

18. It may be appropriate to describe the general condition of the times: Because of Prussian law, the government recognized only one Jewish congregation, a status the Reform movement succeeded in arrogating to itself. Thus, every Jew was automatically considered a member of the Reform congregation and 10% of his income tax was automatically transferred to them. The only alternative would have been to register oneself as "agnostic." Thus, the observant element was under the control of the Reform movement, who exploited this situation most cruelly by closing the *mikveh*, discontinuing *shechitah*, and even enlisting the police to tear children away from private Torah classes and force them to listen to heretical lessons. Finally, R. Samson Raphael Hirsch succeeded to prevail upon the Prussian government to change the law. When the Reform leadership saw that they had lost their dominance, they agreed to permit religious freedom to those who would remain in their framework.

19. See note 5.

20. MT *De'oth* 6:1.

21. *Mikhtav MeEliyahu* II, p. 113.

22. MR Leviticus 34:12: "'And downtrodden poor bring into the house' — That refers to the Torah scholars who enter the houses of the ignorant and slake their thirst with words of Torah."

23. This is how the sages explained why Moses was commanded by God at Mount Sinai to first tell the women (*Pirkey DeRabbi Eli'ezer* 41). Similarly, MR Genesis 17:7 states that everything derives from the wife, and relates the story of a righteous husband and wife who were not blessed with children. They concluded that under these circumstances they were not serving God, so they divorced and both remarried, ending up with evil spouses. Because of his evil wife, the man also became evil, but the woman succeeded in making her new husband righteous.

24. BT *Pesachim* 49b.

NOTES TO CHAPTER 7

1. BT *Bava Metzi'a* 85a.

2. *Higayon Nefesh*, page 2.

NOTES TO PART 4

NOTES TO CHAPTER 1

1. BT *Kidushin* 29b.
2. MT *Talmud Torah* 1:1-3. In *Sefer HaMitzvoth*, too, RaMBaM places teaching ahead of learning, but derives it from another verse. So does *Sefer HaChinukh* (419). All this implies, rather amazingly, that the primary obligation is to teach others, while the obligation to learn seems to apply merely by default. [However, when enumerating the commandments in the introduction to *Mishneh Torah*, RaMBaM writes, "To learn Torah and teach it." *Sefer Yere-im* (25) and SeMaK (105) also cite first the verse dealing with learning, and only afterwards—like an additional commandment—(nos. 26 and 106, respectively) the obligation to teach.]
   Certainly, acquiring knowledge is a major obligation. But the form in which the Torah enunciates it—as an adjunct to teaching others—is also significant. See the beginning of part 3.
3. The centrality of interpersonal obligations in Judaism is evidenced in statements as "What is hateful to you, do not do to your fellow. This is **the whole Torah**." (BT *Shabbath* 31a); "**The whole Torah** is for the sake of peaceful social intercourse" (BT *Gitin* 59b). For an in-depth analysis of this surprising fact, see my treatise in *HaMa'ayan* 28(4):20 (Tamuz 5748).

NOTES TO CHAPTER 2

1. *Pirkey Avoth* 6:1 and MK *Kalah* 8:1.
2. BT *Pesachim* 50b.
3. BT *Ta'anith* 7a.
4. See, for instance, *Beth HaLevi*, as quoted below in chapter 6.
5. Rashi on BT *Ta'anith* 7a says this explicitly: "'*Lishmah*': that is, because my God commanded me, not because I want the title of 'rabbi'." RaMBaM expresses it similarly (MT *Teshuvah* 10:5): "And everyone who studies [the Torah] not out of fear and not because of the reward, but out of love for the Master of the universe, Who commanded it—such a one is said to occupy himself with it *lishmah*." Their source seems to be *Nedarim* 62a: "'To love God...'—a person should not say, 'I will read so they will call me a sage, I will learn so that they will call me a rabbi' ... rather, learn out of love." We can infer that, just like any other commandment, if one learns in order to fulfill the commandment of Torah study, and does so out of love of God, that is called *lishmah*. This is also clearly stated by the "Chatham Sofer" in his glosses (on BT *Nedarim* 81a; and in *Torath Mosheh* on *Tzav*, s.v. *zoth ha-Torah*). He distinguishes between Torah study for the sake of knowing how to serve God and Torah study *lishmah*:
   > For certainly, one who studies only to know how a mitzvah is to be carried out and thus his whole purpose is only to fulfill that mitzvah—this cannot be

considered better than the fulfillment of the mitzvah itself. .... But the essential obligation to study Torah is a separate commandment, "to meditate in it day and night." ... Not merely to study those commandments that obligate him, but to "research and receive reward," that is, the research itself is the reward and it gives God satisfaction. That is Torah study *lishmah*.

This seems to imply that one need not study with the intention of practicing. But this explanation is untenable, as he himself writes elsewhere (as quoted in chapter 3): "For the goal of occupying ourselves with the Torah should be to understand the commandment in order to fulfill it...for this is the primary goal." Clearly "Chatham Sofer" meant to say that the intention of serving the Creator must be combined with the intention to apply what one learns. (Cf. R.Y. Lieberman, Responsa *Mishnath Yosef*, introduction, 4, who interprets "Chatham Sofer" differently).

6. BT *Nedarim* 62a.
7. *Nefesh HaChayim* 4:3.
8. "'Torah' [derived from the root *moreh*] includes the stories from the beginning of Genesis because they guide (*moreh*) people on their way" (RaMBaN, introduction to his commentary on the Torah).
9. Deuteronomy 4:5. Rashi on BT *Ta'anith* 7a cites this verse to explain the meaning of *lishmah*.
10. Rabbeinu Chananel to BT *'Avodah Zarah* 17b.
11. M *Avoth* 4:5.
12. R. Yonah on M *Avoth* 4:5.
13. MT *Teshuvah* 10:5.
    But note RaMBaM's comment on M *Sanhedrin* 10:1 (s.v. *we-kath chamishith*), which suggests that even study itself should be started for the sake of its reward. This apparent contradiction can be reconciled; for there it speaks explicitly of a minor, who is not obligated to fulfill the commandments; when he studies afterwards for the sake of honor, the reference may be to honor accorded him for his conduct, not his studies.
14. Cited by ChYDA in *Chasdey Avoth* on M *Avoth* 4:5.
15. Verbal communication from R. Simchah Wasserman. Also: R. Aharon Kotler, *Mishnath R. Aharon* I 2:11.
16. *Mishnah Berurah, Orach Chayim* 489, note 5, and *Sha'ar HaTziyun* 6 thereto.
17. BT *Pesachim* 50b.
18. BT *Pesachim* 50b; *Nazir* 23b; *Sotah* 22b (see there for a complete listing of citations); similarly in JT *Chagigah* 1:7.
19. MK *Kalah* 8, beginning.
20. BT *Berakhoth* 17a.
21. BT *Ta'anith* 7a.
22. Loc. cit., note 20.
23. BT *Pesachim* 50b and Rashi ad loc.
24. JT *Berakhoth* 1:2, beginning.
25. Note 17, above.
26. BT *Berakhoth* 17a. We translated "*lekanter*" "to dispute." Rashi's wording permits the interpretation of "to provoke," meaning that his whole purpose in study is to

undermine the Torah. However, the wording of Tosafoth (ad loc. and even more clearly BT *Pesachim* 50b) *lekanter chaveraw* indicates that he simply wants to defeat his associate in academic arguments.

Rashi leaves open the status of one who studies without intending to practice, but without evil intentions either. Is intent to dispute, or a similar ulterior motive, a necessary condition, or is the lack of intent to practice sufficient? This question, too, is treated presently.

27. BT *Ta'anith* 7a. Actually, this is not explicit in Rashi's words. He writes: "[Study] *lishmah* [for which the Torah becomes an elixir of life] is study due to a desire to obey God's commandment and not in order to be called 'rabbi,'" implying that one who studies in order to be called "rabbi," studies *shelo lishmah* so that the Torah becomes, for him, "a deadly draught."

The implication could be avoided by postulating an intermediate state: one who learns in order to be honored is in the category of "Your kindness is as high as the heaven." At the same time, the Torah does not become an elixir of life for him, but neither a deadly draught. In any event, however, according to Rashi, one who learns with no intention of practicing is guilty of the evil *shelo lishmah*, as he writes explicitly in (b).

But in fact, it is difficult to assume a *shelo lishmah* which is laudable and yet would negate the "elixir of life" aspect of Torah study. Our Sages frequently described the Torah as such an elixir: "God gave the Torah to Israel, an elixir of life for their entire body" (MT *'Eiruvin* 54a). "To one who uses it, it is an elixir of life; to one who doesn't, it is a deadly potion" (*Yoma* 72b; similarly, *Shabbath* 88b); "'And you shall place them': [a play on words in Hebrew *We-samtam — sam tam*] indicates that the Torah is compared to an elixir of life" (*Kidushin* 30b). All these quotations refer to Torah study as such, *lishmah* or not. It therefore seems impossible to maintain that one who learns in a laudable manner ("Your kindness is as high as the heaven") should be excluded from the concept of the elixir of life. Rather, Rashi must mean to include in the evil *shelo lishmah* the one who wants to be called a rabbi.

28. M *Avoth* 4:5.

29. BT *Nedarim* 62a.

30. The simple meaning of this passage seems to be that the Sages classify such abuse of Torah study as *me'ilah*, deriving physical benefit from a consecrated object; this is punishable by death (divinely executed). Perhaps the deeper meaning of the mishnah is as follows. The essence of sanctity is making one's indulgence in worldly pleasures fully subservient to Torah. It therefore follows that if he uses the Torah to further his enjoyment, he is desecrating the Torah. Since the Torah is "our life and the length of our days," this desecration literally shortens his life and removes him from the world. (See Part 1, chapter 3.) This explains why "removal from the world" does not apply to one who seeks reward in the next world. In support of this, *Yesod Ha'Avodah* (I 1:2) states that the deduction from Belshazzar does not apply under such circumstances. We can make this same distinction in other commandments as well. MaHaRShA (*Kethuboth* 67, s.v. *iba'ith*) distinguishes between one who is motivated by his desire for recognition, who is punished, and one who studies so that his son may be cured or that he himself may share in the next world, which is considered proper piety (BT *Pesachim* 8a; *Rosh HaShanah* 4a).

This means that it is proper to safeguard another's welfare in this world or his own welfare in the next; but if he studies Torah to further his own welfare in this world, he is punished.

Chazon Yechezkel (on *Shabbath* 10a) explains why "one who learns without intention to practice" would have been better off "had his afterbirth been thrust back on him": "The learning and comprehension of the Torah is a matter of soul, not body. But the fulfillment of its commandments requires the body, whose 248 members were given to man for this purpose... Therefore, he who learns without intending to practice does not need his body, and it would be better had his afterbirth been thrust back on him and he would never have seen the light of day."

31.   The opinion that learning must be geared toward practice finds further support in the words of R. 'Akiva (MK *Kalah* 8:1): "For him who reads *shelo lishmah*, it would have been better had his afterbirth been thrust back on him, as it is written (Leviticus 22:31), 'and you shall guard my commandments and you shall **fulfill** them.'" This is even more explicit in the Jerusalem Talmud version: "Whoever studies with no intention of practicing—better he had not been born. R. Yochanan said, 'Whoever studies with no intention of practicing would have been better off had his afterbirth been thrust back on him and he would never have seen the light of day'" (JT *Berakhoth* 1:2). See also *Sifra*, introduction to *Bechukothay* 5, and MR Leviticus 35:7.

32.   This follows from the following considerations: One who learns with no intention of practicing has not fulfilled any commandment and, even if he studies Torah because God commanded him to do so, it does not constitute the fulfillment of a commandment; and, since he does not learn in order to practice, he will also not come to fulfill the other commmandments. Thus, effectively, he has to his credit neither the study of Torah nor the fulfillment of its commandments. Such a person would certainly have been better off not being created, since his creation was only for the sake of his fulfilling the will of his Creator. Cf. the Talmudic conclusion (BT *'Eiruvin* 13b) that, in general, it would have been better for man not to have been created.

33.   BT *Sotah* 22b.

34.   For completeness' sake, we cite here another opinion restricting the study of Torah *shelo lishmah*, as mentioned by ChYDA in the name of R. Shemuel Primo: someone studying with an ulterior motive should do this only with the intent to come to a stage of *lishmah*. "But he who learns solely *shelo lishmah* and his only purpose is ulterior...—better he had not been created." This is similar to the statement of R. Chayim *Or Zarua'* (end of 163): "Every *shelo lishmah* is the same and all are sinful. This transgression is permitted [only] when it leads to the fulfillment of a commandment—like one who saves a woman from a river, or digs a heap of rocks on Shabbath [to rescue a person buried underneath]. This is evident from the passage in *Nazir*, which likens the situation to that of Ya'el. But he who is obstinate will never fulfill a commandment and better he had not been created."

Commenting on M *Avoth* 1:13, R. Chayim of Volozhin is likeminded: "He should learn, even *shelo lishmah*, but in this manner, and with this intention: that by doing thus he will reach the stage of study *lishmah*." But R. Yitzchak Hutner (in *Pachad Yitzchak, Sha'ar Yarcha Telitha-i* 13, note 4) challenges him: "We derive the whole concept of *shelo lishmah* leading to *lishmah* from Balak ... and it is unthinkable that Balak offered sacrifices *shelo lishmah* intending to eventually do so with the purest motives." He concludes: "This question requires further study."

According to all the above, we are speaking here of a precondition to the intent with which he approaches the commandment, which we do not find regarding all other commandments. Why is this commandment treated more stringently than others? R. Shemuel Primo hypothesizes (on *Avoth* 4:5): "Because in fulfilling a commandment, a person is generally rewarded with an inner reverence, for, even though the commandment is fulfilled *shelo lishmah*, he feels that he is performing a good deed. [But] Torah study, approached *shelo lishmah*, is not a good deed at all ... The sages approve of occupying oneself with Torah and commandments *shelo lishmah* only when the study is accompanied by practice, for this purifies the person. Only thus can *shelo lishmah* develop into *lishmah*."

R. Y. Hutner (loc. cit. preceding note) explains: "The passage in *Berakhoth* states that one who has had an emmission is forbidden to learn because, just as the Torah was given with awe and fear, so must be its study for all generations — and it is quite reasonable to say that one who studies *shelo lishmah* does not satisfy this condition."

35. MT *Teshuvah* 10:5.
36. M *Avoth* 4:5.
37. MT *Talmud Torah* 3:10.
38. RYTBA on BT *Yoma* 72b. *Yesod Ha'Avodah* I 3:2, contradicting *Lechem Mishneh* on MT *Talmud Torah* loc. cit.
39. RY, Tosafoth, BT *Pesachim* 50b, s.v. *we-khan*.
40. Cited in the introduction to MR Lamentations 2. See JT *Chagigah* 1:7; MK *Kalah Rabathi* 8, based on Jeremiah 16:11.
41. Jeremiah 16:11.
42. Although our sages interpret the word "guard" to mean study (*Sifra, Acharey Moth* 9:9 and *Emor* 9:3; *Sifrey, Re-eh* 59), in *Avoth* 4:5 "guarding" means practicing—i.e., after learning and teaching. *Tosafoth Yom Tov* explains that the word "guard" there refers to guarding against sin. Furthermore, the phrase "occupying themselves with it" (earlier in this paragraph) refers, according to several Rishonim, to the fulfillment of commandments. See further chapter 4.
43. Tosafoth: BT *Berakhoth* 17a, s.v. *ha'oseh*; *Ta'anith* 7a, s.v. *we-khol*; *Nazir* 23b, s.v. *she-mitokh*. Perhaps this is also the opinion of RY on BT *Pesachim* 50b, s.v. *we-khan*.
44. *Menorath HaMaor* 245.
45. ShaKh on SA *Yoreh De'ah* 246, note 19.
46. *Chayey Adam* 10:7.
47. *Birkey Yosef, Yoreh De'ah* 246, note 12.
48. If we equate the "to be haughty," forbidden by RY (above, note 39) with "to be honored," accepted by Tosafoth (above, note 43), there would be a disagreement between these two. Indeed, this issue is raised in *Yesod Ha'Avodah* (I 6). We can avoid assuming such a disagreement if we differentiate between a desire for honor and haughtiness. Honor is the respect others show for a person, implying a willingness to do his bidding. Haughtiness, on the other hand, is a sense of

superiority, which is very harmful to the personality and is strongly censured by the Torah [see above, part 2, chapter 3, section 4(5)] and not at all implied by the desire for honor. Cf. Meiri, *Chibur HaTeshuvah* (I 5, s.v. *harishon*, p.119). A similar explanation is given by *Darkhey Hashlamah* in the beginning of R. Binyamin Silber's *Mekor Halakhah* on *Shabbath* II, chapter 6, end; and in R. Yosef Lieberman's Responsa *Mishnath Yosef*, introduction, note 3.

49. SA HaRav, *Hilkhoth Talmud Torah* 4:3, citing Psalms 50:16 and the reference of note 40, above.

50. BT *Yoma* 72b.

51. R. Ya'akov Emden, *Mishneh Lechem* (appended to *Lechem Shamayim*), beginning of *Peiah*.

52. *Derekh HaShem* IV 2:6.

53. *Sefer HaChayim*. (Noted by R. P.M. Alter, personal communication.)

NOTES TO CHAPTER 3

1. M *Avoth* 1:17. We find the same idea in *Sifra* (*Acharey Moth* 9:9): "'You shall guard'—This is the study; 'to walk in them'—That is the practice; 'You shall guard to walk in them'—It is not the study that is primary, but the practice." On this RaSh comments, "It is not study that is the main object, but good deeds, which influence a person and bring him to the next world." As a basis for this explanation, *Korban Aharon* writes: "It is not that study entails practice, so that practice is because of study, for then study would be the main object, not practice. ... Rather, practice is the primary goal and it requires study, so study is for the sake of practice." See part 6 (chapter 1, note 7) for an elaboration of this idea by *Iyun Ya'akov*.

2. M *Avoth* 4:5.
    Some Rishonim (Rashi and, following in his foot-steps, RaShBaTz and Ra'AV) maintain that the Mishnah praises only him who learns in order to practice, and explain that "one who learns in order to teach," mentioned earlier in the Mishnah, refers to one who learns in order to be called "rabbi." Their reading of the mishnah is, "... he will **not** be enabled to study and teach."

3. *Midrash David* on M *Avoth* 4:5.

4. *Kesef Mishneh* on MT *Talmud Torah* 3:10, s.v. *ufiresh*.

5. Rabbeinu Yonah on M *Avoth* 4:5.

6. MR Deuteronomy 11:6.

7. Clearly, however, when the Sages excluded those who toil and those who immerse themselves in study, they were not implying that there is no special merit in these activities. God commanded Joshua: "You shall meditate in it day and night" (Joshua 1:8). Furthermore, our Sages have interpreted (*Sifra, BeChukothay,* beginning): "'If you walk in my commandments'—This teaches us that the Omnipresent desires that Israel toil in the Torah." This concept is extremely valuable; but it is not the primary commandment, only a secondary one. This is also how *Korban Aharon* interprets these words: "When the verse says 'You shall guard my commandments and fulfill them'... the positive and negative commandments

are included. How, then, am I to interpret 'If you walk in my commandments?' That one should toil in examining the Torah; and this examination is called 'walking,' because the goal of study is not study, but practice [just like walking is generally a means, not an end]. Therefore, when a person studies and toils in the Torah he should seek a goal beyond it, that is, practice."

8. Meiri on BT *Shabbath* 9b.

9. R. Bachyay to M *Avoth* 1:17, based on Psalms 111:10.

10. *Berakhoth* 17a [and Rashi ad loc.].

11. *Sefer Chasidim* 17, citing Psalms 111:10.

12. Rashi, BT *Berakhoth* 17a.

13. RaMBaM on M *Sanhedrin* 10, following the "five classes."

14. *Derashoth HaRan* 7 s.v. *hinei hokhachnu* (ed. Feldman, Jerusalem, 5737, p. 119).

15. SheLaH, *Shavu'oth*, fol. 32.

16. *Midrash Shemuel* on M *Avoth* 2:5.

17. *Lechem Shamayim* on last chapter of M *Avoth*, beginning.

18. SA HaRav, *Hilkhoth Talmud Torah* 4:3.

19. *Likutey Halakhoth*, first introduction.

20. Introduction to *Or HaChayim*.

21. Alshikh on M *Avoth* 1:17.

22. HaGeRA on Proverbs 23:26.

23. R. Chaim of Volozhin, introduction to HaGeRA's glosses on SA *Orach Chayim*.

24. *Ruach Chayim, Avoth* 1:17. In contrast (loc. cit. 3:17), he writes regarding Torah study that study is primary and knowledge is subsidiary.

25. *Derashoth Chatham Sofer*, pp. 409-410.

26. Preface to *Matzeveth Mosheh*, which is appended to *Chokhmath Adam*.

27. R. S.R. Hirsch, *Horeb* 493 and *Sidur, Avoth* 4:6.

28. R. Yisrael of Salant, *Or Yisrael* 27. There he also points out another advantage of Torah study: "The opportunity to gain wisdom in the Torah, to sharpen the mind, to enrich it and straighten it, to enable one to give and take in the battle of Torah and to uproot mountains with his sharp discourses." But he explains that this advantage is secondary to the primary one of knowledge of the Torah: "[The purpose] of sharpness and discourse is only to enable him to gain knowledge of the Torah."

29. This is alluded to in the statement that the Torah served as a blueprint for the world (MR Genesis 1:1).

30. BT *Berakhoth* 18a.

31. However, *Seder Eliyahu* frequently uses the phrase "Torah study for the sake of Heaven." See the listing in *Talmud Torah Lishmah* by R. N. Lamm, chapter 6, notes 28-33.

32. Commentary on M *Sanhedrin* 10:1, s.v. *hakath hachamishith*.

33. BT *Nedarim* 62a.

34. R. Avraham min HaHar, *Nedarim* 48a, s.v. *Sefarim*.

35. We see from the latter part of his words that enjoyment and gladness of heart are part of the intent of Torah study. However, presumably his intent is not to obligate us to enjoy ourselves when we learn; rather, he means that enjoyment is a direct and inevitable result of learning.

36. Note 15, above.
37. *Nefesh HaChayim* 4:3.
38. *Ruach Chayim, Avoth* 6, beginning.
39. *Derekh Chayim, Avoth* 4:5.
40. BaCh, *Orach Chaim* 47, s.v. *umah shekathav de-amar.*
41. *Sifrey, Wa-ethchanan*, 33.
42. Ibid., *'Ekev* 41. Also cf. RaMBaM, *Sefer HaMitzvoth*, pos. 3 and 5, where he quotes these derivations.
43. For illustrations, see R.Y. Lieberman, Responsa *Mishnath Yosef*, introduction 6ff., especially 9.
44. R. Sheneor Zalman of L'ady, *Likutey Amarim* 6, beginning.
45. *Ruach Chayim* 4:6, beginning.
46. *Nefesh HaChayim* 4:6.
47. BT *Sanhedrin* 71a.
48. Another apparent difficulty is R. Shesheth's assertion (BT *Pesachim* 68b) that he learns for his own sake. Regarding the permissibility of such study, the Talmud concludes that one may indeed begin learning for his own sake.

NOTES TO CHAPTER 4

1. BT *Berakhoth* 11b.
2. Several Rishonim have the text that is now customary ("to occupy ourselves with words of Torah"): RAVaN (142); R. Yehudah HeChasid (*Tosfoth R. Yehudah HeChasid*, BT *Berakhoth* 11b); RAVYaH (39); *Or Zarua'* (Laws of Reading Shema' 24); *Sefer HaMikhtam* (*Berakhoth* I); ROSh and RaN (on BT *Nedarim* 81a); Meiri (on BT *Berakhoth* 11b); R. Yesha'yah DiTrani (in his decisions, *Berakhoth* I). Apparently, however, most Rishonim had the other reading ("...regarding words of Torah"): BaHaG; Gaon R. 'Amram; Rabbeinu Chananel (as quoted by *Or Zarua'*, loc. cit.); RYF; Rashi (quoted in RaShBA's *Chidushim* on BT *Berakhoth* 11b); RaMBaM (in MT *Tefilah* 7:10); R. Avraham Alshevili (*Berakhoth* I); RAH (on RYF); *Agudah* (*Berakhoth* 1:25); and R. David Abudirham (Jerusalem 5723, p. 43). Rabbeinu Yonah's final decision also seems to be such. ROSh and Tur consider it the proper text, though they mention our reading, too. Shulchan Arukh (*Orach Chayim* 47:5) adopts the reading "...regarding words of Torah" exclusively, and, since ReMA fails to comment, he, too, presumably follows it (cf. *Divrey Chamudoth* on ROSh *Berakhoth* I 13, no. 81). But both *Magen Avraham* and TaZ justify our reading.
3. *Beth Yosef, Orach Chayim* 47, s.v. *we-zo nuscha.*
4. RAVYaH 36.
5. *Orchoth Chayim, Din Me-ah Berakhoth* 12. We find support for this interpretation in the fact that the Talmudic sages, too, refer to mitzvah fulfillment as "occupying oneself with Torah," in connection with their interpretation of the verse "which a man shall do and live thereby" (BT *Sanhedrin* 59a; Leviticus 18:5).
6. BT *Sanhedrin* 59a.
7. *Pardes HaGadol* 53.

8. Rashi on BT *Berakhoth* 11b.

9. *Or Zarua'* I 24.

10. Ya'AVeTz (*Sidur Beth Ya'akov* fol. 32a); TaZ (*Orach Chayim* 47, note 1); R. Y.Tz. Meklenburg (*'Iyun Tefilah*).

11. See Note 7 in chapter 3, above.

NOTES TO CHAPTER 5

1. M *Peiah* 1:1.

2. BT *Menachoth* 99b, based on Joshua 1:8.

3. SA *Yoreh De'ah* 246:1.

4. BT *Berakhoth* 35b, based on Deuteronomy 11:14.

5. *Tur* and SA *Orach Chayim* 156: "After [studying Torah] he should go about his occupation, for Torah without work cannot endure and leads to sin."

6. R. Yehudah HeChasid and ROSh to BT *Berakhoth* 35b (see note 9, below). The special review appended to part 1 surveys the ways in which Acharonim dealth with this contradiction.

7. BT *Nedarim* 8a.

8. BT *Kidushin* 30a, on Deuteronomy 6:7.

9. RaDBaZ, Responsa III 416. But see *Sedey Chemed* (*Ma'arekheth waw* 15), who discusses in detail the halakhic basis of the opinion that the requirement of Torah study is satisfied by reading the Shema' twice daily.

   In addition to the Rishonim cited by RaDBaZ, a similar view is expressed by R. Yehudah HeChasid and Tosfoth HaROSh (see *Berakhah Meshulesheth* on BT *Berakhoth* 35b) in reference to the apparently contradictory position of R. Shim'on ben Yochai, who, in BT *Menachoth*, considers it sufficient to read the Shema' twice daily, but in *Berakhoth* objects, "...what will become of the Torah?" They resolve this contradiction by saying that the quote in *Berakhoth* refers only to a generally meritorious deed: to avoid neglect of the Torah.

   Lest it seem that according to all these Rishonim it is enough to say the Shema' morning and evening, it must be pointed out that they apply their statement only in emergencies, as *SeMaG* (pos. 12 and *Hagahoth Maimoniyoth* on MT *Talmud Torah* 1, note 7) states: "If time is pressing, and a person is preoccupied and has no free time, he may rely on R. Yochanan that reading the Shema' twice daily satisfies the requirement of 'they shall not depart...'" Similarly, RYTBA (on BT *Nedarim* 8a) emphasizes that this expedient can only be used under pressing circumstances. Assuredly, neither RaDBaZ nor all the other Rishonim disagree—they merely express the opinion that it is permissible to engage in the ways of the world, in prayer, in acts of kindness, or in other meritorious actions, instead of occupying oneself with Torah study. Clearly this is not to be taken as a license to neglect Torah for things that are neither directly nor indirectly meritorious. Furthermore, he obviously does not consider constant Torah study without merit—"Torah study is as great as all the others together." In his view, constant Torah study is not an absolute commandment but a meritorious deed, as we have seen from the words of R. Yehudah HeChasid and Tosfoth HaROSh—this should certainly not detract from its great importance.

In the same vein, *Shitah Mekubetzeth* (on BT *Nedarim* 8a) cites the opinion that after reading the Shema' "there is no longer a mitzvah [to study]."

Note:

In this context we recall that a merely meritorious deed is not necessarily inferior to an absolute commandment. The latter is merely more urgent, even though the former may have greater influence and may be superior in terms of reward or punishment. Indeed, many actions are not explicitly forbidden, yet their perpetrators have no share in the next world, unlike those who commit idolatry, immorality, or bloodshed. See part 2, where this topic is treated at length.

10. SA HaRav, *Hilkhoth Talmud Torah* 2:3.
11. *Birkath Shemuel* on BT *Kidushin*, no. 27.
12. *Likutey Halakhoth, Pethichah.*

NOTES TO CHAPTER 6

1. BT *Yoma* 19b.
2. BT *Menachoth* 99b; *Nedarim* 8a.
3. *Sifrey*, Deuteronomy 48. The word in our text is "l-m-d," which generally means "studied." But since the statement describes the actions in ascending order, repeating the earlier phrases, the first phrase must be interpreted, "If a person has taught..."
4. RaN to BT *Menachoth* 8a, as discussed in the preceding chapter.
5. SA HaRav, *Hilkhoth Talmud Torah* 3, *Kunteras Acharon* 1 and ibid. 2:12.
6. *Derekh HaShem* III 2:1. Similarly, ibid. II 1:9.
7. *Achar He-asef, Mitzvath Talmud Torah Vechelkeyhah*, beginning.
8. *Or Yisrael* 27.
9. R.Y. Arieli, *'Eynayim LaMishpat* on BT *Kidushin* 29b, note 20, s.v. *we-lakhen*, based on Deuteronomy 11:19 and 6:7.
10. R. S.Y. Zevin, *LeOr HaHalakhah*, p. 206 based on Deuteronomy 6:7 and 4:9.

NOTES TO PART 5

NOTES TO CHAPTER 1

1. SA HaRav, *Hilkhoth Talmud Torah*, beginning.
2. M *Avoth* 5:21.

NOTES TO CHAPTER 2

1. BT *Bava Bathra* 145b and RaShBaM ad loc.
2. BT *Berakhoth* 64b; BT *Horayoth* 14b.
3. Responsa RYVaSh 271; R. Chaim *Or Zaru'a* 163, end.
4. *Shiyarey Keneseth Gedolah* on SA *Orach Chayim* 135, note 9.
5. *Eliyah Rabbah* 136; *Peri Megadim, Orach Chayim, Eshel Avraham* 136, end.
6. R. Shelomoh Kluger's glosses on *Peri Megadim*, loc. cit.
7. R. 'Ovadyah Yosef, *HaKesheruth LeRabanim UleDayanim BiZemanenu*, ["*Torah shebe'al Peh*," Jerusalem, 5739 (1979)] quoting Responsa RYVaSh 271.
8. BT *'Avodah Zarah* 19a.
9. BT *Sanhedrin* 42a.
10. BT *Berakhoth* 6b.
11. See further on, chapter 3, section 2(2).
12. *Orchoth Tzadikim, Sha'ar HaTorah*, based on BT *'Avodah Zarah* 19a.
13. *Yosif Ometz, Seder HaLimud Be'atzmo*.
14. *Yam Shel Shelomoh, Chulin*, Introduction.
15. SA HaRav, *Hilkhoth Talmud Torah* 1:1.
16. HaGeRA, *Even Shelemah* 8:2.
17. R. S. Furst, *Tenu Kavod LaTorah*, p. 10.
18. Responsa *Giduley Taharah* 7.
19. Responsa *Divrey Chayim* II, *Yoreh De'ah* 47.
20. BT *'Avodah Zarah* 19a and Rashi ad loc.
21. BT *Sanhedrin* 99a, based on Numbers 15:31.
22. MaHaRaL, *Derekh Chayim* 6, s.v. *amar Yehudah ben Betzalel*, fol. 116d.
23. *Orchoth Tzadikim, Sha'ar HaTorah*. Also cf. section 2, above.
24. SA HaRav, *Hilkhoth Talmud Torah* 2:4.
25. Quoted in SheLaH, *Torah Shebe'al Peh*, end.
26. SheLaH, *Shavu'oth*, fol. 30.
27. ChYDA, *Berith 'Olam* on *Sefer Chasidim* 288.
28. R. Ya'akov of Lissa, in his ethical testament, 2. Perhaps this was R. Meir Schapiro's source for instituting *daf yomi* in 5683 (1923).
29. *Levushey Mordekhai* on *Bava Kama*, Introduction.
30. Responsa MaHaRYK 167.
31. R. Hillel Ashkenazi, *Sefer Beth Hillel, Yoreh De'ah* fol. 86, in the name of his teacher R. Mosheh Lima, the author of *Chelkath Mechokek*. See R. (Professor) Mordekhai Breuer, *'Aliyath HaPilpul WehaChilukim BiYeshivoth Ashkenaz* in the R. Y. Y. Weinberg Memorial Volume, notes 9-13.
32. R. Avraham Sofer, Meiri on BT *Kethuboth*, preface.
33. *Darkhey HaGemara* 1:16.

NOTES TO CHAPTER 3

1. BT *Bava Bathra* 145b.
2. BT *Temurah* 16a.
3. BT *Shabbath* 31a and SheLaH, *Shavu'oth* 30b.

4. *Pirkey Avoth* 6:5.
5. *Levushey Mordekhay* on BT *Bava Kama*, Introduction.
6. Responsa MaHaRYL, following 220.
7. *Yosif Ometz, Seder HaLimud Le'atzmo*, p. 272.
8. R. Paltai Gaon, quoted in *Sefer Eshkol, Hilkhoth Sefer Torah* 14, fol. 50; also in *Birkey Yosef, Yoreh De'ah* 246:5.
9. Re MT: see Responsa ROSh 31:9; Responsa RYVaSh, 44 end; *Kesef Mishneh* on the Introduction to *Mishneh Torah*; R. Yomtov Lipman Heller (*Tosafoth Yom Tov*), *Ma'adaney Yom Tov, Berakhoth*, Introduction, s.v. *ume-az*.
   Re SA: see MaHaRShA on BT *Sotah* 22a; *Ma'adaney Yom Tov loc. cit. s.v.* we-omer ani, also quoted by *Peri Megadim*, "Kelalim behora-ath...," end; SeMA', *Choshen Mishpat*, Introduction; *Mishkenoth HaRo'im*, "Cheth," 59.
10. MaHaRShA on BT *Bava Bathra* 73b, s.v. *chazinan hay*.
11. *Wikuach Mayim Chayim* on *Torath HaChatoth*, Introduction; Responsa *MaHaRaM Lublin* 135 (at the end of the query).
12. TaZ, SA *Orach Chayim* 47, note 1.
13. BT *Shabbath* 63a; similarly, BT *Ta'anith* 7a.
14. See BT *Berakhoth* 33b for a listing of citations.
15. SA *Yoreh De'ah* 246:12.
16. *Tif-ereth Yisrael*, M *Avoth* 1, note 66.
17. R. Yisrael of Salant, appended to his *Derashoth*.
18. R. E. Wasserman, letter.
19. BT *Bava Bathra* 130b; *Nidah* 7b; JT *Kil-ayim* 4:2; *Shevi'ith* 10:1. Quotation from BT *Gitin* 19a and 37a.
20. Responsa RYVaSh 271.
21. BT *Berakhoth* 36b.
22. BT *Yevamoth* 14a.
23. Responsa R. Y. Weil 164.
24. Responsa *Mayim 'Amukim* 30; *Terumath HaDeshen* 16, end, and 30, end; also see chapter 4, where we quote ReMA's comment that the basic function of the rabbi depends not on learning pilpul, but on being able to arrive at a final decision.
25. BT *'Eiruvin* 13b.
26. *Ya'aroth Devash*, fol. 134.
27. BT *Bava Metzi'a* 96b; *'Eiruvin* 90a; *Bava Bathra* 116b; *Nidah* 33b.
28. Rashi, BT *Chulin* 81a, s.v. *hathra-ath safek*.
29. Responsa RYVaSh 229, Introduction.
30. *Sha-ageth Aryeh, HaChadashoth, Kitzur Diney Chadash* 3.
31. "Chazon Ish", quoted in *Avi 'Ezri, Hafla-ah*. Cf. also *Chazon Ish, Even Ha'Ezer* 14:9; *Kil-ayim* 4:30. Cf. *Seridey Esh* II, end of note to 125.
32. BaCh, *Yoreh De'ah*, Introduction.
33. *Orchoth Tzadikim, Sha'ar HaTorah*.
34. Cited by his disciple, R. Yosef ben Mosheh, *Leket Yosher*, fol. 44.
35. MaHaRaL, *Tif-ereth Yisrael* 56.
36. *Chawoth Ya-ir* 124.
37. MaHaRShA on *Bava Metzi'a* 85a s.v. *de-lishtakach*.
38. The author of *Nethivoth HaMishpat*, in his ethical testament (printed in his hagadah

under the title *Ma'aseh Nissim*), 2.

39. R. S.R. Hirsch, *The Nineteen Letters* 15.

40. I should like to point out a common misinterpretation. To strengthen their Torah learning, children are often encouraged to compete, with the best students receiving prizes. This appears contrary to Torah principles: it pits one child against the other and, by accustoming the child to aggrandizing himself at the expense of another, one may, God forbid, harm his soul, and perhaps even forfeit his share in the next world (JT *Chagigah* 2:1, cited by RaMBaM, MT *De'oth* 6:3 and MT *Teshuvah* 3:14, 4:4). The proponents of this method frequently cite, in defense of their approach, the Talmudic statement: "Jealousy between writers increases wisdom" (BT *Bava Bathra* 21a). But this response is based on a misinterpreation of that statement. Simple reference to the context or to Rashi's commentary there shows immediately that this statement deals neither with competition nor school children. In no way did the Sages mean to encourage self-aggrandizement at another's expense.

Indeed Jacob evidently gave Joseph the striped coat because he was a "wise child", since Jacob taught him all the halakhoth he had learned in the school of Shem and 'Eiver (MR Genesis 84:8, quoted in Rashi's commentary on Genesis 37:3). The Sages then comment (BT *Shabbath* 10b and MR loc. cit.) that a father should treat all his sons equally well (since failure to do so, i.e., awarding Joseph a special garment) resulted in our forefathers' exile to Egypt. We see from this that this national tragedy was the result of a prize which Jacob awarded for Torah study. Furthermore, it is not at all clear that a child should be outstandingly clever; perhaps it is not even something to be proud of. We derive many details of proper prayer from Hannah, who asked God for a child—but not an exceptional one, according to the Sages: "neither tall nor short ... neither [unusually] bright nor [unusually[dull" (I Shemuel 1:11, as interpreted by the Rabbanim in BT *Berakhoth* 31b; cf. Rashi's commentary ad loc.) These words may sound strange to many of the present generation, who were reared in our competitive society. It appears, however, that the majority of the Sages thought otherwise.

It is certainly possible to encourage children by rewarding all those who accomplish above and beyond what is expected of them, in line with the Talmudic dictum (BT *Pesachim* 50b) that one should learn *shelo lishmah*, for this will lead to learning *lishmah*. This will not cause friction—on the contrary, as more children gain recognition, the friendly atmosphere between them will increase.

This is a far cry from the feeling engendered by the competitive atmosphere created by pitting one against the other, creating the feeling that, "I succeeded because of your failure." This kind of training may develop, in the student, attitudes that will continue into later life—to a distorted form of Torah study based on defeating others, which can have dire consequences for one's personal development and for Torah study itself, turning the Torah into a deadly potion (see, above, part 4, chapter 2, note 21).

41. R. S.R. Hirsch, *Nineteen Letters* 18.

42. *Igroth Chazon Ish* I 4 and 12.

43. *Sefer Chasidim* (Mekize Nirdamim ed.), no. 975.

44. *Orchoth Tzadikim, Sha'ar HaSheker*, beginning, cited also by *Yam Shel Shelomoh, Chulin*, Introduction and *Yosif Ometz*, p.272.

45. Responsa MaHaRYK 167.
46. SA *Yoreh De'ah* 242:30, gloss.
47. *Levush* ad loc.
48. MaHaRaL, *Derekh Chayim* on M *Avoth* 6:5.
49. SheLaH, *Shavu'oth* 30 c-d.
50. *'Amudey Sheish* 12.
51. *Shemen LaMaor*, quoted by *Chawoth Ya-ir* 125.
52. *Peri Chadash, Orach Chayim* 66, note 4.
53. HaGeRA on Proverbs 20:17.
54. *Midrash Chakhamim* (see also *Yesodoth Ne-emanim* 2:1). For a similar statement by "Chazon Ish", see below chapter 6, end.
55. *Nethivoth 'Olam, Nethiv HaTorah* 5.
56. SheLaH, *Shavu'oth* 30d.
57. *'Amudey Sheish* 12.
58. SA *Yoreh De'ah* 246:12.
59. Jeremiah 9:22; Isaiah 33:6.
60. *Sefer Chasidim* (Mekize Nirdamim edition), no. 1707. Also cf. *Ba'al HaTurim* in his ethical testament; R. Yosef Ya'abetz, *Or HaChayim*, Introduction; MaHaRShaL, *Yam Shel Shelomoh, Bava Kama* 8:58.
61. SheLaH, loc. cit. note 56, above.
62. *Derush 'Al HaTorah*, end; *Nethivoth 'Olam, Nethiv HaTorah* 5.
63. *'Amudey Sheish* 12.
64. Reprinted in R. S. Asaf, *Mekoroth LeToldoth HaChinukh BeYisrael* I, pp. 85-97, especially p. 90.
65. R. Yisrael of Salant, appended to his *Derashoth*.

NOTES TO CHAPTER 4

1. Rashi on BT *Kethuboth* 57a, s.v. *ha kaima lan*: "Sometimes one reason applies and sometimes another, for the [dominant] reason may change with even minor changes in circumstances."
2. Exodus 21:1 and Rashi ad loc., based on *Mekhilta*.
3. R. Chaim of Volozhin, letter, appended to *Nefesh Chayim 'im Ruach Chayim 'al Avoth*, Jerusalem edition 5733 (1973), quoted in *Yesodoth Ne-emanim* [Beney Berak, 5726 (1966)], 2:33.
4. *Milchamoth HaShem*, Introduction, s.v. *techilath*.
5. TaZ, as cited above (chapter 3, note 12).
6. *Egley Tal*, Introduction.
7. *Igroth Chazon Ish* I 2.
8. "Sevara, that he understands one thing from another, and compares one thing to another." R. Mosheh David Avraham Trevis, *Toldoth Adam* on *Sifrey*, Deuteronomy 1:13 and based on Rashi ad loc.
9. R. S.R. Hirsch on Genesis 41:33, quoted at length at the end of chapter 6.

NOTES TO CHAPTER 5

1. M *Avoth* 1:17.
2. BT *Sotah* 21a, based on Proverbs 6:22.
3. BT *Kidushin* 30a, based on Deuteronomy 6:7.
4. SA HaRav, *Hilkhoth Talmud Torah* 2:3.
5. BT *Kidushin* 40b.
6. *Chawoth Ya-ir* 124.
7. BT *'Eiruvin* 6b, based on Ecclesiastes 2:14.
8. Rabbeinu Chananel on BT *'Avodah Zarah* 17b.
9. *Sefer Chasidim* (Mekize Nirdamim edition), 744, referring to Psalms 112:1 & 1:2. Further, ibid. 648.
10. Rabbeinu Yonah on M *Avoth* 4:5.
11. R. Mosheh of Zurich, commentary on *Sefer Mitzvoth Katan*, (commonly referred to as *SeMaK MiZurich*), 106, note 13, end.
12. Responsa *RYVaSh* 271.
13. Meiri on BT *Shabbath* 9b.
14. SA *Yoreh De'ah* 242:30, gloss.
15. MaHaRaL, *Nethivoth 'Olam, Nethiv HaTorah* 5.
16. Responsa R. Yosef ibn Migash 114.
17. Chapter 3, section 1. See also below, chapter 7, section 4 and in part 2 (chapter 4, section 2).
18. SA HaRav, *Hilkhoth Talmud Torah* 2:1.
19. *Magen Avraham* on SA *Orach Chayim* 290.
20. HaGeRA on Proverbs 13:25, 16:8; *Even Shelemah* 8:7. Further, ibid. 8:11.
21. Introduction to the Gaon of Vilna's commentary on SA.
22. Responsa *Giduley Taharah* 7.
23. R. S.R. Hirsch, *Horeb* 551.
24. *Ma-amar Be'Inyan Chizuk Lomdey Torah* 20. Reprinted in *Or Yisrael HaShalem*, p. 148.
25. "Chafetz Chayim" in the Introductions to *Likutey Halakhoth* and *Mishnah Berurah*.

NOTES TO CHAPTER 6

1. JT *Sanhedrin* 4:2.
2. RaShBaM on Genesis 37:2.
3. Certain Talmudic derivations merely corroborate previously known halakhoth while others actually derive new halakhoth from a verse. Cf. RaMBaM, Introduction to his commentary on the Mishnah, especially, "The third part..."
4. *Yalkut Shim'oni, Shoftim* 49.
5. *Sefer Chasidim* 530; also 745 in Mekize Nirdamim edition.
6. *Shevet Musar* 22. Similarly in *Nishmath Adam*, Hanau edition, 5376, folio 40a; *Or HaChayim* (R. Y. Ya'abetz) 15, beginning; *Reshith Chokhmah, Kedushah* chapter 4.
7. SA HaRav, *Hilkhoth Talmud Torah* 1,1 end.

8.   M *Avoth* 5:21.

9.   See *Mishnah Berurah* 545, note 47; R. M. Blau, *Zikhron Shalom*, Introduction; "Chatham Sofer," *Chidushim* on BT *Shabbath* 140b.

10. BT *Sukah* 27b-28a.

11. BT *Berakhoth* 27b.

12. Some commentaries (e.g., ROSh, Rabbeinu Yonah) explain that the opprobrium applies only if he misquotes his teacher or only in cases of basic principles or important concepts (e.g., *Kether Rosh* 66). Others [RAVYaH (no. 84), MaHaRShA (BT loc. cit.)], however, seem to interpret the words literally.

13. M *Avoth* 2:8.

14. Some authorities (Rabbeinu Yonah, R. 'Ovadyah of Bartinora) maintain that the two tanaim do not disagree—they are merely discussing two different aspects. Others, however, see in this the classical difference of opinion between those who prefer either the "master of Sinai" or the "uprooter of mountains" (*Machzor Vitry, Derekh Chayim, Ruach Chayim*, and *Tif-ereth Yisrael*—all, ad loc.).

15. M *Avoth* 3:15.

16. Responsa *Chatham Sofer, Orach Chayim* 181 and *Yoreh De'ah* 19, (referring to M *'Orlah* 3:9). This is a pun, with *chadash*=new referring to the new crop of grain, which is forbidden until Pesach (cf. Leviticus 23:14).

17. *Kethav Sofer*, Responsa, Introduction to *Yoreh De'ah*.

18. *Magen Avraham* 308, note 17.

19. *Chayey Adam* 10:12, note.

20. R. S.R. Hirsch on Genesis 41:33 (adapted by the author).

21. "Chatham Sofer" Responsa, *Yoreh De'ah*, Introduction.

22. Quoted in *Igroth Chazon Ish* I 4.

23. *Chazon Ish, Yoreh De'ah* 203, s.v. *terem*.

NOTES TO CHAPTER 7

1.   *Yesod Mora*, part 1.

2.   *Chawoth Ya-ir* 124.

3.   *Ma'aseh Efod*, Introduction.

4.   *Teshuvoth HaGeonim*, Amsterdam edition, 5467.

5.   SheLaH, *Shavu'oth*, beginning.

6.   R. Ya'akov Emden, *Migdal 'Oz* fol. 16d, 17a.

7.   HaGeRA, Introduction to commentary on SA *Orach Chayim*.

8.   Responsa *Giduley Taharah* 7. By "grammar" he may be referring to the language of the host country.

9.   R. Avraham Horowitz, glosses on *Yesh Nochlin*, appended to SheLaH, based on Deuteronomy 4:30.

10. *Rosh HaGiv'ah* fol. 11a.

11. *Kether Rosh* 58.

12. NeTzYV, *Kidmath Ha'Emek*, beginning of *Ha'amek Davar* 5.

13. *Derekh Chayim* on *Pirkey Avoth* 6, citing BT *Sanhedrin* 99a on Numbers 15:31.

14. *Chawoth Ya-ir* 124.

15. SheLaH, *Shavu'oth*, fol. 30-31.

16. BT *Bava Metzi'a* 33a.
17. *Kether Rosh* 55.
18. BT *Bava Metzi'a* 33a.
19. SA *Yoreh De'ah* 246:4.
20. ROSh, Responsa 31:9.
21. BT *Bava Kama* 130b.
22. RYVaSh, Responsa, 44.
23. *Nethivoth 'Olam, Nethiv HaTorah* 15, based on BT *Sotah* 22a.
24. MaHaRShA, BT *Sotah* 22a, s.v. *yerei*.
25. *Kether Rosh* 49, cited here. Cf. also SA HaRav, *Hilkhoth Talmud Torah* 2:1; *Mishnath HaRo'im, "Cheth"* 59. Also see *Keneseth HaGedolah, Tur Even Ha'Ezer* 13, note 10; *Pithchey Teshuvah,* SA *Yoreh De'ah* 242, note 8. Also cf. above, part 2 (chapter 4, section 2).
26. HaGeRA, Introduction to commentary on SA *Orach Chayim*.
27. "Chatham Sofer," cited by R. Avraham Sofer in his Introduction to Meiri's commentary on BT *Kethuboth*.
28. MaHaRaL, *Nethivoth 'Olam, Nethiv HaTorah* 5.
29. SheLaH, *Torah Shebe'al Peh*, end.
30. R. Sheftel Horowitz, Testament, section 25 (appended to SheLaH).
31. *Chawoth Ya-ir* 124.
32. *Yosif Ometz, Seder Limud Be'atzmo*, p. 269.
33. SeMA', *Derishah,* SA *Yoreh De'ah* 246; ShaKh's glosses ad loc., note 5; *'Arukh HaShulchan* ad loc., 13; *Mishnah Berurah*, Introduction.
34. *Rosh HaGiv'ah*, fol. 11.
35. "Chafetz Chayim," *Likutey Halakhoth*, Introduction, citing HaGeRA, *Ma'aseh Rav* 60.
36. *Tzofnath Pa'ane-ach* 6.
37. See note 27, above.
38. R. Ya'akov of Lissa, Testament, section 3.
39. *Kether Rosh* 49, 54.
40. *Mishnah Berurah*, Introduction.
41. *Kether Rosh* 49.
42. BT *Bava Metzi'a* 114a.
43. *Rosh HaGiv'ah* fol. 11a.
44. *Sefer Chasidim* 1011.
45. R. Sheftel Horowitz, Testament, section 25.
46. *Rosh HaGiv'ah* 11a.
47. *Mishnah Berurah*, Introduction.
48. *Egley Tal*, Introduction.
49. *Igroth Chazon Ish* I 1.
50. *Levushey Mordekhay, Bava Kama*, Introduction.

NOTES TO CHAPTER 8

1. M *Avoth* 5:21.
2. MK *Sofrim* 16:9.

3. ROSh, *Bava Metzi'a*, 2, end.
4. Introduction to *Ma'adaney Yom Tov, Bava Kama.*
5. BT *Ta'anith* 7b-8a.
6. Ecclesiastes 10:10.
7. BT *Sotah* 44a.
8. Proverbs 24:27.
9. BT *Sanhedrin* 42a.
10. An allusion to Proverbs 24:6.
11. MR Exodus 41:5; MRT *Ki-Thiso* 16; quoted by Rashi on Exodus 31:18.
12. *Sefer Chasidim* 308.
13. Proverbs 22:6.
14. *Nachalath Avoth* 5:21.
15. *Derekh Chayim* 6 (fol. 117b).
16. *Gur Aryeh*, Deuteronomy 6:7.
17. MaHaRaL, *Tif-ereth Yisrael* 56.
18. *Derush 'Al HaTorah*, s.v. *welakhein banay shim'u*, fol. 27a.
19. SheLaH, *Shavu'oth*, beginning.
20. Glosses on *Sefer Yesh Nochalin*, appended to SheLaH.
21. *Wawey Ha'Amudim*, appended to SheLaH, *'Amud HaTorah* 5.
22. R. Sheftel Horowitz, Testament, appended to SheLaH, referring to Isaiah 59:21.
23. MaHaRShA on BT *Sanhedrin* 24a, end, referring to Lamentations 3:6.
24. MaHaRShA on BT *'Avodah Zarah* 9b.
25. Psalms 1:3-5.
26. *Yosif Ometz*, p. 270 and p. 284.
27. Introduction to *Ma'adaney Yom Tov, Bava Kama.*
28. *Chawoth Ya-ir* 124.
29. *'Amudey Sheish* 24, end.
30. BaCh on *Tur Yoreh De'ah* 245, s.v. *hayah minhag.*
31. Shakh on SA *Yoreh De'ah* 245, note 5.
32. Tosafoth, BT *Kidushin*, chapt. 1, end.
33. SeMaG, pos. 12.
34. BT *Sanhedrin* 24a.
35. R. Ya'akov Emden, *Megilath Sefer.*
36. *Migdal 'Oz*, beginning.
37. Note that Shakh's words are disputed by a number of additional authorities. The Talmud states that the Babylonian Talmud combines the three areas of learning required every day. Rabbeinu Tam deduces that there is, therefore, no need to study each of the three separately (cf. note 32). Most commentators interpret this deduction as referring to adults, who have already studied Scripture and Mishnah in their youth, in line with M *Avoth* 5:21 (cf. paragraphs 1, 13, 32, 33, and 38 in the text), and are thoroughly familiar with them. ShaKh, however, understands it as pertaining to children, as well.
38. *Sidur Beth Ya'akov, Hilkhoth Talmud Torah.*
39. *Peri Megadim* on SA *Orach Chayim*, beginning.
40. HaGeRA as quoted by his sons in their Introduction to his notes to *Orach Chayim.*
41. *Even Shelemah* 8:2.

42. *Rosh HaGiv'ah*, fol. 11a.
43. *Toldoth Adam* 3.
44. SA HaRav, *Hilkhoth Talmud Torah* 1:1.
45. Ibid., 6.
46. Responsa *Zera Emeth, Yoreh De'ah* 107.
47. R. Ya'akov of Lissa, Testament.
48. R. S.R. Hirsch, *Sidur, Avoth* 5:25.
49. *Horeb* 551.
50. See the words of Rabbeinu Tam in paragraph 22 above and note 37.
51. *Or Yisrael*, letter 18.
52. *Derekh Chokhmah*, end.

NOTES TO PART 6

NOTES TO CHAPTER 1

1. BT *Kidushin* 40b.
2. See Tosafoth ad loc., s.v. *meivi*, in the name of Rashi; Rashi on BT *Bava Kama* 17a, s.v. *meivi*.
3. MaHaRShA and SheLaH (*Shavu'oth, Perek Barukh Atah*, s.v. *kevar*) offer similar interpretations.
4. R. Yesha'yah in *Shitah Mekubetzeth* on *Bava Kama* 17a; *Peney Yehoshu'a; She-iltoth* on *Lekh Lekha* 7; *Sefer Yere-im* 25; RaShBaTz, *Magen Avoth* on M *Avoth* 1:17; R. A.Ch. Shor, *Torath Chayim* on BT *Bava Kama* 17a. Perhaps Rabbeinu Chananel on BT *Bava Kama* 17a and *'Arukh*, s.v. *gadol* (b), also had this interpretation in mind.
5. Cf. JT *Pesachim* 3:7 and *Chagigah* 1:7, where the same phrase is used, except that "comes first" is used instead of "is greater".
6. *Sefer HaMiknah, Kidushin* 40b.
7. *Binah Le'itim*, as quoted by *'Anaf Yosef* on *'Eyn Ya'akov, Kidushin* 40b. *Korban Aharon* to *Sifra, Acharey* 9:9 makes the same distinction. See note 1 to part 4, chapter 3.
8. BT *Bava Kama* 17a.
9. Tosafoth, ad loc., s.v. *we-ha-amar*.
10. RYTBA, BT *Kidushin* 40b. This interpretation also fits in with other details of the incident reported there.
11. Cf. Rabbeinu Chananel, BT *Bava Kama* 17a; *'Arukh*, s.v. *gadol* (b); *Sefer Yere-im* 25 (although the conclusion of the latter agrees with those who have the usual version).
12. *She-iltoth, Lekh Lekha* 7.
13. Meiri, BT *Bava Kama* 17a.
14. Meiri states this explicitly in his commentary on M *Avoth* 1:17. See section 2 above, where we cite several authorities adopting this interpretation.
15. Cf. R. Chaim of Volozhin, *Ruach Chayim* on *Avoth* 3:17.
16. MaHaRShA, BT *Kidushin* 40b.

17. BT *Megilah* 3b.
18. BT *Berakhoth* 7b: "Personal service [to a Torah authority] is more effective than the Torah he learns [from him]." "Fitting are... " is from Tosefta *Yevamoth*, chapter 8, end.
19. *Ha'amek She-eilah* on *She-iltoth, Lekh Lekha* 7.
20. SheLaH, *Shavu'oth* loc. cit, above 3.
21. On the contrary, from BT *Kidushin* 29b it is evident that the basic obligation of Torah study is teaching others, and only by default does self-study apply.
22. Oral communication from R. Ya'akov Kaminecki, *z.l.*
23. *Ha'amek She-eilah* 7:5.
24. BT *Chagigah* 9b.
25. R. Yesha'yah, *Shitah Mekubetzeth, Bava Kama* 17a.
26. See *Magen Avraham*, SA *Orach Chayim* 687, note 3, in the name of BaCh.
27. M *Avoth* 4:14.

NOTES TO CHAPTER 2

1. M *Avoth* 1:7. Cf. *Magen Avoth* and Meiri ad loc., that this is undisputed.
2. RaShBaTz in *Magen Avoth* and Meiri ad loc.
3. *Yefeh Mar-eh* (*Peiah* 1:1, no. 12), in fact, maintains that the mishnah which takes practice as primary contradicts the conclusion that "learning is great." But this position is difficult to support; furthermore, I have not found a single mishnaic commentary that agrees with it.
4. M *Peiah* 1:1 and R. 'Ovadyah of Bartinoro's commentary ad loc.
5. Proverbs 8:11, 3:15. The bracketed words are based on the commentaries of R. Shelomoh Sirileo, *Peney Mosheh* et al.
6. BT *Mo'ed Katan* 9b; JT *Shabbath* 1:2, end.
7. R. Shelomoh Sirileo; R. Mosheh Margolis, *Mar-eh HaPanim*.
8. We can support *Yefeh Mar-eh*'s interpretation, by citing several mitzvoth which are said to be "equivalent to the entire Torah": *tzitzith* (BT *Nedarim* 25a); *milah* (BT *Nedarim* 32a); charity (BT *Bava Bathra* 9a); Sabbath (JT *Berakhoth* 1:5); kindness (JT *Peiah* 1:1); settling in Eretz Yisrael (*Sifrey, Re-eh* 12:29, no 80). Taken at face value, these would inevitably lead to contradiction. We must, therefore, say that each of these refers only to one particular aspect in which the mitzvah is superior to all others, as *Yefeh Mar-eh* explains in our case of Torah study.
9. R. Ya'akov Emden, *Mishneh Lechem*, appended to *Lechem Shamayim, Peiah* 1:1.

NOTES TO CHAPTER 3

1. JT *Pesachim* 3:7; *Chagigah* 1:7; quoted by ROSh, BT *Pesachim* 3:8.
2. BT *Mo'ed Katan* 9b and Rashi ad loc., referring to Proverbs 8:11.
3. BT *Megilah* 3b, 29a; *Shabbath* 11a; JT *Berakhoth* 1:2, end.
4. The Jerusalem Talmud rules that one fully occupied with learning—like R. Shim'on ben Yochai—need not interrupt his study to recite the Shema'; but

others—such as R. Yochanan—must. However, this rule applies only to the Shema', which is also a form of learning. All agree that everyone must interrupt his studies to build himself a *sukah* or prepare his *lulav*, as codified by RaMBaM, MT *Talmud Torah* 3:4.

5. Cf. BT *Megilah* 29a; MK *Avoth DeRabbi Nathan* 4:3.

6. BT *Sukah* 25b, 26a.

7. RaN, BT *Kidushin* 32a, s.v. *halakhah keIsi*; also quoted by *Kesef Mishneh* on MT *Mamrim* 6:13; RYTBA, BT *Kidushin* 32a.

8. Meiri, BT *Shabbath* 9b.

9. *Birkey Yosef* on SA *Orach Chayim* 38, note 7.

10. *Sefer Hashlamah* and *HaMe-oroth* cite RAVaD to the effect that Proverbs 5:6 comes to guard against the misconception that we should interrupt our Torah study for any mitzvah, even if others could fulfill it. This is also cited by NeTzYV (*Ha-amek She-eilah* 34:5, p. 221 and 103:14, p. 223).

11. *Kehiloth Ya'akov* on BT *Shabbath*, no. 10.

12. BT *Menachoth* 99ab and MaHaRaL ad loc.

13. BT *Berakhoth* 24b, based on Deuteronomy 32:47, *Meshekh Chokhmah* on Deuteronomy ad loc.; *Sefer Chasidim* 952.

14. Meiri, *Bava Kama* 17a.

15. BT *Mo'ed Katan* 9a ff.

16. BT *Kidushin* 29b.

17. HaGeRA, SA *Yoreh De'ah* 242, note 24.

18. BT *'Avodah Zarah* 17b.

NOTES TO PART 7

NOTES TO CHAPTER 1

1. *Baraitha* in the name of R. Meir, cited in Responsa, RaMBaM [Mekize Nirdamim, Jerusalem 5718 (1958), no. 150].

2. BT *Shabbath* 75a, based on Isaiah 5:12.

3. MT *Yesodey HaTorah* 4:12.

4. *Chovoth HaLevavoth, Sha'ar HaBechinah* 2.

5. Rabbeinu Bachyay on M *Avoth* 3, end.

6. MaHaRaL, *Nethivoth 'Olam, Nethiv HaTorah* 14.

7. R. Yaakov Provencali, responsum regarding the study of the sciences, in *Divrey Chakhamim*, R. Eli'ezer Ashkenazi, ed., p. 71. (R. Ya'akov is among those who wrote approbations for *Sefer HaAgur*.) Similar sentiments were expressed by R. Yitzchak of 'Akko, a disciple of RaMBaN, whom we quote in chapter 3, section 1 and another early authority (a disciple of R. Eliyahu Mizrachi)—Responsa *Zekan Aharon* (No. 25; also in TaShBaTz VIII—ms.): "Nowhere do we find that the Sages forbade the study of science."

8. The Gaon of Vilna, quoted in the introduction to R. Barukh of Sklov's translation of Euclid.
9. "Chatham Sofer," *Derashoth*, fol. 112 (*Beshalakh*).
10. BT *Sanhedrin* 90a, 100b, opinion of R. 'Akiva.
11. BT *Sotah* 49b.
12. BT *Berakhoth* 28b. Some explain that logic is part of philosophy (*Menorath HaMaor* 267, and R. Sa'adyah Gaon, quoted in *Nimukey Yosef* on BT *Megilah* 25b). Rashi, in BT *Berakhoth* 28b, explains: "Do not teach them Scripture to excess."
13. *Sifra* on Leviticus 18:4.
14. R. Hai Gaon, quoted in the letters of RaMBaN, *Terem E'eneh* (R. C.B. Chavel edition, p. 350); and in Responsa RYVaSh 45.
15. Rabbeinu Bachyay on Deuteronomy 30:12.
16. *Shir Musar Haskel*. The entire stanza: "Know wisdom and if it is baffling / Know arithmetic and understand healing / And acquaint yourself with the occurrence of the lunations / And the proper time for the festivals, year after year."
17. HaGeRA, SA *Yoreh De'ah* 179, note 13. The word "accursed" has been deleted in the Vilna edition.
18. MR Lamentations 2:13.
19. SA *Orach Chayim* 224:7, based on BT *Berakhoth* 58a.
20. *Beth Yosef* and *Levush* ad loc.; SeMaK 148.

NOTES TO CHAPTER 2

1. *Sifra* on Leviticus 18:4.
2. R. Yosef Rozin, the "Rogoczover," follows a similar line of reasoning in one of his responsa (see chapter 5). He points out that we can conclude from the phrase "do not mix other things with them" that only the mixture of the two is prohibited, not each one separately.
3. This is similar to *Beth Yosef, Tur Orach Chayim* 47, s.v. *umah shekathav rabbeinu*.
4. R. Avraham ibn 'Ezra, *Yesod Mora* 1.
5. Letter of RaMBaM to R. Yehonathan HaKohen of Luneil [quoted in RaMBaM. Responsa III, Mekize Nirdamim, Jerusalem, 5721 (1961), p. 57].
6. R. Bachyay on M *Avoth* 3, end.
7. *Ya'aroth Devash* II 7.
8. HaGeRA, introduction to *Adereth Eliyahu* (commentary on the Torah); R. Yonathan Eybeshutz and R. Mosheh Sofer (both of whom we quote further, later in this chapter).
9. On the precedence of Torah study, see chapter 3, section 1, end. On the precedence of science study, see Tosfoth YomTov, M *Avoth* 3, end; further, section 3 and chapter 5, section 1/2(1).
10. *Zekan Aharon* 25. The Mishnah lists denigrators of Torah scholars among those, who lose their share in the next world (Sanhedrin 10:1).
11. *Igroth Chazon Ish* I 31. Cf. BT *Sanhedrin* 5b.
    In the exposition that follows, the "Chazon Ish" uses the above to explain why a person who is sufficiently learned still requires licensure before rendering decisions,

lest the public misunderstand him. (See BT *Sanhedrin* 5b.) By means of this exposition we can also answer an old question: If we accept a candidate's evaluation that he has learned sufficiently, why can we not rely on his evaluation that he will not be misunderstood? According to the "Chazon Ish," however, this is exactly the problem — he may not be able to assess the situation properly, and may misjudge how people understand him.

12. *Kuzari* II 64.
13. *Ya'aroth Devash* II 7.
14. Song of Songs 7:7.
15. Similar listings can be found in R. Avraham ibn Ezra, *Chibbur HaMeshichah WeHaTishboreth*, Introduction, and R. Bachyay on M *Avoth* 3.
16. Leviticus 11:12; BT *Chulin* 66a.
17. BT *Sanhedrin* 5b.
18. The "Rogoczover" proves the non-Torah origin of Rav's knowledge in this matter in another way; see, below, chapter 5, section 4a.
19. BT *Chulin* 57b.
20. BT *Bekhoroth* 48a.
21. BT *Pesachim* 94b. The discussion there revolves around the question where the sun passes during the night. The Jewish scientists contended that it goes above the sky, while the gentiles asserted that it passes below Earth. R. Yehudah HaNasi found the gentiles' view more convincing. Note that the question has halakhic implications (cf. *Beth Yosef, Orach Chayim* 455, beginning). *Shitah Mekubetzeth* (*Kethuboth* 13b) quotes Rabbeinu Tam as saying that the gentile opinion only appears more correct, but in fact the Jewish scientists are right. In contrast, RaMBaMs's son, R. Avraham, writes, basing himself on this passage, that R. Yehudah HaNasi is called "the Saint" because he was prepared to accept the ṭruth, even from gentiles (*Ma-amar Odoth Derashoth Chazal*, printed at the beginning of *'Eyn Ya'akov*, s.v. we-da').

R. Avraham is merely following in the footsteps of his father, who states (*Moreh Nevukhim* III 14, end): "And the [Sages] spoke of these matters [regarding astronomy] not as having been handed down to them from the prophets, but on the basis of their proficiency in these matters in their generation, or [because they] learned them from the scholars of those generations."

The idea of accepting the truth regardless of its source is also found elsewhere in RaMBam's writings (e.g., in *Shemonah Perakim* and his introduction to *Moreh Nevukhim*): "Be aware that the matters of which I will speak in these chapters ... are matters I culled from the words of the scholars ... and from the words of the philosophers ... and listen to the truth, whoever speaks it." See chapter 3, section 1, regarding the epigram "Love Socrates ... love only the truth more."

RaShBaTz (*Magen Avoth*, philosophical part, Introduction, s.v. we-achar) writes similarly: "It is improper for a scholar to reject truth from anyone's mouth, as [the Sages] have said, 'Accept the truth from him who says it.'" As proof, he notes that RaMBaM quotes gentile works, and the Talmud quotes a fool (ben Tov-al) and concludes that it is proper to accept his opinion since iṭ is reasonable. *Pachad Yitzchak* also takes this approach ("*Tzedah assurah*"): "They have clearly indicated that not every pronouncement in the Talmud is based on tradition, but the Jewish scholars, too, sometimes based their words on logic and investigation...; for otherwise, why would they concede [some points to the gentile scholars]? They would have held fast to their tradition despite any gentile proof." In addition to the above-cited authorities, R. Yesha'yah diTrani (*Tosfoth RYD*) also disputes the aforementioned words of R. Ya'akov Tam. Regarding them, *Minchath Kohen, Mevo HaShemesh* (I 4, beginning) says, "The explanation of Rabbeinu Tam is built on an unsound foundation and a flawed hypothesis—that the sun travels above the firmament at night—for this defies reason and intuition; actually the sun travels on the other side of the Earth, which has been shown by experimentation and cannot be disputed."

22. BT *Nidah* 30b.

23. JT *Kil-ayim* 4:4. This is according to the modern commentators. But in the classical commentary of R. Shelomoh Sirileo even in JT the permissibility is accepted unanimously.

24. BT *Shabbath* 85a; see Rashi's commentary, ad loc., s.v. *gevul re'ekha*.

25. Responsa *Chatham Sofer, Yoreh De'ah* 338.

26. E.g.: Responsa ReMA, 5; R. Yonathan Eybeshutz, *Pelethi*, SA *Yoreh De'ah* 201, note 10; cf. also *Peiath HaShulchan*, Introduction; Responsa *Chatham Sofer, Yoreh De'ah* 167.

27. Responsa *Chelkath Ya'akov* I 84.

28. This discussion concerns the study of nature in general. Apparently, however, some natural laws can be derived from the Torah. Thus, Midrash *Shochar Tov* on Psalms 19 relates that the Amora Shemuel—who was "as familiar with the topography of the heavens as with the topography of [his native] Nahardea'"—became so familiar with the heavens through his Torah study. Another instance concerns the gestation period of snakes (BT *Bekhoroth* 8b). See also RaMBaN's introduction to his commentary on the Torah; however, in his commentary on Genesis 9:12 he himself accepts the opinion of the Greek scientist that rainbows are caused by sunlight striking moist air. He quotes these scientists in several other places (e.g. Genesis 1:20, 21 and Leviticus 12:2). His words are cited by RaN (*Derashoth HaRan* I, s.v. *we-zeh hu 'inyan ha-kesheth*—p. 9 in Feldman edition).

29. *Kaftor WaFerach* 42. (The author was a disciple of ROSh.)

30. *Bitul Moda'ah*, edited by R. Yosef Shaul HaLevi Nathansohn.

31. See chapter 5, section 4.

32. Genesis 1:28.

33. See RaMBaN on RaMBaM, *Sefer HaMitzvoth*, pos. 1.

34. Deuteronomy 10:12.

35. *Sifrey* on Deuteronomy 6:6, referring to ibid. 6:5. When instructing us how to love God, our Sages teach us how to know Him. They clearly consider knowledge of God prerequisite to loving Him. Correspondingly, we do not, here, differentiate between these two obligations.

36. RaMBaM, Responsa (no. 150 in Mekize Nirdamim edition).

37. Psalms 19:1, 29:4; Isaiah 40:26; see also the following text. This is also hinted at in the commentaries on the verse, "Your greatness in the Heavens and on Earth—the actions by which He runs the world" (R. Avraham ibn Ezra on Deuteronomy 3:24) and "This refers to the greatness of nature" (NeTzYV, *Ha'amek Davar*, ad loc.).

38. BT *Shabbath* 75a, based on Isaiah 5:12.

39. BT *Berakhoth* 58b. Astronomy should not be confused with astrology, which is considerd as interfering with Torah study; see the words of MaHaRaL cited at length in section 3 of the next chapter (see notes 28,29, there).

40. MR Leviticus 19:1.

41. *Chovoth HaLevavoth* 2:2, citing Job 35:11.

42. MT *Yesodey HaTorah* 2:2, 4:12; and more explicitly in *Moreh Nevukhim* 3:28 (cf. also ibid. 1:34).

43. *HaMaspik Le'Ovdey HaShem*, p. 15.

44. *Derashoth UFeirushey Rabbeinu Yonah Girondi* on *Wa-Eira*, citing Psalms 8:4.

45. Rabeinu Yonah, ibid. on *Noach*.

46. Rabbis Tzemach and Shim'on, the sons of RaShBaSh and grandsons of RaShBaTz, Responsa *Yakhin UVo'az* I 134:3.

47. *Emunoth WeDe'oth*, Introduction (chapter 6 in R. Y. Kapach edition).

48. Responsa ReMA 7.

49. *She-eiloth Ya'vetz* I 41. Similarly in *Mor UKetzi'ah* 307, s.v. *wekhein sifrey refuah*.

50. *Tosfoth Yom Tov*, M *Avoth* 3, end.

51. "Chazon Ish," *Emunah UVitachon* 1.

52. *Igroth Chazon Ish* I 15.

53. *Shem 'Olam* I, end.

54. MR Genesis 1:1.

55. RaMBaM, *Moreh Nevukhim* 1:34.

56. MaHaRaL, *Nethivoth 'Olam, Nethiv HaTorah* 14.

57. R. Bachyay, M *Avoth* 3, end.

58. R. Bachyay, Deuteronomy 30:12.

59. R. Bachyay, Numbers 33:1.

60. MaHaRShA on BT *Horayoth* 10a.

61. As quoted by R. Barukh of Sklov, Introduction to *Sefer Euclides*, The Hague, 5540. Similarly (*Kol HaTor* V 2:12), "If one lacks knowledge of the laws of nature, his Torah knowledge will lack a hundredfold; and if a Torah scholar understands the laws of nature, his Torah wisdom will gain a hundredfold". The same attitude is reported also by *Peiath HaShulchan*, note 63, below. We thus have three witnesses testifying to the Gaon's authorship of the aforementioned statements. However, the authenticity of *Kol HaTor* has been questioned.

62. *Kol HaTor* V 2:6.

63. *Peiath HaShulchan*, Introduction.

64. This is also evident from his glosses on SA *Yoreh De'ah* 201, note 6. All this evinces a consistent requirement to study the sciences. It is necessary to stress this, because some have cast doubt on the citation of R. Barukh of Sklov (note 61, above), questioning the reliability of his report. However, since all the other quotations are in the same spirit, it would seem reasonable to rely on his testimony. Furthermore, since the translation of Euclid was published eighteen years before the death of the Gaon and he evidently never objected to the quotation to which we have alluded, we can safely assume that the citation is correct.

65. Introduction to *Ayil HaMeshulash* by HaGeRA, R. Ya'akov Mosheh's grandfather.

66. *Malbushey Yom Tov, Orach Chayim* 294, beginning. Similarly in *Divrey Chamudoth, Berakhoth* V no. 43.

67. *Levush* ad loc.

68. *Derekh Chokmah*, end.

69. *Harchev Davar* on Deuteronomy 32:2.

70. *Derashoth Chatham Sofer* fol.112b (*Beshalach*), based on MT *Yesodey HaTorah* 4:13.

71. "Chatham Sofer" to BT *Bava Bathra* 21a.

72. BT *Nidah* 30b.

73. BT *Chulin* 57b, based on Proverbs 19:1.

74. *Derush Or HaChayim* 3; appended to *Tif-ereth Yisrael* on M *Sanhedrin*.

75. The accepted interpretation of this midrash is that when God destroyed the other worlds, he reduced them to naught. However, *Tif-ereth Yisrael's* understanding is also legitimate; MaHaRShaM (*Tekheleth Mordekhai, Bereshith* 2) supports it. Similarly, when the Midrash (MR Genesis 1:9) recounts how a philosopher insisted to R. Gamliel that "God found valuable ingredients that helped Him [in Creation]— *tohu wavohu*," *Tosfoth Aharon* (BT *Rosh HaShanah* 27a) interprets this to refer to the remnants of the previous worlds. Rabban Gamliel replied that these remnants were also created by God.

Support for Tif-ereth Yisrael's interpretation may even be implied in the Talmud (*Chagigah* 16a), which discusses the prohibition to examine "that which went before." The Talmud there compares the world to a palace built on a garbage dump— the king of the palace would not want such a foundation examined. But there is no apparent connection between examining "that which went before" and a garbage dump, unless this world was indeed built on the remnants of others.

76. Jeremiah 1:5.

77. Genesis 12:2.

78. Playing on the identity in spelling of the words *berakhah* (=blessing) and *berekhah* (=pool), the Sages interpret the command "Be a blessing," to mean that Abraham (and his descendants) are to be like a pool (i.e. a *mikveh*) which purifies those who have become impure (MR Genesis 39:11).

79. Exodus 19:6, according to *Mekhilta*, R. 'Ovadyah Sforno, and R. Samson Raphael Hirsch. Rashi and RaShBaM offer another interpretation.

80. The conclusion of a Talmudic debate in BT *Kidushin* 23b.

81. BT *Sanhedrin* 74b, based on Leviticus 22:32.

For examples of the Torah's concern about desecrating God's name before gentiles, cf. Joshua 9:18, Ezekiel 36:20, BT *Gitin* 46a, *'Avodah Zarah* 28a.

82. Deuteronomy 4:6.

83. *Kol HaTor* V 2:1.

84. *Derekh Chokhmah*, p. 116.

85. NeTzYV, *Harchev Davar*, Deuteronomy 32:2.

86. M *Avoth* 5:20.

87. M *Avoth* 2:14.

88. BT *Sanhedrin* 38b.

89. RaShBaTz, *Magen Avoth* on M *Avoth* 2:14.

90. *Nethivoth 'Olam, Nethiv HaTorah* 14.

91. BT *Sanhedrin* 26b and Rashi, ad loc.

92. "Chatham Sofer," *Torath Mosheh, Shoftim*, s.v. *mi ha-ish*, referring to Deuteronomy 11:14.

93.   Genesis 1:28.
94.   See R. S.R. Hirsch's commentary ad loc.
95.   This has been discussed at length in part 2, chapter 3.
96.   Jeremiah 33:25.
97.   BT *Berakhoth* 17a.
98.   MT *Rotze-ach* 11:4, based on Deuteronomy 4:9.
99.   Julius Preuss, *Biblisch-talmudische Medizin*, Berlin, 1921.
100. *Sefer Chasidim*, Mekize Nirdamim edition, section 1469.
101. MT *De'oth* 4; *Rotze-ach* 11 and 12.
102. See chapter 3, section 2.
103. For an extensive listing of authorities citing this argument, see *Sha'arey Talmud Torah*, note to III 2:8(1), end.
104. BT *Berakhoth* 63a; *Kidushin* 29a.
105. BT *Kidushin* 30b, based on Ecclesiastes 9:9.
106. JT *Peiah* 1:1; JT *Kidushin* 1:7. Based on Deuteronomy 30:19.
107. MT *De'oth* 5:11.
108. SA *Orach Chayim* 156, citing M *Avoth* 2:2.
109. Ibid. 306:7.
110. M *Kidushin* 4:14.
111. BT *'Eiruvin* 55b, citing Deuteronomy 30:13.
112. M *Kidushin*, loc. cit.
113. *Kaftor WaFerach* chapter 44, end, and TaShBaTz I 147.
114. Note 7 in chapter 1, above.
115. *Derekh Chokhmah*, p. 116.
116. Below, chapter 3, section 3.
117. BT *Bava Kama* 83a.

NOTES TO CHAPTER 3

1.   Below, chapter 4, section 1(4).
2.   M *Sanhedrin* 10:1.
3.   BT *Sanhedrin* 100b. See chapter 4, section 3, for RYF's reading.
4.   Rav Yosef, loc. cit.
5.   Responsa RYVaSh 45.
6.   BT *Shabbath* 75a and Rashi, ad loc.
7.   SA *Yoreh De'ah* 179:19. But see MaHaRaL's comments on this in the next chapter.
8.   *She-eilath Ya'avetz* I 41.
9.   Chapter 2, section 2, end.
10. Responsa ReMA 5.
11. Ibid. 6.
12. BT *'Avodah Zarah* 17a, based on Proverbs 5:8.
13. Responsa ReMA 7.
14. It is important to emphasize that the only matter under dispute is the study of works by heretical authors. There was apparently no difference of opinion among the Sages or the Rishonim about the study of science itself. See the words of R. Ya'akov Provencali in chapter 1, reference 7.

15. Responsa *Chawoth Ya-ir* 9.
16. ReDaK on Joshua 1:8.
17. *Me-irath 'Eynayim* on *Noach.*
18. See the words of RaMBaM (MT *Yesodey HaTorah* 4:13) and of R. Bachyay (On Numbers — beginning of *Mas'ey*) on the question why it is necessary to have the study of the Torah precede the study of science. Also see NeTzYV, (Responsa *Meshiv Davar* I 44, s.v. *mikol zeh*), regarding the primacy of Torah study: "It is impossible to become a Torah scholar while one is occupied with other matters. And as to all the great scholars who were also well-versed in secular studies, this was only possible because they occupied themselves with secular subjects before immersing themselves in the Torah, or after they had already achieved their greatness." Similarly R. A.Y. Bloch (in a responsum discussed in chapter 5): "It is, of course, improper to neglect Torah study and pursue these studies regularly. Rather, it is possible to begin [the secular studies] in early youth, before the age of Gemara-study — 'at 15 years, Talmud' — when all his time and effort must be directed toward the Talmud."
19. Responsa, RaShBA I 415 and 416.
20. R. Y. Ya'abetz, *Or HaChayim*, end of chapter 3.
21. This parable is alluded to already in the writings of R. Avraham ibn Ezra (*Yesod Mora* 1).
22. BT *Yoma* 19b.
23. Joshua 1:8.
24. Cf. beginning of chapter 2.
25. JT *Peiah* 1:1.
26. BT *Menachoth* 99b.
27. SA *YorehDe'ah* 246:1, gloss.
28. MaHaRaL, *Nethivoth 'Olam, Nethiv HaTorah* 14.
29. MR Deuteronomy 8:6. We may find support for MaHaRaL's suggestion, that the reference here is to astrology, in another Midrash stating that Shemuel learned his astronomy from the Torah (see note 28 in the preceding chapter). Had he learned it from the Torah, he would surely not have studied it in the privy.
30. BT *Shabbath* 75a.
31. R. Samson Raphael Hirsch, *Ges. Schriften*, vol. 4, p. 431-2. Our wording is based on the abbreviated Hebrew citation in *Yesodoth HaChinukh* (Netzach, 5719, pp. 51-53). Quoted by R. R. Katzenellenbogen in *Sefer HaRav Shimshon Refael Hirsch, Mishnatho WeShitatho*, Jerusalem, 5722, p. 90.

NOTES TO CHAPTER 4

1. R. Bachyay, M *Avoth* 3, end.
2. M *Sotah* 9:14.
3. This reading is according to R. 'Ovadyah of Bartinoro's version. Cf. the glosses of R. 'Akiva Eger, ad loc. It is also the text of the Munich ms.
4. BT *Sotah* 49b.
5. Responsa RYVaSh 45.

6. Rashi on BT *Menachoth* 64b.
7. RaMBaM on M *Sotah* 9:14; Meiri on BT *Sotah* 49b; RaShBaTz, *Magen Avoth* 2:14; MaHaRaL, *Nethivoth 'Olam, Nethiv HaTorah* 14.
8. R. Shelomoh Sirileo, JT *Peiah* 1:1.
9. *Me-irath 'Einayim* on *Noach.*
10. ReMaH (*Shitah Mekubetzeth,* BT *Bava Kama* 83a) defines the wisdom of Greek as "star-gazing." Even in his opinion, this is apparently not part of natural science; rather, it is like divination in order to foretell the future, akin to MaHaRaL's interpretation of astrology, which he, too, refers to as "star-gazing" (see notes 28,29 in the preceding chapter).
11. BT *Sanhedrin* 90a.
12. BT *Sanhedrin* 100b.
13. RYVaSh's text stated, "books of heretics" (responsum 45). He prohibited those books concerning nature that tend to uproot the basis of our belief.
14. RYF, *Sanhedrin* 100b.
15. JT *Sanhedrin* 10:1, referring to Ecclesiastes 12:12.
16. Rabbi Yisakhar Dov Eilenburg, *Be-er Sheva'* on BT *Sanhedrin* 100b.
17. R. David Frankel, *Shiyarey Korban* and R. Re-uven Margolis, *Margolioth HaYam,* ad loc.
18. R. A.Y. Bloch, responsum on the study of secular subjects, discussed at length in chapter 5, section 2.
19. *Chidushey* RYTBA, *Bava Bathra* 98b; *Nimukey Yosef,* ad loc.
20. R. N.D. Rabinowitz, *Binu Shenoth Dor WaDor,* p. 300.
21. *Magen Avoth* 3, end.
22. MT *'Avodah Zarah* 2:2, based on Deuteronomy 18:9.
23. MT *Teshuvah* 3:7.
24. See the responsum by R. Elchanan Wasserman (discussed in chapter 5); BT *Berakhoth* 12b, based on the verse in Deuteronomy 15:39, "'Do not investigate after your heart'— This means heresy"; BT *'Avodah Zarah* 17a, based on Proverbs 5:8 and 2:19. That the requirements to distance oneself from heresy are even stricter than those concerning idolatry, is brought in BT *'Avodah Zarah* 27b.
25. BT *Shabbath* 116a. Note that the sanctity of the written name of God is rooted in the intention with which it was written. God's name in a Torah scroll written by a heretic has, therefore, no sanctity.
26. R. E. Wasserman, *Kovetz Shi'urim* II 47. The prohibition of heresy is brought in BT *Berakhoth* 12b, based on Numbers 15:39.
27. BT *Shabbath* 75a and Rashi, ad loc.
28. SA *Yoreh De'ah* 179:19 and ShaKh, note 23.
    Note, also, that R. Yosef ibn 'Aknin, a disciple of Rambam, adduces many reasons to justify the learning from gentiles, and ends thus:
    > The Nagid (Prince), in his work *Ha'Osher,* after having quoted Christian sources extensively, relates that he had a conversation with R. Matzliach ben Albatzak—one of the rabbinic authorities of Scolia—when he returned from Bagdad with an epistle. This epistle contained the life-story of Rabbeinu Hai Gaon, including all his exemplary customs. It relates an incident: one day they discussed the verse (Psalms 141,5), "Oil of primacy will not divert my head,"

and those present were of differing minds about its meaning. R. Hai then asked R. Matzliach to go to the Catholic [primate] to ask him what he knows about the meaning of this verse. When R. Hai saw that R. Matzliach was reluctant to do so, he chid him, saying, "Did not our forefathers and the pious men of yore—who serve as shining examples to us—ask people of other religions for explanation of terminology and interpretations, even shepherds and cattlemen —as is well known." (Comment. to Song of Songs)

It is difficult to understand this in the light of the above halakhah. We have learned explicitly (BT *'Avodah Zarah* 16b-17a) that R. Eli'ezer was sorely tried, because of the enjoyment he derived from a Biblical interpretation he heard from a heretic.

29.   R. Y. Ya'abetz, *Or HaChayim* 8.
30.   *Sefer HaYashar* 6:10.
31.   Responsa RYVaSh 45.
32.   *Magen Avoth, Avoth* 2:14 referring to BT *Yoma* 19b, based on Deuteronomy 6:7.
33.   BT *Berakhoth* 28b.
34.   *Nimukey Yosef*, BT *Megilah* 25b; p. 102 in R. M.Y. Blau edition.
35.   *She-eilath Ya'avetz* I 41.
36.   *'Oleloth Efrayim*, Introduction, s.v. *halo tov lishmoa'* based on Psalms 127:1.
37.   "Chatham Sofer," Responsa, *Orach Chayim* 51.
38.   *Ya'aroth Devash* II 7.
      See also comments of Responsa *Chawoth Ya-ir* 219.
39.   M *Avoth* 5:5.
40.   See note 18, above.
41.   Tosafoth on BT *Shabbath* 116b, s.v. *we-khol shekein*, referring to Psalms 1:1.
42.   ROSh, *Shabbath* 23:1, end.
43.   SA *Orach Chayim* 307:16.
44.   BT *Bava Kama* 83a.
45.   Meiri, ad loc.
46.   JT *Peiah* 1:1.
      See chapter 3, section 3, above, for a discussion of this passage.
47.   *Korban Ha'Eidah* on JT *Shabbath* 6:1.
48.   *Sifrey* on Deuteronomy 18:9.
49.   Meiri on BT *Sanhedrin* 90a.
50.   MT *'Avodah Zarah* 2:2.
51.   RaMBaM on M *Avoth* 2:14.
52.   *Tif-ereth Yisrael, Sanhedrin* 10:1(8); RaShBaTZ, *Magen Avoth* 2:14.
53.   *Lechem Shamayim* on *Sanhedrin* 10:1.
54.   See note 18, above.
55.   *Zekan Aharon* 25, referring to MT *Chagigah* 15b.
56.   *Megilath Sefer* 2.
      One commentator speculates that this is a circumlocution for the privy.
57.   MaHaRaL, *Nethivoth 'Olam, Nethiv HaTorah* 14.
58.   *She-eiloth Ya'avetz* I 41; see extensive quote above (chapter 3, note 8).
59.   *Sedey Chemed, Peiath HaSadeh, Ma'arekheth Alef* 64.
60.   Rabbeinu Bachyay, Leviticus 8:23; RaShBaTz, *Magen Avoth*, philosophical part, 3:1; for additional names, see chapter 2, section 1, and note 21 there.

61. Tosafoth on BT *Shabbath* 116b, s.v. *we-khol shekein*, referring to Psalms 1:1.
62. *Ba-eir Heitev*, SA *Orach Chayim* 307, note 18.
63. *Mor UKetzi'a, Orach Chayim* 307:16. Quoted in the responsa of R. Tzvi Chayoth
     12. This is similar to the words of R. Yitzchak Abarbanel (*Nachalath Avoth* 5:5),
     who gives many reasons why a rabbi may accept a wage, despite the prohibition
     against "making the words of Torah a hoe wherewith to dig." One of these is,
     "Scholars may accept payments from the community for their political efforts on
     the community's behalf, through their good advice and public functions."
64. R. S.R. Hirsch on Deuteronomy 4:32.
65. "Chazon Ish," *Emunah UVitachon* 1:8.
66. *'Arukh HaShulchan, Orach Chayim* 307:9.
67. BT *Shevu'oth* 6b, Rashi.
68. R. Mendel Kargau, Responsa *Giduley Taharah* 7, alluding to Song of Songs 2:15.
69. BT *Sotah* 36b; *Sanhedrin* 17a; *Menachoth* 65a.
70. *Teshuvoth HaGeonim*, quoted by *Sefer Ha'Itim* 175 and R. Yisrael Mosheh Chazan,
     She-erith HaNachalah, p. 13.
71. Responsa *Zera' Emeth* (R. Yishma'el bar Avraham Yitzchak) II, *Yoreh De'ah* 107
     (119).
72. R. Akiva Eger, *Igroth Sofrim*, no. 18, letter dated 1 Shevat 5586 (January 9, 1826).
73. Responsa *Rav Pe'alim, Orach Chayim* 2:22. See *Igroth Mosheh, Yoreh De'ah* III 83
     and *Tzitz Eli'ezer* IX 15 and 16.
74. R. M.C. Luzzatto, *Derekh Chokhmah*, end, cited at the end of Chapter 2.
75. *Derushey HaTzeLaCh* 39.
76. R. Shemuel Landau, *Doresh Tzion*, Introduction.
77. R. S.R. Hirsch, *Horeb* 84.
78. R. D. Katz, *Tenu'ath HaMusar* II, p. 183.
79. See R. A.Y. Schlesinger, *Ma'aseh Avoth*, pp. 39, 63.
80. See R. M.M. Yashar, *HaChafetz Chayim*, chapter 42; R. Z.A. Rabiner, *Rabbeinu
     Meir Simchah*, pp. 149-151.
81. Responsa MaHaRaM Shick, *Orach Chayim* 70.
82. M *Avoth* 5:18.
83. *Likut She-eiloth UTeshuvoth Chatham Sofer* (London 5725/1965) 82:11.
84. R. Avraham ibn 'Ezra, *Yesod Mora* fol. 14a.
85. *Moreh Nevukhim* I 34.
86. *'Ein Ya'akov*, BT *Berakhoth* 28b.
87. *She-eilath Ya'avetz* I 41, end.

NOTES TO CHAPTER 5

1. R. S.R. Hirsch, *Gesammelte Schriften* II, pp. 449-466.
2. The responsa are arranged alphabetically according to the author's name following
    the Hebrew alphabet. See *Sha'arey Talmud Torah*, end, for full text of the responsa.
3. First published in *Proceeding of Association of Orthodox Jewish Scientists* Vol. 1
    (1966).
4. See chapter 4, section 3(2).
5. M *Avoth* 5:21.

6. The halakhic source of this prohibition is somewhat obscure. Cf. section 4d (in the responsum of R. Y. Rozin). Perhaps it is strictly pragmatic.

7. *Kovetz Shi'urim* II 47.

8. MT *'Avodah Zarah* 2:2 and BT *'Avodah Zarah* 27b. In R. Wasserman's opinion, the above-cited interpretation [chapter 4, section 3(2) in the name of Rashi, RaMBaM and Meiri] that the study of this subject is only forbidden if the intent is to follow its precepts — does not apply to such books. This is a more severe interpretation than that of R. A.Y. Bloch, who based his permission on the decisions of Rashi and RaMBaM. R. Wasserman does not relate to these opinions and I therefore do not know on what basis he rejects them.

9. BT *Pesachim* 8b.

10. MT *'Avodah Zarah* 11:1. In a similar vein, the author of *Giduley Taharah* warns (responsum 7): "Many disciplines are not destructive — such as foreign languages and all mathematics — and one need not be on guard against them. But we do need to guard against those who promulgate these sciences and those who seduce others."

11. M *Kidushin* 4:14. The early commentaries all claim that R. Nehorai did not dispute a father's obligation to teach his son a trade. This is discussed at length in part 1, Chapter 2, section 4.

12. *Birkath Shemuel, Kidushin* 27. Compare also *Minchath Yitzchak* (V 79), who writes regarding university study, "Undoubtedly, their teachings, which are based on nature, are included in the 'books of heretics.'" His statement can be reconciled with all the opinions cited in chapter 2 if we assume that he refers to philosophic studies, which are heretical; what we have quoted assumes that God guides the universe directly but He generally follows set guidelines, as we have explained in part 1, (chapter 1, section 2).

13. Published in *HaMa'ayan*, Nisan 5736, pp. 1-9.
    I am greatly endebted to my revered Rav S. Schwab, who gave me the original ms., which had not been previously published. I am also endebted to my revered friend Rabbi Aryeh Carmell, who — together with his sons R. Avraham Chaim and R. David Yehudah — succeeded in deciphering it.

14. Reference is to the case of Rav, discussed in BT *Sanhedrin* 5b.

15. BT *Sanhedrin* 76b.

16. BT *Makoth* 8b. Cf. also RaMBaM, commentary to that Mishnah (2:2). The bracketed phrase was inserted based on the verse cited in support of the permission to strike one's son: "Chastise your son, and he will give you 'nachas,' and present delicacies to your soul" (Proverbs 29:17).

17. R. Ya'akov Gershon Weiss, personal communication.

18. MT *De'oth* 1:4, *Moreh Nevukhim* III 54 (on the verse Jeremiah 9:22).

19. R. Yosef Rozin on Genesis 50:2.

20. *Igroth Chazon Ish* II 50.

21. See chapter 4, section 3(5).

22. R. Ch. Karlinsky, *HaRishon LeShusheleth Brisk*, pp. 381-9.

23. R. Barukh Epstein (author of *Torah Temimah*) *Mekor Baruch*, p. 1013a.

24. Ibid. p. 1012a.

25. Responsa *Meishiv Davar* I 44.

INDEX